Scary Monsters

Scary Monsters

Monstrosity, Masculinity and Popular Music

Mark Duffett and Jon Hackett

BLOOMSBURY ACADEMIC
NEW YORK • LONDON • OXFORD • NEW DELHI • SYDNEY

BLOOMSBURY ACADEMIC
Bloomsbury Publishing Inc
1385 Broadway, New York, NY 10018, USA
50 Bedford Square, London, WC1B 3DP, UK
29 Earlsfort Terrace, Dublin 2, Ireland

BLOOMSBURY, BLOOMSBURY ACADEMIC and the Diana logo are trademarks of
Bloomsbury Publishing Plc

First published in the United States of America 2021
This paperback edition published in 2022

Copyright © by Mark Duffett and Jon Hackett, 2021

Cover design: Lee Brooks

All rights reserved. No part of this publication may be reproduced or transmitted in any form or by any means, electronic or mechanical, including photocopying, recording, or any information storage or retrieval system, without prior permission in writing from the publishers.

Bloomsbury Publishing Inc does not have any control over, or responsibility for, any third-party websites referred to or in this book. All internet addresses given in this book were correct at the time of going to press. The author and publisher regret any inconvenience caused if addresses have changed or sites have ceased to exist, but can accept no responsibility for any such changes.

Whilst every effort has been made to locate copyright holders the publishers would be grateful to hear from any person(s) not here acknowledged.

Library of Congress Cataloging-in-Publication Data
Names: Duffett, Mark, author. | Hackett, Jon, author.
Title: Scary monsters : monstrosity, masculinity and popular music /
Mark Duffett, Jon Hackett.
Description: New York City : Bloomsbury Academic, 2021. | Includes bibliographical references and index. | Summary: "Through a series of case studies, Scary Monsters examines masculinity in popular music culture from the perspective of research into monstrosity"– Provided by publisher.
Identifiers: LCCN 2020036646 (print) | LCCN 2020036647 (ebook) | ISBN 9781501313370 (hardback) | ISBN 9781501313387 (pdf) | ISBN 9781501313394 (epub)
Subjects: LCSH: Popular music–Social aspects. | Masculinity in music. | Monsters.
Classification: LCC ML3918.P67 D85 2021 (print) | LCC ML3918.P67 (ebook) |
DDC 781.640811–dc23
LC record available at https://lccn.loc.gov/2020036646
LC ebook record available at https://lccn.loc.gov/2020036647

ISBN:	HB:	978-1-5013-1337-0
	PB:	978-1-5013-7476-0
	ePDF:	978-1-5013-1338-7
	eBOOK:	978-1-5013-1339-4

Typeset by Integra Software Services Pvt. Ltd.

To find out more about our authors and books visit www.bloomsbury.com
and sign up for our newsletters.

Contents

Acknowledgements — vi

Introduction *Jon Hackett* — 1
1 A night at the Opera: Updating *The Phantom* *Mark Duffett* — 27
2 'His muscles still bulged like iron bands': *King Kong* and the promotion of Lead Belly *Mark Duffett* — 49
3 Colonel Parker and the art of commercial exploitation: The manager as monster *Mark Duffett* — 69
4 The platformed Prometheus: Frankenstein and glam rock *Jon Hackett* — 87
5 The case of Mark Chapman: Extreme fandom as monstrosity? *Mark Duffett* — 109
6 Exhuming the Gravediggaz: Gothic hip hop and monster capital *Jon Hackett* — 137
7 Masculinity on trial: Noir Désir and perverse narcissism *Jon Hackett* — 161
8 Jingle Jangle Man: Jimmy Savile, paedophilia and the music industry *Mark Duffett* — 187

Notes — 230
Reference List — 235
Index — 262

Acknowledgements

First, I would like to thank my co-writer and friend, Jon Hackett. This book was a joint effort and would not exist without his input and guidance.

The volume began to germinate after I attended a conference in Leicester called *The Monster inside Us, the Monsters around Us: Monstrosity and Humanity* in November 2011. I would like to thank Scott Freer and Rebecca Styler, who welcomed me there as a friend.

Since then, I have been invited to quite a few conferences, and organized, or co-organized, some of my own. In particular, I would like to thank Amanda Nell Edgar and Robert Fry, among others, for organizational help during my American visits.

I would also like to thank Cormack Newark, Annette Davison, Clarice Greco, Jacqueline Avila, Leslie McMurtry and others associated with Barbican and Guildhall School of Music's symposium, *Phantoms of the Opera*, held in June 2018.

Finally, beyond Bloomsbury, my own family and partner Julie, rather than single anyone out, I would like to show appreciation for many, inside and outside the academy, for their inspiration (direct and indirect), discussion and support:

Abby Waysdorf, Adam Jones, Allan Moore, Andee Baker, Andrew Crome, Ann-Marie Fleming, Anne Martin, B. Lee Cooper, Beate Peter, Ben Halligan, Bertel Nygaard, Beth Emily Richards, Bertha Chin, Bethan Jones, Bethan Michael-Fox, Catherine Girodet, Christophe Chambost, Clarissa Smith, Claude Chastagner, Clementine Tholas, Cornel Sandvoss, Daniel Cavicchi, David Pattie, Eldon Edwards, Francois Ribac, Fred Vermorel, Gary Burns, Gayle Stever, Georgina Gregory, Heikki Uimonen, Henry Jenkins, Ian Inglis, Isabel Carrera Suárez, James Goff, Jedediah Sklower, Joli Jensen, Julie Lobalzo Wright, Katie Barnett, Kier Keightley, Kirsty Fairclough, Leah Babb-Rosenfeld, Leonike Bolderman, Lincoln Geraghty, Lori Morimoto, Lucy Bennett, Martin Cloonan, Mathias Haeussler, Matt Grimes, Matt Hills, Matthias Stephan, Melissa Avdeef, Michael Bertrand, Mike Brocken, Monique Charles, Murray Leeder, Natalia Samutina, Nedim Hassan, Nigel Patterson, Oliver Carter, Paul Booth, Paul Carr, Paul Clark, Paula Hearsum, Pete Dale, Phil Kirby, Piers Beagley, Pilar Lacasa,

Rasmus Rosenørn, Rebecca Wanzo, Richard McCulloch, Richard Mills, Richard Phillips, Rukmini Pande, Sara Cohen, Sarah Longfield, Shane Brown, Sean Redmond, Sharon Zeng, Shelley Piasecka, Simon Morrison, Simon Warner, Simone Driessen, Stacy Warren, Stijn Reijnders, Tim Wall, Tom Attah, Tom Phillips, Tony Whyton, Valerie Gritsch, Veronica Skrimsjö and Xavier Mendik.

That is not to mention late popular music researchers, including David Sanjek and Dave Laing, friends in the media (especially at podcasts such as ACPG and Pop Unmuted), and many other supportive colleagues at the University of Chester.

I am sure there are others who I have missed out, and for that, in advance, I apologize.

Mark Duffett

I dedicate this book to my mother, father and sister. I would like to thank the following for their help, support and discussions on film and music: Mark, of course, Biswadip Dasgupta, Caroline Ruddell, Dafydd Jones, Damian O'Byrne, Daragh Minogue, Gregory Jackson, Lance Pettitt, Lee Brooks, Joy Mellins, Maria Mellins, Moira Stewart, Peter Howell, Richard Mills, Russell Schechter, Seán Harrington and Sudip Hazra. Thanks to Lee for designing the cover image. I would also like to thank students on the postgraduate module Contemporary Gothic convened by Maria, Caroline and me, with whom some of these ideas were explored prior to their discussion in this book.

All translations in the book from sources listed in French in the bibliography are the authors'.

Jon Hackett

Introduction

Monstrosity has seldom been studied in relation to popular music. Yet myths, performances and discourses associated with it include 'monsters' more often than might be imagined. David Bowie's interest was evident in the title of his 1980 album, *Scary Monsters (and Super Creeps)*. Bowie was associated with an artistically productive flirtation with monstrosity: a performance that was, in part, about interrogating the biases through which we render particular identities as marginal. Dictionary definitions of the term 'monster' tend to talk about frightening, abnormal or imagined creatures, or inhumanly wicked people, though the boundaries between these different ideas are somewhat ambiguous. Precisely in their abject state, monsters can be objects of empathy or pity. Consider, for example, Bowie's almost messianic role as a human alien in *The Man Who Fell to Earth* (Roeg 1976), a film that critic Pauline Kael called a 'sex-role confusion fantasy' (1982, p. 361). Kael explained:

> The wilted stranger can be said to represent everyone who feels misunderstood, everyone who feels sexually immature or 'different,' everyone who has lost his way, and so the film is a gigantic launching pad for anything that viewers want to drift to.
>
> (Kael 1982, p. 361)

We can locate this artistic mission in the clichéd nonconformity of youth culture: if adolescence is a shared space where people grow up by exploring adult identity *through its performance*, flirtation with alterity can become a way to generate inclusivity for those with identities otherwise marginalized by the accepted norms of adult society. Dave Bowie's 'sex-role confusion fantasies' used the clichéd realm of rock'n'roll rebellion to play with an expanded acceptance of gender. After *The Man Who Fell to Earth*, his theatrical performance continued, for instance, in the deliberately challenging 1979 video for 'Boys Keep Swinging'. As the obituary for Bowie on the website *Famous Monsters of Filmland* (*David Bowie Departs This Plane* 2016) explained, 'Even with his movie star good looks, he was an eccentric who, though embraced by the mainstream, was always an oddity, so he appealed to outsiders and oddballs. He got us, and we got him.' Bowie's artistic portrayal of monstrosity was central to that process. As Hawkins and Nielsen (2020, p. 194) recently suggested, monster aesthetics can be about 'being indifferent to difference'. Bowie appears now to have been ahead of his time, anticipating an era when gender is increasingly located as something self-ascribed and individually identified. That raises the question, is grappling with monstrosity always necessarily a 'bad' thing? Perhaps the answer to that depends on what society deems as acceptable, what kind of monstrosity we might mean.

In popular music studies, surprisingly little work draws on the term 'monster' or otherwise examines the subject. Part of the issue is that pop researchers investigate a constellation of associated objects. The field of pop research has multiple, related concerns, including music geographies, scenes and genres, industries and state policies, media, technologies, songs, recordings, live performance, musicianship, amateur musicians, musical instruments, music education, plus, of course, specific recording artists and their audiences. With each of these elements, practice, discourse and identity offer at least three prisms to consider the same foci. Examining music stars alone, we can research their recorded works, performances, celebrity images or implication in different social debates. Monstrosity can relate to almost any of those diverse academic concerns.

In the humanities, monstrosity has become an important, emerging strand of interdisciplinary scholarship. According to Asa Mittman (2012, p. 1), 'In the space of a few years, the study of monsters has moved from the absolute periphery – perhaps its logical starting point – to a much more central position in academics [sic].' Another reason to talk about monstrosity is that it allows us to explore the ways in which popular music texts, in the widest sense, negotiate identity. In relation to music culture, monsters raise issues about transgression, subjectivity, agency and community. Attention to them evokes both the spectre of projection – what monsters are called upon to represent – and wider cultural anxieties, reflecting commonly shared ideologies, fantasies and beliefs. As well as deriving from multiple sources – whether mythical, historical or cultural – since they often serve as the embodiment of difference from a putatively human self, monsters are often called upon to perform 'identity work'. Attention to individuals located by others as monsters can therefore say things about the operation of gender, identity, myth and meaning in popular culture. *Scary Monsters* traces how that process has happened across different times and contexts.

The aim of this book is not to label particular people as monsters – though certain individuals discussed here have been labelled as such – but rather, in part, to explore the *ways in which attributions of monstrosity can function*. By offering a series of in-depth case studies, especially ones that eschew some of the most hackneyed examples, this book aims to explore different aspects of the connection between music, gender and monstrosity. Its argument is that attention to monstrosity is a fruitful way to approach the study of masculinity in popular music culture.

Masculinity

Our case studies focus on *male* monsters, both fictitious and 'real', that have inhabited dark and occasionally fantastical moments in popular music history. Given the novelty of this analytical standpoint, it is helpful to survey the ways in which masculinity and monstrosity have been conceived in cultural and sociological terms, before focusing attention more acutely on popular music case studies in the rest of this book.

It is important from the outset to draw a distinction, albeit hazy, between maleness, male identity and masculinity. On one level there is the association, or otherwise, between a person's physicality and their sex. On another level, are the forms of identification developed around the social attribution of a person as male. Classically, for the psychoanalyst Sigmund Freud, in the context of family life male maturation was associated with the Oedipus complex. In classical myth, Oedipus accidentally kills his father and marries his mother. According to gender researcher Leanne Franklin (2012, p. 76):

> This ancient Greek myth gives its name to the psychoanalytic conflict Freud proposed which involves the attraction of boys to their mother which occurs at the phallic stage ... Once the boy understands how important his penis is, love for his mother becomes transformed into sexual desire and upon this transformation his father, formerly an ally, becomes a rival to his mother's affection.

Girls, according to Freud, experience a parallel process: an Elektra complex that involves romantic bonding to their father. Although Freud's gendered version of psychosexual maturation has been challenged, it did, nevertheless, dominate modern thinking about gender, particularly in the mid-twentieth century, and therefore influence the ideas circulating about gender in popular culture. If some forms of male and female *behaviour* – whether functional or dysfunctional – might have their roots in the cradle of the family, we should distinguish a further level of activity. Central to this is Judith Butler's (1990/2006) famous notion that gender does not come *from* biology, but rather from social expectations created around male and female identity, and the tacit adoption of forms of behaviour associated with those expectations. Discussing Elvis fandom, Duffett (2001, p. 396) therefore offers a basic definition of masculinity:

> Masculinity is the gender paradigm that continues to define most male behaviour in patriarchal society. Masculinity confers male self-esteem by reproducing male privilege. It naturalises gender as difference, and difference as hierarchy, creating shared notions of acceptable and ideal behaviour. Because women are apprehended as the weaker sex, the feminine becomes Othered as an object of scornful disdain and hidden fear. This fear of femininity also permits contempt for 'effeminate' behaviour in men. Masculinity is therefore not just a way to separate the sexes: homoerotic bonding and homosexuality have traditionally been weak and inadmissible forms of male behaviour. On the other hand, independence, rivalry, rationality and self-mastery are recognised as desirable traits since masculinity encourages individuals to compete for status and puts emphasis on defiant achievement (see Easthope 1990). Traditional masculinity turns sex into an arena for the competitive assertion of manhood. Women are reduced to objects of conquest and tokens of exchange.

Much of the sociological literature agrees that theorizing about masculinity has occurred in response to feminism, without whose influence such work might not have seen the light of day. A starting point for the analysis has been traced back to Kate Millett's (1970) study, *Sexual Politics*, in which 'patriarchy', a staple term of debate for second-wave feminism, is delineated. This word, whose etymology implies the 'rule of the father', has become a standard term to describe male-dominated society. Patriarchy has become a framework within which to think of masculinity as a dominant social and cultural norm, all the more powerful given its earlier epistemological invisibility.

Stephen Whitehead (2002) helpfully traces the development of sociological thinking about masculinity, from earlier functionalist and sex role theorizing, to later conceptions developing from the context of second-wave feminism. For Whitehead (2002, p. 88), patriarchy overstates the monolithic dominance of male power, given the advances obtained by women in recent decades. It might be further limited by implying an ahistorical structure that is immune to change and identical across cultures and societies.

A more recent and still important conception of masculinity was outlined by Tim Carrigan, Bob Connell and John Lee in their influential 1985 article. While acknowledging that masculinity is plural and multiple, as well as being subject to change over time and space, the term 'hegemonic masculinity', which derives from Gramscian developments in Marxist theorizing, retains the link between masculinity and power. Connell's more recent work, *The Men and the Boys*, helpfully distinguishes between hegemonic and other masculinities, be they subordinated, marginalized or complicit in relation to the dominant form in any particular social formation (2000, p. 10).

Whitehead's own preference is to speak instead of 'masculinism' as a discourse: 'Masculinism is, then, the point at which dominant forms of masculinity and heterosexuality meet ideological dynamics, and in the process become reified and legitimized as privileged, unquestioned accounts of gender difference and reality' (2002, p. 96). Here Whitehead draws on post-structuralist theorizing, notably that of Foucault, which sees discourse as related to power; as well as being something that both disciplines bodies and enables self-fashioning or subject formation within certain historically contingent limitations. This is in keeping, too, with postmodernist conceptions of identity as a project; here we can make the link with Connell's assertion that we should see masculinity and femininity as 'gender projects' (Connell 2000, p. 28).

The notion of masculinity as a series of ongoing 'gender projects' begins to historicize our understanding of the performance of gender, and relate these patterns of behaviour to the social and economic demands of a changing series of times and places. One phenomenon that is often discussed in relation to these topics is an alleged 'crisis in masculinity', which is culturally diagnosed in part as a response to women's liberation and feminism, and in part as a response to structural shifts associated with business. Globalization – and the global restructuring of capital in late capitalism – leads to the outsourcing of manufacturing labour to the global south, as well as the deindustrialization of traditional manufacturing towns and cities in the global north. This has led in turn to a transition from traditional 'masculine' wage labour in manufacturing districts to allegedly 'feminised' service industries in their place. Feminism has supported an increased presence of women in both the general workplace, and more particularly in male-dominated professions, even though this project remains severely limited by the ongoing domination by men across many spheres. It has successfully contested and challenged social inequalities deriving from gender, plus representations and discourses in the wider culture or mass media that can be designated as sexist or misogynist. The decline of clearly identifiable 'male' roles or identities defined by physical labour in the public sphere, then, is sometimes held to result in a 'crisis' for males unable to adapt to new conditions of work and associated gender roles.

Any notion of a crisis, as thus formulated, is nonetheless open to question. As Whitehead (2002) argues, 'Men (particularly White, heterosexual, Anglo-Saxon men) control, directly or indirectly, most of the world's resources, capital, media, political parties and corporations. It is difficult to imagine this group in crisis' (p. 3). Men overwhelmingly still benefit from the economic and managerial advantages that accrue merely as a result of their gender privilege, a phenomenon that Connell (2000, p. 25) characterizes as the 'patriarchal dividend'. What we can say, however, is there is certainly an increased prevalence of *discourses* of masculinity in crisis (Whitehead 2002, p. 50), not only in relation to work and cultural representation, but also in relation to education and popular culture, among other spheres. In relation to popular culture, Whitehead (p. 49) singles out David Fincher's 1999 film *Fight Club* as an instance of a cultural product that was widely discussed in terms of this alleged crisis. More recently, perhaps, we might point to ongoing attention to masculinity in the cinemas of directors as disparate as Clint Eastwood, Kathryn Bigelow and Jacques Audiard. In contrast to the themes explored by these filmmakers, the less realist and more performative terrain of popular music has been characterized by a play with gender identity that, in a sense, has heralded, reflected upon and sought to solve the 'crisis' by making a wider range of gender identities acceptable among boys and men.

Carrigan, Connell and Lee (1985) popularized the concept of 'hegemonic masculinity' as the dominant version pertaining to a particular culture, even if the majority of men fail to live up to this standard. Construing masculinity in hegemonic terms allows for historical variation, as well as a multiplicity of masculinities existing alongside each other in any given social formation. Connell outlines the prevailing hegemonic masculinity in the contemporary West, namely 'transnational business masculinity'. The notion is defined as 'the business executives who operate in global markets, and the political executives who interact (and in many contexts merge) with them' (2000, p. 51). This valorization of *middle class* forms of masculinity maximizes the benefit accruing from the patriarchal dividend. Transnational corporations have also used elite sportsmen in their marketing materials, bolstering and legitimizing their brands with a focus on older, traditional masculinity defined in terms of athleticism. Contempory forms of masculinity thus gain their justification by subordinating the virtues of previous forms, in this case to create a 'corporate warrior' ethos, which has, since Connell's (2000) study, arguably been augmented or supplanted by a 'geeky' or 'nerdish' reformulation. As Anthony Easthope argues in his study of the 'masculine myth' in popular culture: 'Masculinity tries to stay invisible by passing itself off as normal and universal. Words such as "man" and "mankind", used to signify the human species, treat masculinity as if it covered everyone' (Easthope 1990, p. 1). This idea of 'passing off' captures some of the *work* done by more dominant forms of masculinity, but it does not tell the whole story.

In recent years, research on masculinity has increasingly complicated or moved away from universal formulations (see, for example, Cornwall and Lisdisfarne 2017), and in doing so relegated, challenged or modified notions of hegemonic masculinity (Messerschmidt 2018). Such research considers the specificity of actual masculinities as behaviours and attitudes that are constructed to be performed in *particular* locales or historical situations. Beyond more niche discussions on gendered practices, life cycle roles (such as fatherhood), male identities operating outside heteronormative contexts, racially specific or otherwise intersectional formulations, there has also been work on historically situated performances or embodiments of male identity (for instance, see Cornwall, Karioris and Lindisfarne 2016, Surkis 2018 and Niva 2019). Many of these have referenced particular geographic locations (Hofman and Newman 2014) or institutional context (see Gilbert and Gilbert 2017).

Such studies define masculinities as historically changing, potentially fluid sets of behaviours that can function in positive or negative ways. Specific, 'masculine' behaviours can, for instance, facilitate, dominate, curtail, restrict or challenge those who identify as different. Researchers now say that specific gender projects make efforts to adjust male subjects to their changing roles in an increasingly technological society. Situated masculinities in the contemporary West, for instance, have therefore been constructed around reactionary anger at economic uncertainty and the associated abandoning of the working class (Kimmel 2017), taking a 'tough' approach to survival and resilience, performing residual or 'nostalgic' versions of prior manliness (Albrecht 2016), or achieving alpha status by masterfully exploiting digital technology for social or material benefits. A good example of work recently discussing one situated mode of masculinity is Salter and Blodgett's edited volume *Toxic Geek Masculinity in Media* (2017), which addresses sexist practices, trolling and identity policing associated with the #Gamergate online controversy of the mid-2010s. As their research makes clear, particular social and historical contexts and their associated ideological projects, not only encourage the adoption or practice of particular masculinities – the resulting formulation of gender also does cultural work, *at specific times and places in the real world*. What follows will draw on previous research, theorizing masculinities both broadly and specifically in relation to popular music, attempting to scrutinize the immediate, 'default option' *and* to attain sufficient distance in order to discuss what is it assumes to be deviant or insignificant. We cannot discount the possibility that our own gender will at times mean that we do not succeed unambiguously in achieving this.

Monstrosity

We can now turn to the main term of analysis for this book. Studies of monsters and monstrosity frequently take etymology as their point of departure. Examples of these will appear throughout this study, but monsters are generally derived from Latin words such as *monere*, to warn; or *monstrum*, a warning or portent. Sometimes the link is made with another Latin word, *monstrare*, to show or demonstrate. From this, monsters are deemed to provide warning or cautionary tales; from their beginnings, then, they *make meaning*.

Although monstrosity has not formed a dominant paradigm in popular music studies, monsters have evidently been a concern for certain strains of cultural studies. The ways in which we construe monstrosity will depend in some part on the interpretive frameworks with which we approach it. In this section we will review briefly some of the main approaches from which monsters have been theorized. These various frameworks that follow are competing perspectives from which to interpret or account for this inherently semiotic – or sometimes symptomatic – aspect of monsters and monstrosity. Some might challenge these labels – in many cases, their concerns overlap – but the purpose here is to advance a typology to summarize various influential approaches to aid their exposition. Although this list should not be taken as exhaustive, we will consider folkloric–historical, epistemological–discursive, psychoanalytic/post-structuralist, identity-based, and, finally, realist–materialist approaches.

Folkloric–historical perspectives involve reviewing the cultural history of monstrous representations, often with a long timescale in mind. Such approaches survey the history of representations of monsters from the historical record, often contextualizing them via mythical or religious beliefs. Stephen T. Asma (2009)'s history of the subject begins with classical sources such as Alexander the Great, Aristotle and Pliny the Elder; proceeds via the Bible and *Beowulf*; and through the early modern era, Enlightenment and the theory of evolution. Similarly, Alexa Wright (2013) begins with 'the Monstrous Races' on mediaeval maps and in travel journals; to modern-day serial killers. In each of these cases – and as a regular feature of such accounts – there is a historical 'secularisation' of monsters. Rather than examples of radical evil, supernatural or mythical difference, more recent cases, if not taken from popular culture, derive rather from psychiatry, or abnormal psychology or sociology.

Significant shifts in the conception of monsters are the focus of the 'epistemological-discursive' approaches of Georges Canguilhem and Michel Foucault. Canguilhem's work is not very well known in the English-speaking world, but his ideas on monstrosity have been referred to in various sources, including Wright (2013). His work is interesting because he focuses on the historical evolution of concepts, with a particular focus on the history of science.

One can see the development of conceptions of monsters according to the literature as a change from absolute to relative versions of monstrosity. That is, earlier monsters are mythical, demonic or supernatural entities; or perhaps the result of their intervention in human affairs, for instance, during conception. They are utterly different in kind from the human. Canguilhem by contrast focuses on monstrosity as relative, a particular tendency that departs from normal development, rather than different in kind. This allows him to characterize monstrosity as 'an arrest in development or as a fixation' (2008, p. 15).

Canguilhem's source texts are from the natural sciences. In the original words of one of the sources he references approvingly, the biologist Etienne Wolff (1948, p. 131), 'one might say that the explanation for monsters has taken a decisive step by returning into the framework of the laws of normal embryology'. It is clear from this that Canguilhem's focus is *teratology*, the biological study of monsters, a field where *monstruosité* might also be translated as 'abnormality' or perhaps 'deformity'. Nonetheless, most general treatments of monstrosity from mythical-historical or other perspectives include noted cases from medical history or phenomena such as circus freaks; the overlap between biological monsters and popular culture is therefore pertinent. Perhaps we can see an analogous 'secularisation' of the monster in Canguilhem's account, whereby 'freaks of nature' come to be seen as variants of normality, albeit arrested at a particular point of human or animal development. Where for Asma and Wright, the more recent monster is a psychiatric, psychopathological or sociopathological entity, Canguilhem notes that modern science sees abnormality also from within human and animal (rather than supernatural) development. Elsewhere Canguilhem (1991, p. 278) further outlines the difference between ancient and modern conceptions: 'According to Aristotle, a monster is an error of nature which was "mistaken about matter."' A nineteenth-century scientist such as Isidore Geoffroy Saint-Hilaire, by contrast, is able to define monstrosity as serious, harmful and 'very complex anomalies' (pp. 133–5). The implication is that as particular cases of abnormality, monsters are not radically evil or similarly based on differences in kind. They are, instead, on a scale.

Part of the reputation of Canguilhem in the English-speaking world derives from his influence on Michel Foucault. Indeed, according to Alain Badiou, Canghuilhem is an 'invisible master' of Foucault (Badiou 2009, p. 119). Foucault himself is often referred to in discussions from an epistemological–discursive standpoint, especially for his lectures at the College de France in 1974–5, published in English under the title, *Abnormal*. These lectures outline the 'techniques of normalization' (Foucault 2003, p. 25) that accompany the secularization of the monster in modern times. Specifically, he traces three successive 'figures' in which abnormality is posited in the eighteenth and nineteenth centuries, namely the 'monster', the 'individual to be corrected' and the 'masturbator' (pp. 55–7). The monster itself is the result of 'a natural history organized essentially around the absolute and insurmountable distinctions between species, genus, and kingdoms, et cetera' (p. 62). The absolute and biological distinction of monsters is highlighted in this definition. The later figures of abnormality are human and relativized by comparison. Foucault (2003, p. 131) also mentions Geoffroy Saint-Hilaire as involved in this genealogy; however, his focus in the lectures is on the development of new medico–legal techniques and power during the period in question. One can note the inauspicious decline of the monster, radical and 'absolute' figure of alterity, to be replaced by the less glamorous figure of the furtive adolescent masturbator, as new techniques of power advance.

Recent sources from cultural studies have often taken psychoanalytic or post-structuralist approaches to monstrosity as a figure. Such accounts construe monsters in terms of the unconscious, language and liminality. If the monster is the embodiment of our 'worst fears' (Asma 2009), then this will be accounted for in relation to their significance for the unconscious and fantasy. From a post-structuralist perspective, rather than monsters occupying secure places in taxonomies or distinctions between or among beings, they are border-crossing entities *par excellence*.

Freud's own case studies authorize us to think about monsters, in the obvious sense in which these include a 'Rat Man' and a 'Wolf Man'. The schizoanalytic perspectives of Deleuze and Guattari (1987) rethink these case studies in less Oedipal, more de-territorializing fashion. More widely, the unconscious, as reservoir of repressed thoughts, seems to link with the 'worst fears' that monsters are stated to represent in Asma (2009) and many other surveys. In relation to popular culture, film studies have engaged with psychoanalysis fruitfully in order to interpret monsters on screen. Robin Wood's article 'The American Nightmare' (2003) uses the distinction between basic and surplus repression, derived from Freud, Marcuse and Horowitz. Basic repression in Wood's analysis seems analogous to what Laplanche and Leclaire (1972) term 'primary repression': that which inaugurates the unconscious as such. Surplus repression, for Wood, is 'specific to a particular culture' (p. 63) and so allows us to articulate repressed elements to specific social formations. His article suggests a typology of monsters in relation to the repressed elements they represent, identified along gender, class, race and ethnicity, and age terms. Other influential paradigms from film studies combine psychoanalytic and feminist ideas in order to analyse various types of monster. These often draw from the ideas of Julia Kristeva (1982) on the abject, such as in Barbara Creed's *The Monstrous-Feminine* (1993). In this work, psychoanalytic ideas such as abjection and the archaic feminine are used to analyse a range of films, including those in the *Alien* series.

Other texts take a post-structuralist framework in order to consider monsters as figures. Here, J. J. Cohen's (1996) theses on 'Monster Culture' are emblematic. Cohen's definition of the monster, with its reference to textuality and the deferral of meaning, nods to Derrida's notion of *différance*: 'Like a letter on the page, the monster signifies something other than itself: it is always a displacement, always inhabits the gap between the time of upheaval that created it and the moment into which it is received, to be born again' (p. 4). For Cohen, the difference that monsters represent is often cultural, political or pertaining to racial, sexual or class identity. As with many sources arguing from etymology, monsters are *monitory* figures. Cohen argues that we can extract from them a hermeneutics: 'a method of reading cultures from the monsters they engender' (p. 3). We can find an analogous argument in Weiss (2004), who, once more, presents his ideas as a series of theses: 'In the *Thesaurus Artificiosae Memoriae* (1579), Cosmas Rossellius describes a memory theatre that contains an all-inclusive category, suggesting that *any* monster of *any* sort may be used to signify *any* thing whatsoever, through totally idiosyncratic associations' (p. 124). This, in effect, is to argue that the monster is the ultimate *polysemic* text. In relation to popular music studies, Kobena Mercer's (1986) discussion of the image of Michael Jackson is seminal in this regard, as, following Roland Barthes (1957/2013), he notes that celebrity images can be aesthetic surfaces upon which a society writes its own preoccupations.

A related series of studies on monsters and monstrosity might be characterized as cultural–identity based. These sources often link the concerns of the folkloric–historical surveys, with precise examples taken from literature and folk sources, with an attention to identity that sometimes overlaps with the psychoanalytic and post-structuralist frameworks such as Cohen (1996), Creed (1993) or Wood (2003). Thus, although the sources he refers to are mostly philosophical rather than psychoanalytic, Richard Kearney (2003) argues: 'Whether it be gothic, surrealist or postmodern in genre, the monster continues to hold the subconscious in thrall. And for this reason, the monster remains a personification of our repressed Other' (p. 18). Other theorists consider the political implications of monsters, such as Evelleen Richards (1999), who argues: 'Monsters have always challenged the boundaries of human identity. Typically, they denote physically or morally deviant states of nature' (p. 377). Marie-Hélène Huet (1983 and 1991) analyses the relations between monstrosity and maternity, through a cultural and historicist analysis of philosophical and literary sources from French classicism to the *fin de siècle*. Alongside research by Creed (1993), it is clear that many of the classic studies of monstrosity have implications for the role of women in patriarchal society.

Finally, there have been a number of studies touching on monsters that we might characterize as realist–materialist. The 'realist–constructivist' strain of this work derives from research on the assumptions behind science and technology. To cite one of the best known, Bruno Latour's *We Have Never Been Modern* has been cited in numerous considerations of monster theory and makes mention of monsters in its thesis. Latour's work is a radical questioning of the distinction between nature and culture in modernity. The latter, for Latour, brackets off hybrid objects ('monsters') that partake of both spheres:

> By rendering mixtures unthinkable, by emptying, sweeping, cleaning and purifying the arena that is opened in the central space defined by their three sources of power, the moderns allowed the practice of mediation to recombine all possible monsters without letting them have any effect on the social fabric, or even any contact with it.
>
> (Latour 1993, p. 70)

Instead, Latour calls for a 'Parliament of Things' (p. 142) that includes hybrid objects that straddle the nature–culture divide, constituted by networks that include human and non-human, organic and inorganic actors. Richards, whom we have already mentioned, comes to similar conclusions regarding the marginalization of monsters in relation to anatomy and evolutionary science:

> In sociological terms, biological monsters were marginalized or disempowered in the process of stabilization of a new set of power relations within which it was advantageous to conceive biological and social evolution as generally slow, steady, gradual, and continuous. Where Owen had failed, the Darwinians succeeded in taming the unruly transcendental monster and its radical social implications.
>
> (Richards 1999, p. 411)

Another important theorist from science and technology studies is Donna Haraway, famous, among other things, for her piece 'A Cyborg Manifesto' (1991), which productively recuperates one monster for feminist purposes. In another widely discussed article, Haraway echoes Latour in her assertion: 'In its scientific embodiments as well as in other forms, nature is made, but not entirely by humans; it is a co-construction among humans and non-humans' (Haraway 1992, p. 297). These co-constructions include beings conventionally marginalized as monsters. The rest of the article continues Haraway's interest in identity and politics, specifically what she terms 'inappropriate/d Others'.

The 'materialist' strain of monster theorizing often uses Marxist concepts to think the metaphorical potential of monsters to figure political-economic concepts. As we observe in later chapters, gothic imagery abounds in Marx's own work, in his discussion of the vampiric quality of capital over living labour and so on. David McNally's (2012) *Monsters of the Market* is a survey of such tropes from a Marxist perspective, updating analyses to the present day. Annalee Newitz (2006) also analyses the relations between monsters and capitalism, in relation to American popular culture. Another strain of this materialist strand is associated with the concept of hauntology – derived from the work of Jacques Derrida (1993/2006) and his own reading of Marx – developed in critical commentary on popular music by writers such as Simon Reynolds (2012) and Mark Fisher (2013, 2014). Here, logics of temporal disjuncture are used to figure political-economical aspects of labour and unrealised futures, something that has been linked to both aspects of recording technology – as well as untimely or discredited political ideas, both of which make ghostly returns in the chapters that follow. It should be noted that the 'realist–materialist' studies that have just been enumerated are elsewhere characterized as 'constructivist' – though there is faith in objects and/or material processes, this is in tension with a focus on monsters, with ghosts and imaginary creatures bearing the same ontological status as 'real' and actual ones.

This typology has been offered as a way of ordering a disparate set of works that consider monstrosity from a number of perspectives. It will have been evident from the discussion that many of the studies straddle many of the categories enumerated; some would question our placing certain works in one category rather than another. There are edited collections on monstrosity that feature articles drawing on a number of these perspectives within the same volume (e.g. Hackett and Harrington 2018, 2019). Furthermore, if we take the post-structuralist idea that monsters are border-crossing entities seriously, then any typology is inherently open to question. The list of approaches has been offered here as a heuristic for purposes of exposition, rather than as a rigid classification.

Monstrous masculinities

To begin thinking about monstrosity in relation to masculinity, we can point to a relatively mythical conception of masculinity, elaborated by Sigmund Freud in his 1913 work, *Totem and Taboo* (Freud 1913/2001). This work, and in particular the myth of the father of the primal horde, has frequently been taken up by later writers on masculinity. Anthony Easthope (1990, pp. 19–23), for instance, analyses the canonical Western, *Red River* (Howard Hawks 1948) in order to elucidate the logic of Freud's theory. Freud attributes the 'primal horde' myth to Darwin and employs it as a sort of thought experiment in order to explain some of the 'phylogenetic' aspects of the mind – our psychic inheritance from an evolutionary perspective as a species. It is advanced as a conjecture to illustrate the psychic mechanisms he has been identifying, derived largely from anthropology and traced from totemic cultures to the mental life of what Freud characterizes as modern civilization. In particular, this forms part of Freud's theorizing of the genesis of the superego, the agency of conscience, guilt and religion.

Freud evokes a 'primal horde' or tribal civilization, in which a dominating father monopolizes access to all women. This is to the absolute exclusion of his sons, who are relegated resentfully to a band united in their hatred of the father and lack of access to love objects, including their mother. Freud theorizes that this horde of brothers at some point unite and kill the father, later feasting on his remains. He traces this as the event that prefigures the totem meal identified in the anthropological accounts he had studied, involving a binge consumption of the totem animal that is otherwise taboo for the tribe. Freud observes that totemic feats are followed by mourning for the loss of the animal killed 'by dread of a threatened retribution' (p. 201). As such, this foreshadows the existence of a separate agency of guilt, morality and conscience that Freud names the superego.

The myth of the primal father connects Oedipal issues (male competition in the family) to capitalism (male competition in society). It perhaps gains full development in the later elaboration of this text in Lacanian psychoanalysis. In the latter, the most familiar instance of the father in psychic life is the father as 'paternal metaphor', that is, as the transcendental signifier in the symbolic order of language and law. Where Freud's Oedipus complex was theorized apparently in more flesh-and-blood terms, the place of the father in Lacan's 'structuralist' elaboration of the theory is much rather in terms of linguistics and of the unconscious structured as a language. Where Freudian psychoanalysis elaborated the Oedipus complex in terms of a fantasy of the infant about a real threat of castration at the hands of the father, in Lacan the emphasis is more on an irreducible lack that is instituted on the infant's entry into the symbolic order of language and law.

Now, in Lacan's later thinking, the 'primal' father of the horde retains an existence in the psyche as the 'real' father outside the symbolic order. If the paternal metaphor of the symbolic order is structuring it *as being* absent, then the primal father returns as all-too-present when the symbolic father is in abeyance. This is why Slavoj Žižek can characterize the real father as 'the obscene, uncanny, shadowy double of "the Name of the Father" … a kind of "master of enjoyment," a paternal figure which comes closest to what Kant called "radical evil,"' (Žižek 2001, p. 158). Furthermore, and crucially, the real father emerges at a time when the paternal metaphor is under attack or in decline. Žižek's particular example here is taken from American film noir. For Žižek, the obscene father allows us to make sense of this film genre; its weak, compromised male protagonists; and its deadly femmes fatales; in terms of a wider cultural crisis in masculinity. Although the primal father may appear primordial, Žižek characterizes it as 'a thoroughly *modern* entity' (2001, p. 159).

Now we can return to Connell's earlier formulation of hegemonic masculinities and supplement it with a psychoanalytic conception. Connell can be seen as conceiving of hegemonic masculinity in terms of a specific, situated 'gender project', one based on transnational business masculinity, propped up in marketing terms through the visual display of the bodies of elite sportsmen. Interestingly, Connell observes that the entrepreneurial masculinity has displaced its recent rival, 'the rigid, control-oriented masculinity of military command, a variant of which is the military-style bureaucratic dictatorships of Stalinism' (Connell 2000, p. 54). Although it may sound glib to state this in such bald terms, what else are the current leaders of the first and former second worlds – Trump and Putin – but two versions of this hegemonic masculinity personified?

Putin is the most straightforward case – a resurgence and revival of what Connell (2000) had understandably written off in 2000 – the oligarchic dictator modelled on Stalin (albeit with all reference to communism removed). Trump can now be characterized by us as a hybrid between Connell's (2000) transnational business masculinity and Freud's primal, obscene father. His oft-noted business acumen is arguably fused with the sadistic and libidinal impulses that the 'civilised' post-Oedipal Westerner must repress, but that Trump is allowed to indulge with no reservation ('grab them by the pussy' and all). Indeed, these two leaders are by now notoriously compatible with one another, leading to a rather obscene complicity of hegemonic masculinities, modern and primordial, aggressive and instinctual. To complete this scheme, the decline of the symbolic version of masculinity, the 'name of the father' or the law, can be linked to the widespread backlash against a straw-man construction of the 'liberal elite'.

Popular music, gender, and monstrosity

Having discussed monstrosity and masculinity, we are now in a position to return to popular music. Simon Frith and Angela McRobbie's classic 1978 article, 'Rock and Sexuality', is an early landmark on the subject. By reinforcing dominant norms regarding masculinity and femininity in the sphere of consumption, they said, popular music contributed to an individual and collective 'sexualization of leisure' (p. 395). More specifically, the two researchers consider the gendered nature and 'patriarchal dividend' inherent in rock music as a genre, taking this to operate through '*construction* of sexuality' (1978/1990, p. 373; emphasis in original). In relation to this, we might consider the performance of specific, contextual masculinities in popular music through at least two associated lenses: *spaces* (of musical culture) and *texts* (or their performers, whose public identities are intertextual constructs).

In terms of spaces of performance, Frith and McRobbie (1978/1990) parallel the claims of Laura Mulvey's 1975 *Screen* article on the gendered nature of visual pleasure in narrative cinema, only they consider a musical genre: 'The music business is male-run; popular musicians, writers, creators, technicians, engineers, and producers are mostly men' (Frith and McRobbie, 1978/1990, p. 373). This claim was developed by Mavis Bayton (1998) in her work on the music industry. Concern for the gendering of spaces of musical culture – and, frequently, the associated sexism (or resistance to it) – was extended from there, across music education (Green 1997), music journalism (Davies 2001) and, notably, local music scenes.

We mention in this regard the pioneering studies of particular, regionally and genre-specific scenes, their practitioners and audiences. To mention just two, Sara Cohen's (1991) study of popular music culture in Liverpool and Barry Shank's (1994) monograph on the scene in Austin, Texas, each situate gendered practices of production and consumption with precision in relation to carefully delineated contexts. Such research has been paralleled by the rise of work examining dynamics in particular music genres. Matthew Bannister's (2006) study of masculinity and indie rock argues that genre is generalizable across multiple music scenes in different countries and continents, and can therefore be privileged over 'scene' as an analytical framework. Other researchers, such as Neil Nehring (1997) and Robin James (2015) have explored how particular music genres have been *appropriated* because they afford non-traditional expressions of gender identity which therefore broaden accented ideas of how each gender can behave. Marion Leonard's (2007) study of women playing indie rock notes, however: 'Indie music may be understood as offering an alternative articulation of masculinity rather than operating as a gender-neutral or pro-female category' (p. 48). Leonard's analysis extends the consideration of cultural spaces through examination of the ways in which studio, touring and press practices tend to marginalize the participation of female performers in these spheres; her study is well-supported through interviews with some notable as well as aspiring musicians in the genre. She therefore highlights specific musical spaces in which gender is performed and which serve as locales for endorsing and sometimes challenging normative gender constructions. Other examples of gatekeeping practices that might serve to exclude potential female musicians are considered by Mary Ann Clawson (1999 and 1999a) and Carey Sargent (2009), among others. Clawson's two articles track the ways in which male domination is enforced through recruitment of band members during adolescence, usually along gendered lines; as well as relegation of female musicians to limited choices of instrument through the more recent vogue in certain forms of rock music for female bassists. In relation to the first of these questions, Clawson argues: 'Being a boy served, in these early years, as a form of social and cultural capital. Girls lacked access to an entitlement that seemed to be assumed by boys: the cultural authority to initiate band formation' (Clawson 1999, p. 111).

A concern for the gendering of specific locales is reflected by work on spaces fully devoted to music consumption as well as production. Several scholars have pointed to the traditional record shop as a prime example of a *masculinised space* in popular music. Will Straw (1997) explores record collecting as 'nerdish homosociality' (p. 15) that avoids the most obvious locations for the exercise of hegemonic masculinity, while simultaneously carving out a masculine space through exclusionary curatorial practices. This will likely operate differently according to musical genre concerned: contemporary R&B operates differently to, say, black metal. A more recent study by Matthew Bannister (2006) sees the record shop as central to indie rock in providing a locus for gatekeeping practices:

> I suggest re-envisioning indie as a history of record collectors – the importance of rock tradition to indie, of male rock 'intellectuals' and secondhand record shops; a narrative suppressed because of the normative emphasis on rock as a folk discourse, spontaneous, instinctual, closely allied to a 'natural' masculinity.
> (Bannister 2006, pp. xxvi–xvii)

Straw's and Bannister's analyses bring out the fraught and often contradictory practices involved in indie's simultaneous *rejection* of some hegemonically masculine presentation (and self-presentation) styles, together with its *reproduction* of certain alternative yet still dominant styles enforced through cultural capital.

A second research trajectory to emerge from Frith and McRobbie's (1978/1990) seminal work considers popular music texts and their performers, and, in particular, the ways in which these *perform* gendered identities. Like the music itself, popular music studies have been part of a cultural movement that has reconsidered the nature of gender, helping to locate it as cultural rather than natural. Commercial music has, perhaps, lent itself to this because, while appearing to express authentic, one might even say bodily, identities and emotions – Barthes's (1977) classic notion of the 'grain of the voice' is an example – it is, at the same time, open to creative artistic and political projects, technologies and modes of stage performance that serve to *denaturalize* gender. Musical performance is, furthermore, so wide-ranging that it is a place where different gender identities are exposed, expressed, negotiated or constructed. In this context, Frith and McRobbie's 1978 article discussed a genre of rock that embodied hegemonic, heteronormative masculinity, namely 'cock rock'. The latter was contrasted with 'teeny bop', which the authors identified with males performing softer, romantic masculinities primarily for a young female audience. These two styles represented different performances of masculinity that were 'predicated on sexual divisions in the appropriation of rock' (p. 375). For performers, gender roles could also be delimited by music in other ways: Frith and McRobbie (1978/1990) mention 'the singer-songwriter/folkie lady' (p. 377) and the 'ambivalent sexuality' or 'camp' of glam rock (p. 382).

Returning to Freud, 'cock rock' obviously has phallic connotations. If it is not too fanciful, we might consider the dubious appeal of Donald Trump as in some ways related to the apparently less sinister appeal of iconic rock or hip hop musicians. Whitehead (2002) identifies the nineteenth- and twentieth-century instances of transnational business masculinity:

> He is the self-made man carved out in the image of Ford, Hurst, Hughes, Goldwyn, Carnegie, Rockefeller, Beaverbrook. His contemporaries are global entrepreneurs such as Bill Gates, Donald Trump, George Soras [sic], Richard Branson and Rupert Murdoch.
>
> (Whitehead 2002, p. 122)

Whitehead (2002) then supplements this with a more recent list: 'However, unlike the singularly besuited (White) Rockefeller or Ford, contemporary global icons of (heterosexual) male potency are just as likely to include Ice T, Michael Jordan, David Beckham, Brad Pitt or Eminem' (Whitehead 2002, p. 122). Further credence to these parallels comes from Imani Perry, whose study of poetics and politics in hip hop notes that 'Donald Trump, Bill Gates, and Bill Clinton, White men who have played the game successfully, are often appreciated in depoliticized form as role models for street players in hip hop' (Perry 2004, p. 124). Given the prominence of their respective corporate brands, we might go back to earlier forms of popular music, such as rock, to consider such figures as Mick Jagger, Robert Plant and Ozzy Osbourne as further 'cock rock' candidates who fuse thrusting masculinity and business success.

One contention here might be that visibly successful male musicians in certain dominant musical forms, such as 1970s rock, or more recently hip hop, often share this fusion of hegemonic entrepreneurial masculinity with the monopoly on enjoyment of the obscene father. Here we can allude again to Simon Frith and Angela McRobbie's claim, 'Cock rock performers are aggressive, dominating, and boastful, and they constantly seek to remind the audience of their prowess, their control' (1978/1990, p. 374). In hip hop the performer as not only monopolizing enjoyment, but also becoming a one-man corporation, is highlighted even further, with artists like Jay-Z ('Girls, Girls, Girls' and Rocawear), Dr. Dre (with his multi-million Beats headphone business) or 50 Cent (from 'P.I.M.P.' to his Formula 50 soft drink, to later forays into film production and other ventures).

'Cock rock' is not, however, the be-all and end-all of performances of masculinity in popular music. In reality, just like in the case of musical spaces such as scenes or collective genre cultures, the gendering of performance texts is a form of communication that is both specific and responsive to particular cultural contexts. A number of useful books on popular music have focus on this (con)textual performance of gender since Frith and McRobbie's (1978/1990) pioneering work. These include edited collections by Whiteley (1997), Jarman-Ivens (2007) and Lee (2018), as well as monographs by Hawkins (2009) and Auslander (2006) and White (2011). In recent years, queer studies have helped to reformulate approaches to gender identity, both in academia and in the commercial marketplace, leading gender theorists such as Jack Halberstam (2012) to take a deeper interest in pop performance.

It is to questions of gender performance in popular music texts that most of the trickle of work on popular music and monstrosity has, so far, spoken. Beyond occasional surveys of Halloween recordings and similar material (see Cooper 2006), existing discussions of monstrosity often talk about performers who have pushed accepted notions of gender or other boundaries. In recent years, inspired by artists such as Bowie and Jackson, a range of performers have continued to challenge the naturalization of gender and have been examined in relation to the idea of monstrosity. Seth Cosimini (2017), for example, has studied Nicki Minaj in this respect. When Lady Gaga emerged, she extended this playful engagement with monstrosity, labelling herself 'Mother Monster' to a community of 'Little Monsters' and in doing so, helping a diverse range of fans improve their self-esteem (see Corona 2011; Varriale 2012; Click, Lee and Willson Holladay 2013). In seeming contrast to the playful theatricality of pop, monstrosity has also been studied in other genres as a mode of *authenticating* gender. Niall Scott (2007), Stan Hawkins and Nina Nielsen (2020), for instance, have considered heavy metal. Questions around the meaning of hyper-masculine modes of rock performance raise the idea that 'toxic masculinity' may itself, particularly in light of the #MeToo era, be perceived as inherently 'monstrous': angry, cursed, guilty, capable of acting out violence. This notion of White nihilistic masculine self-hatred is, to some degree, associated with and performed through various rock genres, such as metal and emo.

Having made this brief, disciplinary survey, it is in the analysis of particular case studies in this book that the variety of masculinities on display in popular music cultures will emerge. It is not our intention here to side with any singular academic conception of masculinity or masculinities at the exclusion of others. Some of these approaches will be more fruitful for particular chapters in the current study, but they are all conceptual tools that will inform the case studies on some level, even if implicitly. With the help of these different ideas, we have found much to say about masculinity and monstrosity in relation to popular music culture. Staking out this broad territory has situated the study in relation to more general discussions, some departing from our own objects. Previous research on both masculinity and monstrosity in other disciplines has also helped to sharpen our ideas. We aim to signal the specificity of popular music as a medium where pertinent. Our survey of popular music and gender in this introduction has only sketched part of the subject, saying relatively little, for example, on masculinity and race, sexual orientation or music genres like electronic dance music.

Chapter outline

Various chapters in this volume engage with this problematic of dominant masculinities as performed in popular music. In most cases, masculinity is questioned or troubled, if not in some crisis or other. In this section, we will outline the contents of the chapters that follow, locating them in terms of the ideas discussed in the previous parts of this introduction on masculinity and monstrosity. Chapter 1 offers an analysis of adaptations of Gaston Leroux's classic novel *The Phantom of the Opera* (1911) on stage, screen and record. Leroux's appealing story explores the fraught, but romantic, relationship between female projection and masculine monstrosity in a way that allows it to be reinvented as a way to speak about different issues at different moments. Drawing on Steven Schneider's (1999) notion of monsters as uncanny metaphors, this chapter explores how the disfigured Phantom has been updated to express changing anxieties about popular music in an age of mechanical reproduction. Taking in questions of Oedipal spectrality, the chapter begins to consider damaged or alternative masculinities. Different versions of the Phantom story – particularly film adaptions such as Brian de Palma's *Phantom of the Paradise* (1974) and *Kiss Meets the Phantom of the Park* (Hessler 1978) – are therefore contrasted to explore the ways in which they portray the uncanny, twilight figure of the Phantom in relation to monstrosity, masculinity and music as the product of a business based on pleasure.

Race provides a way, for Connell (2000), to subordinate certain masculinities to hegemonic versions; we begin to explore this terrain in the second chapter, which considers perceptions of the Black artist Lead Belly in relation to the 1933 RKO blockbuster, *King Kong*. Cooper and Schoedsack's film alludes to a racial theme in the proclamation of its director protagonist, Carl Denham, 'I tell you that there's something on that island that no White man has ever seen.' A year after the film's release, folklorist John Lomax recorded the music of a convicted murderer named Huddie Leadbetter in the Louisiana penitentiary. Although there are of course significant differences between the two stories, both narratives involve mythic encounters that were publicly staged in ways that drew upon shared assumptions about the place of the Other. Both performances played to primitivist anxieties about male Blackness as an implicit threat to the fabric of civilization. This chapter connects to an epistemological–discursive treatment of monstrosity, using its approach to examine race-making in popular music and the wider culture.

Chapter 3 picks up the psychoanalytic thread established by the first chapter to study the infamous manager of Elvis Presley, Colonel Tom Parker, a man who has been widely perceived as a kind of monster. Not only did the Colonel keep up to half of the profits made by his client, his legend also cast him as someone who never cared for Elvis as anything other than a commodity (Bertrand 2011). Worse still, it eventually suggested that Parker had a shadowy background that almost certainly involved con tricks and may have included murder. This chapter will argue that Parker's public image embodied the venal, rapacious side of the music industry (epitomized in the idea of the carnival), that his primary role in the Presley myth was perceived as an Oedipal one (in effect an inescapable 'bad father'), and ultimately that Parker carefully engineered and played upon his monstrous reputation. While on the surface he resembled an 'obscene father', such attribution underplays the agency of his charge: in certain cases Elvis was keen to use Parker as an alibi for his own unstated agency.

In terms of our typology of monstrosity outlined earlier, we might say that partly due to our focus on mass-mediated popular music, folkloric–historical perspectives play a relatively minor part in the study. Nonetheless, an attention to a popular literary text, its mediation and contemporary reception, has a considerable role in Chapter 4. Here the post-structuralist idea of monsters as metaphors and boundary-crossers returns. Having already analysed *The Phantom of the Opera*, this chapter considers how *Frankenstein* has created an enduring myth that has been highly mobile across a range of media forms. In particular, our case study considers glam rock. At the start of the 1970s, bands as diverse as the New York Dolls and Edgar Winter Group recorded songs bearing the monster's name – originally its creator's and then 'misread' as the creature by pop culture. Two years later, *The Rocky Horror Picture Show* (Sharman 1975) drew on science fiction, horror movie nostalgia and camp to create gender trouble. Dr Frank-N-Furter epitomized the reshaping of the legend in the context of marginalized masculinities. Parliament's 1976 album, *The Clones of Dr. Funkenstein*, combined funk and glam aesthetics in service of an Afrofuturist agenda. These glam texts embody the 'excessive interpretability' that Halberstam (1995) has suggested characterizes monstrosity generally. Tracing Frankenstein as a cipher moving between radically different entities, this chapter is the nearest the book gets in its study of monstrosity to following Latour's approach. It explores Frankenstein as an adaptive self-perpetuating metaphor across a range of popular music texts and performances.

Some masculinities are widely considered 'beyond the pale'. Chapter 5 explores the discursive construction of extreme fandom as monstrosity. In December 1980, Mark Chapman was convicted of fatally shooting John Lennon. Chapman has been described as a deranged fan or 'fame monster' who thought that he could achieve notoriety by killing a famous person. Although the reading has gained currency among media commentators, by failing to take Chapman's mental illness into consideration, it proves inadequate to fully understand his crime. Yoko Ono, John Lennon's widow, meanwhile, has attempted to deny Chapman fame or freedom by locating her husband's death as a public trauma, in effect, without meaningful cause. This chapter argues that such a reading not only draws attention away from the complexity of Lennon's celebrity image, it also helps to reduce both the killer and his victim as entities that take on their meaning through a meaningless act. Like the final two chapters, this one explores fraught discursive battlegrounds in which the cases at hand are made sense of by a wider culture.

Monstrosity can provide a discourse in which to address social and political issues obliquely. After the decline of Black nationalist and Muslim themes in rap music (Reeves 2008), in the early 1990s a new subgenre emerged in hip hop called 'horrorcore'. A series of artists appropriated monstrous imagery from horror films. Gravediggaz, for example, had a first album titled *6 Feet Deep* in the United States, which was released elsewhere as *Niggamortis*. The focus of Chapter 6 is on the cultural work performed by monstrous tropes in the context of the group's music. More specifically, we will consider how horrorcore imagery can be related to both monstrous and supernatural metaphors in Marx's work and notions of the 'Black gothic' read in the narratives of Toni Morrison and Richard Wright. Oral folklore frames for monstrosity are considered here. The argument is that horrorcore represented a displacement of political and economic concerns into a new lexis inspired by the supernatural. This allowed it to avoid some of the constraints of a hegemonic spectacular masculinity associated with mainstream gangsta rap.

The general 'secularisation' of the monster, from mythical beast to human, all too human, is reflected in the trajectory of the chapters towards the end of our book. Continuing a previous focus on violent crime, Chapter 7 looks at the French rock band, Noir Désir, asking what happens when a rock idol does something unambiguously monstrous? From the late 1980s, Noir Désir became one of the biggest French rock bands of their era. The group fell from grace when its lead singer Bertrand Cantat was incarcerated in Lithuania on a charge of murder committed with indirect intent (*dolus eventualis*) following the death of his girlfriend, the actress Marie Trintignant. In the aftermath of his crime, *Paris Match* called Cantat 'a monster and a saint'. Commentaries on the events of Vilnius and succeeding the trial took very different perspectives in relation to domestic violence, gender relations and doomed love (*amour fou*). This chapter examines the coverage in both French and British media by looking at discourses used to interpret Cantat's crime. In particular it considers how a vocabulary of doomed romance, and monstrosity and damnation, was used to articulate the case with wider cultural and gender politics. The chapter also considers the psychoanalytic concept of narcissism.

Finally, we turn to another 'monster' of rock music, famous radio DJ, TV presenter and charity fund raiser Jimmy Savile. When the British entertainer died, it was revealed that he had committed sexual assaults against hundreds of innocent young people, including children of both sexes. Savile's offences were long-rumoured, but their industrial scale came as a shock to many.

Some speculated that Jimmy Savile was never bought to justice because he was protected by the 'deep state'. Chapter 8 focuses on Savile's celebrity image, suggesting that it positioned him as a kind of 'spiv' who used the permissive reputation of the music industry as a way to abet his 'hiding in plain sight' and bragging of his crimes.

Both masculinity and monstrosity are relatively recent objects of study, at least in the cultural sense; their mutual implication in the analysis of music is an under-theorized field. This introduction has sketched dominant paradigms in the cultural study of masculinity and of monstrosity, before outlining the contents of the chapters that follow. In the case studies in this book we aim to establish the pertinence of these frameworks for the study of popular music culture, by presenting a variety of examples and a range of musical styles, scenes and contexts.

1

A night at the Opera: Updating *The Phantom*

Music and monsters often go together. Nowhere is this clearer than in Gaston Leroux's perennially popular story *The Phantom of the Opera*. When it was published in 1909, Leroux was churning out two novels a year – thirty in his lifetime – and saw himself as a commercial writer. He was, in a sense, an early exploitation merchant, a figure who specialized in turning subjects such as mutilation and cannibalism into commercial product. Leroux's tale of the Phantom was about unrequited love and the haunting of a talented young singer. Christine Daaé's father has died. As she slides into a state of madness, she hears a voice which she believes is the Angel of Music, sent by him to protect her. It turns out to be Erik, a physically disfigured character who lives underneath the Paris Opera House. Erik falls in love with Christine and teaches her how to excel as a singer. She cannot be his, however, both because he seems mysterious and tainted with death, and as she loves her childhood sweetheart, who is now Vicomte (Viscount) Raoul de Chagny. When Erik realizes that Raoul wants to kill him, he kidnaps Christine and threatens to blow up the Opera House. She then goes along with his ideas and pledges to marry him. In the story's climax, Erik's emotions are turned by their first kiss; after it, he frees Christine to be with Raoul and takes his own life.

A few years before Leroux finished *The Phantom of the Opera*, in *The Interpretation of Dreams*, Sigmund Freud (Freud 1900/1997a) talked about the family romance. His conception of psychosexual development centred on the way that our first relationship – that with our parents – shapes our understanding of intimate personal relationships. In brief, Freud believed that until they found ways to move on, boys became possessively attached to their mothers (the Oedipus complex) and feared they might be punished by their fathers (castration anxiety). For girls, the situation was a mirror image, with the father as repressed object of initial romantic stirrings. We are all challenged to move beyond the ties that bind us to such first relationships without losing appreciation for our parents' unending love. Especially if anything goes wrong in early childhood, it can be hard to understand that you will always be your parents' son or daughter, without always being their child. The family romance animated gothic literature well before Freud invented psychoanalysis, and *The Phantom of the Opera* was in the tradition. Beginning in 1764 with Horace Walpole's *The Castle of Otranto: A Gothic Story*, the death-obsessed genre of gothic literature often included ghastly family curses and secrets uncovered by hapless innocents; it pointed to the diminishing role of fatherhood. Talking about gothic art, Gilda Williams (2007) adds:

> The Gothic is escapist, retreating into distant landscapes, lost eras and outlandish personal appearance. It celebrates depression as a kind of desirable, living death. This inclination to transcend the ordinary, cultivate the anti-social and experiment with the sexual unknown makes Gothic a perfect haven for adolescence.
>
> (p. 15)

She adds that 'the Gothic remains indebted to an expansive group of broadly related themes' (p. 16) which include a 'perpetual erotic subtext' (p. 17).

The Gothic sensibility is sensual, uncanny, refined, aesthetic, vampiric, abandoned and excessive, bringing together things that should have been kept apart; it rejects common sense, rationality, science and hard work. In short, it offers a kind of receding refuge from the harshness of the modern world; a chance for us to live it again in a different way. This refuge is also, however, a means of entrapment. With its emanating and enveloping, supposedly possessing quality, perhaps nothing is as gothic as music. Sound can therefore challenge the fixity of boundaries of the Self. In classic gothic literature, a vessel for the self is the haunted house. It becomes a dark expression of family patterns being handed on from the past. Leroux sutures Phantom to this tradition when he describes the Paris Opera House: 'They were almost alone in the huge, gloomy house; and a great silence surrounded them' (p. 67). Erik nevertheless has a saving grace. He is a hideous, masked 'monster' (Leroux 1909/2011, p. 137), but he is also a maestro: a composer and music maker. He explains that he has been working on a piece called *Don Juan Triumphant* and adds, 'I began that work twenty years ago. When I have finished, I shall take it away with me in that coffin [where I sleep] and never wake up' (p. 133).

The *Phantom* story rests on a number of assumptions about music based on romanticist thinking that emerged slowly and were prominent by the time Beethoven's work was celebrated. Music professor Nicholas Cook summarizes:

> There is, in short, a nexus of interrelated assumptions built into the basic language we use of music: that musicianship is the preserve of appropriately qualified specialists; that innovation (research and design) is central to musical culture; that the key personnel in musical culture are the composers who generate what might be termed the core product; that the performers are in essence no more than middlemen, apart from those exceptional interpreters who acquire a kind of honorary composer's status; and that listeners are consumers, playing an essentially passive role in the cultural process that, in economic terms, they underpin.
>
> (Cook 2000, p. 17)

Cook suggests that such assumptions led to the idea that music could be collected together in a museum, an archive that both registers the creative contribution of particular individuals from the past and, as collection or canon, keeps alive the memory of originators.

As a composer, Erik occupies a privileged place in this social process, yet as a ghost he is impotent in getting his music heard by anyone other than the performers who sing in his name. The voice promises to return Christine to the plenitude of her first romance with her father, despite his passing, through musical performance: 'I will play "The Resurrection of Lazarus", on the stroke of midnight, on your father's tomb and on your father's violin' (p. 124). Inspired by the memory of her father, Christine channels the perfect music which Erik makes available. His music forms part of the sentimental attachment that draws Christine to him. Describing a performance of his piece *Don Juan Triumphant*, Christine explains that it 'seemed to me at first one long, awful, magnificent sob. But, little by little, it expressed every emotion, every suffering of which mankind is capable. It intoxicated me; and it opened the door which separated us' (p. 136). Christine is, in some ways, Erik's fan. She displays traits stereotypically associated with fandom, having a hysterical, 'highly strung imagination' (p. 86). She is also possessed, explaining, 'Alas, I was no longer mistress of myself: I had become his thing!' (p. 124). Then, 'I can tell you the effect that the music had upon me. It seemed to command me, personally, to come, to stand up and to come to it ... I believed in it' (p. 125). When Christine vanishes, Raoul ponders, 'What influence has she undergone. What monster had carried her off and by what means?'

(p. 94) Raoul realizes the danger: 'I saw your ecstasy *at the sound of the voice*, Christine … And that is what makes me alarmed on your behalf. You are under a very dangerous spell' (p. 108). He adds, 'When a man adopts such romantic methods to entice a young girl's affections, the man must either be a villain, or the girl a fool: is that it?' Christine replies, 'Raoul, why do you condemn a man you have never seen, whom no one knows and about whom you, yourself know nothing?' (p. 109) Christine's possession is a point which conjoins the gothic to mass cultural assumptions about fandom,[1] because it suggests an abdication of personal autonomy (she cannot guide her own thoughts) and perhaps also subjectivity (she is no longer herself).

Christine's tutelage from Erik is in part a matter of him bringing down the music of the spheres, but also of her reaching inside herself to find her soul. Raoul, meanwhile, *is also Christine's fan* and finds empathy in *her* sorrow: 'Oh Christine, my heart quivered that night at every accent of your voice. I saw the tears stream down your cheeks and I wept with you' (p. 123). As Raoul said, 'No professor can teach you accents such as those' (p. 61). He recalls:

> Christine and I knew that music; we had heard it as children. But it had never been executed with such divine art, even by [her father] Monsieur Daaé. I remembered all that Christine had told me of the Angel of Music. The air was The "Resurrection of Lazarus", which old Monsieur Daaé used to play to us in his hours of melancholy and of faith. If Christine's Angel had existed, it could not have played better, that night, on the late musician's violin.
>
> (p. 65)

On one level, we can read Erik simply as crass, commercial culture penetrating the Opera House, a grand bastion of high culture. After shocking his own parents, Erik found employment exploited as a 'living corpse' in fairs across Europe (p. 274).

Aural spectrality: Music in the age of sound recording

> For several months, there had been nothing discussed at the Opera but this ghost in dress clothes who stalked about the building, from top to bottom, like a shadow, who spoke to nobody, to whom nobody dared speak, and who vanished as soon as he was seen, no one knowing how or where. As became a real ghost, he made no noise in walking. (Leroux, 1909/2011, p. 8)

Erik begins as a ghost in Leroux's story. Unseen as he is, here, he represents a phantom spectator, perched up in Box Five of the grand tier of the theatre: both an upper class subject ('in dress clothes') and an isolated nonentity. Christine's friend Meg Giry concludes, 'The ghost is not seen … You only hear him when he is in the box. Mother has never seen him, but she has heard him' (1909/2011, p. 14). The theme of exclusive audibility recurs when Raoul eavesdrops on Christine's dressing room, where he hears a man's voice demand that she love him. Leroux pointedly quips, 'What a position for Chagny! To be caught listening behind a door!' (1909/2011, p. 24). The Angel of Music is similarly, an audible experience: 'No one ever sees the Angel; but he is heard by those who are meant to hear him' (p. 55). Christine explains, 'I had heard him for three months without seeing him. The first time I heard it, I thought, as you did, that that adorable voice was singing in another room' (p. 121). That Raoul hears the voice too is important; Leroux follows it by a passage where the Vicomte sees multiple reflections of his lover in a mirror and wells up with tears, as if he is both aware that she is his own projection, and he is also drawn into her world of melancholic madness.

On another level, Erik himself conforms to the mass cultural notion of the demented fan. He is initially deceptive to Christine, telling her that he is indeed the Angel of Music that her father had promised to send after his death (p. 121). He also runs an extortion racket, demanding 240,000 francs per year in allowances from the Opera management (Leroux, 1909/2011, p. 33). Like a stalker, he lives in the shadows and threatens another singer called Carlotta so that Christine can take her place. At one point Erik writes, 'If you appear tonight, you must be prepared for a great misfortune at the moment when you open your mouth to sing … a misfortune worse than death' (p. 74). His interest in Christine is both a matter of unrequited love, and the idea that he can vicariously express his living essence (his creativity) through the voice and body of a 'real' living proxy. When Carlotta cannot perform and croaks like a frog, her lost voice signifies Erik's own impotence: 'But everyone knew how perfect an instrument her voice was; and there was no display of anger, but only of horror and dismay' (p. 82). Indeed, the House managers, who are in the audience, in Erik's box, immediately feel his presence and croak themselves, 'smarting under the ghost's attacks' (p. 83). They 'distinctly heard his voice in their right ears, the impossible voice, the mouthless voice' which tells them the chandelier is about to come crashing down (p. 84). This 'mouthless voice' is a voice that appears to evoke what Michel Chion, calls acousmatic listening, 'a situation wherein one hears the sound without seeing its cause' (1994, p. 32): a form of sound and perceiving it that both confounds the listener's understanding of its source and allows them to focus on it as *sound qua sound*.

Leroux's novel was written in the wake of the early emergence of electronic media and audio playback technology. Recordings of the human voice date back to around 1860, when a phonautogram inscribed a twenty-second recording of the French folk tune, 'Au clair de la lune.' It was a short step from here to Thomas Edison's phonograph, which allowed in 1877 for virtually instantaneous playback, and Emile Berliner's gramophone, a decade later, which played the flat discs that were the forerunner of vinyl records. Music historian Keir Keightley (2015) has shown that the assumptions that emerged around canned food suggesting something tainted or mediocre were transferred into discussions of music. By 1895, critics had begun talking disparagingly about 'canned music' as something compromised and made inferior. This gradually led to the idea that commercial imperatives had driven the adoption of sound carriers that both preserved music and, in a sense, destroyed its beauty or spirit.

Erik haunts. Tainted by death and sweetly singing with a 'mouthless voice', he is arguably positioned as a kind of contagion emerging from the newly ambient technology of canned music. 'Hauntology' is a term developed from the work of philosopher Jacques Derrida (1993/2006) to think about the way one thing can almost imperceptibly influence another, with time being out of joint (see Fisher 2013, 2014). In popular music research, the term has gained currency as a way to talk about how sound recordings give an illusion of rooted experience when what they actually present is a mere surface of sound. Recent academic discussions of 'hauntology' do not so much point to actual audience experience; audiences have rapidly become accustomed to the creep of mimetic media and only have an 'eerie' experience of it when commentators frame it that way. Instead, hauntology has become a kind of educative reading, designed to highlight the prominence of 'dead labour' in the production process. While Marx did not use the term, he outlined the concept in *A Contribution to the Critique of Political Economy*:

> The sole antithesis to objectified labour is non-objectified, *living labour*. The one is present in space, the other in time, the one is in the past, the other is in the present, the one is already embodied in use value, the other, as human activity-in-process, is currently engaged in the process of self-objectification, the one is value, the other is value-creating.
>
> (Marx 1859/2010, p. 35)

As technology moves forwards, the increasing predominance of dead labour in the production process is only meaningful insofar that it displaces and marginalizes living labour, rendering workers unemployed and changing their role. As Marx (1939/1993, p. 705) explained in the *Grundrisse*, as labour gets objectified, it 'no longer appears so much to be included within the production process; rather, the human being comes to relate more as a watchman and regulator to the production process itself'. The progressive waves of industrialization have both transformed our daily occupations and continually reshaped our modes of entertainment. Seen this way, *Phantom of the Opera* reads as a novel about the coming of sound recording as a force of creative destruction that upset the live music industry. Before an epilogue, it ends by saying, 'Erik is dead'; a phrase that takes on the status of a realization if we interpret Erik as the embodiment of documented sound. Journalists often talk about 'the day the music died' to be a tragedy that silences a community by robbing it of a key music maker: Buddy Holly, Elvis, Kurt Cobain or whoever. Yet sound recording itself kills music – ends its liveness and relocates the present as a memory. The miracle of 'dead' music, though, is that it comes alive when played, unless it is buried. In the prologue to his story, Leroux shares a letter from 'General D' about the kidnapping of aristocrat Vicomte de Chagny and disappearance of Chistine Daaé:

> It will be remembered that, later, when digging in the substructure of the Opera, before burying the phonographic records of the artist's voice, the workmen laid bare a corpse. I was at once able to prove that this corpse was that of the Opera ghost. I made the acting-manager put this proof to the test with his own hand; and it is now a matter of indifference to me if the papers pretend that the body was that of a victim of the [Paris] Commune.
> (Leroux 1909/2011, p. 5)

The notion of burying the records and finding a corpse is reminiscent of fans who declare their wish to be buried with music, like the dedicated Status Quo fan in the record shop documentary, *Sound It Out* (Finlay 2011):

> I mean, I've already said –, I've been doing research into this. This sounds morbid, I know, but one of the things I've looked into –, I would begrudge selling this [record collection] on to somebody, because I don't know if they would actually look after it. I don't have any children myself. I don't have a partner. And I've thought, well, what's the one way I'd like to be 'thinged' with my records? I thought, well, how about being buried with them? I was actually talking to an undertaker. He said, 'Did you know that there is actually two or three companies

that can actually melt your vinyl down and make it into a coffin?' So that's one of my things in my will. It's to have all my vinyl melted down and be buried with my vinyl, in a vinyl coffin. It's my idea of taking it with me, because it means so much to me.

However, the workmen who bury the records below the Paris Opera House are not so much interring a fan as repressing memories, and in that act of repression/sublimation, they encounter the evidential body of the ghost – they find him by going deep in an effort to bury the vinyl, to stop the music talking. There is much evidence to suggest, though, that Erik can never quite stop talking. As Simon Reynolds (2012) explained online in *The Wire*:

> Edison originally conceived the phonograph as a way of preserving the voices of the dearly beloved after their demise. Records have habituated us to living with ghosts. We keep company with absent presences, the immortal but dead voices of the phonographic pantheon, from Caruso to Cobain.

Such claims raise the issue of spatial, temporal and emotional distance from celebrities. From one perspective they are always already distant (stellar), but we can gain access to them through alienated products, whether sound carriers or digital files. This means that our closeness to them emerges despite inevitable separation and always reflects a sense of loss; recording, physical death and temporal distance (their turning from event to memory) merely intensifies and reinforces the feeling. However, we might also say that such ideas play into the hands of mass cultural thinking that posit audiences as duped into believing that 'dead' products carry 'living' traces of our favourite performers. Perhaps the most important clue in *The Phantom of the Opera* is that Christine is kidnapped by Erik in the middle of her public singing, the implication being either that her passion for the music has emotionally 'transported' her as she has nostalgically surrendered herself to it, or that, in the middle of her performance, she has, in effect, been dematerialized by the same spectral force that haunts the Opera House. Leroux says that while she is singing "'My spirit longs with thee to rest!' It was at that moment that the stage was suddenly plunged into darkness' (p. 149). Once we add Erik's tendency to speak as a disembodied voice, his ability to use simulations against people – notably recreated animals and an iron tree – plus his propensity to extort money, he appears rather like capital, a force that both tempts workers and threatens their world with destruction. Not only does Erik trouble the realm of high culture by threatening to extort and destroy the edifice of the Opera House, but he can only leave a shell in its wake. His previous palace at Mazenderan was ruined: 'From being the most honest building conceivable, he soon turned it into a house of the very devil, where you could not utter a word but it was overheard or repeated by an echo' (p. 224).

Like almost anyone who listens only to audio recordings, Christine is fascinated by the source of Erik's real identity; she says, 'Suddenly, I felt a need to see beneath the mask. I wanted to know the *face* of the voice' (p. 134). When her wish is fulfilled, she greets the reality of Erik's deformity with horror. Christine does eventually consent, under duress, to entering a more intimate union with Erik: 'Yes, she was waiting for me ... waiting for me erect and alive, a real, living bride ... as she hoped to be saved' (p. 265; ellipses in original). In other words, she wishes her life to be preserved ('saved'), but all Erik's grip of death can offer is a kind of (sonic) residue. Ultimately, Christine is reduced to an echo of her former self: 'What had become of that wonderful, mysterious artist of whom the world was never, never to hear again? ... I shall hear the lonely echoes of the North repeat the singing of her who knew the Angel of Music' (p. 270). Raoul, meanwhile, suffers an even worse fate. After continually contesting Erik – and by extension, perhaps, what he stands for – he is consigned for eternity to an inaudible place (outside, as it were, of sonic preservation): 'the Communists' dungeon, which is the most remote part of the Opera, below the fifth cellar, where no one ever comes, and where no one ever hears you' (p. 265).

If Erik represents the momentous shifts in music consumption engendered by sound recording, as a 'monster', he is not wholly other or entirely evil. On one hand, he is the worst kind of murderer as he drives Joseph Buquet to suicide through torment based on illusion. However, Leroux discusses Erik's evil exploits through the eyes of a character called the Persian. Like other parts of the story, this term smacks of Orientalism, the type of discourse described by Edward Said (1978/2003) which justified Western colonialism by rendering the lands beyond its borders absolutely different and exotic: wild places that could both satisfy sensual desires and evoke mortal fears. The Persian knew that Erik had specialized in the lethal art of strangulation – the 'Punjab lasso' – and had taught his evil muse, the 'Little Sultana' this deadly skill (p. 223). Leroux is not simply being Orientalist here; he is using references to aspects of the (imagined) Orient to evoke the realm of the unconscious mind. The strangling 'lasso' also silences.

Erik's 'extraordinary ugliness' (p. 274) is double-edged in its consequences: alienating him from others but also rendering him an object of pity. Having captured Christine, at one point he explains to her:

> I can't go on living like this, like a mole in a burrow ... I want to have a wife like everybody else and to take her out on Sundays. I have invented a mask that makes me look like anybody ... You are afraid of me! And yet I am not really wicked. Love me and you shall see! All I wanted was to be loved for myself ... You don't love me!
>
> (p. 256)

Such passages rouse us by revealing the profound and somewhat undeserved nature of Erik's social isolation. In explaining his predicament, he shows that he has needs that are commonplace ('all I wanted was to be loved for myself'), but the social stigma created by his physical appearance leaves him unfulfilled. Seen this way – even though Christine explains her refusal to be intimate with Erik as part of her own general predisposition, it could be read as another example of prejudice, something that may give rise to feelings of guilt on her part. From this perspective, Erik's vicious backstory is both somewhat explicable (he turned after being so unloved) and ultimately functions to exonerate Christine from the burden of rejecting him as she is not ignoring him on the basis of his looks alone. Leroux ends his book not with her story, but with Erik's:

> Shall we curse him? He asked only to be 'some one,' like everybody else. But he was too ugly! And he had to hide his genius, *or use it to play tricks with,* when with an ordinary face, he would have been one of the most distinguished of mankind! He had a heart that could have held the empire of the world; and, in the end, he had to content himself with a cellar. Ah, yes, we must needs pity the Opera ghost.
>
> I have prayed over his mortal remains, that God might show him mercy notwithstanding his crimes. Yes, I am sure, quite sure that I prayed beside his body, the other day, when they took it from that spot where they were burying the phonographic records. It was his skeleton ... And now, what do they mean to do with that skeleton? Surely they will not bury it in the common grave! ... I say that the place of the skeleton of the Opera ghost is in the archives of the National Academy of Music. It was no ordinary skeleton. (p. 277; emphasis in original)

The novel's final words here not only emphasize that Erik's genius has gone unrecognized because of his looks, but links him to recording ('phonograph records') and notes that his talent is used to 'play tricks' – as if denoting the comparative gimmick-based field of commerce. Contrary, to, say, the cries of the Opera's management (who might dismiss Erik's conduct as venal extortion alone), the true 'place' for his decaying body (of work), however, is the National Academy, somewhere that would secure his creativity an appropriate level of cultural recognition for producing enthralling, quality music.[2]

A living legend

Music genres are social contracts, promises to express certain formal conventions. David Brackett (2016) also recently showed that they are living cultures that change as history plays out. Like genres, popular narratives do not exist outside of time. Instead they are remade and updated as the concerns of society, or different groups in it, change at particular times. We should be careful not to apply the distinction between high and low culture too quickly to the early twentieth century, as it was a gradual product of the mass reproduction created by electronic media. Nevertheless, one of the key aspects of the Phantom story, as it has been retold is what Ann Hall (2009) has called 'lowbrow appreciation for highbrow art expressed in what was then considered a low brow art form … opera for non-opera lovers' (p. 44). This has been referenced in a number of ways which can be productively explored through the idea of *spectrality*. For Derrida (2006), 'The revenant is going to come' (p. 2) and 'One cannot control its comings and goings because it begins by coming back' (p. 11). In other words, spectres are displaced in time, and Janus-faced in their historical resonance. Not only do they, as revenants, walk out of the past and infect the present with unfinished business (often family secrets), but they also confound any separation between the present and the future, as if forthcoming concerns are already implicated in the process of time unfolding now, or as Simon Reynolds (2012) explained it, they can 'turn up brandishing portents'.

One of the interesting things about the Phantom story is how much it focuses on the idea of the disembodied voice as something essentially ambiguous and hard to pin down. In *The Phantom of the Opera*, Erik's voice takes on a mysterious quality. When Raoul witnesses it, the mesmeric voice emerges like a signal, initially faint, then getting stronger:

> She seemed to be listening … Raoul also listened … Whence came that strange sound, that distant rhythm? … A faint singing seemed to issue from the walls … yes, it was as though the walls themselves were singing! … The song became plainer … the words were now distinguishable … he heard a voice, a very beautiful, very soft, very captivating voice … but, for all its softness, it remained a male voice … The voice came nearer and nearer … it came through the wall … it approached … and now the voice was in the room, in front of Christine. Christine rose and addressed the voice, as though speaking to someone. (pp. 101–2; ellipses in original)

Passages like this one suggest that the novel, which was written just before the first public radio broadcast in January 1910, was also in a sense pre-empting the rise of radio as a public technology that allowed spectral voices to enter the nation's living rooms. The broadcast had come from New York's Metropolitan Opera House. Opera broadcasts became associated with the franchising of popular prestige.

Carl Laemmle produced a major film version of the story for Universal in 1925 starring Lon Chaney; Hall (2009) saw it as 'a propaganda film about film' (p. 41). At that time, as a silent medium, cinema had to make its points by visual means. This meant manifesting the Phantom. The first film version both offered the spectacular setting of a lavish Opera House and popularized opera as a spectacle – opening it up, as it were, to poorer and less cultivated audiences (film goers, not opera enthusiasts). Chaney's hideous make-up was a focus of public discussion, as if finally revealing the Phantom's unseen truth. The first Phantom film was notable for extending Leroux's story to feature a lynch mob who chase the Phantom, something that was not included in the novel (Babilas 2018). Ironically, when Laemmle sought the opportunity to screen his film at the Met, he was rebuffed by its management (Hall 2009, p. 42).

Unlike Leroux's story, in the 1925 Universal film version of *Phantom*, an already able Christine is not entrapped by her pre-existing love of music, but 'inexplicably' drawn towards the public stage, perhaps under the Svengali-like grip of the Phantom (Hall 2009, p. 43). When he entices her in the film, the Phantom says:

> Christine, tonight I placed the world at your feet! To you I have imparted the full measure of my art. You will triumph – all Paris will worship you! But I must warn you, you must forget all worldly things and think only of your career – and your Master!

Before kidnapping her, he adds, 'Christine – It is I, your master. Look not upon my mask – think rather of my devotion which has brought you the gift of song.' When she is captured, she pleads, 'If you love me, as you say, let me go. I promise to be your slave forever!'

The notion of a hypnotic, master–slave relationship had already been popularized by one of the most globally successful 'chillers' of the silent period, Robert Weine's gripping *Das Cabinet des Dr. Caligari* (1920), where the grubby character of the title, a circus side-show hustler who doubled as the boss of a psychiatric asylum, arguably stood as an allegory for the charismatic leaders who had beguiled the German people in earlier times and made them complicit in nefarious deeds. In Universal's *Phantom*, Erik is not merely an ambiguous 'spook' who lures Christine with his magnificent music. He is positioned as a form of industrial competition, a talent farmer who works in direct opposition to the Opera management. What is interesting about this is that commercial music was, by this point, locked into competition with itself as formats challenged each other. The rise of radio meant that record labels initially took a cut in their profits. Victor's sales declined by half in the four years up to 1925, while Columbia went from declaring a net income of $7 million in 1919 to filing for bankruptcy in 1923 (Titon 2014, p. 200). In Laemmle's film, Erik has no complex Oriental backstory; he is simply a mad man, escaped and on the loose, wreaking havoc where ever he goes. As the Opera House owners discover in a written message: 'ERIK: born during the Boulevard Massacre. Self-educated musician and master of the Black Art. Exiled to Devil's Island for [the] criminally insane. ESCAPED. NOW AT LARGE.'

One of the escape routes that the major record labels pursued before radio began to primarily rely on recorded music was to create markets based on communities of less wealthy consumers. For this reason the 1920s and 1930s saw the rise of vernacular market places in American recorded music, particularly hillbilly (country) and race (blues-based) music (Tschmuck 2012, p. 59). ASCAP, the first established performing rights organization in America to collect songwriters' royalties, was launched in 1914. In 1939, however, it was challenged by another national organization called BMI.[3] The new body's strategy was to create rivalry by appealing to writers who were having their songs played on the radio, but tended to go unserved by ASCAP because they worked in the vernacular genres. Vernacular music was associated with compelling live performances aimed at ordinary listeners: fiddling contests, barn dances, moments of communal jamming and improvisation.

Arthur Lubin's 1943 remake of *The Phantom of the Opera*, again for Universal, reused the set of Laemmle's 1925 original. Where the first version started by lingering in dark recesses under the Opera House, Lubin's starts with the pleasure of musical performance and the joy of held notes, as Edward Ward's score is played by an orchestra. This time, the Phantom is a called Erique Claudlin and he is a beleagured composer – former violinist of the Opera House (memorably played by Claude Rains), who cannot bring in the income he needs to stay afloat. Claudlin submits one of his concertos to the music publisher Pleyel & Desjardins, but gets no reply. When he visits Maurice Pleyel to see what has happened, he realizes that his composition has been taken without giving him creative or financial credit, and snarls, 'Thief! You've stolen my music! Thief!!!' The two men grapple and Claudlin tries to strangle Pleyel, but the publisher's assistant Georgette comes to the rescue, throwing a tray of etching acid in Claudlin's face and setting him up to become the Phantom.

In Lubin's version, then, the Erik character is natural, not supernatural. That he is maimed by a woman, almost accidentally (in self-defence, attempting to avert a murder), raises the issue of gender relations. Leroux's original novel contains a passage where the Phantom explains to the Persian: 'My mother, daroga [officer], my poor, unhappy mother would never … let me kiss her … She used to run away … and throw me my mask! … Nor any other woman … ever, ever!' (p. 265; ellipses in original). The Phantom's confession offers an Oedipal explanation for his descent: his mother uses his disfigurement as an excuse not to love him, so he cannot resolve his first relation with her and is consumed by a sense of grief and hatred.[4] In Lubin's version, Claudin subconsciously prompts a situation where an innocent female character acts out his issue and plays the role of 'bad mother' for him, only this time it is she who literally disfigures him in the process, again sending him – and consequently his victims – into a dark, nightmare world.

Lubin's scenario raises complex questions in relation to monstrosity, because the publisher Maurice Pleyel, his assistant Georgette and the composer Claudin all seem to act in monstrous ways. In that sense, it may also reflect the era of the Second World War in which it was made; the characters do what they need to do, but nobody comes out unscathed. It also elevates the idea of financial exploitation (in the guise of song theft) to a central place in the *Phantom* story – an issue connected to the concerns of the performing rights organizations because it was based around the dire potential consequences of composers not getting their due. Indeed, Claudin is an essentially sympathetic character who has neither the complexity of Leroux's original Erik, nor the macabre inscrutability of Lon Chaney's 1925 Phantom.

Song theft became an issue for those working in the music industry in the years to follow. After the 45 rpm vinyl single was introduced, records became more profitable than sheet music. Teenagers became a key market for popular songs. The Tin Pan Alley style of music production – where music publishers dominated the industry and jobbing songwriters shopped their compositions to entrepreneurs who liaised with famous singers – was soon modified and challenged by vernacular musicians of different types who worked in self-contained bands. Rock'n'roll brought Black music to the mainstream, with its Tin Pan Alley side sometimes raising the question of whether Black songwriters were being exploited as White performers 'diluted' R&B for mainstream audiences. Mainstream popular music culture diversified at that point: in the civil rights era the blues became celebrated by middle class White fans in part as a form which allowed poor Black singer-songwriters to receive their due; other Black genres such as soul then funk went mainstream; more cross-over records appeared, and even as they drew upon the blues, White musicians formed combos: beat groups and rock bands which wrote and performed their own songs. By the 1960s Tin Pan Alley was in decline (Barfe 2005, p. 213). As acts like Bob Dylan and the Beatles took 1960s rock in musically complex, artistically adventurous and politically relevant directions, the elitist attitudes which gave the *Phantom* story its resonance began to retreat. Nevertheless, its myth was repurposed for a new generation, not least since the intense responses of young music fans during the era evoked criticism that arguably helped to position rock as an enchanting, *gothic* phenomenon: an encounter with the sublime in which male rock stars 'haunted' the waking lives of dedicated female audiences, making fans twist and shout with excitement.

In the 1960s, Bob Dylan and the Beatles spearheaded a movement in which artists wrote their own material, using it for intimate personal expression and social protest. After rock'n'roll, it became a form of common knowledge that the music industry exploited both fans and artists, with rock managers gradually emerging as shrewd, tough, mediating agents. The two trends come together in Brian De Palma's 1974 film *Phantom of the Paradise*, which structured the Phantom myth almost entirely around financial and creative ownership. In De Palma's film, Paul Williams plays Swan, a corporate svengali for Death Records who sends his heavy out to acquire some tunes.[5] When singer-songwriter Winslow Leach, an intellectual hippie type, is approached to sell off his songs so that they can be performed by 1950s revival outfit The Juicy Fruits, he contends, 'I'm not going to let my music be mutilated by those grease balls. I'm the only one that can sing Faust!' After visiting Swan's office, Leach gatecrashes an audition only to bond with a female singer played by Jessica Harper and realizes that his song has been stolen. He is in the powerless position of trying to meet the man who has stolen his music, but is beaten up, framed for drugs and literally rendered toothless in jail. After an accident involving Swan's record press, the unfortunate songwriter falls into the East River and emerges as the monster. Released between the Broadway and film version of *The Rocky Horror Picture*

Show, part of the cult appeal of *Phantom of the Paradise* is that it inverts Leroux's subtext and places the recorded music industry centre stage.

By the late 1970s, Kiss were the epitome of the commercial rock band. Branded with their painted faces, and popular with students across high schools throughout America, Paul Stanley, Gene Simmons and bandmates licensed over 2,500 lines of merchandise and even flirted with the idea of a stock market flotation. In their 1978 variant of the legend, *Kiss Meets the Phantom of the Park*, directed by Gordon Hessler – which was not animated, but nevertheless produced by Hanna-Barbera – the Opera is re-imagined as the entertainment industry, actualized as an amusement park with its spectacles, emotional thrill rides and shadowy ghost walks. As a depiction of consumer capitalism, the leisure or entertainment park was featured a decade earlier in ITV's psychedelic British spy series *The Prisoner* (McGoohan and Markstein 1967–8). It is worth noting that a similar setting was used for James Goldstone's 1977 exploitation film *Rollercoaster*. The idea of subversive agents attacking locations that reflected modern leisure was a staple plot for several disaster movies from the era.

In the Kiss version of the Phantom story, the park's financial health starts declining, so the most popular rock bands in the world are brought in to revive its flagging fortunes. Abner Devereaux, meanwhile, is the mad scientist who designed half the park's attractions. When it transpires that he tested them too early, without due care for customers, he is given the sack.[6] This Phantom figure then vows to take his revenge. A first step is to transfigure human captives into a series of animatronic, android figures that he uses to do his bidding. When the Kiss show opens, he uses one to photograph the four participants of this arena rock spectacle. The charismatic musicians demonstrate 'a little star power' by telecommunicating to and possessing a female visitor called Melissa who is seeking her boyfriend. That night, however, a carefully crafted Gene Simmons lookalike attacks some police and smashes a concessions stand. The next day, the cops visit Kiss, who are lounging by the pool, still in full makeup. Trying to protect his investment, the park owner intervenes and aims to prevent their arrest. In an avuncular style, he explains, 'I know rock'n'rollers tend to get rowdy, but all we want is a nice show tonight boys. Get some rest.' The subsequent rock show involves a (fan) girl in awe who symbolizes 'a cosmic force field which protects our talisman'. A band member adds, 'without them [fans], no powers' and 'we're just ordinary human beings'. Bugging the conversation, the Phantom menacingly retorts, 'You are mistaken my friends. You are ordinary. And soon, you will be even less than ordinary. All of you.' When the Phantom's servant tries to steal the talisman, Kiss come back to the park at night, only to have to fight off a barrage of remote-controlled assassins which take the shape of leaping white werewolves. Simmons's voice is computerized, and he stalks with big boots plus breathes fire like Godzilla. Safe, meanwhile, behind his revolving console of controls, Abner Devereaux quips, 'Let the dance begin' and sends in a karate team. The band then enter the dungeon ghost walk area, where they fend of a series of animatronic monsters that resemble iconic spooks from the 1930s Universal film cycle. Finally, the band are captured and replaced by clones on stage.[7] As if to symbolically reaffirm their authenticity, they escape and fight their alter egos on stage, then rally the concert crowd with, 'Are you ready for the real KISS?' In an ensemble ending which would have suited one of Hanna-Barbera's other properties, *Scooby-Doo*, the band and park owner enter Devereaux's lair and restore his servant, Sam, to humanity. In a scene that echoes the discovery of Mrs Bates's corpse in the horror film *Psycho*, the ageing genius wheels round, dead. Locating Devereux as a competing rock manager, the park owner philosophically laments, 'What a waste. A brilliant man. A true genius. He created Kiss to destroy Kiss. And he lost.' Flat and rather clichéd, *Kiss Meets the Phantom of the Park* thus used a broadly Oedipal trope – with Abner Devereaux personifying the generation gap in a version of Erik's 'bad father' role – to celebrate the protagonists' supposed rock authenticity. It was relegated in the Kiss canon, however, as both the fans and band thought that it portrayed them as buffoons; in other words, though *Kiss Meets the Phantom of the Park* attempted to see through the familiar sham of mass culture, it arguably offered an uninspired instance of the commercial exploitation upon which it was trying to comment.

In November 1980, the presidential election that saw Ronald Reagan voted into office symbolized a broad change of mood for America, from a capitalist society open to progressive change and permissiveness towards one structured around materialist self-centredness. Individuals in this new society were encouraged to commodify themselves by being more entrepreneurial and focusing on self-improvement. The zeitgeist was reflected in MTV, a music video cable TV channel that launched in the summer of 1981. Music videos were characterized by stars who played with gender and made dynamic spectacles of themselves. A few months before MTV appeared, the ABC channel launched *Dynasty*, a soap opera centred on the Carrington family in Denver, Colorado, which explored the power play between an elite coterie of affluent men and women. The show was known for the way its female characters employed power dressing, particularly wearing dresses with shoulder pads, to emphasize their Amazonian determination in business. In other words, there was a sense of growing female empowerment, even if it was formulated as superficial glitz and gladiatorial competition. Robert Markowitz's 1983 rendering of *Phantom of the Opera* appears relatively traditionalist, but begins to focus on both the superficiality of glamour and the reworking of gender. Its plot centre on the opera conductor Sandor Korvin who teaches his wife Elena for her role in a performance of Faust. When the owner of the Opera House is unsuccessful in his attempt to seduce Elena, he engineers a bad review of her performance, and she drowns herself. Korvin confronts the review's writer and in the fire that accidentally ensues he is disfigured by an accident involving acid. Five years later, he emerges to spot Maria, a chorus girl who resembles his dead wife. Though she loves the new opera conductor, he tutors her and decides to terrorize those who stand in her way. With shades of Hitchcock's 1958 film *Vertigo*, the plot features a glamorized, contemporarily styled Jane Seymour as *both* Elena and Maria.[8] When the Phantom is unmasked, his speech references the vertiginous interplay of signifiers that characterized the MTV era, where the mediated image took centre stage: 'You want to see what's behind it? Perhaps another mask; a mask behind a mask. No, you cannot tear this one off. It's me, me, me!'

Italian horror director Dario Argento's 1998 take on the story, *The Phantom of the Opera*, starred the British actor Julian Sands and was panned by critics as straight-to-video kitsch. It arrived two years after the patent for MP3 encoding was issued. Though music had been digitized on CD for years, its spectrality was about to increase with the expansion of broadband internet, and – two years after the film was released – introduction of Apple's iTunes music store. A year after iTunes appeared, the peer-to-peer file sharing platform Napster was about to bring a metaphorical chandelier down on the music industry. To put it another way, the proliferation of freely shared MP3 files represented 'the popular liberation movement in music' which threatened once-dominant major labels with 'an inevitable price meltdown' (Dolgin 2009, p. 11). In a post-analogue environment the copy can be of the same quality as the original, so digital reproduction raises issues of identical duplication and deceptive cloning. Argento researched his story by immersing himself in the Opera Library in Paris, listening to recordings in 'a music archive of all the operas staged over the past decades' (2019, p. 248), as if sonic reproductions rather than live music experiences would help him understand the practice. In his version, a long-haired Sands is not disfigured on the outside as the Phantom. Instead, he is, imperceptibly, disfigured on the inside, with loyalty to another realm. Raised by rats, and protective of them. At one point he explains, 'I am not a phantom, I'm a rat.' In other words, 'his mask is figurative, but the duality persists' (Hall 2009, p. 90). After chasing a woman through a series of catacombs (basically, a series of rat warrens), he bites out her tongue. This capacity to silence is paralleled by the idea that he may be a projection: when the female diva first appears, she is in an empty auditorium – a theatre of the mind's eye space where the Phantom, alone, is watching her – as if he is her projection, or maybe she is his. He sees her, meanwhile, in his dream. Some scenes from the original story are reprised: in one moment, an usherette is convinced she has seen him; in another, he brings down the chandelier. When he kills the diva and offers her role to his muse, she says that she does not want it, and that she hates him. He replies, 'But hate and love are one.' She is trapped, not only with him, but in effect with a philosophy that does not discern such things from their doubles. As film commentator Ann Hall (2009) noted, film versions of Leroux's story depend on a tension between what is seen and what is heard, but Argento's film relegated the music in favour of Christine and the Phantom having visually signified moments of mutual telepathy. Because, in this incarnation, the Phantom can force Christine to sing, music does not feature as a seductive vehicle for connection, but as 'a means for transcendent torture' (p. 91).

Joel Schumacher's 2004 version of *The Phantom of the* Opera based itself on Andrew Lloyd Webber's phenomenally successful stage musical of the story and represented a high water mark. Even adjusting for inflation, its mammoth $80 million budget was around eight times larger than any previous cinematic version of the story, but critics again dismissed the film, not for its gory kitsch, but instead for its generic, mainstream quality, highly sanitized grandiloquence and distinct lack of edge. In the *New Yorker*, Anthony Lane (2004) quipped:

> The plot is impressively free of anything that does not smell of unpasteurized melodrama … The irony is that, as visual habits go, there is none more threadbare than this brand of subterranean gothic, at once fussy and lumpen, with its frankly unhygienic mixture of lingerie and dungeons. It reminds us that 'The Phantom of the Opera' is a period piece, and that the period in question is not 1870 but 1986, when Lloyd Webber first presented his production to the world. We should not be surprised, then, if this bellowing beast of a movie looks and sounds like the extended special-edition remix of a Duran Duran video.

Schumacher's blockbuster came out less than six months after Sony Music Entertainment had merged with the Bertelsmann Music Group, a union which ended a century of rivalry between Columbia and Victor Records. The unprecedentedly large merger occurred after six months of heated debate about whether the corporate behemoth would itself be an 'unhygienic mixture'. The merger of the two giant media groups was not about sponsoring new music, but instead amassing vast collections of lucrative back catalogue assets, material which could be reproduced with costs saved through economies of scale. BMG's Chairman and CEO Rolf Schmidt-Holtz used the digital reconfiguration of the music industry as an austerity-based justification. Framing the union as a circling of the wagons, he explained, 'The creation of Sony BMG Entertainment is a historic opportunity for us to build a new company that we believe can thrive creatively and financially in a highly challenging worldwide music marketplace' (Jelassi and Enders 2008, p. 556). In other words, corporate survival was a case of *playing it safe*: capital shoring itself up, as it were, against the exigencies of competition. In relation to the *Phantom* project, Sony Music released the movie's soundtrack, and also, at that point, worked with another safe bet, Duran Duran, whose eleventh studio album *Astronaut* had just come out on the Epic Records Label.

Ann Hall's (2009) analysis of Schumacher's picture highlights some of the ways in which commercial pressure underwrote a conservative approach to cultural expression: Lloyd Webber only came on board once his stage show had found its own success and he realized from the film *Chicago* (Marshall 2002) that there was a significant market for movie musicals, critics decried the Phantom as too handsome (almost using his mask as a fashion accessory), the film's damsel in distress plot left little room for the idea of Christine as a complex woman who struggles to choose between two men, and visual spectacle – with its dynamics of looking – is prioritized in the narrative over a spectral tension between what is seen and what is unseen (i.e. audibly heard). In her analysis, the stage show's commercially shrewd creator, Lloyd Webber himself, almost became the Phantom:

> It is easy to assume that Lloyd Webber purposefully created a weak film in order to keep up the interest in the stage play … given the Lloyd Webber team's ability to manage and manipulate marketing, perhaps the film was a kind of planned obsolescence similar to those used in the creation of computer technology and electronic entertainment. (Hall 2009, p. 126)

The corporate opulence and nostalgic focus of Schumacher's *Phantom* arguably reflected an era where a sheen of expensive corporate spectacle both illuminated the ubiquity *and* the dangerously mercurial movement of capital as *it* dematerialized – like Erik – but here across expanding digital networks. This *Phantom's* characteristically conservative tone was revealed by Lane (2004) when he noted that a reported 80 million people had attended Lloyd Webber's show since its inception. Music and movie spectacles were now fully spectral: consumer *content* to be instantaneously circulated online. YouTube was only a year away.

In conclusion, this chapter has not only suggested that *The Phantom of the Opera* story uses music performance as a medium for its gloomy, sentimental, monstrous romance, one that deals with the relationship between what is heard and what is seen; it suggests the story has been periodically reformulated on screen to reflect the shared experience of a changing mediascape. While the novel dealt with the coming of sound recording and its ability to upset hierarchies of refinement, its film versions have connected with the rise of radio and heyday of cinema, the triumph of vernacular music, portrayal of songwriters as the industry's victims and more recent era of digital file sharing and corporate mergers. If Phantom has remained a buoyant commodity, perhaps, then, we might consider Mark Worrell's (2014) phrase that the commodity itself, with its increasingly erratic spin cycles, is the 'ultimate monstrosity'. Drawing on Marx, Marshall Berman (1981) assessed the experience of modern life as one in which *All That Is Solid Melts into Air*. In an age of digital content, entertainment mergers and the over-accumulation of (sonic) information, there was *no need for the solid part*. Music itself could be used to extort money then disappear like the Phantom.

2

'His muscles still bulged like iron bands': *King Kong* and the promotion of Lead Belly

In 1933 *King Kong* (Cooper & Schoedsack) burst into the public imagination thanks to a new RKO blockbuster movie. The film showed an anthropomorphized yet violent beast transported from the mysterious Skull Island by an obsessive film maker called Carl Denham. *King King*'s racial theme was more than a subtext: early in the movie, Denham proclaimed, 'I tell you that there's something on that island that no White man has ever seen.' A year after the film's release, folklorist John Lomax recorded the music of a convicted murderer named Huddie Leadbetter in the Louisiana penitentiary. The connection between *King Kong* and the frisson around John Lomax bringing Lead Belly to New York was made by Lomax's biographer, Nolan Porterfield (2001):

> When Lomax and his folk-singing ex-con arrived in Manhattan on the eve of the new year 1935, people were talking about another exotic phenomenon which had descended upon them less than two years earlier. King Kong, the landmark fantasy-adventure movie released in March 1933 for a long run in Manhattan, had captured the public's fancy ... The relationship between Hollywood and real life ... is a subject best approached with caution. But certain key similarities between *King Kong* and what was about to be reported in the press are unavoidable and perhaps help to explain the sensation which Lead Belly created among New Yorkers: a savage being, primitive and violent, is discovered by a White man, put in bondage, transported to Manhattan, and placed on public display.
>
> (2001, p. 347)

The entry of Lead Belly into New York as a live performer, and placing of his recordings into the Library of Congress, was carefully staged and stage-managed to suggest the ultimate in cultural collision between the South and the modern metropolis. Though there are, of course, significant differences between the two stories, both narratives involve mythic encounters that were publicly staged in ways that drew upon shared assumptions about the place of the Other. Both performances played to anxieties about Blackness as an implicit threat to the fabric of civilization. Race has sometimes been constituted through racist practices, discourses and power relations which attempt to attribute monstrosity.

By exploring parallels between the stories of *King Kong* and the promotion of Lead Belly, I will suggest that we can learn more about the cultural work of inter-racial myth-making in 1930s America. I therefore use comparison as a methodological strategy to expose the pervasive framework of racial Othering that characterized 1930s America and that placed evolutionary conceptions of primitivism at the centre of the American public sphere (see Hiller 1991). In doing this I aim to excavate a preconscious shared form of racial Othering that was central to the operation of both American society and its culture of popular music. The story emerges in three sections. The first sets the scene of 1930s New York in terms of the sociology of race and urbanization. The second explores the racial dynamics of Cooper and Schoedsack's original film as a product of that society. The final section examines Lomax's packaging of Leadbetter as Lead Belly: a seemingly primitive and dangerous figure who embodied White desires and fears about Blackness. The chapter aims to trace the operation of social projection motivated by White anxiety that has Othered Black identity in American society.

Competition from 'The New Negro'

Monsters, real or perceived, can reveal social anxieties in relation to race (McIntosh 2018). It is therefore important to understand something about contemporary notions of racial culture against which the American folklore movement – including Lomax – pursued its project. The freeing of slaves which went with Reconstruction in the 1870s gave hope to African Americans. However, a generation later, according to Peter Conn, under the next regime, called Jim Crow, segregation had been violently restored: 'the American South had become little more than an armed and organized system for intimidating Blacks, and the American North had been reduced to bored collaboration' (1983, p. 149). Henry Louis Gates has taken the White supremacist writings of

Reconstruction-era journalist Henry Grady and his justifications for the New South as a starting point for this Jim Crow period:

> Grady's clever declaration of the birth of the New South unfolded as part of what we might say amounted to a terrorist campaign against the freedmen and freedwomen, waged not only through physical violence and intimidation, but also through a massive wave of propaganda hell-bent on permanently devaluing the freed people's very humanity – often referred to in scientific literature of this period as 'the nature of the Negro' ... This propaganda war as so brutally effective that it demanded a response from Black people themselves ... as evidence that the disparaging claims about the Negro's beastlike 'nature' were horribly mistaken.
>
> (2019, p. 33)

Throughout the Jim Crow era, Black intellectuals dreamed of a modern African American contribution to national culture. At the dawn of the new century it was reflected in W.E.B. Du Bois's concern that each modern African American would escape from stereotyping:

> [He] would not Africanize America, for America has too much to teach the world and Africa. He would not bleach his Negro soul in a flood of White Americanism, for he knows that Negro blood has a message for the world. He simply wishes to make it possible for a man to be both a Negro and an American.
>
> (1903/1973, p. 3)

Economic betterment through migration from the South gave hope to many African Americans. In 1900, 90 per cent of Black Americans lived in the South, most of them on farms. America's urban population was only 22 per cent Black. By 1930 this figure had almost doubled, so that African Americans constituted 40 per cent of the urban population. The shift was not just reactive or geographic, but was associated with Black populations asserting their new role in American society, aspirating to take their place as a more mannered and sophisticated urban labour force (see Leland 2004, pp. 75–6). Coming in the tradition of Du Bois, Howard University professor of philosophy Alain Locke's essay 'The New Negro' was a call for the African American community to 'enter a new dynamic phase' (1925/1997, p. 4). The 'New Negro' was not only a poet, playwright or musician, but a sharecropper, steelworker or domestic servant. Locke declared that the 'New Negro' was self-confident, sophisticated and assertive.

The 'New Negro' movement called more public attention to civil rights concerns, pointing out the fallacy of fighting for democracy abroad while denying equality to African Americans at home. Increased memberships in national, regional, and local protest and racial pride organizations, large numbers of migrants moving from southern rural areas to northern cities, and a greater emphasis on collective action, were just a few manifestations of the 'New Negro'.

The Harlem Renaissance was part of the 'response' to racism described by Henry Louis Gates insofar that it clearly indicated that New York's African America citizens had developed a sophisticated, metropolitan community based around 'civilized' arts and culture. It peaked for five years before the 1929 stock-market crash. By the 1920s, in general, American popular culture had begun to transform and diversify in relation to race. The jazz age had arrived, and, as Phillip Blom explained, 'Black music … did not remain in a cultural ghetto' (2015, p. 109). He cited performers as diverse as the dancer Josephine Baker and actor-singer Paul Robeson, who were both accepted by White audiences, in order to reference the racial complexities of the era: where the uninhibited Baker played up to colonial stereotypes, Robeson's manner was more serious and dignified (pp. 110–12). Speaking about a prominent critic of the time, cultural historian Peter Conrad (1998) noted:

> André Levinson, Amazed by Baker's 'simian suppleness,' watched as she regressed through the centuries, rejoining 'our common vision of our animal ancestors' … Did a dance have the power to reverse all the effortful victories of civilization? Levinson knew that Josephine Baker had come from the wilderness by way of industrial America.
>
> (p. 366)

In other words, 'From Baker, [as cross racial entertainment] popular music inherited a mission to redefine the boundary between civilization and wildness' (p. 367). This notion of a cultural approach to the performance of race that would 'redefine the boundary' posited its depiction as somehow Janus-faced – transitional, compromised, contradictory or confused – during a rapidly changing time that internationally formed the heyday of the colonial period. Writing on the persistence of blackface minstrelsy a decade later, John Strausbaugh suggested:

> In the encyclopedias and world books at least through the 1930s, you can see the well-intentioned authors struggling, with varying levels of success, to shed the worst excesses of Victorian cultural smugness while still pandering to readers' curiosity about exotic peoples. (2006, p. 53)

In other words, Jim Crow was a time of both segregation and slow transition. Exoticism, primitivism and nostalgia provided a forum within which both regressive and more positive depictions could emerge and contest each other. Four years after the Harlem Renaissance had period ended, in the depths of the Great Depression, *King Kong* was released, the same year that Lomax first recorded Lead Belly. Two years later, race relations in the United States had soured to the point that a riot was sparked by rumours of the beating of a teenaged Puerto Rican shoplifter by the White employees at a five and dime store in Harlem.

King Kong as monstrous metaphor

Well before the twentieth century, Western thinking in the slave era defined Black Africans as different to European Whites, more savage and more bestial. In his classic study of the subject, the University of Mississippi historian Winthrop Jordan (1974) talked about this as 'an exercise in self-inspection by means of comparison' (p. 13) in which acts like cosmetic mutilation, polygamy, infanticide, ritual murder and cannibalism were imagined or seized upon as a justification for slavery that 'seemed somehow to place the Negro among the beast' (p. 15). He continued by saying:

> Slave traders in Africa necessarily handled Negroes the same way men in England handled beasts, herding and examining and buying, as with any other animals which were products of commerce. If Negroes were likened to beasts, there was in Africa a beast which was likened to men. (p. 15)

This led to confusion: hypotheses that Black Africans were the offspring of apes, or that apes were the monstrous product of human-animal interbreeding. Jordan explained:

> The sexual association of apes with Negroes had an inner logic which kept it alive: sexual union seemed to prove a certain kind of affinity without going so far as to indicate actual identity – which was what Englishmen really thought was the case. By forging a sexual link between Negroes and apes, furthermore, Englishmen were able to give vent to their feeling that Negroes were a lewd, lascivious, and wanton people ... Lecherousness among Africans was at times for Englishmen merely another attribute which one would expect to find among heathen savage, beastlike men.
>
> (1974, p. 18)

Colonialism and slavery were justified by projections of savagery established by noting a departure from Western, Christian standards. This philosophy associated Blackness with the same animal qualities thought to characterize African apes – brute strength and sexual aggression – because those things underpinned assumptions about the threatening nature of Black men unchecked, their supposed urges to seize White women and the need for Whites to keep them in line through practices of organized labour. From at least the era of the Minstrel Show onwards, such assumptions have reverberated through and been reformulated by popular culture. One form they have taken is the parading of what Rosalyn Poignant (2004) has called 'professional savages': non-White people exhibited as objects of cross-cultural curiosity rather than individuals. It is important to note, however, that in the United States, Aboriginal performers were often used in such roles, as 'White Americans (for most of the nineteenth century) saw slaves of African origin as domesticated "other," and attributions of savagery tended to be reserved for Native Americans' (Poignant 2004, p. 83). The era which started with Reconstruction at the end of the 1870s, however, changed things significantly. Blacks were segregated during the Jim Crow era, and ideological justifications needed to be found.

King Kong's origins lay in Orientalism (see Said 1978/2003). The film's creator, Merian Caldwell Cooper, was fascinated by a prototypical version of the story at six years old, when his uncle gave him a copy of French explorer Paul du Chiallu's (1862/1985) book *Explorations and Adventures in Equatorial Africa*. As *King Kong* historian Ray Morton explained:

> The book kindled in young Cooper a passionate desire to travel to distant lands and explore the far-flung reaches of the earth. A story in one of the chapters about a tribe of ferocious giant gorillas that attack a native village also caught his eye. An incident in which one of the apes carried a female villager off into the jungle especially intrigued him. While this depiction of gorillas as vicious, rampaging beasts is quite at odds with the shy and gentle nature of the real animals, it was very much in line with the popular conception that characterized these noble, mysterious creatures as rapacious and terrifying monsters. Enthralled, the young Cooper began a life-long fascination with gorillas.
>
> (Morton 2005, p. 6)

In adventure stories, the gorilla becomes a mythic projection of an essence of otherness that contrasts with civilized society. It is located as primitive, animalistic, vicious, rampaging, rapacious, a menace ever-ready to unpredictably emerge from another realm to endanger life and cause mayhem. The ape here is 'ferocious', 'giant' and able to carry off 'a female villager'. Before the ape in *King Kong* had a name, the film makers simply called it the 'Giant Terror Gorilla'; 'cutesy moments' scripted to show the screen gorilla's softer side 'were eliminated to toughen Kong's character' (Morton 2005, p. 27).

The film begins with an Arabian saying created by Cooper that locates it within an Orientalist mystique, saying that the beast was made impotent by an interest in beauty. In the first version of the script that Cooper had commissioned from Edgar Wallace, protagonist Carl Denham had been portrayed as big game hunter. Cooper changed his role to movie maker, as if to imply that photography itself was an invasive, predatory action. Denham is introduced as a reckless and ruthless White photographer and film director, able to face a lion in order to bring back a picture and looking for a female lead for his new movie. He defends his taking a girl into danger by saying she is already imperiled in New York City, though the dialogue reveals that this is *known danger*, as opposed to the *unknown danger* of the jungle. Denham's relationship to Fay Wray's character Ann Darrow is structured around the issue of trust. After they set sail for Skull Island, Ann pats Iggy the monkey aboard ship, and Denham quips, 'Beauty and the beast, eh?' He explains his movie idea to ship hand Jack Driscoll by saying 'The beast was a tough guy too. He could lick the world, but when he saw beauty she got him. He went soft. He forgot his wisdom and the little fellas licked him.' Denham explains that the natives on Skull Island have walled-up something they fear:

> Denham: I tell you that there's something on that island that no White man has ever seen.
> Driscoll: And you expect to photograph it?
> Denham: If it's there, you bet I'll photograph it.

As if to emphasize that this venture will be mediated and contained through its mediation, still aboard ship Denham screen tests Ann by asking her to scream for her life. Once Denham's crew arrive on the island, the different races first encounter each other when Denham and his team are caught voyeuristically filming the native's ceremony to offer a bride to Kong. In a tense exchange, the natives decide they want to buy Ann, but Denham backs off. After Driscoll announces he loves Ann, the natives steal her from the ship that night. When the ship's Chinese cook finds out, he announces that the 'crazy Black man' has been on board. After Ann is taken by Kong, the team shoot a dinosaur in the jungle:

'a prehistoric beast ... that brute'. The crew fight Kong and the natives with technology: gas bombs and gun powder. Kong represents the chaotic essence of the primitive: fighting dinosaurs, trampling and biting people, smashing property. When Dehman captures him, he announces: 'We're millionaires, boys – I'll share it with all of you!' Back in New York, a theatre crowd prepares to see the new live exhibit. After one audience member has it explained at the theatre that Denham has a personal appearance, and it's not with a safari movie this time, another female in the audience asks, 'Say, what is it anyhow? I hear it's a kind of gorilla. Gee, haven't we got enough of them in New York?' Denham explains:

> Ladies and gentlemen, seeing is believing and we – my partners and I – have bought back the living proof of our adventure ... He was a king and a god in the world he knew, but now he comes back a captive; merely a show to gratify your curiosity.

King Kong is enraged by the flash bulbs of the press and retaliates with a rampage, traumatically biting a White man in half and dropping another struggling woman before stealing Fay Wray. He heads for the Empire State building, but, in the classic final scene, is shot down by planes. Denham says, 'No – it wasn't the airplanes; it was beauty who killed the beast.'

King Kong was an unparalleled success. Opening in New York at the Radio City Music Hall, it was preceded by a stage show called *Jungle Rhythms*. With ticket prices ranging from $0.35 to $0.75, the movie took $89,931 in four days (Morton 2005, p. 78). *King Kong* temporarily saved RKO from bankruptcy and spawned two sequels by the same team: *Son of Kong* (Schoedsack 1933) and *Mighty Joe Young* (Schoedsack 1949).

Though there are other readings, it is not hard to see a racial subtext in the movie.[1] Cooper's adjustments to Wallace's script included a scene where the natives worshipped Kong. Their racial difference is used to form a transition to the realm of the monster. The tribe's Witch Doctor was played by Nobel Johnson, a founder of the Lincoln Motion Picture Company, a firm dedicated to making 'race' pictures for Black audiences. In a history of race and horror cinema, Robin Means Coleman explains:

> Kong is 'Blackened,' or racially coded, when juxtaposed against the presence of Whites in the film. Kong is the colour Black, emerging from a 'lower,' primitive culture in which he is surrounded by Black natives – or mini-Kongs when they dress up like apes to worship their big Kong. The soundtrack that accompanies scenes with Kong and other Blacks in the film consists of drums, an auditory cue

that is typical of jungle films and the appearance of Black natives. The film also continued to confine understandings of Blackness to wildness, and its sexuality to savagery, adding fears of the big Black phallus.

(2011, p. 41)

Coleman's 'Blackened' reading assertively interprets the movie and arguably misses some of its nuances. Nevertheless, one can broadly agree, 'The implicit narrative goal is to keep the beast out of the (White) boudoir' (p. 44). This interpretation is shared by James Snead in *Black Screens/White Images* (1994, p. 8):

> In all Hollywood film portrayals of Blacks, I am arguing here, the political is never far from the sexual, for it is both as a political and as a sexual threat that the Black skin appears on screen. And nowhere is this more plainly to be seen than in *King Kong* ... he makes off with not just a woman, but with a *White* woman. *King Kong*, then, is a noteworthy, though perhaps surprising, instance of 'coded Black' – in this case the carrier of Blackness is not a human being, but an ape, but we shall see that the difference can easily be bridged.

Certainly, the film was engineered to hint at a sexual threat to White women popularly associated back then with Black masculinity. Encouraging Fay Wray to wear a wig, director Merian Cooper made sure that the White girl captured by the ape was an innocent blonde. He and co-director, Ernest Schoedsack, perceived Kong such a threat that they portrayed themselves as the fighter pilots who finally destroyed him. Kong's entry into New York City is accompanied by him breaking his chains, rampaging through the city and climbing the Empire State Building, perhaps an analogy for Black social aspiration.

Ever since the first version appeared, *King Kong* has become a way for people to talk about race in America. The racialized reading of the movie was never more clear than in the civil rights era. In November 1968, in Fullerton, California, Frank Zappa spoke a few words to introduce a thirty-one-minute version of an instrumental called 'King Kong' by the Mothers of Invention. The rendition (eventually released in 1992 on the album *Our Man in Nirvana*) performed a song that was soon aired in several variations on his 1969 album release *Uncle Meat*.

> The name of this song is 'King Kong'. It is also included in our new album [*Uncle Meat*]. It occupies all of side four of the two record set and uh, it's actually the story of a large gorilla. You all know the story I'm sure. The gorilla is on an island, eats bananas, has a good time all day long. Plays out there in the bushes and

uh, some Americans find out about the gorilla and they hear how big he is, you know. They're very impressed with the size of the beast. So they make it to the island, you know, they check out the gorilla. And they get a thing and they catch him, you know. They catch the gorilla, and they stick him in a boat and they bring him back to the United States. And they show him off to everybody. And they make a bunch of money on the gorilla, and then they kill him.

Frank Zappa

Zappa's introduction to 'King Kong' came at the height of the civil rights era: in April 1968 Martin Luther King had been assassinated in Memphis and President Lyndon Johnson had signed the Fair Housing anti-discrimination act. That summer the Black Power movement targeted the Olympic games in Mexico City. In the midst of a phase of tumultuous social protest where the notion of a unified melting pot had been stretched to its limits, Zappa evoked the *King Kong* myth to remind audiences of the history of racist oppression that included the transportation of Black Africans to the new world as slave labour. In some ways the analogy was banal in its familiarity: since its original silver screen portrayal in 1933, *King Kong* had become part of the furniture of Anglo-American, and increasingly global popular culture.[2]

Lead Belly positioned as *King Kong*

By the early 1930s John Lomax lost his job working in a bank to the financial consequences of the Great Depression. In the wake of his redundancy, with his adolescent son as his assistant, Lomax switched career and set out to capture a record of America's disappearing folk music. His work was part of a larger project to understand an American way of life as something before and outside of industrial civilization (Filene 2000, p. 57).

This raises the issues of projection. Drawing on the work of psychoanalyst Melanie Klein, Cornell Sandvoss (2005) has described projection in relation to media fan culture:

> Processes of projection and introjection can not only manifest a bond between the fan and the object world (and its dominant social system), but can equally function to construct a hated 'Other'. Klein herself describes the projective control and fantasies of power and omnipotence as the prototype of aggressive object relations. Klein (1946/2000) labels the dislocation and containment of

'bad' parts of the self through imagined control over the object of projection as a 'projective identification', a process whereby the boundaries between self and object are increasingly blurred. (Sandvoss 2005, p. 82)

In other words, projection is not just a matter of imposing an *a priori* interpretive grid on the world, but it is one where 'internal "bad" feelings are channeled and assigned to an external object' (Sandvoss 2005, p. 80).

The Lomaxes pursued their work with a veneer of objectivity, yet as Benjamin Filene explained:

> In depicting themselves as unbiased preservers, the Lomaxes' use of the portable phonograph was their most powerful methodological statement ... The recording machine, they believed, removed the collector as a source of bias and captured all of a song's nuances. Instead of a scholar's representation of a song, the machine preserved a folk singer's entire performance, unadulterated.
> (Filene 1991, p. 617)

This notion of capturing 'sound photographs' of 'Negro songs' allowed Lomax to conclude that he had not interfered with the recording process, though he evidently took for granted his own role as a White song hunter who had selected the locations, singers and songs to record. Indeed, Lead Belly became a kind of inverse 'native informant', singing to other potential performers to demonstrate the kinds of songs that Lomax aimed to record (Filene 1991, p. 618). In the face of this expanding repository of traditional art and customs, the prevailing notion that no distinctive African American culture existed, or that such culture that did exist was one of either fossilized African survivals or debased imitations of White models, began to gain ground. Reviewing John and Alan Lomax's book *American Ballads and Folksongs* for *The New York Times*, Dorothy Scarborough (1934/1968) explained:

> College professors and their like are convenient persons to chase down folksongs and print them in books, a useful service in this day when such songs are being killed off by civilization, but John Lomax has done more than that. He grew up among folk songs, has sung them, lived with them, loved them for so long that he is like a brave ballad himself .... Recently Mr Lomax and Alan made the round of a number of penitentiaries and prison camps in Texas and other Southern States, hunting Negro folksongs, in the belief that in such places they might find Negro lore little influenced by White sophistication.

What is evident here is that Whiteness is connected to the sophistication of 'civilization', a form of development that made folksongs an endangered species.

The Lomaxes could then come in as 'hunters' aiming to both capture and rescue the music. The hunter metaphor recalls colonial control and sophistication, turning the encounter into a safe adventure. In his efforts to find the 'purist' of folk music, John Lomax located its makers in something parallel to a mythic deep jungle environment (the penitentiary) where he could find 'the Negro who has had the least contact with jazz, the radio, and with the White man ... [Where] convicts heard only the idiom of their own race' (Filene 2000, p. 51). Using the music as the holder for a kind of primitivized racial essence, this approach symbolically connected cultural purity with criminality and savagery. It was, moreover, *unlike* the approach of Francis Child or other musicologists, who had come before and sought to show how folk ballads had European roots (Filene 2000, p. 15). Of Lead Belly, Lomax claimed that 'his eleven years of confinement had cut him off from the phonograph and the radio' (Filene 1991, p. 609). This was not true, as Lead Belly had learned some of his song craft from phonograph recordings and sheet music. Nevertheless, to preserve the musical (ethnic) purity that they encountered, the Lomaxes aimed to prevent him from playing recent popular songs at concerts, and they encouraged him to tell stories of Southern life between his songs.[3] They also recorded his songs without other musicians accompanying him in order not to 'taint' recordings with the interpretations of outsiders (Filene 1991, p. 617).

Positioned to offer a supposedly unmediated voice, Lead Belly represented, for Lomax, a *locus of authenticity*, one that bought a new *realism* to the gramophone record *as a medium*. One *New York Times* reviewer explained:

> Negro folk songs fall into two categories: spiritual and sinful. The notes inform us that 'Huddie Leadbetter – better known as Lead Belly – early decided that he preferred frankness, flesh and the devil to sanctimoniousness without a guitar.' ... Alan Lomax, who collaborated in the publication of his songs and in the writing of his life, believes that this is the first authentic album of American folk music, and in all probability it is. As he points out, radio and gramophones have encouraged distortions. Hearing these records is enough to confirm his claim. There is nothing quite like them on any other list.
>
> (Parkenham 1939, p. A6)

Lomax's engagement with Lead Belly needs to be seen in the context of the changing Left liberal politics of the 1930s. Modelled on the British Labour Party, the American Labor Party was formed in the mid-1930s to unite Social Democrats and trade unionists. In a sense, the folk music movement was its cultural wing, positioning working-class Whites and Blacks as comrades and celebrating African American music as a unique contribution to the vernacular sounds of America.

Towards the end of February 1939, Lomax presented Lead Belly in a show of *Negro Music: Past and Present* on the Labor Stage 'with Albert Moss's exuberant [twenty voice] choir singing songs of a sorrow, a hope and an exaltation that belong uniquely to the Negro race'. The concert packaged a series of artists 'tracing the history of Negro music from the African period with its tribal dances to the latest type of racial manifestations in the art'. The Labor Club teamed up with John Velasco to create the event; Velasco was one of the organizers of the Negro People's Theatre, which fed into the Federal Theatre Project. Lead Belly was placed on stage in his informal work attire at a number of other events in New York and elsewhere. In August 1940, he sang 'work songs' and blues in the American Common section of the World's Fair. Early the following year he participated in New York's Cavalcade of American Song. By the mid-1940s, he was performing as an 'old-time' American folk singer.

John Lomax died of heart failure at the start of 1946, Lead Belly, however, continued touring, but died of a bone infection at the end of 1949. A memorial concert was held at the start of the following year featuring Woodie Guthrie, WC Handy and Count Basie. It culminated in the screening of a famous film strip of the singer's life – a newsreel which guided perceptions of his performance and is worth further consideration. In 1935 Lomax and Lead Belly restaged the beginnings of their association for a *March of Time* newsreel, which began in the Louisiana State Penitentiary (*colujomes*, 2009). The completed footage begins with the headline, 'Angola, La!' – a title which functions both as a reference to its location – the penitentiary was known as 'Angola' after the plantation that was there before it was rebuilt as a prison on a curve in the Mississippi at the end of Highway 66. Together with the faces of the Black convicts, however, it also resonates with notions of the African country.

Dressed in his convict uniform, Lead Belly sings 'Goodnight Irene' for an audience of his fellow prisoners while 'Curator' Lomax – who wears what seems to be an Indiana Jones-style hat, khaki shirt and brown tie – records him over again ('Just once more, Lead Belly'). Lomax then offers his endorsement: 'That's fine Lead Belly, You're a fine songster. I've never heard so many good negro songs.' Lead Belly asks John Lomax to beseech a governor with the song to help turn him loose. The convict is then seen three months later, guitar in hand, but now dressed as a hobo or manual labourer, and presumably a free man, entering Lomax's office-cum-hotel room in Marshall, Texas:

> Lomax : Lead Belly, what are you doing here?
> Lead Belly: No use trying to run away boss, I came here to be your man. I'd like to work for you for the rest of my life. You got me out of that Louisiana Pen.
> Lomax: You can't work for me. You're a mean boy. You've killed two men.
> Lead Belly: Please don't talk that way, boss.
> Lomax: Have you got a pistol?
> Lead Belly: No sir, I got a knife.
> Lomax: Let me see it. What would you do with that thing?
> Lead Belly: I'd use it on somebody who bothered you, boss. Please boss, take me with you. You'll never have to tie you shoe strings no more as long as you keep me with you.
> Lomax: Alright Lead Belly, I'll try you.
> Lead Belly: Thank you, boss. Thank you! I'll drive you all over the United States, boss, and I'll bring all those songs with you! You'll be my big boss and I'll be your man. Thank you, sir, thank you!

Next an upper-class newscaster who acts as narrator explains that Lead Belly became Lomax's 'man' and travelled with him. Then Lead Belly is seen in Connecticut, in a suit and bow tie, serenading his new Black bride, Martha, who was brought up from the South to be with him. The film ends with Lead Belly's songs going 'into the archive of the great national institution along with the original copy of the declaration of independence'. Lomax, now in a suit, plays his recording of 'Goodnight Irene' to two tweed-suited White librarians who sit in a Library of Congress drawing room.

The *March of Time* newsreel is more complex and interesting than it first appears as there are several tropes at play. On one level, Lomax is portrayed as a song hunter who appears to have gone from one end of the class system and civil society to the other, on an expedition to collect and retrieve folk songs as his lost treasure. Lomax has modern technologies at his disposal: typewriters and recording equipment. Lead Belly is a singer who has only his knife and guitar. Nevertheless, the convict forms a pact with the song collector ('I'll be your man') that is almost entirely through his own agency, with only limited effort from Lomax. Finally, Lead Belly's change of clothing is used to indicate a process in which he is increasingly civilized and raised up through the social hierarchy. Indeed, Lead Belly became the Lomaxes' 'man' for eight months until March

1935: they used him as a chauffeur and house servant at their home in Wilton, Connecticut, where he was given a room, board and an allowance in exchange for Lomax keeping all of his concert earnings. The *March of Time* film is only one of a number of instances – including the recordings themselves – where 'authentic' (working) folk culture was *restaged* as an object for emotional identification. Cast as a savage genius, Lead Belly was described by English scholar John Wright (1989, p. 96) as 'in one rough frame the bruised and imbruted "man farthest down" for whom Booker T. Washington and the organizations of racial uplift had lowered their proverbial buckets'.

John Lomax's interventions continued with the work of his son, Alan. Interviewed by Harvey Breit for the *New York Times* book review in 1950, Alan Lomax explained that his father would read Shakespeare aloud to him. He added that, 'The ordinary people are alive and have kept alive truth and beauty' (p. BR7). In February 1961, *The New York Times* published a letter by the anthropologist Margaret Mead explaining:

> At no point in the review can the reader discover where the work of John Lomax, the father, ends, and the work of Alan Lomax, the son and author, begins. Such continuity between father and son is so rare in our culture that perhaps it is also responsible for the reviewer's failures to recognize that Alan Lomax's outstanding contribution – a genuine integration between cultural theory, geographic specificity and folklore style – is too new to have been made by anyone in his father's day, and is still on the very growing edge of our knowledge.

At a Carnegie Hall Concert he staged on 3 April 1959, Alan Lomax said, 'The time has come for Americans not to be ashamed of what we go for, musically, from primitive ballads to rock'n'roll songs' (Wilson 1959, p. 13).

Lead Belly and *King Kong*

About three years after *King Kong* was released in cinemas across the country, reviewing the Lomaxes' *Negro Folksongs as Sung by Lead Belly*, one *New York Times* reviewer explained how the Black singer was touted in front of 'curious-minded and sensation-loving audiences' in the 'clubs, colleges and universities' of the North. The reviewer added:

> Fortunately the editors have permitted Lead Belly to tell the story of his life in his own graphic vernacular. For the most part it is a recountment [*sic*] of sordid, semi-savage emotions and episodes revealing nature endowed with an

admirable sense of the dramatic and an insatiable lust for life. *Primitive in his heart and mind, his desires and aspirations are likewise primitive and always of the flesh.* He has too much of the earth to be concerned with thoughts of the spirit; therefore he never approaches anything resembling a poetic attitude of mind, the common inheritance of his race. Even when he sings, his half-inarticulate, groping mind is concerned with thoughts of bodily enjoyment, and he is always the boastful, self-satisfied satyr, conscious of his musical gift, but proudly aware of his physical force.

(Kennedy 1936, p. BR7, emphasis mine)

Press stories from this first visit labelled Lead Belly a 'Murderous Minstrel', 'Virtuoso of Knife and Guitar' and 'Sweet Singer of the Swamplands Here to Do a Few Tunes between Homicides' (Porterfield 2001, p. 347).

One of the key tropes through which the Lomaxes occasionally represented Lead Belly was animalism. Alan Lomax recalled that the singer was offered a chance to show 'to a streamlined, city-orientated world that America had living folk music – swamp primitive, angry, freighted with great sorrow and joy' (see Filene 1991, p. 609). In the fall of 1934, according to Barker and Taylor (2007, p. 18), John Lomax wrote:

Lead Belly is a nigger to the core of his being. In addition he is a killer. He tells the truth only accidentally ... He is as sensual as a goat, and when he sings to me my spine tingles and sometimes tears come. Penitentiary wardens all tell me that I set no value on my life in using him as a travelling companion.

According to Barker and Taylor (2007, p. 18), Lomax told New York reporters that Lead Belly 'was a "natural," who had no idea of money, law, or ethics and who was possessed of virtually no restraint'. They add, 'Needless to say, there was little truth in these remarks – Lead Belly was a soft-spoken, gentle man who was well aware that his drunken, frenzied murder attempts had been wrong; his understanding of money, law, and ethics was solid and strong.'

For the live New York audience, Lomax acted as a privileged interpreter who could bring them something more authentic from across the Mason-Dixon line. According to John Lomax in 1935:

Northern people hear Negroes playing and singing beautiful spirituals, which are too refined and are unlike the true Southern spirituals. Or else they hear men and women on the stage and radio, burlesquing their own songs. Lead Belly doesn't burlesque. He plays and sings with absolute sincerity. Whether or not it sounds foolish to you, he plays with absolute sincerity. I've heard his songs a hundred times, but I always get a thrill. To me this is real music.

(in Byrne 2015)

As a frame for how to hear the performer, Lomax's introduction locates Lead Belly as Southern, sincere and unmediated: natural, sensual, expressive, unrefined, unstaged and perhaps threatening. The Black singer's musicality was understood as an essential component of this, a kind of natural expression akin to the famed 'hollers' of Southern field workers. Since gender has been used as a way to talk about race, it is also important to also note that Lead Belly's performance style was desexualized and rendered sentimental for his White metropolitian audiences: in the *March of Time* film, he can be seen eventually monogamously coupling-up with his Black female partner.

Writing in her book *Monstrosity, Performance and Race in Contemporary Culture*, Bernadette Calafell (2015, p. 1) has noted that 'monsters are made, not born'. More specifically, as Susana Loza (2017, p. 7) notes, blackface minstrelsy and the 'monsterization' of Black subjects has been 'inextricably linked' in White supremacist thinking. These associated forms of racial mimicry, for Loza, both indicate the durability of White (settler) colonialism. She argues, 'Seeing monstrosity as a technology, a vehicle through which race is made, helps us understand why the West is so consumed with this liminal figure' (p. 2). Though selection and redemption, John Lomax both made *and unmade* Lead Belly's perceived monstrosity. While he capitalized on White privilege, it would be too simplistic to brand John Lomax a monster himself. The field recordist's philosophy was complex in that it involved a utopian moment of social assimilation pursued through a pronounced recognition of musical and social difference. His notion of the 'sound photograph' constructed identity in the process of claiming to record it. It located Black folk as American citizens, but in effect as discontents and holders of sub-altern identity, the lowest social grouping in a regional hierarchy of modernity based on one notion of shared progress. Lomax was, of course, not alone in his racialized vision of the blues and ballads as American folk music. Before meeting Lead Belly he had persuaded MacMillan to publish a book of songs, enlisted a charitable foundation to support his venture and contacted the Library of Congress's Archive of American Folk Song to supply recording equipment and archival storage for his results (Filene 1991, p. 602). Social interest in his project before it had started, while not necessarily indicative of widespread racism, at least indicated a shared conception of racial patronage, perhaps fuelled by the already segregated marketing of 'race' records.

A detour into cinema may help illuminate the complexity of Lomax's position. Matthew Hughey's (2014) study of a more recent film narrative he calls 'the White saviour' film is instructive here, as a 'genre in which a White messianic character saves lower- or working-class, usually urban or isolated, non-White character from a sad fate' (p. 1). White saviour films are largely a recent phenomenon. Hughey cites films such as *Avatar* (Cameron 2009) and *The Blind Side* (Hancock 2009) as examples. The difference may account for the urban location of the African American victim characters, but the process of rescue has some parallels. Hughey argues that Othering is a key to understanding film examples:

> Such imposing patronage enables an interpretation of non-White characters and culture as essentially broken, marginalized and pathological, while Whites can emerge as messianic characters that easily fix the non-White pariah with their superior moral and mental abilities. While some might argue such racially charged saviourism is an essentially conservative, postcolonial device that rationalizes right-wing paternalism, I argue that it knows no political boundaries and is pliable to contradictory and seemingly antagonistic agendas.
>
> (p. 2)

As his book unfolds, Hughey shows awareness here of the unstable qualities of Whiteness itself: tacitly claiming supremacy, in the shape of White normativity, but constantly having to justify its relative position on the basis of moral superiority. In one sense, the journey to find Lead Belly and its reverse – the journey to showcase him in New York – were pitched to resemble Carl Denham's trip to find the mythic giant entity on Skull Island:

> They did not just document the native traditions of the Other, but captured him, brought him back to their culture, and asked him to remake it in his image (or in their image of his image). The matter was further complicated because the Lomaxes not only held Lead Belly up as an exemplar of a foreign culture but also as an important vestige of America's *own* culture – the culture that was slipping away in the twentieth century.
>
> (Filene 1991, p. 616)

If Lomax was a 'White savior', he was therefore more than just that.

In conclusion, at a time when Black aspiration was a threat in some quarters of American civic life, the Lomaxes used the idea of an untainted folk music to stress class distinctions between races. As Benjamin Filene (1991, p. 604) explained: 'The Lomaxes claimed to be impartial folklorists who documented an existing tradition, but they had a personal vision that has powerfully influenced how Americans remember their musical heritage.' It would be easy to blame John Lomax and his son individually as unthinking racists who essentialized stereotypes in their pursuit of 'pure' folk music. Yet they were evidently ambiguous agents in a much larger social process. Compare, for example this affectionate tribute to Lead Belly given by the folk singer Pete Seeger in a 2001 interview. After declaring, 'Lead Belly was one of the greatest performers I ever knew,' Seeger continued:

> He didn't write many songs on his own, but he changed every song he sang, adding to it, using a different harmony, etc. He was ambitious. If he hadn't been a musician, he would have been a great athlete. In his sixties his muscles still bulged like iron bands.[4]

Seeger's evocation of Lead Belly combines appreciation for his musical contribution with a focus on the African American singer's physical strength. We could say that, well, Lead Belly was simply strong and muscular, but in the context of this history, such statements are not innocent. We might even say that Seeger was performing his Whiteness here, through an implied contrast between his subject and himself. It would, however, be mistaken to assume that we, as contemporary observers, are fully free of White supremacy, or that that Seeger was fully committed to it. It be wrong to miss the human admiration that the White folk singer felt for his African American friend. Equally, rather than fully locate the folklorist John Lomax as monstrous, it is perhaps better to understand him in the context of his time, as somebody updating attitudes to race in a context of residual racism. Examining John Lomax's *Adventures of a Ballad Hunter* for the *New York Times* book review, Horace Reynolds explained:

> Never before I heard the records he made of the Negro work songs, did I quite realize the Negro genius for making art out of work ... One of the things I like about this book is its sincerity. Nothing in it tastes synthetic. These people really existed, said and did and sung these things. If anybody ever did, John Lomax really heard America singing.
>
> (Reynolds 1947, p. BR7)

3

Colonel Parker and the art of commercial exploitation: The manager as monster

Those who treat others as inhuman render themselves as monstrous. As the infamous manager of Elvis Presley, Colonel Thomas Andrew Parker has been widely perceived as a kind of monster. In a synopsis for their unproduced documentary about his life called 'The Real Colonel Parker', Charles Stone and Peter Phillips wrote, 'The three main biographies that have been written about Parker are all variations on the same theme … The "Colonel" was a bullying, manipulative control freak who turned into a monster whilst cynically ignoring his protégé's cries for help.'[1] Reviewing Alanna Nash's biographic portrait of Tom Parker, *The Colonel*, Fred Goodman (2003, p. 11) noted in the *New York Times* that the singer and his manager had already 'become an American fable: the apple-cheeked plowboy and raw sexual dynamo who is born to the throne but can never escape the nefarious grasp of his kingmaker, a Southern-fried amalgam of Rasputin and Cardinal Richelieu'. He added that any 'responsible biographer' had a duty to prioritize less colourful facts over more appealing legends.

However, Parker had always been a creature of legend. Nash's biography speculated that in his former incarnation – a life so secret that nobody knew Parker's identity as an illegal alien – the Colonel's motivation for leaving his native Holland to come to the United States was that he could have committed a murder at home. The idea that Parker dispatched Anna van den Enden is a classic conspiracy theory, devoid of proof, based only on limited, circumstantial evidence. Nevertheless, it has become an integral and pervasive part of the discussion about the Colonel, because it so clearly appeared to fit his own mythic profile. In 2012, *Smithsonian* magazine, for example, published an article asking, 'Was He a Killer on the Lam?' (Dash 2012) To understand the pervasiveness of such ideas, it is relevant to consider way in which the larger myth of Elvis Presley has symbiotically created space for the Colonel. What follows will examine how Parker has been perceived, the basis of myths about him, and less obvious aspects of Elvis's phenomenon that they reveal. I argue that although the Colonel has been seen as an uncanny exploiter and perhaps even a symbolic 'bad father', popular understandings need to be contextualized in wider questions of class and agency.

Perceptions of Parker

Especially in later descriptions, Elvis Presley rarely appeared alone. Moving towards a theory of famous actors, Quinn (1990, p. 154) suggested, 'The genealogy of celebrity has reached an extraordinary state of extension.' As Elvis's fame spread and fans craved more information, writers began to reveal a cast of other figures around him. Relatives, friends, business associates and co-stars all became well-known through their connections. On one hand there was his family. When he became a national star, his parents Gladys and Vernon were sold as part of the story (Dundy 1995, p. 255). At Ellis Auditorium in May 1956 the spotlight was put on Elvis's parents. In turn, during the next decade new wife Priscilla and daughter Lisa received publicity. By the 1970s fans sent gifts to Graceland for Elvis's Grandma Minnie Mae and Lisa (Yancey 1977, pp. 47, 175). On later tours not only did Elvis ritualistically introduce the band to give himself a breather midway through each show, but he also presented friends and family to the audience as well. Priscilla (Presley 1985, p. 281), a four-year-old Lisa (Gordon 1996, p. 190), karate mentor Ed Parker (1978, p. 45), Mafia foreman Joe Esposito (Presley et al. 1980, 163), his father Vernon Presley and final girlfriend Ginger Alden (Geller 1989) were just some of the individuals Elvis introduced, to great applause. Once the singer divorced Priscilla, his new girlfriend Linda Thompson would sign autographs for fans from in front of the stage (Goldman 1982, p. 659). Uncle Vester became famous to fans working the Graceland gates. Cousin Billy Smith entered the spotlight too, with writings on and interviews with him. Also the public came to know others such as the Memphis Mafia: Elvis's male entourage of aides and bodyguards who got their name from press reports following *G.I. Blues* (Presley et al. 1980, p. 128). The star's immense iconicism resulted in a hyper-extended state of celebrity genealogy which meant exceptional things regularly happened. For example, Elvis's army sergeant Rob Fuller got *his own* fan mail (Haining 1987, p. 72). Soprano Kathy Westmoreland and side man

Charlie Hodge had *their own* fan clubs (West et al. 1977, p. 173); Kathy also had an impersonator (Westmoreland 1987, p. 132). The acquaintance, fan, collector and merchandiser Paul Lichter even sold a marketing firm the rights to *his* name and likeness (Hopkins 1980, p. 251). In light of Elvis's immense stardom, it was hardly surprising that Colonel Thomas Andrew Parker, who was Presley's third, final and main manager, was a consistent focus of attention. Parker had his own celebrity virtually as soon as Elvis became nationally famous in the 1950s. After the singer first appeared on television in January 1956, 'The Colonel Presents … ' sometimes prefixed Presley's live billing (Gordon 1996, p. 54). Parker did his own interview with *Time* magazine (Dundy 1995, p. 193), became a regular part of Elvis's press, and received his own fan mail (Hopkins 1974, p. 178). The vitriol Parker received after his death in 1997 related to a widespread perception that located him as a master manipulator.

Elvis's responses to the Colonel were varied. Initially he said, 'I can't get it into my head that I'm property,' because he could so frequently do what he liked. Reporting on a Nashville DJ's convention singer Minnie Pearl said, 'They had him on display' (Hopkins 1974, p. 90). By mid-1956 the star told friend June Juanico that in three years he could lead a life of his own (Guralnick 1995, p. 313), suggesting a pact with his manager. Much of the time Elvis impotently accepted his role, giving in to the Colonel's challenge (Wise 1987, p. 14). Yet he grumbled to friends, even telling director Hal Kanter at the end of 1956 that he envied a dog they passed on the street because it had a life of its own (Guralnick 1995, p. 372). In this rendering, Elvis had become Colonel Parker's puppet (Fortas 1992, p. 268; Clayson 1994, p. 52): reduced to a cartoon character in his movies (Marsh 1992, p. 122) or treated like what he called a 'chunk of meat' and forced to constantly tour across America (Haining 1987, p. 162; Hodge 1988, p. 186).

The Colonel's role as exploitative manager was a central part of his own celebrity image. It was symbolized in the theory that Parker once kept dancing chickens. This story went that live performances incurred a $20 entertainment tax unless they were classed exhibits, so the Colonel carried farmyard animals, usually two chickens, in his truck, to place in a box marked as an exhibit before Eddy Arnold's country music shows. If Arnold was too sick to appear, the Colonel hung up a sign saying 'Colonel Parker's Dancing Chickens'. He then stood the chickens on a hot plate strewn with straw inside a cage left on stage. When the hot plate was plugged in, the heat-agitated chickens entertained onlookers. Accompanied by the recorded sounds of Bob Wills and his Texas Playboys, doing 'Turkey in the Straw', they 'danced' trying not to burn their feet

(Fortas and Nash 2008, p. 40). It was a story that the Colonel told himself with reference to his ingenuity at outwitting local officials, but it contained themes of the exploitation and abuse of performers that were hard to miss. The 'dancing chickens' story appeared in Jerry Hopkins's seminal, *Elvis: A Biography*. The phrase formed part of a chapter title in Alanna Nash's (2003) biography, *The Colonel*. Nash argued that because Parker was an animal lover who 'treated animals with more dignity than he treated humans' (p. 66), the story proved apocryphal (p. 67). Nash also cites Gabe Tucker, who claimed that Parker appropriated the incident as something that made a good story; the real animal act belonged to Dub Albrittan, who told him about it in 1945 (Nash 2003, p. 67).

The 'dancing chicken' trope did not just belong to Parker, but eventually it became part of popular culture. A good example of this is in the climax of Werner Herzog's fictional feature, *Stroszek* (Herzog 1977), where the lead character, Bruno, is mesmerized by the sight of actual dancing chickens. The image conjures up both entertainment and entrapment. Some ex-members of the singer's entourage, the Memphis Mafia, thought Colonel Parker hypnotized his client (West et al. 1977, p. 264; Goldman 1982, p. 513). Luc Sante (1981, p. 22) claimed Elvis's manager encouraged his ignorance to make manipulation easier.

When Parker's ability to extract revenue for himself is added to the equation, this picture of the manager as someone having *Caligari*-like powers of control over his charge tips into perceptions bordering on vampirism. Not only was Parker 'on the take', he operated a 'bleed-em-white' strategy even against the Presley estate (O'Neal 1996, p. 73). Early band-mates Scotty and Bill feared he would 'cut their throats' as soon as look at them (Guralnick 1995, p. 266). It was Chris Hutchin's obituary of the Colonel in *The People*, complete with a photo of Parker jokingly holding a knife to Elvis cousin's throat that drove home the interpretation. Here Colonel Tom 'bled Elvis dry' because he was a 'cut-throat wheeler dealer' (1997, pp. 6, 8). He was seen as inhuman, numb and 'unfeeling' (Broeske and Brown 1997a, p. 32).

Monstering of the Colonel extended to portraying him as pathologically violent or emotionally dead: a walking corpse, craving (financial) blood, but incapable of human empathy. *Time* magazine called Parker a 'dead eye' promoter (Cocks 1977, p. 24). TV movies showed him signing merchandise contracts over Elvis's coffin (Esposito 1994, p. 143). 'Colonel will drink cup after cup of scalding hot coffee that would make another man scream with pain,' hatchet-job biographer Albert Goldman (1982, p. 54) emphasized in his best prose. 'If the old man is in a good mood he may even take a flaming match and lower it down his throat.'

Central to such monstrous portrayals of Colonel Parker is the idea that he treated his charge as nothing but a walking dollar sign. Though Elvis's bodyguards saw their boss as 'valuable human property' (West et al. 1977, p. 2) and 'living bullion' (Crumbaker and Tucker 1981, p. *back cover*) it was Colonel Tom who supposedly took that view to extremes. He became the arch villain in Elvis Presley's life story. The Colonel treated Elvis inhumanely like a piece of merchandise (Dundy 1995, p. 195). Parker wanted his charge to become a 'respectable middle class commodity' (Fortas 1992, p. 58), so for the Colonel, 'Elvis was the purest of postwar products' (Guralnick 1995, p. 240). The Colonel only saw Presley in terms of money (Buskin 1995, p. 60). Again, the ways of the almighty dollar were emphasized by Chris Hutchins (1997, p. 6) writing *The People's* obituary for Colonel Parker: 'To Parker, Elvis was a six foot dollar sign.'

Sometimes the Colonel's perceived monstrosity has been cast in familial terms. It is notable that Presley was born a quarter century after Parker; the two men were a generation apart. Given the prominence of the generation gap during Elvis's heyday, it is not surprising that Parker was sometimes portrayed as a kind of father of his client. Certain aspects of Elvis's image allowed this perception to emerge. In the early days, Elvis told the press, 'Colonel is almost like a second daddy to me when I'm away from my folks' (Farren 1981, p. 80). Vernon Presley, Elvis's real father, has also been portrayed as illiterate (Slaughter 1995a, p. 4) or seen as 'a bible belt Hillbilly' (Broeske and Brown 1997b, p. 52) and borderline 'White trash' with all its connotations of being mean, lazy, shiftless, quick tempered, criminal, tasteless and sexually immoral (Fortas 1992, p. 15; Marsh 1992, p. 1). At worst, some grim moments are highlighted, in a history of hatred involving secret parental alcoholism and the shame of past crimes (Dundy 1995, p. 295). Elvis put Vernon in charge of finance, but the elder Presley was supposedly mean and hated the Memphis Mafia. To him they drained the family fortune (Goldman 1982, p. 658; Fortas 1992, p. 265). In the late 1930s, Vernon served time for fraud while his three-year-old only son protected his distraught mother, placing Elvis as a kind of surrogate father (Fortas 1992, p. 67).

Vernon was therefore, in effect, in the role of *his own son's child* (Parker 1978, p. 78; Crumbaker and Tucker 1981, p. 26). This Oedipal inversion of the typical parent-child relationship frames Vernon as an utterly inadequate male. His wife Gladys called him castrated: 'steer cotted' (Goldman 1982, p. 440). She, meanwhile, encouraged her son by transmitting her positive ethics (Aparin

1988, p. 24). After describing the Southern matriarchy, biographer Elaine Dundy (1995, p. 13) said of Elvis's mother, 'In short, she was the person with the greatest power.' Gladys supposedly mistrusted the Colonel and his contracts (Dundy 1995, p. 237; Guralnick 1995, p. 207). One thing therefore implied by Parker's portrayal is that the Colonel supplanted Elvis's strong, supportive mother – while ineffectual father Vernon did nothing about it, he 'stole her baby' (Flippo 1994, p. 17). At best, Vernon could be shown as the dumb butt of Elvis's practical jokes; fooled by his son's bogus plan to release an X-rated version of 'Hurt' (Westmoreland 1987, p. 244). Later on, Vernon was seen mainly as a taker in his son's life (Crumbaker and Tucker 1981, p. 37). Above all, in these versions of his story, Elvis is considered only accountable to the Colonel.

Ten years after Elvis died, a few British fans actually met Colonel Parker in Las Vegas during their anniversary tour. During my PhD research in the mid-1990s, I talked to some who went to the convention. One said, 'I think Parker was a bad influence myself. I've not got great love for him at all. We've met him and we didn't like him very much' (Duffett 1998, p. 91). Another explained that Parker almost split the fan club, because members who had pictures taken with him were ostracized by others. Hearing of Tom Parker's passing, Elvis's early girlfriend June Juanico told one interviewer, 'That really does prove one thing; only the good die young and he was not a good man' (in Haynes 1997, p. 18).

Evidence for the monstrous perception of Parker

As Memphis writer Jackson Baker (1997, p. 33) noted, 'No one connected with the Elvis Presley phenomenon has undergone such drastic ups and downs on the reputational flow chart as "Colonel" Tom Parker.' This suggests that Parker's actions can be perceived in different ways and may not have been a case of pure exploitation. Instead, the evidence is mixed. Rather than it simply being a case of complete parasitism, any thorough analysis of Parker's actions unearths greater complexities, including things he did to serve himself and his client at the same time. Evidence for the widespread perception of Parker as an exploiter is further confused by the constant shell games he played with his own 'snowman' image.[2]

Was Parker an uncanny exploiter, as was widely perceived? Elvis's first major biographer, Jerry Hopkins, painted the relationship as a 'classic symbiosis' (Hopkins 1980, p. 21). Yet it was also a cordial one. From a mishap managing country singer Eddy Arnold, the Colonel realized he had stayed out of his charge's personal life. He referred to the star as 'Mr Presley', gave credit to fans rather than himself for making Elvis great (Levy 1962, p. 49) and would not let others belittle his charge (Crumbaker and Tucker 1981, p. 114). *Before* the Colonel, while supported by Bob Neal, Elvis asked many others – mostly radio DJs – to manage him, including, by some accounts, Dewey Phillips (Hazen and Freeman 1997), Bill Randle, Tommy Cutrer, Bill Perryman and 'Yankie' Baharovich (Cotten 1995, p. 97; Burk 1997, p. 161). Once Colonel Parker took over from Bob Neal and ditched his own partner Hank Snow, the situation was more stable. However, countering the idea that Parker greedily muscled in for his own gain, there have been reports he tried to sell part of the deal to Oscar Davis and Ernest 'Uncle Dudley' Hackworth (Cotten 1995, p. 49). Although an average manager's commission was 15 per cent – Scotty Moore had taken 10 per cent then Bob Neal 15 per cent from Elvis – the Colonel began on 25 per cent of Elvis's pre-tax earnings as manager (Hopkins 1974, p. 101).

While Parker always took a larger percentage than was typical, he defended it by saying that Presley got full attention as his only client. He was an astute deal-maker, a tireless promoter and friend to the fan clubs. The Colonel's early deal as Elvis's promoter then manager gave him a big incentive to look after his charge and get the best deals he could. He got Elvis on to RCA, a major label, without a demo (Clayson 1994, p. 51) although the singer already had a string of Sun hits. Colonel Parker found more promotion for Elvis and a royalty rise from 3 per cent to 5 per cent which initially meant 2 cents per record (Guralnick 1995, p. 231). Also he shrewdly turned RCA's recoupable signing into a gift, meaning that Elvis's future royalties would not be spent paying back Sun for the sign-over. Colonel Parker secured a top publicity agent, national television exposure and entry into Hollywood without his client having previous acting experience (Guralnick 1995, p. 261). Furthermore, he obtained an initial film contract with unprecedented pay, even for an established star (Esposito 1994, p. 25). Some say Elvis would not have been a star without the Colonel (West et al. 1977, p. 128), others suggest he would have made it much slower (Lacker et al. 1979, p. 23). The singer told his friend Ed Parker (1978, p. 25) how well the Colonel had served him. Elvis's movies may not all have been interesting, but they were made so quickly he could earn millions without working most of the year. Tom Parker also advised other singers for free and helped upcoming actors like Nick Adams and Tommy Sands (Guralnick 1995, p. 460). Tom Jones and the Beatles may have asked the Colonel to be their manager too (Esposito 1994,

p. 98). When Elvis was alive, Parker helped to arrange for UK fan club members to attend Elvis's American concerts (Slaughter 1995b, p. 1). RCA producer and guitarist Chet Atkins said the Colonel was capable of real generosity (Guralnick 1995, p. 169). Colonel Parker gave the Memphis Mafia bonuses (Fortas 1992, p. 132) and sent toys to children of the Graceland staff (Yancey 1977, p. 179).

If evidence of Parker's less venal side begins to suggest a counter-argument to the claims he was a total vampire, it is also relevant to note that the Colonel *played up* to his infamous image. With an honorary rank, carnival background and mystery origin, Colonel Thomas Andrew Parker of Virginia, née illegal Dutch immigrant Andreas Cornelis van Kuijk, was already a prominent performer himself. He would dress up in various costumes, act out daft scenarios and recount tales of his own dubious past (Fortas 1992, p. 162). Alfred Wertheimer (1994, p. 97), who Parker knew was RCA's man, reported how he conned a poor porter into shifting baggage. When Elvis got his $110 army pay cheque (Cortez 1978, p. 43), in front of a ranked media the Colonel yelled, 'Don't forget my commission!' Parker evidently knew his venal image was good for business and he stuck to it. The sign over his MGM office ambiguously read 'Elvis Exploitations' (Geller 1989, p. 83). He was the manager who said he was willing to sell 'I Hate Elvis' badges if they too made a profit (Buskin 1995, p. 64). As Jackson Baker (1997, p. 33) also said, 'To call Parker a con man is merely to give him his due.'

Elvis's feature films were arguably a conduit through which mythic notions of his image were shaped, in part because the pictures were marketed as vehicles in which the star was always more prominent than the story. The public saw Elvis inflected, as it were, by each new character he played. Parker had a lot to do with these films: he approved of their contents as technical advisor (Dundy 1995, p. 282). Consequently, it is worth considering how singers and their managers were portrayed. In particular, *Jailhouse Rock* (Thorpe, 1957) set a pattern by suggesting that a singing hero could be victimized by criminals from the music industry. As Vince Everett, Elvis spends time in prison, having accidentally killed a man in a bar room dispute he never started. His cellmate Hunk Houghton suggests a career in singing. Coming out, Elvis steals the show and a classy female plugger succumbs to his charms. She initiates him into the music industry and Elvis/Vince becomes an over-night sensation, but his dubious old cellmate reappears and craftily becomes his manager. At *Jailhouse Rock*'s climax, the singer and manager have a fight in which Vince/Elvis loses his voice. The film ends with relief, as it returns to him. This is significant because it parodied the music industry and painted Elvis's manager as his most expensive flunky. Through such Hollywood features, Elvis's audience was encouraged to see his industry and manager in a way which gave them further opportunities for empathy. Years after *Jailhouse Rock's* release, Raquel Welch was shocked by the Colonel's condescending invitations to see 'the boy' when she was in Las Vegas: 'He was talking about Elvis Presley as if he were White trash!'[3] When Lisa Marie's appointed legal guardian Blanchard Tual conducted an investigation in 1981 he found RCA and Colonel Parker indulged in 'collusion, conspiracy, fraud, misrepresentation, bad faith and over-reaching' (Goldman 1982, p. 717).

Claims of 'over-reaching' raise the spectre of the Colonel as a 'bad father', but again the evidence is limited for that. Some of the Colonel's behaviour could be interpreted from a Freudian angle. On his orders, no girls were initially allowed, for example, in the picture of Elvis's life. Arriving at Fort Chaffee the new recruit refused to pose with his showgirl companion Dotty Harmony, saying she was not connected with the event (Levy 1962, p. 11). Dotty later claimed the Colonel wanted nobody female getting close to Elvis (Guralnick 1995, p. 391). After Elvis's girlfriend June Juanico did a press interview in August 1957, Parker told his charge they did not need that kind of publicity (Guralnick 1995, p. 317). Similarly, his army superiors strictly forbade photo coverage of female partners (Levy 1962, p. 26), although they broke that rule by strategically displaying a WAC for Elvis to kiss as he left for Germany (Guralnick 1995, p. 485). The 'no girls' rule can be perceived as Freudian insofar that it appears to keep Elvis in a commercially appealing state of pubescent arrest. Its flip-side was, in a situation akin to Freud's *Totem and Taboo* (1913/2001), that Parker, as the 'bad father', in theory kept all the women of the tribe to himself.

While Parker was arguably trying to add a frisson of romantic availability to Elvis's image, the initial lack of romantic associations in public raises the question of how much control the manager had over his client's image. Was Elvis psychologically in thrall to the Colonel? People thought Colonel Parker might have hooked Elvis on drugs or even hypnotized him, forgetting that Parker had both the contracts and contacts necessary to keep him there. The public did not know Elvis's father Vernon had been in jail for forging a cheque years earlier; that scandal broke in *The Midnight Globe* after Elvis died (Presley et al. 1980, p. 78). Biographer Elaine Dundy (1995, p. 288) suspected Colonel Parker may have blackmailed his charge, humiliatingly forcing him to act out his father's story. However, Dundy's scenario seems far-fetched, especially since Elvis and Vernon told at least one friend their family 'secret' (Guralnick 1995, p. 358). Singing prisoners already existed: apart from Lead Belly a few years earlier, the Sun label had hits with a group of inmates from Nashville State Penitentiary called the Prisonaires. Priscilla Presley (1985, p. 233) said her ex-husband was an 'obedient child' to his manager, but Elvis bucked the Colonel on several key occasions. For example, a defiant Elvis did not stay away from Charlotte until show time in June 1956 (Guralnick 1995, p. 288). He also agreed with producers of the 1968 *Comeback Special* against the wishes of Parker (Goldman 1982, p. 510) and took up songs for which he had no publishing rights during the subsequent American Sound Studios session (Fortas 1992, p. 290).

The idea of the Colonel as someone who 'stole Gladys's baby' partially rests on portrayals of Vernon Presley as spineless and inadequate. There is plenty of evidence to counter such portraits of Elvis's father. Vernon actually came from a class slightly above his own wife (Dundy 1995, p. 31), and his tastes may have been less extreme than his son. For instance, Elvis furnished the Jungle Room at Graceland with chairs Vernon hated (Flippo 1994, p. 115). For such a 'shiftless' man he had been remarkably stable in Memphis, working at the United Paint Company for five years before Elvis made the big time (Hazen and Freeman 1997, p. 9). Vernon was not quite as spendthrift as perceived, either: occasionally *Elvis* tried to stop *Vernon* overspending (Crumbaker and Tucker 1981, p. 36). Priscilla Presley also made efforts to curb Elvis's profligacy, though she was never perceived of as 'White trash' (Goldman 1982, pp. 467 and 563). Although Vernon was supposed to be subordinate to Elvis and therefore way below the Colonel, at first he bucked Colonel Parker by re-signing the Hayride contract (Guralnick 1995, p. 213). That was not the way it would usually be described. What such evidence suggests is that things are more complex than often perceived. Views of the Colonel's relationship with Elvis have undergone several revisions. Initially they were portrayed as a happy pair (Goldman 1982, p. 439). Years later, Parker said, 'I never looked upon him as a son but he was the success I always wanted' (Hutchins 1997, p. 8). This suggests that further elements have been at play in creating the negative perceptions of Colonel Parker as manager.

Motives for the monstering of Colonel Parker

It was really only after Elvis died that negative readings of the Colonel began to dominate (Fortas 1992, p. 168). Grey areas could then be exploited. In his analysis of Parker's misdeeds, the Southern historian Michael Bertrand (2011) used the Colonel's inappropriate dress at Elvis's funeral to signify a lack of human compassion. Writers have made much of the fact that Colonel Parker came to Elvis's wake dressed in a Hawaiian shirt and admiral cap and never cried or looked inside the casket (Goldman 1982, p. 702). However, Elvis told friends he did not want his mourners to wear black (Brewer-Giorgio 1990, p. 84). Some others avoided funeral garb or never attended at all (Esposito 1994, p. 251; Moore 1997, p. 227). Presley's nickname for his manager was also 'the Admiral' (Goldman 1982, p. 203). While Bertrand's historical analysis is strong on evidence – in other words, the Colonel really did financially over-reach – it is also true that myth is a way of telling each story that proves satisfying to the popular imagination, regardless of the facts (see Duffett 2013, p. 210).

To understand Parker's role, we need to look at Elvis's own image. Locked together as giver and taker, the singer and his manager form a double act in writings about his life. Elvis maintained his primary reason for performance was the love shared with fans. In other words, Elvis's role is as a giver. In their 1997 Candlelight Vigil pamphlet his Country Fan Club explained, 'Elvis was a humanitarian, a man of giving ... and he did it his way.' He was celebrated as a great humanitarian (Guralnick 1995, p. 443). Presley was known for freely distributing all sorts of material items – including jewellery and cars, occasionally even houses – to family, friends, fans and complete strangers: people in material need and those who were not. Elvis was more than a donor. He was understood as a natural resource (Lacker et al. 1979, p. 98), and his motives have been widely analysed. Biographers often include whole chapters on Elvis's generosity.[4] His giving *was* well known by the mid-1970s, as news reports mentioned it (Parker 1978, p. 127). He gave to make others happy (Geller 1989, p. 158) and got his own thrill out of it. The singer once told his foreman Joe Esposito (1994, p. 33) that giving things away let him feel the same buzz as being on stage. At one concert in 1976 he read out a Cadillac bumper sticker which said, 'I paid for this – Elvis didn't buy it' (Hopkins 1980, p. 186). In fans' perceptions, Elvis's generosity is framed as an indication of his naivety: 'The man didn't have any inclination about money,' one lamented when interviewed in the 1990s, 'He never knew what he was giving away. That's why he was such a generous person' (in Duffett 1998, p. 103). Elvis is therefore portrayed as naïve about money, rendering him a tragic figure, someone whose lack of financial savvy opened the way to his exploitation.

The Colonel's image worked in relation to a tragedy of exploitation scenario. A dollar sign, property, worse than a dog, a puppet, cartoon character, a chunk of meat – Elvis Presley was tragically degraded by the Colonel who supposedly made show business deals on *his* own terms, sapped the singer's money, held him inhumanly to contractual obligations and denied his creativity. The Colonel arranged nightmare options for his client: endless roles in boring formula movies or grinding tours. As such, the singer supposedly became dehumanized, manipulated and kept subordinate to his manager. Seeing such concern the other way around, however, perhaps the Colonel, in his image, became a kind of notional remainder that had to be sacrificed in order for Elvis to be perceived as innocent and free from any role as a self-interested financial exploiter himself. After all, a gift made for the wrong reasons becomes something different entirely. If Elvis Presley's performance was an action of giving, it had to be framed by verifying attitudes of humility, loyalty and generosity on his part. For motives behind it to be perceived as sincere, it could not have been interpreted as anything else, such as an act of manipulation or an obligation. In other words, Elvis faced a problem. Despite being a diplomatic person sometimes he was inevitably forced to be unpopular and say no to people. One grey area was why Elvis did no tours outside North America; with illegal immigration status the Colonel was blamed. Both Elvis and the Colonel insisted their show would go (Firth 1965, p. 19; Moore 1997, p. 198); some later said that Elvis used his manager as an excuse (Hopkins 1980, p. 144; Esposito 1994, p. 197). Customs would have checked Elvis's firearms and Europe's indoor arenas were too small to be profitable for him at that time.[5] Elvis never said no; the Colonel did. So Elvis used the Colonel for image protection (Esposito 1994, p. 416; Guralnick 1995, p. 416) saying in private, 'Colonel doesn't mind taking the blame' (Presley 1985, p. 161). Colonel Parker's persona of authority was an important deterrent, which functioned *pre-emptively* towards that end. The same shielding function fell previously to Presley's first manager Scotty Moore (1997, p. 83). Requests or services to fans that were not lucrative could be located as things of which the Colonel disapproved. In turn, the Colonel often used the market place as a way to keep out insignificant bidders, demanding a cool $1 million, for example, for Elvis's film engagements or tour performance packages. In his concern to get a (financial) piece of Elvis, Parker could be read as a kind of substitute: a stand-in for the market itself or the fans who make demand happen.

Cultural commodities embody 'holy moments'. Many depend on the fact that, from one angle, they are not commodities at all: they are authentic traditions, real people, unique experiences (access to which is paid for as tickets). Elvis was no exception as his image consistently combined roots and show business.

Studying entertainment law Jane Gaines (1992, p. 153) caught the dilemma of its approach by stating that 'the entertainer *is* the product ... At the same time, however, the performer is not a product.' That particular contradiction is negotiated in different ways by different groups. While the industry, represented by *Billboard* magazine, saw Elvis as pure merchandise (Guralnick 1995, p. 155), and the singer plus some commentators recognized *both* sides, his fans aim to see him purely as a human being. For instance Ann Stowe (1987, p. 15) told *Elvis Monthly* readers that, although RCA treated Elvis as a dollar sign, *they* should treat him as a man. For such fans, industrial views are not ignored but recouped as tragedy. The Colonel did not simply hold these views, he personified their worst aspects. As well as financially exploiting Elvis, Parker's over-reaching therefore also performed the mythic function of palpably limiting the star's agency.

Deleuze and Guattari (1992, p. 19) have described American popular culture as a rhizomatic network of capital flows. Power accumulates and gets transferred. In show business everybody knows that popularity is converted into money. As one German fan (in Levy 1962, p. 102) exclaimed, 'When he sings, gold comes out of his throat!' As purveyors of products who are also not products, singers not only commodify their voices, but they also personify the plight of individuals selling their skills in a labour marketplace.

In the 1950s, the press did not ask Elvis about music (Wertheimer 1994, p. 59) but rather about his latest cars, clothes and girlfriends. Music critic Mick Farren (1981, p. 7) claimed it was an opportunity missed, but in one sense cars, clothes and girls were as important to his public image as songs and stage moves. There has been a desire to know how much of his due Elvis could get, and what he could do with his power. With his first $5000 signing bonus from RCA, Elvis got his mother the famous pink Cadillac even though she could not drive (Geller 1989, p. 44). He soon had more things than he could ever need, and said so (Farren 1981, p. 107). He told a journalist in 1956 that he had three Cadillacs, forty suits and twenty-seven pairs of shoes (Crane 1956, p. 46). Eventually flashy tastes and the power to turn everything into a personal metonym meant that Elvis Presley had the most famous suit and car in the world (Flippo 1994, p. 149). So cars, clothes and girls were part of his story, not because Elvis's fans were envious of his riches, but because they were taken to symbolize the immense value of his vocal talent. This meant that material 'takers' – both including and beyond the Colonel – have been perceived as unwelcome. In a book written for fans, for example, Memphis Mafia wife Patsy Lacker (in Lacker et al. 1979, p. 215) claimed she did not feel sorry for Vernon's second wife Dee getting divorced, because the settlement meant Dee would indirectly be taking Elvis's money. This attitude appeared in relation to other cases too.

The notion of Elvis Presley as a kind of naïve golden goose at the mercy of his environment has extended to perceptions of his career. Elvis's performance always had an expressive quality, and his vocals were loved by fans, and yet, because he was not a songwriter, commentators rarely position him as a creative force.[6] In their readings, all that is left is that he represents instinct and opportunism: a gifted singer who beats out the competition to achieve the American dream. The flip side of this is that Elvis has been perceived as having a rollercoaster career, a stance which assumes he has ridden the vicissitudes of capitalism with no moral resources or leverage to guide him. In other words, Elvis has been stereotypically framed almost like a child: someone so eager for commercial self-gratification that he acted to his own detriment. In such stories, when he plumbs ever-increasing depths of self-commodification, the only mechanism to hold him in check as a cultural worker – to maintain the artistic value of his work, or his own wellbeing – is one built into the marketplace itself. Fitting this notion on to the actuality of Presley's career has led to a kind of *double dip* narrative.

The rollercoaster hypothesis dovetails neatly with questions of Elvis's social relevance. It suggests that the ride started when his rapid rise to fame occurred through rock'n'roll because he defied sexual repression and heralded racial integration. Next, his rebellious superpowers waned when he was conscripted in the army and his talents were squandered by Hollywood. His fortunes supposedly turned when commercial failure forced him into creative innovation: first in his 1968 NBC television show, then in a triumphant return to live performance. Unfortunately, however, in this popular version of Elvis's biography, Vegas became its own treadmill, and he descended once again, this time into a final phase of personal tragedy.

The rollercoaster narrative strategically ignores some key facets of Elvis's career, such as the self-created grandeur of his 1960s gospel albums, or the occasional music heights of his final days on tour. Nevertheless, it is rather ingrained in popular culture. Eugene Jarecki's 2017 documentary, *The King*, for example, mounts an America road trip in Elvis's 1963 Rolls Royce, using the rollercoaster story to explain the descent of the United States as a nation into a hellish netherworld of *casino capitalism*. In this formulation, Elvis is framed as a cautionary tale: a dumb Southerner for whom celebrity ascent ultimately meant personal descent, because he had become alienated, as a modern subject, from authenticating resources – religion, community, love – that might have acted as a bulwark against his own exploitation. In that context, his manager Colonel Parker could only be framed as a gateway to debasing temptations or an irresponsible surrogate father. According to one writer, by the mid-1970s, 'Elvis was a very unhappy person. His marriage had ended in divorce, Colonel Parker was gambling away his fortune at the Hilton, and his health was going down hill' (Curtin 1998, p. 273).

Mutually assured destruction

Parker's image represents a kind of shell game in which it is hard to spot the true cause of Elvis's downfall. Exactly what the Colonel mythically personifies, however, is open to question. A prominent candidate here is that Parker, by speaking for the marketplace, was acting purely on behalf of Elvis's fans: the King's customers. Consider Elvis's market-orientated career management: back in the 1950s the star said it was foolish to try something new if he was pleasing audiences (Farren 1981, p. 39), so music commentator Dave Marsh (1992, p. 126) blamed fans for their stifling loyalty. The 1960s were supposedly Presley's 'I walked like a zombie' phase (Marcus 1977b, p. 198), where, under contract to MGM, the Memphis singer drifted through countless formula films and would have been 'better off dead' if he wanted to become a serious actor (Fortas 1992, p. 190). With a poor choice of songs to record for soundtracks, Elvis was 'embalmed in celluloid on planet Hollywood' (Baker 1997, p. 31). Making good-humoured family pictures where he almost invariably sang, the star was obligated to serve his fans. They only wanted to see him in musicals (Presley 1985, p. 189). This idea itself represents a kind of unmasking, which blames audience complicity for the star's descent. In such a formulation, Parker becomes a kind of necessary alibi: somebody who affords Elvis's audience the opportunity to deny its role in working him into oblivion. That notion, however, raises the issue of *who* abused Elvis. It asks whether his audience was an insatiable force, an exploited cash cow, an unpredictable (highly variable) quantity or all of those things. A critical problem here, however, is that the rollercoaster strategy was not about giving the audience what it notionally wanted – Elvis at his creative and commercial centre – or simply exploiting demand until it was fully exhausted. What the rollercoaster idea misses is that survival, for Parker and for Presley, was a case of *constantly shifting* media, music genres, locations and audiences. In the end, Elvis was touring America's secondary live market places: smaller, interstitial locations, big towns and small cities. His recorded music career was by no means fully exhausted. Yet his spirit was gone.

Beyond the conception that Parker saw Elvis only as a cash resource is the idea that *both* men eventually *squandered* the pots of income they secured. Elvis never had a particularly close eye on the money and Parker purposefully neglected some areas of operation. Since agreements with RCA were not renegotiated the largest royalty Elvis ever received was an abysmal 5 cents per record (O' Neal 1996, p. 12). Parker let the IRS figure out his star's taxes and they were frequently overpaid. Elvis never collected publishing royalties on his fifty-one BMI songs and RCA were not audited for their handling of his sales account. Joe Esposito (1994, p. 202) claimed that rather than the Colonel selling Elvis's entire back catalogue in 1973 because he wanted to, it was *Elvis* who demanded the sale and Parker who bargained up RCA. Even if this was the case, the singer only got $750,000 out of the $5,500,000 arrangement (Tobler and Wootton 1983, p. 154). One of the Colonel's specialties was to cut *other* parties out, always making it look like he took larger percentages of Elvis's money. For example, Parker took 75 per cent to 82 per cent of Elvis's posthumous merchandising (Goldman 1982, p. 696), a figure which seems outlandish. However, when Elvis first began licensing his image in the 1950s, income was split down the middle with organizer Hank Saperstein (Guralnick 1995, p. 354). The Colonel simply moved in on Saperstein's territory when his contract ran out, becoming licenser, which together with a manager's fee created the result.

Both the star and manager squandered their respective money, but through bad deals and neglect, Elvis *owed* the Colonel $1,500,000 when he died (Goldman 1982, p. 634). This led Presley's hairdresser Larry Geller (1989, p. 44) to name his friend as one of the most mismanaged stars in history.

The most famous celebrities could be seen as rather like astronauts in that they go first into places where others go later. They are increasingly required to commodify aspects of themselves (including information); losing personal privacy, constantly under surveillance, entrepreneurial, brand-aware, in competition, over-worked and undermined by the market. However, as specifically neoliberal subjects, we have not so much succumbed to temptation – which is surely a biblical frame – but have, rather, been *worked upon* by ideologies (pointing to austerity, but advocating entrepreneurialism), become dislocated in global mechanisms of economic competition, and been mined for various resources (time, creativity, data) as our personal boundaries have quietly been under-cut.[7] Jeremy Gilbert (2016, p. 13) has noted, in relation to the state, neoliberal subjects seem 'to have been characterized by a consistently interventionist approach'. Perhaps we are therefore not so much tempted as compelled into increasingly inhuman depths of self-commodification. In other words, rather than being enticed, we have been (re)shaped. In that sense perhaps we can feel nostalgic about the human frailty of Elvis, even in his decline.

Here the Colonel exists, in both his and Elvis's end game, as a kind of throwback to earlier times. The culture industry demands its front men and women give more of their identities to the public than other workers. In such circumstances, star's bodies may be their final property. In mythic narratives, as a superstar, Elvis supposedly continued an inverted parent-child relation because Vernon had less power than him. As Vernon could not assert authority, Elvis tended to over-indulge (Presley 1985, p. 209). Shock biographer Albert Goldman (1982, p. 397) said the Colonel's power increased as Elvis's declined, since Parker could use him to lever large entertainment corporations. However, according to Presley (1985, p. 198) nobody restrained Elvis after Gladys died because Vernon was weak. It stands to reason that Parker was weak, too. After all, Parker ultimately failed to allow Elvis's creativity and commerciality to merge in a way that could both generate greater demand and keep his client happy. It appears that later on *both* Elvis and the Colonel seriously considered leaving each other (Presley 1985, p. 285; Goldman 1982, p. 634). Furthermore, in the 1970s, as his charge put on weight and increased drug prescriptions, the Colonel was even less in control (Crumbaker and Tucker 1981, p. 169).

Rather than being an alibi or shield, what fans are left with is a scenario in which an over-reaching Parker became the abyss into which Elvis's talent was thrown. On one hand, the Colonel's gambling got out of control, as if to show that money had no meaning to him, and all his years of shrewdly getting the best deal were not about the revenue, they were about *the con*. This idea separates Parker from the corporate machinations of capital, but fails to place him above his class roots. Dismissing both the singer and his manager, the *Washington Post* ran a story that said, 'Parker and Presley represent the convergence of two characters from carnival culture: the poor country boy who grabs the brass ring and the mysterious stranger who fleeces the innocent' (Nash 2003, p. 303). 'Carnival culture' was arguably used as a polite euphemism there for the commercial desperation of the lowest class. If Elvis's father Vernon and the Colonel were twinned as inappropriate fathers in Elvis's myth – the one inadequate and other exploitative – eventually the singer himself, his manager and his audience all, in a sense, became seen as *id*: embodiments of the primitive, insatiable, addicted mind. Presley had his pills, Parker (now a permissive father) had his roulette wheel, and the fans had Elvis. Each could make use of the other, but as the 1970s wore on – in the mass culture myth at least – none was quite enough to rescue an icon. Ironically, then, although Elvis was the *most* commodified person of his era, in such formulations he never quite got his due *because* he failed, in a contemporary sense, to embrace his position and entrepreneurially brand himself.

4

The platformed Prometheus: Frankenstein and glam rock

In 1986, Jon Stratton was able to ask the question, 'Why Doesn't Anybody Write Anything about Glam Rock?' According to his article, glam rock had rather suffered in studies of popular music at the expense of alternative genres that were more closely identified either with class identities, often theorized in terms of subcultures, or with anti-commercial underground music practices. Until recently, this neglect was still apparent; Andy Bennett's article of 2007 features a title that aptly summarizes his thesis: 'The forgotten decade: rethinking the popular music of the 1970s.' Once more a general neglect by popular music studies is diagnosed – here on the scale of an entire decade.

At least in terms of glam rock, things now appear to be looking up. Bennett acknowledges the publication of Philip Auslander's (2006) pioneering study, even if he feels that the emergent literature of which it is part 'is by no means comprehensive, nor, it could be argued, representative in its coverage of the 1970s' in its entirety (Bennett 2007, p. 6). Since then, at least for glam, as well as scattered articles and book chapters, there has been an international collection on the genre edited by Ian Chapman and Henry Johnson (2016) as well as a major survey by a leading music journalist, Simon Reynolds (2016). Stan Hawkins's (2009) academic study of *The British Pop Dandy* also features glam prominently; there have also been book two tie-ins with exhibitions (Pih 2013) and museum collections (Turner 2013) that testify to a contemporary interest in the genre. Plus, of course, there was the huge success of the Victoria and Albert Museum's *David Bowie Is* exhibition, as well as the large media coverage of Bowie's death and final album release; both confirmed ongoing interest in glam rock's prime mover.

This chapter will consider the prevalence of Frankenstein imagery in relation to glam rock, in both lyrics and song titles, as well as discussions of the genre and its performers. It will involve taking 'Frankenstein' in the loosest sense, to denote *both* creator and creature (a slippage popularized by James Whale's film adaptations), across media. Other writers on glam have noticed this affinity between trope and genre – Auslander devotes a section (2006, pp. 63–6) on the presence of Gothic tropes including Frankenstein specifically in glam; other commentators also make the link. In Reynolds's recent, compulsively readable volume, Frankenstein is invoked in discussions of Alice Cooper (Reynolds 2016, p. 125), David Bowie (p. 252), the New York Dolls (p. 397, in relation to their song of that title), Roy Wood of Wizzard (p. 412), *The Rocky Horror Show* stage play (p. 426) and even the 'digital glam' of contemporary music video production (p. 618).

My purpose here then is to expand on the ways in which Frankenstein figures in glam rock in relation to various artists and performers who have invoked this cultural precedent. Furthermore, this will involve consideration of Frankenstein's significance as metaphor – perhaps, as Chris Baldick (1987, p. 1) argues, 'a modern myth'. It will be my contention, authorized in part by Mary Shelley's invocation in the 1831 preface to *Frankenstein*, 'And now, once again, I bid my hideous progeny go forth and prosper,' that Frankenstein's monster is something of a self-actualizing metaphor, or what we will call later in this chapter, an *entelechy*. That is, Frankenstein – often as metonymy for the creature, or an erroneous pop-cultural displacement from the creator to the creature – appears to generate new assemblages compulsively across different media. Here we might allude to Halberstam's (1995) arguments that 'Gothic novels are technologies that produce the monster as a remarkably mobile, permeable, and infinitely interpretable body' (p. 21). This or similar arguments have been advanced previously by Halberstam and others in relation to the novel and film; more rarely has this metaphoric or mythic power been considered in popular music, though there are exceptions (on a very different musical genre, for example, see McCutcheon 2007).

In the *Cambridge Companion to Mary Shelley*, Anne K. Mellor argues in the opening chapter that 'Frankenstein can claim the status of a myth so profoundly resonant in its implications that it has become, at least in its barest outline, a trope of everyday life' (Mellor 2003, p. 9). Of course, Victor Frankenstein and his 'creature' or monster first appeared in Mary Shelley's 1818 novel *Frankenstein*, which was revised and published with a new and famous preface in 1831. Though there is much to merit an attention to the source text – and how this has been adapted and sometimes distorted in subsequent representations – this will not be my main concern here. Rather, it is the metaphorical or figurative properties of the proper name Frankenstein, by now a 'trope of everyday life', that will be considered in relation to the musical genre under study. As stated, I am taking Frankenstein to be what Baldick characterizes as a modern myth, a concept he elucidates helpfully as follows:

> The vitality of myths lies precisely in their capacity for change, their adaptability and openness to new combinations of meaning. That series of adaptations, allusions, accretions, analogues, parodies, and plain misreadings which follows upon Mary Shelley's novel is not just a supplementary component of the myth; it *is* the myth. (Baldick 1987, p. 4)

In popular music, 'Frankenstein' might serve as lyrical or discursive shorthand for a cluster of hazily adumbrated, but resonant concepts or affects – which might well involve 'plain misreadings', in strict literary terms.

Frankenstein as myth and metaphor

Perhaps due to the very ubiquity of Frankenstein as a cultural trope or myth, various critics have interrogated the ways in which its meanings proliferate and multiply, from a number of perspectives, sometimes based on the source text and sometimes looking to wider discursive formations.

Chris Baldick traces some literary precedents for Mary Shelley's novel both in the Gothic fiction emerging in the wake of Ann Radcliffe's novels and in political pamphlets responding to Edmund Burke's reflections on the French revolution (1987, p. 16). He further tracks the legacy of the creature after the publication of *Frankenstein* through nineteenth- and early twentieth-century literature. Following Michel Foucault, he also reminds us of the early modern usage of monstrosity: 'a "monster" is something or someone to be *shown* (cf. Latin, *monstrare*; French, *montrer*; English, demonstrate)' (p. 10). In simpler terms, it could be said that *Frankenstein* is a cautionary tale, one that delivers a moral lesson.

Baldick (1987) warns against several common interpretations of the Frankenstein myth, the first being an 'archetypal', ahistorical interpretation alluding to 'our deepest fears', abstracted from all concrete reference (p. 6). Perhaps even more common, is what he terms 'the technological reduction', which 'sees the story chiefly as an uncanny prophecy of dangerous scientific inventions'

(p. 7). This is implicit in innumerable newspaper headlines involving 'Frankenstein science', a notion which has evolved from a supposedly religious injunction against overstepping the limits of the finite and mundane, to a secularized though similar version of it as applied to contemporary innovations in the life sciences, for instance. As Fred Botting (2003) argues, '"Frankenstein" enters the language, somewhat ambiguously applying to both creator and creation, to name any product of experimentation that causes concern in crossing the borders of humanity and nature' (p. 341). In fact, as Markman Ellis (2000) has argued, Mary Shelley's novel, at least, serves more as a warning against alchemy and the dangers of secretive, non-peer-reviewed pre-scientific practices than as a caution against technological progress, as such.

Notably, Baldick (1987) asserts that misreadings, creative or uninformed as they may be, are involved in the constitution of Frankenstein as *myth* (p. 4). Above all, it is the adaptations of *Frankenstein* in other media that has contributed to its cultural mythologization, first of all on stage and later in James Whale's film and successive on-screen representations. Crucial to this adaptation and translation is 'the difference between visible and invisible monsters' (p. 5) that narrows some of what Baldick characterizes as the openness of the literary text to a more visually delimited set of meanings, embodied notably by Boris Karloff's lumbering and inarticulate monster.

Staying with the novel itself, Daniel Cottom (1980) highlights the radical openness in Shelley's text by characterizing the monster as figuring a crisis of representation itself. The novel is, as with many Gothic novels, an epistolary narrative that involves a succession of narrators and embedded narratives, which raises the question of their reliability and the authenticity of transcription between different diegetic levels. What Cottom points to is 'a breakdown in representational orders which leads to the confusion of identities drifting among different individuals rather than adhering to a specific figure' (1980, p. 62). Frankenstein's creature is a *Doppelgänger* of Victor Frankenstein, but he has other doubles in Clerval and Walton (p. 63). The relation between Victor and the monster doubles – perhaps replaces – that between Victor and his betrothed, Elizabeth. And scientific discourse itself, as a representation, creates a further double: 'representations of man as a representation' (p. 65). All of this means, for Cottom (1980), that 'Frankenstein's monster images the monstrous nature of representation' itself (p. 60).

The status of the Frankenstein metaphor in relation to contemporary science is explored further in a fascinating article by Fred Botting (2003). First of all,

Botting argues, contemporary science's denunciation of popular discourses of 'Frankenstein science' nonetheless betrays the ongoing haunting of modern science by Gothic monsters in the latter's own self-conception: 'The very fact of contemporary science arguing over Romantic texts testifies to a continued irritation that is put down to the effects of fiction' (Botting 2003, p. 342). Elucidating the arguments of Lily Kay, Botting discerns an ongoing presence of the ineluctability of metaphor in science in appeals to coding as the 'book of life' in the contemporary life sciences (p. 353). According to Botting, we have evolved from a distinctly modern conception, whereby monsters 'are formlessness figured, figures disfigured, misshapen shapes that lurk on the outer reaches of systems of classification and representation' (p. 346), to a condition in which 'all births and monstrosities [are] coded on the same informational plane as no more than simulations that are optimizations or enhancements of prior simulations' (p. 361). Monstrosity and metaphor, henceforth ubiquitous, are now redundant.

The monstrosity of metaphor, however, is still alive and kicking in pop-cultural terms. At least for popular music, and popular culture generally, the determinant actualization of the Frankenstein metaphor has been Karloff's hulking presence in James Whales's *Frankenstein* (1931) and *Bride of Frankenstein* (1935). Though a feature of discussions of stage adaptations in the nineteenth century too, the monster's arrival on screen cemented the transfer of the proper name 'Frankenstein' from Victor to the creature in common usage. In addition, as Anne-Marie Adams (2009) argues, 'Ever since then, Mary Shelley's hyper-articulate and philosophical Creature has been clearly overwritten by James Whale's stylized celluloid monster' (p. 403). Nonetheless, Adams (2009) does highlight the fact that for all its liberties with its source text, Whale's adaptation did at least have the courtesy in its framing narrative to 'foreground Shelley's importance as author' (p. 403).

Glam studies

Before we consider the presence of Frankenstein both explicitly and implicitly in glam rock, a brief summary of responses to the genre in popular music studies is in order. Early considerations of the genre are inflected by the particular concerns of the Birmingham Centre for Contemporary Cultural Studies (CCCS), notably with the paradigm of subcultures as counter-hegemonic resistance. A pioneering article by Ian Taylor and Dave Wall (1976) both summarizes the prevalent notion of glam – at least in its 'hard' versions exemplified by Slade, the Sweet and Gary Glitter – as an evolution from skinhead culture, reducing the reactionary and alienated character and violence of the latter while broadening its class appeal; and takes its distance from this hypothesis as being short on specifics that explain how glam serves as a solution to working-class concerns.

Taylor and Wall further specify glam's appeal with regard to the decline of an anti-commercial hippie underground and aggressive marketing of glam rock to working and middle class audiences:

> The demise of the underground is such that it can provide no alternative; and the collapse of the skinheads is in turn to be explained in terms of the appeal of a class-based Glamrock version of exotic but passive entertainment.
>
> (Taylor and Wall 1976, p. 119)

David Bowie is taken to be the charismatic figure that inspires this passively consumed spectacle.

A more favourable take is presented by Dick Hebdige, who, while retaining the CCCS's emphasis on subcultures and resistance, expands the parameters of what counterhegemonic practices might oppose. Therefore, rather than the passive duping of working-class resistance, glam alters its target: 'In glam rock, at least amongst those artists placed, like Bowie and Roxy Music, at the more sophisticated end of the glitter spectrum, the subversive emphasis was shifted away from class and youth onto sexuality and gender typing' (Hebdige 1987, p. 61).

In advancing this argument, Hebdige is explicitly taking his distance from the rather distasteful attitude evinced by Taylor and Wall to Bowie's gender-bending, whose music supposedly left the underground legacy in glam rock 'imperceptible, *emasculated* and effectively irrelevant' (Taylor and Wall 1976, p. 116; emphasis is mine). Their further specification of him as 'a bisexual short-haired mod who preaches a spiritual nihilism (in counter-cultural form) to an audience across the class and age groups, but to the backing of a working class rock beat' (p. 111) similarly contrasts Bowie unfavourably with a more virile, hetero, working-class authenticity.

Hebdige's account has been more influential in the long term, since many more recent accounts of glam rock stress its subversion at the level of gender typing and sexuality; as well as a camp insistence on artifice and self-fashioning. The influence of queer theory has lent studies of the genre a boost in terms of its highlighting of performance and cross-dressing. An informative account of the visual and performative aspects of glam is provided by Georgina Gregory, who argues 'In some ways, the flights of fantasy offered by glam rock were more personally liberating than the self-centred heterosexual hedonism offered within the hippies, mods or progressive rock subcultures' (2002, p. 52). Writing from a US perspective, Mike Kelley (2000) also makes an interesting case, *pace* Taylor and Wall (1976), for the continuities of glam (or glitter) with the counterculture, arguing that the latter had evolved to share glam's interest with artifice and superficiality, as well as gender subversion.

In terms of recent academic treatments of the genre, by shifting the emphasis from reception on to performance, Philip Auslander's (2006) monograph was pivotal in encouraging further work. The author's background in performance studies facilitated closer textual analyses of the artists' music and lyrics, and above all, visual and performance styles. Chapman and Johnson's (2016) edited collection emphasizes both the genre's transnational status (with precise studies of national music scenes) and the primacy of presentation in their definition of the genre: 'It is because glam is a music style that is primarily defined by its non-musical elements that it so fittingly lends itself to non-musical definition' (Chapman and Johnson 2016, p. 3). There is much to say nonetheless about the specifically musical qualities of glam rock, especially in terms of the prominence of studio production and some emblematic music producers and mixing styles – which so aggrieved some Stooges fans on the release of the band's Bowie-produced *Raw Power* (1973) – as well as 'hard' glam's stomping drums and simple, anthemic song structures. Further discussion of this in general terms, however, goes beyond the scope of this chapter.

The platformed Prometheus

One of the most intriguing themes in Simon Reynolds's recent book on glam rock is its recurrent analysis of a series of quasi-magical connotations of the musical genre. First, and most obviously, there is the derivation of glam from 'glamour', a term popularized by Walter Scott and originally referring to visual illusions. There is also 'an etymological connection between glamour and word-magic' (Reynolds 2016, p. 22), which might put us in mind of Slade's orthographic licence in song titles such as 'Mama Weer All Crazy Now' (1972), a refrain that might also serve as a performative speech act, resembling word magic on a willingly suggestible audience.

Other signifiers of magic are present in the discussion of glam's spearhead, Marc Bolan, who used to boast of a sojourn in Paris with a 'wizard' as part of his own myth-making, especially in tall tales to interviewers. As Reynolds argues, 'The concept of magic – and the conception of himself as a magical being – was central to Bolan's outlook and work. Words like "magic" and "spell" crop up continually in his interviews and frequently in his lyrics' (p. 21). Reynolds follows this with a discussion of Roger Melly's assertion that 'magic is far more important than talent' in popular culture (Reynolds 2016, p. 61). Specifically, Melly alludes to 'charisma', which Reynolds traces to the ancient Greek *charis* before its adoption by Christianity, referring to 'grace'. Reynolds's modern gloss, which captures the collectivity of both the early Christian church and modern musical subcultures, is 'collective single-mindedness' or 'vibe'. A further set of magical references are present in a discussion of another central glam figure, David Bowie, and his interest during his wayward Thin White Duke phase in the occult. Of Bowie during this period in his self-imposed exile in Los Angeles, Reynolds observes, 'The Devil finds things for idle minds to dwell on' (p. 502).

The magical lexis moves glam rock as a genre, closer, once more, to the Frankenstein myth. Mary Shelley's novel was subtitled 'Or, the Modern Prometheus', alluding to the Titan of ancient Greek myth who rewarded man with the gift of fire. In Romantic treatments of the myth the emphasis is on the Titans' creation of man – hence its relevance to the novel: Victor Frankenstein himself as the Modern Prometheus. As Markman Ellis (2000) emphasizes, it is the alchemical arts and not modern science that is the object of this cautionary tale, and which provides Victor with his supernatural agency.

Conversely, in the novel, charisma is aligned firmly with the creature; unlike in the celluloid version, Shelley's creation is articulate, keenly perceptive and decisive where Victor is faltering. When cajoling Victor into creating a mate for him, after the former has destroyed his work so far, the creature commands him: 'You are my creator, but I am your master; obey!' (Shelley 1818/1986, p. 437). Though unsuccessful in this command, the creature's influence on the events in the novel before and after this utterly confounds Victor's own capacity for action. This turning of the tables from creature to creator anticipates perhaps the popular usage's transfer of the proper name Frankenstein itself. In terms of popular music, perhaps the 'collective single-mindedness', according to Reynolds's gloss of popular culture following Melly, at least potentially represents a more democratic version of the creature's demand for recognition in the novel.

Here the glam 'scene' itself and relations between audience and performers might reinstate this.

Another affinity of the glam rock genre with the Frankenstein myth is in Victor Frankenstein's method of creation, which has notable affinities with the *bricolage* emphasized in Dick Hebdige's (1987) account of style in musical subcultures. The creature is composed of bits and bobs, human and animal; glam rock too has at times been characterized as a hybrid or motley assortment of stylistic and musical influences. In relation to David Bowie, for instance, Richard Mills (2015) argues that 'Each Bowie look is an assemblage of fashion curiosities, a hotchpotch of clues to Bowie's influences' (p. 183). This ties in with what Margaret F. Savilonis (2013) characterizes as 'the overt construction of multiple personae facilitated by the conventions of glam' (p. 155).

There may indeed be something magical or alchemical in the artifice and animation of as disparate a series of stylistic ingredients as are present in glam style and performance. This is present in the various identities, costumes and musical styles that glam assembles with self-conscious and shameless artifice. But in case these observations appear rather fanciful or impressionistic, some case studies of particular glam performers are in now order.

I can make you a man

One of the first appropriations of the Frankenstein myth in popular music that springs to mind is surely that in the quintessential cult film, *The Rocky Horror Picture Show* (Jim Sharman 1975). In terms of characterization, the cross-dressing alien, Frank-N-Furter, played by Tim Curry, is a camp, glam variation of Victor Frankenstein, while the inarticulate beefcake Rocky – played by Peter Hinwood and billed as a 'creation' – is a more photogenic if pudding-basined mutation of Boris Karloff's role. I will not summarize the plot to any extent here; but it is clear that the Frankenstein narrative provides just one of a number of inter-texts for a film that also borrows from science fiction, musicals, creature features and the counterculture. If the borrowings from previous versions of *Frankenstein* are made with extreme licence, their presence in an emblematic glam-era film text nonetheless underlines the centrality of the Frankenstein myth to glam.

Amittai F. Aviram (1992) describes Frank-N-Furter in the title of his article on the film as a 'Postmodern Gay Dionysus'. Glossing this reference to Dionysus,

Aviram makes a link to the Prometheus featured in Mary Shelley's subtitle to her novel: 'There is already in Greek religion a vague association between Prometheus' gift in defiance of the gods and that of Dionysus, the intoxicant fruit of the vine' (1992, p. 187). Aviram also discerns a reference to a canonical creature feature, *King Kong* (Cooper and Schoedsack 1933), in Rocky's carrying away of the body of his creator at the end of the film in a camp *Liebestod*:

> After Frank has already received the death-charge of Riff-Raff's laser gun, the woeful Rocky carries the body of his erstwhile maker as he scales up the radio tower of the old RKO logo in a visual allusion to King Kong's abduction of Faye Wray.
>
> (Aviram 1992, p. 190)

Already we have a series of literary and mythic intertexts, as well as those from pop-culture, in a characteristically camp glam synthesis.

Many other commentators have been struck by the subversion of gender and sexuality in *The Rocky Horror Picture Show*. For Michael Eberle-Sinatra (2005), the film represents 'probably the most daring interpretation of the sexual politics of the novel, a treatment of Shelley's story that arguably enriches in turn any reading of the sexual aspect in *Frankenstein*' (p. 185). Victoria Tickle takes a similar line, citing Judith Butler's conception of gender as performance as finding an analogue in the film's rhetoric: 'He [Frank-N-Furter] represents the deconstruction of gender roles and sexuality and the representation of gender performativity' (Tickle 2014, p. 148). We can see this emphasis on gender and performance in the film as consonant with many analyses of glam rock, from Hebdige (1987) and Hoskyns (1998) to Auslander (2006).

Interestingly, a number of critics have seen the film's subversion of norms of gender and sexuality as limited or perhaps even compromised by the film narrative. Steven Beverburg Reale is perhaps the most damning of these critics, since he argues that '*The Rocky Horror Picture Show* affects a subversive, prurient demeanour while engaging in an indoctrination of conventional sexual ethics' (Beverburg Reale 2012, p. 159). According to this author, the film's structure of *Bildungsroman* – that is based on the conventions of the novel of personal development – contains or even constrains the subversion of its play with gender norms. On Beverburg Reale's reading, this plot concerns the spiritual education (if this is not too elevated a way of putting it) of Brad and Janet, with Frank-N-Furter subservient to this narrative – to the extent that his flirtation with femininity and passivity is punished with death.

One of the most interesting aspects of Beverburg Reale's study is his discussion of the timbre of Frank-N-Furter's voice, often of a rockist masculinity that belies his ostensible flirtation with feminine dress and gesture. In the number 'I Can Make You a Man', for instance, 'Frank's "cock rock" voice communicates complete control as his blasphemous words claim utter potency: the power to "make a man"' (p. 146). The author also makes an interesting link between Frank-N-Furter, the fictional character, and glam rock musicians in their appropriation of femininity while retaining male privilege: 'Thus, like glam rockers, Frank appropriates femininity as a transvestite (not as a transsexual) because his masculinity offers the freedom to make such an appropriation' (Beverburg Reale 2012, p. 146).

There is a possible counterargument to Beverburg Reale's arguments in relation to the film narrative, however. His argument that the film resembles a *Bildungsroman* relies on us interpreting Brad and Janet as central to the film's diegesis. However, such is the scenery-chewing prominence of Frank-N-Furter, enhanced by the fortunate casting of Curry, who is identified with the role that one can make the argument that this is the film's central – or at least most memorable – character. If this is the case, then Frank's showy gender-bending will exceed the conventional frames of closure and re-equilibrium that the narrative advances. In so doing, the return to gender norms and normality have been subverted from within the narrative itself, the narrative resolution being sufficiently desultory that it does not undermine the central spectacle of Frank. In making this assertion, I am advancing a similar argument to Richard Dyer (1998) in relation to Rita Hayworth's 'resistance through charisma' to the conventional femme fatale role assigned her in the film *Gilda* (Charles Vidor 1946).

In any case, Beverburg Reale's arguments about Frank-N-Furter's rockist masculinity (and vocal timbre) belying his flirtation with femininity are less easy to argue against and find support in the analyses of Betty Robbins and Roger Myrick (2000). Here again, the authors argue that Frank-N-Furter's masculine control overrides the ambiguity involved in donning drag: 'Throughout the film, as shifting as Frank-N-Furter's surface appeal and objects of desire are, his control and domination of scenes, characters, and the audience remain constant' (Robbins and Myrick 2000, p. 274). Their thesis is based on general arguments about male adoption of feminine garments: 'given the ultimate power held by the male performer, he is also able to take control of women's image through the drag performance' (p. 271). It is beyond the scope of this chapter to discuss their construal of drag in gender terms, which might be open to question in terms of apparently discerning an evident binary 'beneath' the drag performance.

The limitations of *The Rocky Horror Picture Show*'s subversion of gender and sexuality might be analogous to those in glam rock. For the duration of a participatory screening – or of a concert or television performance, perhaps – the fantasy of a blurring of rigid gender binaries is entertained. But at the close of the screening or exit of the concert venue, normality may be restored. This is how the film's critics often characterize the viewing experience of *Rocky Horror* – though there is more to say about how its fans' practices linger in fact after the screening has finished.

I have suggested elsewhere that a strong argument for glam's subversion of gender identities lies in its importance for a subsequent generation of musical performers such as Siouxsie Sioux, Boy George and Neil Tennant, as well as directors of New Queer Cinema such as Todd Haynes (Hackett 2015). According to these artists at least, who in different ways defied norms of gender performance, glam was not the ultimately conservative form diagnosed by some of its critics since it provided an inspiration for their own subsequent performances and cultural production.

Guys and Dolls

In Mary Shelley's novel, Victor Frankenstein recalls his appalled reaction to viewing his creature alive for the first time, an assemblage made out of limbs and features selected specifically for their beauty:

> Beautiful! Great God! His yellow skin scarcely covered the work of muscles and arteries beneath; his hair was of a lustrous black, and flowing; his teeth of a pearly Whiteness; but these luxuriances only formed a more horrid contrast with his watery eyes, that seemed almost of the same colour as the dun-white sockets in which they were set, his shrivelled complexion and straight black lips.
> (Shelley 1986, p. 318)

That this might bring to mind at least one glam performer is implied by Van Cagle's description of the on-stage countercultural impact of Alice Cooper: 'Cooper [Vincent Furnier] pranced about the stage sporting greasy shoulder-length hair, his face accented by macabre black makeup that darted from his eyes and mouth' (cited in Auslander 2006, p. 34). A contemporaneous reviewer,

Steve Turner, described Alice Cooper (singer and band) as 'the Frankenstein of the cathode tube ... a product of a sick society rather than a responsible human with the power to choose' (cited in Reynolds 2016, p. 125).

It might seem harsh or at least over the top to compare Vincent Furnier, visually, to the monster described by Mary Shelley – but such was the shock value (pre-punk) of the *grand-guignol* makeup and schlocky horror antics of the group, and its singer in particular, that, then and now, these comparisons are unsurprising. Indeed, in the 1970s, an interesting transposition of proper name 'Alice Cooper' from the band to the singer later – when it became Furnier's solo act – mirrors the pop-cultural metonymy of 'Frankenstein' from Victor to the creature. Auslander notes the gothic tropes present in the standout track from the group's 1971 album, *Love It to Death*, namely 'Ballad of Dwight Fry'. Perhaps given the lyrics' concern with insanity and confinement, a closer comparison in terms of gothic literature would be with Edgar Allan Poe rather than Mary Shelley.

In a recent piece, Ian Chapman makes a sustained case for *grand-guignol* being an appropriate framework with which to interpret 'glam rock's preeminent problem child' (Chapman 2016, p. 113). Chapman highlights Alice Cooper's sometimes marginal status as glam performer, often located in terms of subgenres such as 'glitter punk' or 'glam metal', even while being cited by some as glam's originator (p. 114). As a case for including Alice Cooper solidly in the glam canon, Chapman alludes not only to the – for him decisive – focus on theatricality, effeminate dress styles and visual presentation, but also Alice Cooper's address to pre-teen to mid-teen audiences, as well as a willing self-presentation as carnivalesque or freakshow entertainment while insisting on audience participation, that is shared by other glam performers.

Though taking place after the glam era I am discussing in this chapter, Alice Cooper in his solo avatar recorded a track entitled 'Teenage Frankenstein' for his 1986 LP, *Constrictor*. The track is a straightforward identification of Furnier with the titular character, who is also described as the 'local freak' with a 'twisted' mind. A few years later, 'Feed My Frankenstein' appeared on the 1991 album, *Hey Stoopid*, whose video features Wayne and Garth from *Wayne's World* (Penelope Spheeris 1992). Both tracks reflect the return of Alice Cooper as performer to an occasionally perfunctory, glam-metal musical style, though with an endearingly schlocky stage show in evidence in the videos.

One artist who recorded a track titled 'Frankenstein', even if he is rather marginal to glam rock – Auslander asserts that he had a 'glam phase' (2006,

p. 63) – is Edgar Winter, with the Edgar Winter Group in 1972 (this is another track listed by Auslander in his round-up: 2006, p. 63). The group's name, as with Alice Cooper, is another instance of slippage of a proper name from creator (Edgar Winter) to creation (his group), or from singular to plural perhaps. As well as being a single, the track appears on an LP with a glam and goth-sounding title, *They Only Come Out at Night* (1972). The single reached number 1 in the US charts despite being an instrumental; its influence has been cited by Dave Grohl of Nirvana and Foo Fighters at his SXSW festival keynote speech as an early inspiration for him wanting to become a rock musician (Gold 2013). The track is sufficiently rock'n'roll to be a frequent feature of rock anthem anthologies, especially of the 1970s. However, its drum and saxophone breaks make it also sufficiently funky to have composed part of DJ Kool Herc's Bronx block party sets, which are often cited as one of the origins of hip hop (Batey 2011).

It is, above all, the construction of Winter's 'Frankenstein' – its mode of production – that qualifies it as a Frankensteinian track in more than name. Matt Hurwitz relates that that the track originates in what Edgar Winter originally referred to as 'The Double-Drum Song' since it facilitated a dual drum solo in its live performance. The track was invigorated by Winter's purchase of an ARP 2600 synthesizer, which Winter was able to wield like a synth-axe through the use of a strap (Hurwitz 2011, p. 18). Both in the Moog-like synth squiggles and the live performance aspect that freed Winter from a static playing pose, the ARP revitalized the track's sound and delivery.

More pertinent, for our purposes, was what happened in the studio once 'The Double-Drum Track' was recorded for the LP. Three full takes were recorded, ranging from 11 to 15 minutes (Hurwitz 2011, p. 19). In fact, the final track was made by directly splicing the best bits (like Frankenstein's prime cuts) of master tapes for the various takes. A second round of edits reduced the track length to 4 minutes 45 seconds. On hearing the final playback while tracking the various edits involved, it was drummer Chuck Ruff who remarked, 'Wow, man, it's like Frankenstein,' thus renaming the track both for its hybrid nature as assemblage and perhaps for its 'studio technology gone mad' production history. This latter interpretation is supported by Winter's own recollection: 'The whole idea of Frankenstein was technology running amuck, with me as the doctor, and the song itself, the creation, as the Monster' (Hurwitz 2011, p. 19).

But the first track many would think of as a glam rock anthem to this creator–creature (and the track that first inspired this chapter) is 'Frankenstein' by the New York Dolls, which appears on their self-named debut LP of 1973. For Van

Cagle, what was characteristic of the Dolls was their reversal of the emphasis in US rock of 'paying your dues', the obstacle that has frequently prevented the crossover of UK and other non-US acts across the Atlantic. Instead of the band having to earn respect through an arduous touring schedule, the onus was placed on their followers: 'the maxim of "paying your dues" became one that was applied to devotees, not to the band itself' (Cagle 2000, p. 132). This was due to the band's confrontational presentation style (as evidenced in the cross-dressing, bouffant hairdos, perilously high platform boots and plastered makeup on their debut album cover), as well as their proto-punk amateurism (in terms of musical ability). Fans were, well before punk rock had made this more common, forced to accept and indeed embrace unprofessionalism as well as the band's obvious flirtation with gender-bending and drug cultures.

Perhaps for this reason their appeal in the United States rarely spread further than Manhattan. As indeed with the Pistols after them, by the time of recording their debut, the Dolls were far from a sloppy, completely amateurish racket, despite the early accounts of their chaotic gigs. Singer David Johansen's Jaggerisms are complemented by bluesy riffing along the lines of the Stones and the Faces. In this respect, it is perhaps the Dolls' visual presentation that is their most obvious contribution to glam.

This extended to their fans and the scene that built up around them at the Mercer Arts Center, which led to a fierce loyalty on the part of certain influential music journalists, as far as *Creem* magazine in Detroit and its celebrated critic, Lester Bangs. The favourable *Rolling Stone* review of 1973 describes the band's fans in the following terms: 'boys and girls of indeterminate gender, males with earrings and flashing orange hair, females with ducktails and black leather, interchangeable clothes, makeups and postures, maybe gay, maybe not' (Glover 1973). It locates them in a solidly glam/glitter locus of gender subversion. These magazines' readers were sometimes, but not always, as convinced of the band's virtues as their critic champions – as is evidenced by the Dolls' polarizing positions in the *Creem* 1973 readers' poll: simultaneously as best new band *and* worst new band in separate categories (Cagle 2000, p. 133).

'Frankenstein (Orig.)' itself is one of the highlights of *New York Dolls* (1973). David Johansen drawls 'Something must have happened over Manhattan' before invoking, in rather obscure terms, the rise of a Frankenstein figure of ambiguous appeal, with shoes that are too big and a jacket that is too small. Asking how 'you' – the fans, the listener or perhaps Johansen addressing himself? – could ever love such a thing, here Frankenstein seems to be a floating signifier, standing in for the band, its loyal fans, its music or its dress sense. The song's rather doom-laden portentous sound is complemented by bluesy riffs, resulting in a tension between proto-goth minor chords with jangling open strings on the one hand, and more conventional rock'n'roll chugging on the other. The track builds to a crescendo over 6 minutes before juddering to a halt with Johansen asking whether you could 'make it with Frankenstein?'

The Dolls may have been marginal to glam rock in some accounts, with some favouring punk instead as a descriptor. They did, nonetheless, play a gig in London's glam mecca, the Biba clothing emporium (Turner 2004, p. 79), which underlines one aspect of the music genre – its status as transnational music style. In this respect, as Pete Lentini (2003) points out, it prefigures punk rock for which it was in some respects an influence: 'Punk's precursors – David Bowie, Lou Reed, Iggy Pop and the New York Dolls – were all involved in processes of transatlantic exchange' (p. 169).

The Rocky Horror Picture Show had transported Frank-N-Furter, notionally a space alien but with the cut-glass vowels of the English upper class, to Ohio. Alice Cooper's 'School's Out' coincided with the British Pupil Power movement, causing the family values campaigner Mary Whitehouse to call for a *Top of the Pops* ban for the single (Reynolds 2016, pp. 140–1). The New York Dolls were also, for a while, clients of Malcolm McLaren, future manager of the Sex Pistols, and gigged in the UK in the early 1970s. Bowie, of course, made the reverse journey, first under the wing of Tony Defries and MainMan in New York City; later strung out in Los Angeles around the time of his appearance as a space alien in *The Man Who Fell to Earth* (Nicolas Roeg 1976). In this respect glam rock's musicians are prefigured, if this does not seem too fanciful, by Victor Frankenstein's chase of his creature across another ocean, to the North Pole.

Frankenstein to Funkentelechy

In the previous sections we have discussed the oft-noted subversion of norms of gender and sexuality in glam rock. As we have seen, the sometimes confrontational aspects of this emphasis in some glam performances are intimately tied to Frankenstein tropes, especially perhaps with Frank-N-Furter of *Rocky Horror*. However, so far little has been said in this chapter about the possible involvement of discourses and representations of race in popular music's Frankenstein imagery. Remaining in the mid-1970s, this section will therefore extend the analysis beyond glam rock proper to the music of Parliament and its leader, George Clinton.

Howard L. Malchow's discussion of Mary Shelley's novel echoes the emphasis that Chris Baldick places on the context of politics and revolution in the genesis of *Frankenstein*, adding another important constituent:

> Indeed the peculiar horror of the monster owes much of its emotional power to this hidden, or 'coded,' aspect, and the subsequent popularity of the tale through several nineteenth-century editions and on the Victorian stage, as well as in satire, derived in large part from the convergence of its most emotive elements with the evolving contemporaneous representation of ethnic and racial 'Others.'
> (Malchow 1993, p. 92)

If this is the case, then analysis of Frankenstein tropes in glam-era popular music might fruitfully be extended to questions of race and ethnicity, as well as those of gender and sexuality.

Parliament's 1976 album, *The Clones of Dr. Funkenstein* is most obviously pertinent to Frankenstein's glam lineage. As J. Griffith Rollefson observes, 'the album's narrative draws heavily on the Frankenstein story and the trope of the mad scientist' (Rollefson 2008, p. 97). In the album's 'Prelude' listeners are treated to an origin story of specially designed 'Afronauts' capable of 'funkatizing' galaxies, revealed early on to mankind but buried in the pyramids until humans might be more ready to 'clone the funk'. Implicit in the imagery of Parliament's albums of this time (and indeed sister band Funkadelic's (1978) *One Nation under a Groove*) is a notional battle between Afrofuturist funk on the one hand and inauthentic copies on the other. In the 1976 LP, Dr. Funkenstein is the guarantor of authentic funk in an era of synthetic disco hybrids, as well as being the latest alter ego for George Clinton.

We can note incidentally that the trope of a Black science buried in the pyramids places P-Funk imagery here rather close to some of the Nation of Islam ideas (see the related discussion on the Five Percenters in Chapter 6), whereby White men were asserted originally to be the creation of a mad scientist, Yakub. In Clinton's mythology, this is located in terms of a battle between authentic funk and diluted copies. In *The Clones of Dr. Funkenstein*, the funk is cloned effectively and authentically in the 'children of production'. In the later LP *Funkentelechy vs. the Placebo Syndrome* (1977), the album title itself gives us an opposition between self-actuating funk (now identified with the Starchild character) on the one hand and an ersatz vanilla replacement on the other.

J. Griffith Rollefson attributes the critical power of Afrofuturism to 'the racialized tension between future and past, science and myth, robots and voodoo' (Rollefson 2008, p. 86) and this is especially so in the case of P-Funk due to its fruitful inclusion of Frankenstein tropes that complement these tensions productively. On the one hand Dr Funkenstein is a science-fiction avatar of the band's (1975) *Mothership Connection*; on the other, he is a mad scientist using voodoo (akin to alchemy as a pseudo-science) to create funky clones (or robots). Kesha Morant traces the Mothership's lineage back to the plantation: 'The Mothership of the 1970s operates in same role as the chariot during enslavement: as a vehicle sent to take Black people to freedom' (Morant 2011, p. 79) and Horace J. Maxile, Jr. sees the P-Funk Mothership as 'a rational extension to the train trope' found in earlier twentieth-century African American musical forms such as the blues, a trope for freedom, liberation and transit (Maxile, Jr., 2011, p. 601).

Most of the literature on glam rock previously referred to in this chapter excludes African American music from its purview; Parliament and Funkadelic are most often and correctly discussed from the perspective of soul and funk genres. Nonetheless, two articles have convincingly made the case for Clinton's groups to be considered in relation to glam – not only for their activity during the same era but specifically in terms of their presentation styles. Margaret F. Savilonis discusses Parliament and the female trio Labelle as combining the flamboyant styles of Sun Ra and Sly Stone with 'the overt construction of multiple personae facilitated by the conventions of glam' (Savilonis 2013, p. 155). In connection to the foregoing discussion, Dr Funkenstein and the Starchild play a similar role in Clinton's evolution in the 1970s, to, say, Ziggy Stardust and Aladdin Sane for David Bowie.

Furthermore, Mark Willhardt and Joel Stein have likened Clinton's bands' attire to 'a cross between David Bowie, Gary Glitter, and *The Wiz*' (Willhardt and Stein 1999, p. 145), referencing here two prime British glam figures as well as Sidney Lumet's (1978) retelling of *The Wizard of Oz* (Victor Fleming 1939) with an African American cast. Indeed, these authors note (p. 167 n.) that Larry Gatsby, costume designer for *The Wiz* (Lumet 1978), fitted out the band for the Mothership tour, on which Clinton claims to have spent $350 million in terms of production budget. This places Parliament–Funkadelic in the realms of high glam in terms of flamboyance and presentational excess. (We might think perhaps of Queen's stadium glam as equivalent in scale.) These writers also cite Clinton himself as authority for us to link his bands with the genre: 'If it's gonna be about glitter, then it's got to be glitter of the highest order' (George Clinton, cited in Willhardt and Stein 1999, p. 164).

Savilonis's (2013) recent article emphasizes in particular the on-stage presentation of Starchild and Dr Funkenstein during the 1976 *P-Funk Earth Tour*, in which the extra-terrestrial imagery of the album covers is played down (thankfully only slightly) to render these characters on stage outlandish yet still identifiable in terms of identifiable African American and Native American archetypes:

> Because Star Child and Dr. Funkenstein are so clearly in command – of themselves, the band, and the audience – they ultimately resist caricature, and the exaggerated markers of race become positive reinforcements of Star Child's and Dr. Funkenstein's status as enlightened Others.
>
> (Savilonis 2013, p. 174)

According to Savilonis, where Labelle used glam iconography and personae to expand limited definitions of gender for 1970s female vocal performers, in Clinton's bands the emphasis was transferred from gender to racial politics, in the manner described above.

Finally, we can observe with interest the 'Funkentelechy' coined by Clinton for Parliament's 1977 LP, *Funkentelechy vs. the Placebo Syndrome*. Drawing on the compact OED, Willhardt and Stein characterize this term as follows:

> Thus when Clinton cops the term 'entelechy,' or 'the condition in which a potentiality has become actuality,' and makes it the 'Funkentelechy' that fights the Placebo Syndrome, he is talking about the 'scientific' and existential realization of The Funk.
>
> (Willhardt and Stein 1999, p. 159)

So this term, a combination of Aristotelean metaphysics and Clinton's P-Funk is one more mutation of the Frankenstein myth as self-actuating metaphor. A metaphor for which potentiality has become actuality, which *makes itself real*. Indeed, this scholastic term perhaps recalls Victor Frankenstein's unhealthy fascination with the likes of Cornelius Agrippa, Paracelsus and Albertus Magnus (Shelley 1986, pp. 297–8). Furthermore, as Halberstam (1995) reminds us, this actualization is not without displacement into other media, genres and idioms, since 'Gothic novels are technologies that produce the monster as a remarkably mobile, permeable, and infinitely interpretable body' (p. 21). George Clinton's Funkentelechy is therefore one further technological mutation of the Frankenstein myth as self-actuating metaphor.

Glam has never been modern

Simon Reynolds has pointed to an important aspect of glam rock, which he refers to as 'fashion logic'. Glam rock follows such a logic 'in the sense that fashion was the first area of popular culture to treat its own archive as an auto-cannibalistic resource' (Reynolds 2016, p. 417). In a related point, discussing Bryan Ferry and Roy Wood, Philip Auslander suggests that the 'inauthentic voices of glam rock' (Auslander 2006, p. 192) render these singers hard to identify with an individual style, due to their impersonation of singing styles from previous eras of popular music.

Furthermore, there is in glam rock a pervasive return to 1950s rock'n'roll, before the counterculture, present from Marc Bolan onwards and exemplified in popular glam's revival of the 7-inch single (compared with progressive rock's disdain of the shorter format). We could of course characterize such practices of pastiche, as Reynolds does, as postmodernism *avant la lettre*. What is interesting in glam rock is that this incorporation of elements from rock's past is combined with a simultaneous exoticism of the alien or the monster.

As a final paradigm for considering these cultural phenomena, we may allude to the arguments of Bruno Latour, in his work, *We Have Never Been Modern* (1993). In this book, Latour makes some general points against conceiving of contemporary societies in terms of modernity, supporting this position with arguments derived from his own study of scientific practices:

> [The] word 'modern' designates two sets of entirely different practices which must remain distinct if they are to remain effective, but have recently begun to be confused. The first set of practices, by 'translation,' creates mixtures between entirely new types of beings, hybrids of nature and culture. The second, by 'purification,' creates two entirely distinct ontological zones: that of human beings on the one hand; that of nonhumans on the other.
>
> (Latour 1993, pp. 10–11)

For Latour (1993), modernity facilitates the creation of new beings, hybrids that are neither entirely natural nor entirely cultural; while simultaneously relegating them to separate spheres and disregarding or attempting to forbid their mediation. Indeed, Latour identifies his hypothesis in the book as being that modernist 'purification' has in fact been the driver for 'translation', the creation of new hybrid beings. The injunction against conceiving of hybrid entities facilitates their multiplication.

It is interesting that Latour (1993) founds his argument on an analysis of 'objects fabricated in laboratories', both in the age of Hobbes and Boyle (p. 27) and our own (p. 21), to which we might add Mary Shelley's also. His thesis is that such fabricated objects involve the creation of networks and the agency of human and non-human actors. This latter process of mediation is precisely what modernity cannot admit. Perhaps this might account for the potentially unmasterable proliferation of Frankenstein mutations from book to page, screen to stage and so on.

At any rate, Latour's (1993) arguments provide us with an interesting way of articulating modernity (or non-modernity) with hybrids and monsters, one which seems immensely suggestive in relation to the simultaneous existence of glam's retro elements together with its exotic and monstrous performers, and its new hybrids of fashion, gender, identity and style. On this reading, a certain lineage of modernism in popular music has nonetheless produced, through its forbidding of nostalgia, new hybrid identities that it cannot (for a while perhaps) comfortably admit into the canon. Hence the wariness that glam performers met in terms of their 'hotchpotch' of styles and influences; perhaps too, in relation to their new hybrids of race (Funkentelechy), class – those 'passive', effeminate glam fans of Taylor and Wall (1976) – and gender (Frank-N-Furter) discussed throughout this chapter.

Perhaps Latour's model is more convincing in relation to the cultural sphere than as an analysis of contemporary societies. One of Latour's targets in his book is the idea of revolutionary history, which he takes to be part and parcel of a modernity that for him is discredited:

> The idea of radical revolution is the only solution the moderns have imagined to explain the emergence of the hybrids that their Constitution simultaneously forbids and allows, and in order to avoid another monster: the notion that things themselves have a history.
>
> (Latour 1993, p. 70)

Conversely, what readers such as Baldick (1987) and Malchow (1993) underline is precisely the importance of political revolution as a backdrop to the creation of Mary Shelley's *Frankenstein*. Perhaps, that is, Latour's argument that 'we have never been modern' might be taken as one more mutation of the Frankenstein myth, one which (applied here) models this species of retro-rock's profusion of new hybrids and monsters, and which acknowledges the tendency of mutants to proliferate paradoxically, the more we produce cautionary tales against them.

Conclusions

Glam rock, then, can be seen to have an affinity with Frankenstein and his monster, which extends further than their presence in lyrics and song titles. Both the musical form and the cultural myth involve a bricolage of existing cultural detritus fashioned into new and rapidly proliferating forms. Furthermore, the anxiety produced by new hybrids of the human and the animal through alchemy finds a parallel in the new creations conjured up by glam's performance styles. Novel, hybrid audiences are formed, merging lumpen skinheads with bourgeois prog rockers; style and fashion are used to assemble new counterhegemonic masculinities; in Funkentelechy, race is brought into the mix in glam's tendency to mutate and find new hybrids.

Of course, one of the most striking things about glam is its short initial lifespan. That is, if Marc Bolan is taken as the genre's initial figurehead, for many, glam's heyday ended in 1975 or so, with Sparks, Queen and one or two others as a decadent finale to the genre, and Bowie and Roxy Music largely dropping glam rock elements from their musical and presentation styles. Yet this is, perhaps, to fail to see how glam rock's Frankenstein re-emerged in new hybrid forms in later popular music styles. Although the question takes us beyond the scope of this chapter, it could easily be argued that the creature lumbers on through punk, goth and New Romantic styles, to say nothing, for example, of Lady Gaga or Anohni. This should cause us no surprise and is entirely consistent with Frankenstein technologies, which are liable, as Halberstam (1995, p. 21) reminds us, to 'produce the monster as a remarkably mobile, permeable, and infinitely interpretable body'.

5

The case of Mark Chapman: Extreme fandom as monstrosity?

Monstrum (monster) means 'the exception that cannot be accounted for in rational terms alone' (Davis 2009, p. 17). Four decades after it happened – as long, in effect, as the life of its victim – the murder of ex-Beatle John Lennon retains its emotional force as a 'flash bulb memory': a day, in a sense, that the earth stood still. When he pulled the trigger, a previously unknown Mark David Chapman was thrust into the glare of the public spotlight, defined through his shocking act and immediately located as a monster. The poet Allen Ginsberg compared Chapman's heinous act to 'slashing a Picasso' (Cott and Dounda 1982, p. 92). This eloquent word picture located the crime entirely on the terrain of art, giving its victim all the creative connotations of Picasso (individuality, innovation and perhaps macho misogyny), yet it also placed the star *as the artwork*: 'a' Picasso, not 'the' Picasso. This approach did not see the human body as God's art or say that taking a life offended its maker. Rather, it framed the killing of John Lennon as an act of artistic desecration, locating Lennon's celebrity image as an artistic statement made through self-fashioning. Ginsberg's dictum positioned Chapman's monstrous act as a case of nihilism masquerading as criticism – indeed a peculiarly extreme, brutal and Manichean act of criticism, or rather of *critique*: holding Lennon up to absurd moral standards, finding him lacking and deciding that execution was the only appropriate reward.

The idea of making a 'slash' connoted Chapman's complete lack of grace, forgiveness, of understanding. Indeed, Chapman's name has now started to become synonymous with violent negation in popular culture; witness, for example, the description of Alex Rawls as the 'Mark David Chapman [the man who killed John Lennon in 1980] of the blogosphere' (Doss 2011, p. 29). There is something reductive about such descriptions. Cases involving monstrosity inevitably raise moral dilemmas, questions such as whether monsters deserve our pity and whether, in our rush to condemn them, we are becoming monstrous ourselves. The aim of this chapter is to consider Mark Chapman's act in relation to monstrosity, fandom and celebrity.[1] It argues that 'bare celebrity' has emerged as a defining currency in explanations of Lennon's murder because different stake holders have found it useful to address different issues, some of which existed *before* the murder took place. These issues included the ambiguity of Lennon's own celebrity image, his wife's reputation, and Mark Chapman's motivations.

How did the killer understand the crime?

In December 1992, Lennon's killer went on the *Larry King Live* television show, because, he said, he was mentally well enough. The interview was revealing and replete with ironies. Here was a (still) young man, who had fallen into the abyss of insanity, a place from which he had committed an extraordinary crime a decade earlier. He had, evidently, been schizophrenic, sociopathic, and suicidal at the time of the attack. Karen Halttunen (2001) has argued that murderers have become treated in America as 'mental aliens'. She explains that insanity replaced evil as an explanation for killing in a post-Enlightenment world, but when that happened the perpetrators of violence became ontologically separated from their communities:

> The most important ideological work done by this new construction of the criminal offender was to protect the understanding of human nature as rational and well-intentioned, by creating a kind of moral quarantine to contain the agents of the most shocking of human transgressions. But the construction of that moral quarantine for criminal transgression carried a heavy cultural cost: the peculiarly powerful horror evoked by the spectre of the murderer as madman.
>
> (Halttunen 2001, p. 234)

In other words, the emergence of the insanity diagnosis (initially as 'monomania') and, eventually, the insanity defence helped to position the murderer as a 'mental alien': a mentally disturbed and morally distanced Other, someone whose monstrous acts evoked gothic anxiety and dread. Mark Chapman's status as a 'mental alien', however, never quite allowed what he did to be seen as a tragic and unfortunate accident, the upshot of a severe attack of mental illness during which the perpetrator was literally out of his mind. Chapman himself knew that the crime took preparation and that the idea of a bout of blinding insanity was indefensible. Initially, he was marooned, in terms of explaining the moment both to himself and to the world. Twelve years later, he went on *Larry King Live* via a video link to his prison and said:

> Mark David Chapman was a failure in his own mind. He wanted to become somebody important, Larry. He didn't know how to handle being a nobody. He tried to be a somebody through his years, but as he progressively got worse – and I believe I was schizophrenic at the time ... Mark David Chapman struck out at something he perceived to be phoney, something I was angry at, to become something he wasn't, to become somebody.

Chapman evidently needed to commit the crime to satisfy his own psychological impulse, yet he also needed to dissociate himself from it. He therefore oscillated between discussing what happened in terms of his insanity and taking responsibility. He hovered uneasily between the roles of victim of mental illness (a proven schizophrenic) and cold-blooded killer (someone pursuing a premeditated crime). If Chapman was going to act out his murderous impulse, he first needed to repress his motives and dissociate himself from his actions. Equally, if he was, afterwards, to cope with the horror, guilt and shame of what he had done, he needed to separate himself from the person who pulled the trigger. It is logical therefore to read this dualistic approach to culpability as a kind of ongoing mental necessity on Chapman's part. Playing both roles allowed him both to commit his crime (as someone systematically enacting a 'disturbed' psychology) and to explain it (as somebody dissociated, looking at his actions as those of someone else). He also had to find a way to explain what he did that was acceptable to himself and to others.

Mark Chapman lived in the same world of media consumption as everybody else (Caughey 1984). Within that world, in order to explain his notionally inexplicable action, he used his resourcefulness. His crime offered *no rational motive*. Contemporary stereotypes of fan behaviour formed his lifeline: a shared cognitive and discursive resource. In Chapman's hands, shared assumptions from the mass culture critique became connecting bridges, responding, in some ways, to the deductive frames imposed on him. A first such bridge was the idea that the audience lacked agency and was in effect a manipulated end product of media production. Henry Jenkins (1992) has suggested that fan stereotypes have traditionally included the idea that 'the naïve spectator, drawn too close to the text emotionally, loses the ability to resist' and becomes 'unable to separate fantasy from reality' (pp. 62 and 10). Chapman explained to Larry King that at the time of the shooting he was 'a confused person' who was 'literally living inside a paperback novel – J.D. Salinger's *The Catcher in the Rye*'. He added:

> What happened before I pulled the trigger, and after, were two different scenes in my mind: before, everything was like dead calm and I was ready for this to happen. I even heard a voice inside of me – my own – saying, 'Do it! Do it! Do it! Here we go'. Then afterwards it was like the film strip broke. I fell in upon myself. I went into a state of shock … I was stunned. I didn't know what to do. I took *The Catcher in the Rye* out of my pocket. I paced, I tried to read it – I just couldn't wait, Larry, until those police got there.

This confession suggested that Chapman had been a victim of media effects. Rather like the adolescents who played *Pokémon Go*, he lived in an augmented reality, one in which the real and fantastic blended imperceptibly. He 'entered into' Salinger's book, signing it as 'Holden Caulfield', writing '*This* is my statement' and leaving it at the crime scene. In this explanation, unlike the more 'authentic', rebellious stance of *Catcher*'s hero, Holden Caulfield, John Lennon symbolized the 'phoniness' of commercial culture, and that enraged Chapman. His frame of reference was therefore to claim the identity of the fictional Holden Caulfield.

Post-war American youth culture has formed itself around the idea of the misunderstood juvenile delinquent. This fictional persona gave Chapman a sense of 'cool', a sense of justification for refusing to grow up and accept the compromises of adult society.[2] In the novel, Caulfield only *fantasizes* about killing someone. He imagines it as a drama, seeing 'my guts, blood leaking all over the place' (Salinger 1945/2010, p. 94). Caulfield continues:

> Then I'd ring the elevator bell. As soon as old Maurice opened the doors, he'd see me with the automatic in my hand and he'd start screaming at me in this very high-pitched, yellow-belly voice, to leave him alone. But I'd plug him anyway. Six shots right through his fat hairy belly. Then I'd throw my automatic down the elevator shaft – after I'd wiped off all the finger prints and all.
>
> (p. 94)

At the end of the same paragraph, echoing a media effects position, Caulfield concludes his fantasy by surmising, 'The goddam movies. They can ruin you. I'm not kidding' (p. 94). Commenting on the passage, Harold Bloom noted:

> As a pastiche of Chandler or Hammett or Erle Stanley Gardner this script would take some beating – film noir from an expert. But Holden is also 'scripting' his

own part, an author-director writing himself into his own text. The way ahead has once more been richly indicated.

(Bloom 2000, p. 101)

Like Caulfield in his fantasy, Chapman used a gun to kill *then blamed a fiction* (though this time it is Salinger's novel, not Hollywood noirs). Also like Caulfield, he used his fantasies to envision or 'script' his actions and thereby disown his motives. However, the similarity ends there.

The next set of explanations that Chapman employed related to what we might call the 'attention economy' of celebrity. What is interesting about this, however, is that Chapman has said only *in retrospect* that issues relating to the attention economy motivated his actions *before the crime happened*. We can therefore say that, just like he used the media effects idea, he also used the notion of an 'attention economy' to justify his motives. For Larry King, he forged a link between his damaged self-esteem and notoriety, explaining it as part of a wider social phenomenon:

> After, you disintegrate again. You become nothing. So if you have nothing to start with, and your life consists of fantasizing about celebrities or being with them, that can become very dangerous, and that is a phenomenon in this country now that has to be addressed. That's why the secret services have been talking with me, to try and find out what was ticking in this thing here. [Points to head.]

Drawing on such readings, Janne Mäkelä (2004, p. 217) suggested, 'It was the conflict between the image of a socially active rock hero and the image of a passive and irresponsible recluse that, in a sense, incited Chapman to pull the trigger.' He then adds, as if to moderate the claim, 'Certainly, this is conjectural and should be presented as such' (p. 217). The problem with it is that nothing 'incited' Chapman except for impulses in his own mind, and initially they did not admit external frames of rational justification.

After Lennon was shot, perhaps the most immediate discursive resource that the media had to hand was the idea that Chapman was a 'deranged fan'. After all, seemingly, there was a good fit. The killer had been a Beatles enthusiast earlier in his life. He had asked John to sign an autograph on his copy of *Double Fantasy* earlier that day at the Dakota building. For Antony Elliot (1999a, p. 139), the murder therefore reflected a 'curious sort of violence intrinsic to fandom'. Thinking along this line, *Daily Mail* reporter Tony Rennell, for example, reasoned:

> A rootless adult who never settled into a proper job, he found solace for his empty life in the music of The Beatles. A loner himself, he identified with the

reclusive side of Lennon's insecure, mixed-up personality. But revelations of Lennon's vast wealth and burgeoning business empire turned Chapman's hero-worship on its head. He felt betrayed, personally insulted. He stalked and shot his erstwhile hero out of a weird sense of retribution – coupled with a desire to be famous for something.

(Rennell 2010)

By suggesting that John Lennon's assassin was a Beatles devotee whose 'hero-worship' was 'turned … on its head', Rennell portrayed Mark David Chapman as an otherwise normal fan who descended from love to resentment, rage and murder due to forces beyond his control. This explanation is mythic insofar as it neatly accounts for an inexplicable act by telling a story that is popular and 'satisfying': after all, no individual star is so available that he or she can offer anything near the kind of equal attention that thousands of followers supposedly crave. There is just not enough time in the day to give each one full and proper personal attention. It is then a case of the fan with the lowest self-esteem becoming the weakest link, and eventually snapping.

The 'slippery slope' idea assumes fans always and inevitably desire equal attention from their creative heroes. Behind this theory is actually a critique of capitalism: that it sets up idols who inevitably cannot deliver on their supposed performative promise. I have challenged such deductive reasoning elsewhere, and questioned the evidence, pointing out that there is no innate logic in fandom that sends people down a 'slippery slope' towards murderous resentment (see Duffett 1999; 2013, p. 107). In this particular case, what the idea does not account for is the role of Chapman's mental illness and the nihilistic nature of his crime.

Mark Chapman was *not* a disgruntled Beatles fan in 1980. His interest in the band had ceased a decade earlier and he had no concern for their music. Instead, he *posed* as a Beatles fan in order to get closer to Lennon. The idea that Chapman was a Lennon 'anti-fan' (Gray 2005) holds a little more water, insofar that he loved Todd Rundgren's music at the time, and Rundgren had a feud with Lennon. Nevertheless, such rationalizations fail to accommodate Chapman's own insanity, which is something that guided his behaviour, in effect offering a motive that could not be rationalized by the murderer, the fans, the commentators, the newscasters or anyone else.

An associated interpretation located Chapman more squarely as a 'fame monster' who, in what Charles Fairchild called the 'attention economy', was using Lennon as a way to change his position as someone in 'competition for attention' (2007, p. 359). Many commentators believe that Chapman committed Lennon's murder precisely for the *public* attention that he would receive. From this perspective, the crime was a seizure of resources, something almost akin to Freud's *Totem and Taboo* (1913/2001) or, supposedly, like a recreation of the macho final scene from *The Shootist* (Siegel 1976), where three local cowboys attempt to assassinate a widely celebrated gunslinger, played by John Wayne, as a way to establish their reputations.[3] The rules of the system that Chapman entered, however, were different. By pulling the trigger, he exchanged obscurity *not* for mass fame, but for *mass blame*, infamy and notoriety on a spectacular level. Some readings of the crime have posited that Chapman was so desperate or deranged that he could not tell the difference. For example, one American studies student at Wesleyan wrote in her thesis:

> Mark David Chapman has become a household name by eliminating John Lennon, which clearly was his intention. Chapman clearly staged Lennon's murder; he chose the setting, set the scene, and even brought along a prop, his copy of *Catcher in the Rye*. But he did not erase Lennon; rather he ensured an explosive, and unforgettable, end to a legend. It is clear that the media's focus is on the slain superstar, but his killer makes his way into the limelight as well.
> (Kass-Gergi 2012, p. 59)

This reading paints Chapman as a protagonist whose mental instability is almost irrelevant to his crime: although his act remains unconscionable, it was calculated with the logical assumption that fame is a currency that can be acquired through high profile association (see Gunter 2014, p. 12). What has happened is that Chapman's own readings of his crime have increasingly come to fit the 'fame monster' interpretation, as he has pursued the inevitable interest in his case as a spokesperson and interviewee. *In his explanations*, he has suggested that each famous person 'was somebody', associating the acquisition of fame with self-esteem, and perhaps implying that murder is potentially less forgettable than, say, throwing a custard pie or some other banal way of forging a high profile association.

Accepting the 'fame monster' reading allowed Chapman a way to both socially justify and dissociate himself from his crime. He was, he surmised, not someone possessed by evil but a selfish and vulnerable 'idiot', someone who struggled with self-esteem and got tempted by the rewards of the fame game. Even in this assumption, however, he was mistaken. He carefully recanted on his position to King, saying that the album signing was a 'real' ethically positive moment in which the star recognized his fan, if not as an equal, then at least as someone whom he made time for: 'He was not a phoney, by the way: he was very patient and he was very cordial, and he asked me if there was anything else.'

Such readings may actually have allowed Chapman to come to terms with his responsibility for the crime and explaining it to other people. He said on CNN's *Larry King Live* show:

> It was me, Larry, and I accept full responsibility for what I did. I've seen places [in the media] where I'm blaming the devil. I hope that [explanation] isn't kept going after this interview. I'm not blaming the devil, I'm blaming myself, but, in a major sense, it wasn't me, because I'm better now: I'm normal. I'm functioning. I have a lovely wife and we have a great marriage, as much as can be had from here – from Attica [prison]. I'm not the same person, in a major sense. Because back then, I was lost, and I didn't know who I was, but now I do ... I didn't have a personality then, and I do now.
>
> Mark Chapman on *Larry King Live* (1992)

By the time of the *Larry King Live* interview, Chapman had settled on the side of culpability, also saying at this point, 'It was definitely pre-meditated.' This implied that although he had been insane, he now recognized that it was an evasion not to locate himself as someone with an intent to kill. It was therefore as if he was not fully responsible (as someone acting on a mental disorder), but nevertheless, accepted full responsibility. He explained to King, 'People who've read the book [about why I did it] will see, this is a monstrous act, but perhaps not done by a typical monster.'

Explaining his crime as the calculated acquisition of fame helped Chapman to justify it in a way that mitigated *both* his insanity and personal responsibility. The currency of fame reading, however, had further consequences. While many saw Chapman as a monster for pulling the trigger, his act unleashed monstrous invitations to profit that went far beyond his personal situation.

First, Chapman's crime was fetishized by the media. Audible through emotionally straining voices, rock music is often envisaged as a romantic form: the public expression of private sentiments, a baring of the soul. It uses the body to place something notionally private into the public sphere. Culturally, murder is a very unusual, 'extreme' event, equal and opposite to music in some ways. It violates the body and extinguishes life. It enacts a desire so repulsive that it cannot be brought near, but that also makes murder a focus of commodification. Television screens, crime novels and feature films can never 'bring home' the full horror of the victims' families authentic emotions, so viewers are left to vicariously imagine how strong its effects truly feel. Like love, murder is therefore both uncommodifiable and constantly commodified, becoming media content because it acts as a kind of strongest possible justification for media texts. Discussions about it start with a dead body, logically assume an act, begin to deduce a motive, and trace the identity of the killer. While the disgusting nature of the act keeps its commercial analysis in the realm of 'low culture', we therefore apprehend it in a similar way to art: looking for signifiers of intent, and one might even say of 'authorship'.

Second, beyond Chapman's own fame, macabre items connected with the murder have fetched high prices. Such items of memorabilia are 'part of history', enticing their owners to exchange them for increasing monetary rewards and thus cross ethical boundaries. In 2016, the Dakota building concierge Jay Hastings sold the bloodstained shirt that he had tried to help Lennon while wearing; it fetched £31,000. Garry Shrum of Heritage Auctions told the *Daily Mirror*, 'He is not exploiting John Lennon's death. He is telling the story of how he tried to help John Lennon in the last few minutes of his life' (Koncienzcy 2016). The copy of *Double Fantasy* that Lennon signed for Chapman was acquired by Manhattan building superintendent Philip Michael, from Hamburg, New Jersey, after Chapman dumped it in a large flower planter located beside the security guard booth of the Dakota building (he placed it there between the star signing it earlier in the day, and returning at 10.40 pm, the time when he was shot). First, it was given to the police for analysis. Next, 'The authorities offered the album to Ono, but she didn't want it. They also offered it to Chapman because it was his property. But Chapman didn't take it either, so it was returned to the man who first discovered it. He later sold it to a collector on the U.S. West Coast' (*John Lennon's Final Autograph to his Killer Part of PNE Exhibition 2015*). It was returned in August 1981 with a letter of thanks from the district attorney. Chapman himself wrote to a memorabilia dealer with the aim of getting the album returned to him in April 1986. He wanted to sell it on behalf of a children's charity and also enquired after any available Stephen King and J.D. Salinger letters. The bid was unsuccessful. After keeping it safe for almost two decades, however, Michael put it up for auction with Moments in Time in 1999. The auction house sold it for $460,000. The company's owner, Gary Zimet, later claimed that he had made the figure up for advertising purposes and actually sold it on a site called ehammer.com for $150,000. Michael sued him for breach of contract, claiming the asking price was $1.8 million, of which

Zimet's company was to get 5 per cent (Goldbaum 2003). At a 2003/4 resale, the album supposedly exceeded its reserve price of $525,000/£327,357 (Lifton 2012). However, other estimates suggest a £274,000 asking price, with Zimet saying the $525,000 was made up (Taylor 2012). In 2010, the same company offered it again, supposedly for $850,000 (*Album signed* 2010). Its new custodian was Peter Miniaci, the curator of a special Beatles exhibit. He showed it at the PNE Centre in Vancouver (*John Lennon's Final Autograph* 2015). The company placed it on the market again in mid-2017, complete with 'police reports, fingerprint documentation, letters from the District Attorney' (*Double Fantasy* 2012). The new asking price was $1.8 million and the company's president Gary Zimet justified it by saying, 'It is arguably the most important rock'n'roll artefact in history, even if it is a little morbid' (Boyle 2017). In 2013, Chapman's arresting officer, Stephen Spiro, also put a series of letters that Chapman wrote to him in 1983 up for sale at $75,000/£48,000, saying he wanted to pay his medical bills (he had cancer), and 'I wanted to publicise them to the world because they're part of history' (*Letters Written by John Lennon's Killer up for Sale 2013*). All these incidents demonstrate the 'dark forces' at work in the case of Lennon's murder have not simply sprung from Chapman's mental instability. They have emerged from the way that the profit motive has constantly challenged what is acceptable in terms of taste.

Beyond the calculus of celebrity murder

As Antony Elliot (1999b, p. 839) said, 'Lennon was, suddenly, no longer; but his death, and in particular our relationship to it, remained a problem.' A different take on this 'problem' is to say that the meaning of a person's death can reflect back on the meaning of their life. From the viewpoint of those sympathetic to John Lennon, on top of his murder, Chapman's public profile created an issue. He had achieved notoriety: mass news coverage, a footnote in history, a place in generational memory, fame and infamy. The *New York Post*, for instance, offered ten pages about the crime and star's death in its 9 December 1980 edition. The story of what was going on inside Chapman's mind became the grist of several documentaries, true crime books and other media products. Such commodities, largely following the stereotypical clichés, took their audiences 'face to face with pure evil' and 'inside the mind of a killer'. Because pursuing such a heinous act can take us out the realm of rational motivation, most of the realist or documentary texts attempt to wrestle with the idea of evil, and explore what could have been going on in the killer's disturbed mind. In effect, then, the social interest in mediated murder strangely parallels an interest in artistic intent. In the genre of true crime reporting, the criminal's monstrous mind becomes *a mystery to be solved.*

For his televised interview with Mark Chapman in 1992, Larry King adopted the clichéd parlance of the true crime genre. He explained to viewers that he was intent on 'probing the criminal mind ... various sides of a complicated and disturbed man: a caring relief worker who aided Vietnamese refugees, a bashful Georgia boy who volunteered at the local Y[MCA], a suicidal alcoholic, a deadly celebrity stalker'. Chapman readily participated in such fare too, continually explaining his bizarre story to his interviewer. To Larry King, he said of Holden Caulfield, 'he probably would not have killed anybody as I did, *but that's fiction and reality was standing in front of the Dakota*' (emphasis mine). At another point, he explained, 'A few minutes later there was a blood-curling scream from someone, and it put the hair on the back of my neck straight up.' In other words, because he felt as dissociated from the murder as viewers who were not there, Chapman was willing to re-perform the experience and offer people the opportunity to vicariously participate in it. He became a privileged witness, someone able to offer a window on a real moment reconfigured as an imagined memory.[4] This stance, as a dissociated observer of his own acts, simultaneously aligned him with King's audience, but also, ironically, placed him as an 'insider': someone who 'was there' and experienced what happened at close range. Furthermore, he received social recognition for his act in a variety of ways. He explained to Larry King that he did not have what he called 'fans', but he *did* receive the full spectrum of correspondence, from deathly curses to Christian messages about forgiveness. From the perspective that framed Chapman's mission as an attempt to receive mass attention by killing an icon, he had, to some extent, succeeded. The enormity of his one simple act has threatened to overshadow the artistic contribution of its victim, swamping years of edifying music and insightful social commentary with the media's fetishistic tendency to report true crime as a question of collectively exploring the perpetrator's motives.

Nobody who knew John Lennon wished his killing to overshadow what he was about or what he stood for. In that sense, Chapman's monstrous action had to be kept 'unauthorized'; those close to John did not want to comprehend his killer's confused reasoning. They wanted John to have the attention. Understandably, then, Lennon's friends rarely mentioned the killer by name and never pretended to care about his motives. Paul McCartney did not tour for a decade after his friend was killed. He said relatively little in public about Lennon's death, framing it as an atrocity without a palpable cause. Years later he recalled for Larry King, 'My manager called me ... that was just the shock of all shocks.' On ITV's *Jonathan Ross Show*, McCartney elaborated:

> I just got a phone call. It was like, – ?! [Shrugs] I think it was like that for everyone. It was just so horrific. You couldn't take it in – I couldn't take it in. Just for days, you just couldn't think he was gone. It was just a huge shock, and then I had to tell Linda ... That was like a really big shock in most people's lives. It was a bit like Kennedy ... For me, the biggest thing was, that the guy who's took his life, the phrase just kept coming in my head, "Jerk of all jerks." It was just like, this is just a jerk. It was not a guy who was, like, politically motivated. Just some total random thing, like, "Hey!" Bop!

McCartney's explanation understandably saw his friend's murder as relatively inexplicable, thereby marginalizing and moralizing the role of Chapman's mental illness ('just a jerk ... just some total random thing'). He implied that a political assassination would have been a more 'fitting' and meaningful end for John, because it would have continued the singer's participation in social struggle. Instead, the crime was seen as an expression of nihilism, something unconnected with the meaning of Lennon's image: a random act that merely reflected one interloper's private demons. However, even the idea of 'some total random thing' acted to actively shape interpretations of Lennon's celebrity persona. Janne Mäkelä (2004) astutely captured the wider differences such interpretations made to John's image:

> Lennon's brutal murder evoked parallels with 1960s political assassinations, rather than resembling the mythology of [indulgent and] premature rock star deaths. Lennon was thus shifted from the realm of stardom to the realm of heroism, coming to serve as an exemplary and iconic figure for a particular community, that of the Sixties generation.
>
> (Mäkelä 2004, p. 217)

John Lennon was a real person, but all icons are mediated, offering their audiences 'intimacy at a distance' (Horton and Wohl 1956). They are produced through mediation as spectral figures, people who are screened and, in a sense, 'here' and 'not here'. In that respect, any celebrity's death actualizes a tendency in our experience of their image to find them 'not there' in our lives. At least while they are flesh, while they are 'available' to mediation and generational memory, this phenomenon of screening celebrity also, in an important sense, makes them experienced in a way that is understood as situated, yet simultaneously perceived beyond personal embeddedness in historic time. Celebrity studies scholar Sean Redmond recently explained this, talking about a GIF image that united different faces from the career of one of his own heroes, David Bowie:

> If you watch it, there is no beginning and no end, in a sense. It's not linear time, it's not chrononormative time, because beginning, middle and end – in terms of his career trajectory – are all wrapped together in this beautiful relay ... Stardom and celebrity operates in relation to time in two distinct ways. One, it does support linear time ... we can see aging happen on our stars, we can see their corporeality ... [Second] stars offer us a different version of time ... sort of a Deleuzian, phenomenological movement, which isn't linear, but multidimensional, which one accesses, not at the beginning or at the end, but at any point, and follows it in succession or out of succession ... there's something potentially transgressive about that.
> (Redmond in *Marshall, P. David* 2016)

Seen in relation to this, Lennon's murder is both something that happened *in time* and something *out of time*. His assassination was not the last global moment in popular music history – Live Aid, for instance, came five years later – but perhaps the last time a star's body was justification for such a global moment. It signified a sad moment of togetherness, on the same level of (Western) global unity as the Beatles 1967 satellite broadcast or George Harrison's 1971 Concert for Bangladesh. In death, Lennon became the subject of a 'heroic' narrative, but he was more than a hero. His biographic story significantly complicated his construction as 'bare celebrity'. During his lifetime and beyond, his public persona had been understood in a variety of ways by different people. In order to further analyse the competing interpretations of his murder, it is therefore useful to examine his evolving image.

Moving from beat music (updated rock'n'roll), through pop and into art rock, with associated chemical, musical and spiritual experimentation, the Beatles used artistic creativity to express an ethos of personal liberation. The group helped popular music, as a field of cultural activity, graduate from its 1950s incarnation into an artistic medium that spoke directly and creatively about changing times, politics, ethics and the human condition. Although Lennon retreated somewhat from his own fame in the 1970s, he had been among the most prominent public figures of the 1960s and his image caught the public imagination. Like some other figures of the time, notably Spike Milligan, he was eccentric, quirky, acerbic, thoughtful, surreal and funny.

The first generation of British rock'n'rollers, from Cliff Richard to Tommy Steele, mixed evocative performances with relatively 'safe' attitudes. Lennon, in contrast, was a rebel. His appeal as a celebrity came in part because he coupled his creative musical talent with an appealing sense of ordinariness. He flatly contradicted old notions of deference and decency associated with middle England, offering a rougher masculinity that made him seem all the more authentic. To put it another way, John refused to accept the traditional British society equation, eschewing best behaviour and received pronunciation, opting instead for wearing his regional identity on his sleeve, for outspokenness, frankness and sharp wit. Gently propagated in the films *A Hard Day's Night* (Lester 1964) and *Help!* (Lester 1965), Lennon's witty and rebellious stance helped his band ride the tide of Beatlemania and conquer America, but it began to cause problems for his group when *Datebook* syndicated his comment that the Beatles were 'more popular than Jesus' in July 1966. His comments raised the ire of Christians across America (see Sullivan 1987). While he recanted on what he said, the apology was somewhat ambiguous: 'I just said what I said and it was wrong. Or taken wrong' (Lawrence 2005, p. 77). Although the Beatles did not lose all their fan base because of the 'Jesus' comment, other issues arose to complicate things for both Lennon and his band. Many of his personal qualities resembled those associated with juvenile delinquents and other non-conformists: irreverence, anti-establishment attitudes, not being guarded in what he said. As film scholar Des O'Rawe (2006, p. 66) noted, Lennon was 'a patient keeper of the anti-authoritarian flame.'

A complex icon – and his wife

To the public, Chapman's victim was not simply a hallucinated 'straw man', but (notionally) a real person, someone who gave rise to a set of media performances that in turn defined him. When he died, he left a 'living' archive. Because people experienced his image as 'authentic', they had a greater purchase of understanding: at a distance, but in parallel, in a sense, 'experiencing' the shock of his death, too. The issue with Lennon's personal history, however, is that, as Antony Elliot said, it 'confronts us with too much' (1999b, p. 838) to clarify his meaning as an icon: beyond any superficial glance, the ex-Beatle's celebrity image appears too rich, multi-faceted and contradictory to accommodate any simple classification. Janne Mäkelä (2005) pointed out that since his death, John Lennon's image has therefore been subject to competing interpretations. The struggle between them ranges across different media forms, including biographies and documentaries. As Mäkelä (2005, p. 172) notes, 'If stars die, but star images do not, it is therefore reasonable to suggest that we have not reached the end of John Lennon's story ... [while] his meaning is still discussed.' The positive 'Imagine' reading of Lennon as an angelic peacenik, for example, contrasts strongly to interpretations that put his faults centre stage. While Albert Goldman's biographic portraits of rock stars including John Lennon have been roundly rejected as grotesques (see Mäkelä 2004, p. 219), historian Dominic Sandbrook (2015) still ventured that the ex-Beatle 'was a nasty piece of work who epitomized our age of self-obsession'. One might reasonably say that however 'nasty' Lennon was, he never deserved to die, which is absolutely true, but that is the point: a specific interpretation of John's untimely death has been used to draw attention to particular aspects of his image. The consequent reading of Lennon has shaped how we see (or, indeed, do not see) his killer, understand why he committed the crime, and decide what justice he deserves.

Lennon's constant search for freedom authenticated his image by pushing against everything that might be held dear – the security of show business and the Beatles, the Royal Family, the church, the counterculture – and yet he assented to monogamous love. In May 1968, he moved in with Yoko Ono, a successful avant-garde artist. The new couple had fallen deeply in love and began making art together. They were both rebels. Yoko was a highly successful conceptual artist, and she gave John license to more freely express himself. By dint of John's immense popularity, the pair instantly became a very prominent celebrity couple, one that used their place in the spotlight as an outreach forum for political activism based on artistic collaboration. Rebelliousness was always at the centre of what they did together. Rejecting what he once described as the 'bloody tribal rites' of celebrity and mass fandom (Northcutt 2006, p. 136), John embarked on series of three albums with Yoko that were, at first, almost unlistenable: highly experimental, arguably 'indulgent' and flatly rejecting the modes of aural pleasure offered by the Beatles.[5]

Initially, people did not know quite what to make of Yoko. In his 1969 diary, Kenneth Williams (1993, p. 352) observed:

> The Beatle who is married to an Asiatic Lady was on the *Frost* programme. The man is long-haired and unprepossessing, with tin spectacles and this curious, nasal, Liverpudlian delivery: the appearance is either grotesque or quaint & the overall impression is one of great foolishness.

The idea of Lennon's image being that of a 'foolish' person was a reflection on both his cryptic humour and his political idealism. The couple exploited their celebrity by turning their honeymoon into two 'Bed-ins for peace'. They used John's 'foolishness' to promote his activism in Amsterdam and Montreal, forwarding an idealistic, artistic plea for global pacifism.

In his classic book on celebrity, *Stars* (1979), Richard Dyer noted that there is a tendency in media coverage of high profile activists to direct public attention towards the celebrities rather than to their causes. Biographer Hunter Davies (2016, p. 139) reported:

> [John's friends watched him] ranting on to the press, pushing his message of peace, attacking the war in Vietnam, Christianity, politicians, going on about hair, often not making complete sense, but watching the press write it all down ... he had meant every word.

In 'Give Peace a Chance', which was recorded at the second Bed-in, and 'Imagine', released two years later, John affirmed his image as an idealist by inviting listeners into a community formed around himself, his wife, and the values of love and peace they shared. According to Martha Bari, in a doctoral study of Lennon's 'Bag-In' events:

> The power as well as the quirkiness of Ono and Lennon's 1969 events owes much to the couple's romantic and intellectual fixation on each other. Their mutual obsession was a mark of what they felt was an intoxicating new love relationship that caused them to look at the world afresh and to search for novel ways to fuse their different artistic and musical interests into a united force.
>
> (Bari 2007, p. 18)

Because of this cross-pollination of talent and interests, privileging one artist over the other in their collaborations becomes problematic. Yet, most writers tend to do so, or quickly skim over this period of intense joint activity without much comment, so that in some studies, Ono's role shrinks to that of a maternal figure or of a muse to John, while in others, critics see Lennon as an artistic subordinate to Yoko Ono. Often, scholars diminish or eclipse Ono or Lennon's creative role in order to accommodate a separate, heroic narrative for the other

(Bari 2007, p. 19). What is interesting here is that the Lennons' marriage could instead be framed as a *trade off*: John, who was already a successful popular musician, gained access to the artistic credibility of the avant-garde and, in a sense, became a verifiable 'global' person just as Yoko became a central and essential part of his celebrity image. Speaking of the John Lennon Museum, located in Saitama, Japan (2000–10), for example, Saeko Ishita said, 'While the JLM was a museum about John Lennon, it was also a museum of the world's most celebrated Japanese wife, Yoko Ono' (2016, p. 146). Yoko was already a successful avant-garde musician and artist, but with John, she gained access to popular celebrity, something primarily achieved by association rather than making hit records. Indeed, her association with John was in effect the start of her use of popular music as an idiom through which to pursue her art. Yoko's music, however, has never eclipsed her husband's in terms of its commercial success. According to Theodore Gracyk (2007, p. 7), if one 'classifies music as popular or unpopular according to how many people actually endorse it … perversely, we might question whether Skip James or Yoko Ono made popular music … [meaning] music that is intended to be widely accepted'. Neither was the association necessarily good for her artistic reputation. One art student called Judy (2014) visiting an exhibition that featured her work recently mused, 'When it came to Yoko Ono, I was so conscious of her celebrity status that I found it difficult to see the art.'

Williams's understanding of Lennon as 'foolish' was shared, for a different reason, by some Beatles fans, who saw Yoko as influencing the break-up of their much-loved band. The couple courted and faced a certain unpopularity for forging ahead in spite of the concerns of their audience. This, however, had been the case right from the early phases of their love affair. Marion Pinsdorf (2002, p. 288) has summarized the image problem that Yoko faced:

> Critics were not kind to her. One *New York Times* feature began: 'She's every woman's worst nightmare'. 'Her art was ridiculed for decades. Her music reviled while her husband's was celebrated'. Her greatest achievement? Single handedly 'destroying the most popular music group of the century'. Her greatest lasting achievement? Brainwashing her third husband into marrying her. 'He was, in the end, a god. She was, all along, the Devil'. Obviously, Ono could only improve upon her image, and she did.

Pinsdorf's summary may have selected some of the comments made about Yoko, but she is right in saying that Yoko's role was not always appreciated as something positive. Parodying reactions to their *Two Virgins* album, Lennon once quipped, 'This Japanese witch has made him crazy.'[6] According to Scott Wilson:

> Ono's famous association with love as a transformative power was, like Che Guevara's, also nursed by hatred – both her own and the intense hatred that she attracted. 'You see many people hated me', recalled Ono in an interview with Beth Ditto in 2007. 'Well I used that hatred as a power, as an energy, and it's a great power, my God'.
>
> (Wilson 2013, p. 28)

However, the 'hate' directed at Yoko came from a range of different sources.[7] It may also have come from Beatles fans, who assumed Yoko had taken John away from them. It came from conservative authorities, who saw the couple as rule breakers. This positions John and Yoko as disaffected, idealist romantics, flowers entwined in their romantic 'double fantasy', living on a planet on which hell was other people. Such readings are interesting, insofar that they charge John's popularity with a set of atheistic, humanitarian values. During the 1970s, Lennon's way of moving forward, personally and politically, was to address his own inner demons through primal scream therapy and engage with feminism. For John, by this point, there were no apparent lines between his personal struggle and his art; his issues were reflected in songs such as 'God' (1970), 'Mother' (1970) and 'Woman Is the Nigger of the World' (1972). As Mäkelä (2005) so eloquently put it, 'Lennon as an artist strove for authenticity and represented a star seeking to reconfigure utopianism and realism, politics and aesthetics, celebrity and genuineness' (179).

Lennon's engagement with feminism aligned his personal struggle over his marriage with a politics that demanded women were respected as equals. Such a formulation helps us to interpret his less public, late 1970s phase as a 'house husband' as a further act of rebellion: eschewing an ego-led life as a rock star in the public sphere for the sake of helping his wife. If his 'lost weekend' was an indulgent fall from monogamous grace, its aftermath indicated he reached a plateau of maturity, as exemplified by the music on the *Double Fantasy* album – a more melodic (and therefore, arguably, less abrasive) record than his early 1970s offerings. Towards the end of 1980, it appeared that he had, at last, found greater personal peace. Though his early 1970s activism was a strong part of his public image, John Lennon was now starting over: talking about love again without picking on enemies.

Murder is unusual in that the injured party is gone and other people have to speak for them. In commenting on public desires to know the 'real' celebrity, even John's more abstract art pieces with Yoko appeared to offer a view of John's private life.[8] After he died, she was the only mediator left who could offer an inside account of life with and without him. Sometimes this has included comments on her feelings as John's widow. DVD viewers of David Leaf and John Scheinfeld's 2006 documentary *The U.S. vs John Lennon* (Leaf 2006) were offered an extra feature – Yoko Ono reading the letter she sent in September 2000 to the New York State Division of Parole asking for the Board to ignore Mark David Chapman's petition for release:

> [When Chapman killed my husband] darkness prevailed ... the power of destruction [was] at work ... [Releasing him would] give a 'go' signal to the others who would like to follow ... [and] bring back the nightmare, the chaos and confusion once again ... Violence begets violence. If it is at all possible, I would like us to not create a situation which may bring further madness and tragedy to the world.

Yoko speaks here, sincerely and poetically, of John's specialness, of the cruelty and injustice of his killing, of her denial and pain, of the loss incurred to his family and to the world, of how releasing Chapman could endanger the public and of how he should stay incarcerated for his own safety. In a powerful, moving performance, Yoko describes her own state of mind: 'I was screaming inside myself ... the memory of that night has never left me for the last twenty years.' Chapman, meanwhile, is not understood as a sick individual, but as a keeper of the flame of chaos, an incidental agent of destructive forces. Ono's language is almost biblical and, no doubt, genuinely expresses the horror that the loved ones of any murder victim must feel. It is also publically offered by a global celebrity who has social privileges and access to financial and other resources that most people do not (see Gunter 2014).

Establishing the trauma reading

Yoko never remarried and constantly acts as an archetypal widow: a spokesperson for Lennon's artistic legacy. In that sense, John Lennon's assassination had two victims: the star himself, and his wife, the wronged person whose life is defined around her loss. Seeing the crime this way both locates the assassination as a crime between genders, and something resembling a war situation: an event which traditionally leaves behind grieving women. Furthermore, in her grief, Yoko is locked into her secondary celebrity, as the woman who lost her star husband, and aligned with his audience, bonded through the loss they share with her. Consequently, there is a sense in which she cannot speak (as only John matters to her, and he is gone) and yet she has to speak (for John, for herself, for the fans and for their sense of injustice). These twin pressures have shaped almost four decades of her artistic ventures. Yoko's widowhood thus invites interpretations as both a public service to Beatles fans and a reflection of the hate that they are imputed to feel, not towards her, but towards Chapman. This is important, because, according to Marion Pinsdorf (2002, p. 288), when John died, 'Widow Yoko Ono faced two tasks: rehabilitating her own image, then assuring through her songs, actions and memorials that her husband Beatle John Lennon be remembered her way.'

Lennon's assassination understandably devastated his widow, but would it be accurate to call it a social trauma? Jeffrey Alexander (2004) introduced one of the most widely cited discussions of the concept explaining, 'Cultural trauma occurs when members of a collectivity feel they have been subjected to a horrendous event that leaves indelible marks upon their group consciousness, marking their memories forever and changing their future identity in fundamental and irrevocable ways.' He then defines what he calls a 'lay theory' of the phenomenon. In this reading, the event itself *inevitably causes* the change in group identity. Alexander immediately complicates this, however, by saying:

> [Trauma] illuminates an emerging domain of social responsibility and political action [because] ... social groups ... not only identify the existence and source of human suffering, but "take on board" some significant responsibility for it ... [as they] define their solidary relationships in ways that, in principle, allow them to share the sufferings of others.
>
> (2004, p. 1)

This claim opens a space between the event and how people respond to it, a space where trauma is imagined, attributed, performed, mediated and accepted. What this means is that suffering can also *fail to translate* into trauma if 'carrier groups have not emerged with the resources, authority, or interpretive competence to powerfully disseminate these trauma claims' (p. 27). Part of the 'meaning work' that helps to persuade a wider audience that it has been traumatized by an event or experience is the establishment or verification of a connection between the victim and wider audience:

> To what extent do the members of the audience for trauma representations experience an identity with the immediately victimized group? ... Only if the victims are represented in terms of valued qualities shared by the larger collective will the audience be able to symbolically participate in the experience of the originating trauma.
>
> (p. 14)

Lennon's deplorable killing certainly fits the 'horrendous event' category and, no doubt, it has left its mark upon collective consciousness. However, in important ways, his murder did *not* automatically generate *social* trauma. 'Trauma' is too strong a word. After all, it was – for most – not a blow to the public's individual psyches so sharp that nobody could effectively react, so intense that it had to be repressed, so alienating that it impaired full communality. Quite the opposite: the shooting represented a shared defeat, one that created very public mourning, *bringing together* an extended community (Fogo 1994).

It is clear here that, in her artwork, Yoko offers glimpses of her own arrested life as a focus for our empathy. She therefore acts as the central agent in the 'carrier group' that continually brings her husband's death back around, in effect re-establishing our ongoing 'symbolic participation' in it, if not as a collective trauma in the strict sense, then at least as a kind of traumatic scene. Her first effort in this direction was the *Season of Glass* LP (1981). A reviewer for *Rolling Stone* commented:

> There are several highly charged fragments that relate directly to the murder. 'I Don't Know Why,' Yoko Ono's one song of outright grief, is a compelling incantation with a coda in which her voice rises in fury: 'You bastards! Hate us ... /Hate me ... We had everything ....' It's a devastating moment, because its non-specificness underlines its universality. 'You bastards' could be everybody who ever resented the couple for their happiness and success. They could be the critics and commentators who scorned Ono's art and blamed her for breaking up the Beatles. They could be the fates themselves. They're probably all this and more ... Another number is prefaced by the sound of gunshots. Finally, there is Yoko, disconsolate and terribly alone, as she answers the telephone. Some people will find these references exploitative. But imagine how callous Ono would have appeared if she hadn't alluded to her husband's death at all.
>
> (Holden 1981)

In the shadowy world that the album constructs, Yoko's one-way phone conversation references issues of privacy and celebrity, while the 'fury' in her voice as she shouts at those (left unspecified) who hate her, or her and John, could equally be directed at fans. More controversial, however, was a use of John's blood-spattered glasses on the cover of her album, *Season of Glass*. Antony Elliot (1999b) argues that Lennon's death was felt as a great loss, in part because we are in 'denial of the existential significance of death in contemporary culture' (p. 841). He sees it as a point of 'radical otherness': unpredictable, non-rational, limiting our emotional self-mastery, repressed and sequestered. It is made part of the media spectacle, but is inevitably trivialized by such treatment. Lennon's death, for Elliot, was not entertainment; it acted against celebrity, to re-individualize him as someone contingent, historical and mortal. He cites Yoko's statement about *Season of Glass* – 'People were offended by the glasses and the blood? John had to stomach a lot more' – as evidence that we wish to avoid the physical and psychic messiness of death itself. However, this could apply to any death, of course, except that we care about Lennon. What I find more interesting here is that Yoko speaks both for and about her husband's victimhood, thus using the incident to align herself as a kind of ambassador. When biographies – notably Albert Goldman's (1988) – came out questioning John's saintly portrayal, Yoko again said, 'John isn't here to answer the things said about him' (Mäkelä 2005, p. 175). Such responses are understandable and expected, but my point is that Yoko takes on the role of curating and re-inscribing the 'real' John as an absence which she can present. This complicates the idea that John is a 'blank slate', a space of projection made and remade in the image of his fans, instead adding to his complex image the idea he is now more like a 'blank surface', no longer able to be apprehended at all, abolished by an act of violence that has redefined him as an absence, a place where people can put their sense of loss.

Yoko's music has been characterized by 'screams from the heart' (Brown 2012b). As Antony Elliot (1999b, p. 849) has explained, 'The raw emotional material of pain is perhaps a central starting point because it brings into view that which is felt most intensely in the private and public realms, and underlines the defensive markings of identification in any event'. In other words, Yoko's expressions of pain bring the private and public spheres together, evoking public empathy in a way that deflects attention from any residual animosity people may have felt about her. Now someone else has removed (the living) John from his public place, someone who – like his fan base and his second wife – supposedly did not love him. As Marion Pinsdorf (2002, p. 288) explained:

> Critical Beatle fans viewed the couple's relationship as problematic – Yoko as cipher or, worse, that she lured him away from the Beatles. Still, in his death she was the most visible link – akin to 'the widow of a head of state acting out rituals to console the masses grieving over their fallen leader'.

What is interesting about Yoko's art is that it does not, because of this, mention or acknowledge Chapman. When she has opposed clemency in his case she has said that his release would 'bring back the nightmare, the chaos and the confusion once again' (in O'Rawe 2006, p. 64). Here, even Chapman's agency cannot be named and is only implied. Instead Yoko frames the traumatic incident of her husband's murder in relation to New York, a world city, a metropolis at the heart of society, a place characterized by the hustle, bustle and violence of modern America. For example, in 1994, she endorsed a musical:

> Critics dubbed the 1994 musical 'New York Rock,' a contemporary love story of a man and woman destroyed by New York City violence, as the latest chapter in Ms Ono's 'continuing eulogy of her relationship with the slain rock star'. The latest mythic version 'of a perfect couple separated by tragedy', emotionally wounded, but still idealistic.
>
> (Pinsdorf 2002, p. 288)

The complexity of this 'New York' reading of John's death was that the city, in some ways, represented a kind of potentially threatening chaos he could and did embrace, yet Mark Chapman was not some native New Yorker goaded into violence by the stresses of America's capital city. Yoko's own art continued this approach. Her 2014 piece *Mended Cups*, for example, is described by Vera Mackie (2016):

> The sixth cup and saucer bear the name of New York City. This is not, however, a reference to the terrorist attacks on the World Trade Centre on 11 September 2001, as might be expected. Rather, the date is 8 December 1980, the day Ono's partner John Lennon (1940–1980) was shot dead by Mark Chapman outside the Dakota Building. *How can you mend a broken heart?* At first it seems as if time has stopped on 8 December 1980, with the sixth cup and saucer referring to the day, thirty-five years ago, when John Lennon was shot. This reflects the experience of trauma or bereavement, where the individual is often unable to move beyond the traumatic event.

The anonymous, 'New York City' reading of Lennon's murder is followed not just by Yoko and Sean Lennon, but by other members of the carrier group for Lennon's trauma. Elliot (1999b, p. 840) suggested, 'For those straining to cope, let alone understand the reasons for Chapman's murder of Lennon, the world had seemingly become unmanageable.' For Beatles fans, Chapman has been described as, 'He whose name shall not be spoken' (*Book Review* 2016). Pop studies academic David Shumway analysed the *Lennon NYC* documentary, saying for example:

> The murder itself is handled exceptionally well. The killer's name is not mentioned, and the event is discussed by interviewees in terms of their reaction to the news. We hear from Yoko how difficult it was to have to listen to the public singing John's songs in the street outside her window. We can only imagine how difficult the loss was for Sean. Yoko's question, 'Why would someone want to kill an artist?' sums up the horrible absurdity of this event. No one, however, addresses the irony that the city Lennon loved was located in a country where nuts have easy access to guns. New York had permitted Lennon to live a more normal life than had London, but he could not escape his celebrity.
>
> (Shumway 2011, p. 302)

Chapman's nobody/somebody dichotomy was actually serviced by Paul McCartney who located him as 'the jerk of all jerks', implying, as Yoko said, 'it didn't matter who pulled the trigger.' Here we might consider the relevance of Giorgio Agamben's (1998) concept of 'bare life'. For Agamben, 'bare life' is the life of *homo sacer*: a criminal, judged in the Roman legal system, for a very specific kind of crime, who, may legitimately be killed, but not ritually sacrificed. *Homo sacer* is 'bare life' insofar that his rights to citizenship are revoked. He is, in effect, assigned the role of a common animal: biologically alive, but not a functional entity within the social (here religious or judicial) system. The term emerges from ancient society, but it is invoked by the theorist to chart the failure of democratic states to escape their creeping convergence with totalitarianism:

> Today politics knows no value (and, consequently, no non-value) other than life, and until the contradictions that this fact implies are dissolved, Nazism and fascism – which transformed the decision on bare life into the supreme political principle – will remain stubbornly with us.
>
> (Agamben 1998, p. 10)

If humanity consists of 'living beings who have language', then it also creates subjects who remain alive but are devoid of humanity: they have 'bare life', existence without enfranchisement, without rights, without a voice. Agamben uses the notion of 'bare life' in a judicial sense: the subject who is ascribed 'bare life' is an 'in between' subject – alive (for now), but not given basic human rights.

While Agamben talks here of concentration camp inmates, the concept has been extended to include asylum seekers (Darling 2009). One might further extend it to include criminals – as was the word's root – whose acts have been judged so monstrous that, it is sometimes argued, they do not 'deserve' the treatment accorded to civilized human beings. Agamben's ideas are arguably relevant to Chapman's case because the nature of the act is perceived as negating any identity. Yoko's statement that 'it didn't matter who pulled the trigger' evidently spoke her personal truth, prioritizing the husband that she loved and reflecting her horror at losing him. For others to agree with such statements, however, furthers the erasure of Chapman's identity, by refusing to service his ego or self-esteem, or by negating his mental illness. It is as if to say, the 'fame monster' reading is basically correct, but its putative rewards must be denied on moral grounds. Going along with this reading, meanwhile, has allowed Chapman to exculpate himself, by safely jettisoning the husk of a past actor. At his ninth parole hearing, he told the board that he had a sociopathic mind and killed Lennon because he wanted to be famous. The Parole Board's denial of appeal was on the same grounds, citing the 'premeditated and celebrity seeking nature of the crime' (Alexander 2016).

With its basis in over 150 hours of interviews with mental health doctors, Chapman's trial was described by a journalist for *People* magazine as 'a long and clamorous drama ... [with] a considerable element of farce' (Gains 1987). Qualified professionals offered their assessments of whether Chapman was afflicted with a psychosis or had a less severe personality disorder. Seemingly taking responsibility, but perhaps also aiming to repress the possibility of a self-image that admitted insanity, in the end Chapman withdrew his psychiatric defence and pleaded guilty to murder. He was, nevertheless, ordered into psychiatric treatment, as well as sentenced to incarceration. This suggests, in a judicial sense that he *was* responsible, rather than *only* insane, because his mental illness was not severe enough to have removed his culpability. However, there appears to be no clear motive that does not admit some kind of delusion on the killer's part. For Antony Elliot (1999b, p. 839), 'One of the most striking things about Lennon's death was the way that, despite endless media information about the shooting, it remained incomprehensible, inconceivable, as if cut off from cultural self-knowing.'

To conclude, for Yoko Ono, denial may well serve personal psychological functions, but, simultaneously, it also acts in public, performing 'meaning work' in a wider, social sense, directing attention back towards the innocent side of John's celebrity persona. In making it morally unacceptable to give Chapman any limelight in a sense we both freeze and render him – at least as he was back then in 1980 – 'bare life': erasing any basic human rights he may have left. However, even murderers, like other criminals, retain some rights under the law. Those who have served their sentences and no longer considered a threat are regularly set free, regardless of the wishes of their victims' families: over 1000 in the three years to 2014 in California alone, for example (*1,400 'Lifers'* 2014). One only needs to think of the differences between, say, crimes of passion, assassinations, serial killings, vigilante attacks, infanticides and honour killings, to realize that murder is always a culturally specific phenomenon. It means different things in different contexts. The judicial system has the awkward task of measuring the enormity of each crime, dispensing justice and assessing rehabilitation. This is not to suggest that Mark Chapman should now be set free, but rather to indicate that celebrity is used as a shared way to judge the enormity of his crime, to place it in a different category, and to make him, in a sense, because of who he chose to kill, a placeholder for more widespread public concerns about the injustice of murder itself.

Media scholar Johnathan Gray has defined 'anti-fandom' by saying, 'Opposed and yet in some ways similar to the fan is the anti-fan: he/she who actively and vocally hates or dislikes a given text, personality, or genre' (2005, p. 840). On the thirtieth anniversary of Lennon's death, one smiling family man, holding his toddler and standing next to his wife, explained to a UK TV newscaster, 'I think it might be a good idea for him [Chapman] to stay in prison, because there's a lot of people who are more Lennon fans than we are that could take that to extremes [and attempt to kill him]. I think his life would be in danger' (*TheUnauthorizedStory* 2015). By turning himself into a Lennon anti-fan and killing an icon, Mark Chapman has inevitably, such statements assume, generated a legion of anti-fans of his own. To be a Beatles fan is, automatically then to be a Chapman anti-fan, and – depending on *one's own* violent proclivities – to potentially possess the interest and capability of ending Chapman's life in a kind of hypothesized fannish mob justice. This idea justifies Yoko's lawyers in their continuously successful attempts to rebuff his appeals, not least on the grounds that Chapman's incarceration is *for his own good*. It also draws on the stereotype that behind love for the Beatles there is a kind of residual hate, tempting dedicated fans to violent irrationality. In reality, sane individuals are responsible for their own actions. Fan allegiance can, at the end of the day, be used as a socially acceptable alibi or excuse to cloak behaviour that has other causes. No love is completely blind. John Lennon, no doubt, would not have been lost on the irony. His later career centred around the rebellious testing of his inescapable commercial popularity; he never acceded to 'bloody tribal rights', except in death – the one time that popular sentiment and the 'dark forces' of commerce finally spoke for him.

Notions of Mark Chapman as a 'fame monster' offer a form of sanely explicable *insanity*. By rendering John Lennon a *victim* (someone in the wrong place at the wrong time), perceptions of Chapman's arresting, monstrous act serve to frame and configure the unruly complexity of the ex-Beatle's public image. His killer's initially hypothesized, inevitably misguided motive necessarily affirms Lennon's artistic activity as something more meaningful than can be encapsulated by any commercial calculus of 'bare' celebrity. The double bind of Lennon's death, then, is this: by acknowledging the profound *meaningfulness* of the star's life, we are asked to accept the compassionate obligation to discount any meaningfulness to Chapman's identity, to see him as defined through one monstrous, unredeemable act, *only* as a 'killer'. In McCartney and Ginsberg's words, Chapman has been seen as 'just a jerk' who 'slashed a Picasso'. Yet in order to discount any potential of the horrific *meaningfulness* of Chapman's action, we have also chosen to consider him non-existent, suggesting that John died, in effect, when he encountered chaos. Was Chapman's act so monstrous that we should effectively therefore choose to say there was *no subject* there who actually did it?

6

Exhuming the Gravediggaz: Gothic hip hop and monster capital

The early 2010s saw a number of interesting hip hop releases that took an allegedly 'gothic' turn. Records like Kanye West's 'Monster', Killer Mike's 'Big Beast' and Tyler the Creator's 'Yonkers' incorporated 'dark' imagery and sound in the music, and horror iconography in video production. Kristen Sollee (2015) presents a comprehensive list, while making links with fashion explicit in her analysis. When these records were released, a number of commentators noted the trend for a distinctly gothic aesthetic entering hip hop. Pusha T, an MC who initially found fame with Clipse, was moved to assert: 'I'm sick of this gothic, hip hop, nasty look' (Bustard 2013).

What was pointed out less frequently was the relatively long tradition of using gothic and horror themes in rap music as a vocabulary with which to approach African American experience. In particular, various hip hop artists from the early 1990s, dubbed 'horrorcore' at the time by the media, used such imagery extensively for just such a purpose. Sollee is surely right that in the 2010s, although significant and widespread, adoption of gothic imagery in hip hop was often a temporary tactic, for the duration of one release, before it was 'on to the next one' (Sollee 2015, p. 254). However, a couple of decades earlier, horrorcore artists presented a more sustained engagement with this aesthetic that persisted over successive releases.

In this chapter, my concern is to consider the cultural work performed by gothic imagery of the undead in the music and visual identity of Gravediggaz, one of the most noted of the horrorcore groups, whose name clearly signals the centrality of such monstrous tropes to their work. At first the analysis might seem of limited potential – but this is only at first sight, since the group as well as their music can be taken as a case study for themes linking apparently disparate wider cultural phenomena. First, to analyse the iconography and themes of Gravediggaz is to consider the relations between the gothic and African American popular culture more generally. Second, to explore the era in which the band arose, just after the high-point of political hip hop or 'message rap', means to consider the political implications – or absence thereof – of gothic rap and of Gravediggaz' music in particular. Finally, much discussion of this genre of popular music foregrounds the way hip hop artists negotiate their relations to capitalism and commodification.

These are all of course very large questions. However, I would like to suggest that to give attention to this group is to attend to aspects of wider historical or cultural phenomena that are often sidelined in dominant formulations of the concepts in question. The gothic, for instance, despite notable New England and Southern variants from the United States, is often seen as solidly European and White in its makeup. It is also rather ironic that recent appropriations of the gothic in popular culture have often been compared unfavourably with original, now canonical gothic literature, even though the early gothic novels were roundly perceived as popular culture when they were first published.

Many have pointed to the close relations between gothic novels and slavery; Wendy Walker (2016) notes that 'All four of the first Gothic novelists – Horace Walpole, William Thomas Beckford, [Matthew] Lewis and Ann Radcliffe – were significantly involved with plantation slavery and/or its abolition, the great cause of the day.' Other scholars have noted the importance of colonialism to texts such as Charlotte Brontë's *Jane Eyre*, for which Jean Rhys's *Wide Sargasso Sea* has often been seen as a postcolonial response (Spivak 1985; Parry 1994).

In addition, discussions of capitalism as such can sometimes elide the persistence and importance of economic subordination that is specifically racialized – the persistence of the legacy of the plantation on US social and economic life. Both of these large frameworks – namely gothic iconography and imagery, and a reflection on African Americans' relations to capitalism and the music industry – form part of Gravediggaz' main themes, with their concerns expressed both in lyrics and in interviews.

Therefore, some of the discussion in this chapter will provide a very broad context in which to locate the band's work. Perhaps at times it might appear that I am burdening discussion of the group with rather too general cultural, political and economic frameworks. Nonetheless, the distinctive mixture of influences informing their work allows us to trace a synthesis of various cultural categories often kept apart in discussions of the gothic, capitalism and African American cultural forms and experience. It is hoped the discussion on the specificity of

Gravediggaz' themes will demonstrate the imaginativeness of their particular syncretism of cultural influences.

Despite some similar concerns, in making links between political economy, race and music, I will be taking a different approach to Richard L. Schur, whose 2009 book *Parodies of Ownership* makes the convincing case of the pertinence of a critical engagement with intellectual property law for hip hop. In this respect, he is following the lead of critical race theory in interrogating the racialized assumptions of the legal framework. Schur's emphasis on legal issues is unsurprising given the association of hip hop with sampling, something which led to a series of lawsuits that ultimately transformed the music from a form dependent on sampled breakbeats to a more clean-sounding, programmed style. Schur argues that 'Hip hop aesthetics reenacts the slave narratives' desire to become the subjects of property law' (Schur 2009, p. 8). I certainly agree that rap's emphasis, from the 1980s on, has been on 'getting paid'. I am interested here, however, in a more pessimistic conception of the economic base – and the way in which a gothic lexis, specifically from within hip hop, might figure this relation as an ongoing historical problematic.

As a final observation for the introduction to this chapter, I note that I run the risk, as a White European academic who writes about this group, of presenting their work and its significance in ways not congruent with the manner in which it was envisaged by the producers or received by original audiences. Focusing on various Marxist notions and ideas such as gothic, I will likely betray the marginality of my own position in relation to other discussions about their work. Nonetheless, by supporting my arguments with material from the group and academic debates informed by Black studies, I hope to mitigate some of the effects of this inevitably partial account. Rather than see African American expressive culture as having a tangential relation to gothic, I also suggest that attention to their *interrelation* can provide an important corrective to hegemonic discourses about gothic that locate the latter too solidly within one specific cultural tradition.

Exhuming the Gravediggaz

Gravediggaz were formed in 1994 and are often seen as a hip hop 'supergroup'. Prince Paul and Frukwan had been in pioneering jazz rappers Stetsasonic, signed to Tommy Boy Records. At the same label had been Too Poetic, another member of the new group. All of these artists had recently lost their recording contracts. In an early interview, Prince Paul joked: 'Gravediggaz are a bunch of Tommy Boy rejects' (McCann 1994, p. 22). In addition to being dropped by Tommy Boy, Prince Paul's record label, Doo Dew Man Records, a subsidiary of Def Jam, had been shut down by rap mogul Lyor Cohen for being too uncommercial. Neil Kulkarni attributes the dark sound and themes of Gravediggaz' debut partly to this latter setback: 'It's Prince Paul's clear frustration at the collapse of his Doo Dew label that accounts for the album's sheer darkness' (Kulkarni 2004, p. 66). Prince Paul had, in fact, despite these career upsets, found fame as the producer of De La Soul's 1989 debut, *Three Feet High and Rising* and its two successors. The fates of the other MCs in the group would also invite cynicism regarding their place in the music industry.

The fourth member of Gravediggaz, the RZA, had previously found limited success as Prince Rakeem. His debut as producer and MC for the famous Wu-Tang Clan had come out in November 1993, and he combined duties for Gravediggaz and Wu-Tang Clan over the next four years or so. As was customary in hip hop of this era, the various group members devised alter egos for the new band: Prince Paul became the Undertaker, Frukwan was the Gatekeeper, Too Poetic was known as the Grym Reaper, and RZA answered to the appellation, the RZArector.

Gravediggaz' first LP was called *6 Feet Deep* in the United States; in the rest of the world, their original title was uncensored and the LP was released as *Niggamortis*. It is frequently compared to other albums that came out around the same time using gothic and horror imagery, by groups such as Flatlinerz; Bone, Thugs and Harmony; Geto Boys; Three 6 Mafia; and others. The ensuing term, 'horrorcore' was rejected by the group; in interviews around the time of their second LP in 1997, Prince Paul called the term a 'distraction' (Crysell 1997, p. 16); Poetic dubbed it a 'media invention' (Holley 1997, p. 24). Nonetheless, the term aptly describes both the supernatural imagery used by the band and those lumbering piano-driven tracks that manage somehow to sound simultaneously funky and sinister, something that RZA also achieved with his productions for the contemporaneous debut from the Wu-Tang Clan, *Enter the Wu-Tang (36 Chambers)*. Richard Middleton (2007) deftly characterises the sound of the Wu-Tang debut, which also applies to the RZA's productions with his gothic side project: 'The backgrounds combine abstract, near-atonal riffs and nostalgic, even "cheesy" samples' (p. 112).

The group's second LP, *The Pick, the Sickle and the Shovel*, was released in 1997. This maintained the imagery of the first album but with a more melodic, less sinister sound. The contributions of Prince Paul to the production on this release were fewer compared with the earlier record.¹ However, the group's political ideas were at least as prominent in their second LP as in their debut, notably themes ultimately deriving from the Five Percent Nation.

The dead men were alive

The various tropes of death, gravedigging, ghosts and so on in Gravediggaz' music can fruitfully be compared to African American appropriations of the gothic in fiction. In his article on this writing, including the novels of Toni Morrison and Richard Wright, Cedric Gael Bryant (2005) argues:

> African American literature situated within gothic discourse opens up discursive spaces in which revisions of identity are possible and geographies of the imagination can be remapped. Within these narratives, the 'gothic' becomes a recuperative, revisionary idea that makes monstrosity not only a fixed, paralyzing moment of horror, but also a catalytic space where agency and progress, hope and being are possible.
>
> (p. 550)

It is this progressive aspect of the gothic that Gravediggaz too are engaging with – many people have described their songs as cautionary tales and the MCs in the group represent themselves as spirit guides or prophets leading their constituency out of the darkness. As we have seen, their fortunes in the industry necessitated a self-reinvention, one of the things that according to Bryant can be facilitated by gothic tropes and imagery. This is to present a 'catalytic space' apart from the claustrophobic urban spaces that form the backdrop of their tracks.

We can take the comparison with Richard Wright even further. In an essay on gothic themes in Wright's *Native Son* (1972), James Smethurst (2001) argues:

> Yet despite this use of the terminology of the supernatural and the uncanny, there is nothing supernatural in *Native Son*. What these terms represent is both an instinctual understanding of the results of the capitalist system in the United States and a mystification of the laws of that system.
>
> (p. 32)

I think it's overstating things to say there is 'nothing supernatural' in Gravediggaz, since the group clearly relish the *grand guignol* opportunities gothic presents both in their rhymes and in the mediated spectacle of their videos. However, the insight that this imagery represents both an understanding and mystification of the relations of African American men in capitalism seems pertinent.

In his 2009 book, *The Tao of Wu* – an exuberant synthesis of autobiography, self-help advice, and musings on Eastern wisdom, kung fu movies and rap aesthetics – the RZA devotes two short chapters to monstrosity. He recalls happy childhood visits to his uncle Hollis in North Carolina as a respite from the trials of living in the housing projects of Brooklyn. In particular, he memorized a Southern folk rhyme that Hollis would intone and that he would later riff on in his Gravediggaz lyrics:

> Never cry when a hearse goes by. Because you may be the next to die. They'll cover you with a white sheet. They'll put you down about six feet deep. It's not so bad the first few weeks, until you start to mumble and creep, and the worms crawl in and the worms crawl out, and the ants play pinochle on your snout, your stomach turns the sickest green as pus runs out like thick whipped cream.
> (RZA 2009, p. 12)

As well as folk rhymes, movies are another source of the imagery. Another chapter in *The Tao of Wu* considers George A. Romero's zombie films, namely *Night of the Living Dead* (1968) and *Dawn of the Dead* (1978). These films are notable for having Black men playing leading roles as protagonists. In addition, for the RZA, *Night of the Living Dead* prefigures the rise of crack cocaine in the 1980s; and (as many others have also noted) with its zombie hordes shuffling around a shopping mall, *Dawn of the Dead* serves as a metaphor for consumerism. In general terms, RZA observes: 'The dead were alive, but they were blind, deaf, and dumb. So to me, they were symbolic of Black men in America' (RZA 2009, p. 45). Furthermore, the nature of this death is mental – one of Gravediggaz' repeated refrains in their music is that they are liberating the mentally dead; 'Twelve Jewelz' is an exemplary track in this respect. To further explore this concept, it is necessary to mention the RZA's main *political* influence – the Five Percenters. We will come back to this later in the chapter.

More broadly, the folk rhymes and supernatural imagery that feed into Gravediggaz' lyrics can be seen in relation to US Black cultural precedents: 'Tales of ghosts who seek vengeance against oppressors appear frequently in African American folklore, along with tricksters – animal, human, or otherwise – who even the odds between the weak and the strong' (Fulmer 2002, p. 430). In this quotation, Jacqueline Fulmer is discussing the gothic horror film, *Tales from the Hood* (Rusty Cundieff 1995), a film released around the time of the group's second LP that shares its use of gothic to present cautionary tales about urban life. It was not the only film to make such a connection: *Candyman* (Bernard Rose 1992) and *The People under the Stairs* (Wes Craven 1991) have both been discussed in relation to race and capitalism. More recently, of course, we have seen Jordan Peele's films: *Get Out* (2017) and *Us* (2019). Between these cycles, there was an interesting Snoop Dogg vehicle, *Bones* (Ernest Dickerson 2001) that foregrounds hip hop in soundtrack and cast. Of this film, Richard Ravalli (2007) observes: 'The moral message of African American ghostlore also remains in its inner city manifestations' (p. 289). So Gravediggaz' use of supernatural imagery in its lyrics not only parallels analogous use in narrative media formats such as cinema, but also draws on conceptions of conjure men, tricksters and ghosts in oral folklore traditions.

Gothic Marxism

In fact, taking ghosts seriously in terms of their political or sociological import also informs a number of interventions in the human sciences that emerged around the same time as Gravediggaz' first two LPs. These ideas were sometimes discussed in relation to the term, 'hauntology', the neologism coined by the philosopher Jacques Derrida in his work *Specters of Marx* (1993/2006). Another work that emerged with some cognate themes was the US sociologist Avery F. Gordon's work *Ghostly Matters* (1997/2008). The arguments of these works are far from identical, but the thematic attention to haunting, ghosts and revenants found obvious application to literary and cultural studies where such themes have been used to figure historical or political events and problematics. We can locate Smethurst's (2001) and Bryant's (2005) work broadly in this tradition – especially since Gordon's (1997/2008) book also featured an analysis of Toni Morrison's *Beloved* as a prominent part of her work.

Derrida's foundational text is too involved to be summarized very easily, ranging as it does from reflections on the thesis of the end of history recently advanced by Francis Fukuyama (but compared by Derrida to earlier debates following Alexandre Kojève and others in the 1950s in France) to consideration of the legacy of Marx to contemporary thought (as well as what he alleges is Marx's own warding off of the ghosts in his own work), and a rethinking of philosophical ontology in the light of Derrida's arguments about the trace, *différance* and the non-coincidence of the self-identical, etc. It is this strain of reflections on Marxism specifically that is most pertinent to the arguments I will consider in this chapter.

It is not Derrida alone who has noted the prevalence of ghostly or supernatural imagery in the writings of Marx and Engels. Most obviously, perhaps, there are the opening lines of the *Communist Manifesto*: 'A spectre is haunting Europe – the spectre of Communism. All the Powers of old Europe have entered into a holy alliance to exorcise this spectre' (Marx and Engels 1848/1968, p. 35). Later on in the same text, when Marx and Engels discuss the transition from capitalism to socialism, they write: 'What the bourgeoisie, therefore, produces, above all, is its own grave-diggers' (Marx and Engels 1848/1968, p. 35). It is my contention that 'Gravediggaz', the hip hop group, also has a keen sense of political significance in relation to capitalism – albeit of a very different register.

Another strain of gothic imagery occurs in Marx's historiography. In the second paragraph of the *Eighteenth Brumaire*, Marx writes:

> The tradition of all the dead generations weighs like a nightmare on the brain of the living. And just when they seem engaged in revolutionising themselves and things, in creating something that never existed, precisely in such periods of revolutionary crisis they anxiously conjure up the spirits of the past to their service.
>
> (Marx and Engels 1848/1968, p. 93)

On the same page he dubs this the 'world-historical necromancy' that sees revolutionaries conjure up previous historical figures, almost to be possessed by them in the absence of contemporary guidelines or landmarks.

If these sources use ghostly imagery to refer to revolutionary situations, another strain of supernatural lexis is used in 'later' Marx to refer to capital itself. In the notebooks preparatory to *Capital*, later published as the *Grundrisse*, Marx refers to capital ('dead' or 'congealed' labour) as preying on living labour in the following terms: 'Capital posits the permanence of value (to a certain degree) by incarnating itself in fleeting commodities and taking on their form [...] But capital obtains this ability only by constantly sucking in living labour as its soul, vampire-like' (1857/1993, p. 646). There is a near repetition of this in the first volume of *Capital*: 'Capital is dead labour which, vampire-like, lives only by sucking living labour, and lives the more, the more labour it sucks' (Marx 1867/1976, p. 342).

Apart from the metaphorical significance of such tropes in Marx's work in order to figure the categories of political economy, is there any wider significance or pattern to its usage taken as a whole? Derrida's own answers to the question are nuanced and complex, acknowledging both the ethical and conceptual advances that the gothic analogy brings to Marx's own work, as well as making an attempt to exorcise spectres and spectrality that Marx is himself not wholly able to master. For the purposes of our chapter, a more general insight into the *thematic* significance of ghostly imagery for Marxist or Marxism-inspired theorizing is more obviously relevant, even if this might miss some of the acuity of Derrida's arguments.

In the rest of this section, I will summarize some arguments that have been made as to the significance of supernatural or undead imagery in Marx's work or that inspired by him, by several recent writers. Avery Gordon's *Ghostly Matters* (Gordon 2008) advances a bold thesis about the general relevance of haunting for sociological thought: 'Haunting is a constituent element of modern social life. It is neither premodern superstition nor individual psychosis; it is a generalizable social phenomenon of great import. To confront social life one must confront the ghostly aspects of it' (p. 7). Bringing out the affective register of haunting allows Gordon in the book's final chapter to consider haunting in terms of Raymond Williams's (1977) notion of a 'structure of feeling' (p. 128). In order to explore the significance of haunting for social life, Gordon departs from the empirical data of much sociology and looks instead to the novel, in particular Luisa Valenzuela's *Como en la Guerra* (1977) and Toni Morrison's *Beloved* (1987). It is in relation to the latter novel in particular that Gordon (2008) outlines the relevance of haunting for African American culture in general terms:

> Whatever can be said definitively about the long and varied traditions of African American thought, writing, and radicalism, the social reality of haunting and the presence of ghosts are prominent features. The capacity not only to live with spectres, in order to determine what sort of people they were and could be, but also to engage the ghost, heterogeneously but cooperatively, as metaphor, as weapon, as salve, as a fundamental epistemology for living in the vortex of North America.
>
> (p. 151)

We can compare this with the more recent observations by Frank B. Wilderson III (2009), which also articulate the structure of haunting with slavery: 'This structure of feeling is palpable even in the place-names "Africa" and "the Caribbean," names whose articulation (grammar) and memory (ghosts) would not be names at all were it not for the trade in human cargo' (p. 119). Other commentators have outlined the significance of other, perhaps more material, monsters for figuring the workings of capital. Discussing the displacement of the aristocratic vampire by the zombie worker in late capitalism, Steven Shaviro (2002) argues: 'monsters are intrinsic to the ordinary, everyday reality of capitalism itself' (p. 281). Dracula appears rather quaint, according to Shaviro, alongside the zombie hordes of contemporary capitalist imaginaries, not to mention the more inhuman nature of capital itself, which appears positively Lovecraftian in the late capitalist era.

David McNally (2012), finally, devotes a book to the significance of monsters for the analysis of capitalism. On Marx's own use of such imagery, McNally argues:

> If there is a Marxist Gothic, then, it is one that insists, among other things, on journeying through the night spaces of the capitalist underworld, on visiting the secret dungeons that harbour labouring bodies in pain. Another shared feature with the Gothic is a fixation on corporeal vulnerability. Bodies are always imperilled in Gothic tales, threatened by invasion and dismemberment.
>
> (p. 138)

What McNally's book tracks throughout modern history is the development of the relations of capitalism to the precise nature of monstrosity and bodily dismemberment, from the ghoulish body snatchers sourcing the barber-surgeons in London and the enclosures and parcellation of the commons in the early modern era to Frankenstein as a figure of the French Revolution in the era of the Gothic novel, and on to Marx's own analyses of the disfigurement of the labouring body as a sort of Victorian Gothic, before finally turning to vampires and zombies in contemporary African popular culture, from Nollywood to urban myth, in our own day.

Ghosts of primitive accumulation

In *Ghostly Matters*, Avery F. Gordon asserts, 'The presence of the ghost informs us that the over and done with "extremity" of a domestic and international slavery has not entirely gone away, even if it seems to have passed into the register of history and symbol' (Gordon 2008, p. 168). This insight about a haunting of contemporary capitalism by the legacy of slavery brings us to the thorny issue of the relations between capitalism as mode of production and chattel slavery. One of the controversies between Black studies and Marxism has been precisely the centrality of the latter to the former. Was slavery a premodern mode of production that contributed to the 'primitive accumulation' that made capitalism possible? Or are the histories of capitalism and slavery much more contemporaneous – perhaps even something like mutual? Such claims also raise the question of the relations between Marxism and African American political thought and movements. This is a very big question, one covered extensively by Cedric Robinson in his 1983 work, *Black Marxism*. Some of the most prominent twentieth-century Black American intellectuals traversed Marxism, such as W.E.B. Du Bois, C.L.R. James and Richard Wright who are discussed by Robinson. Sometimes they passed through it to something else, sometimes they maintained a partial identification with it. Though it is beyond the scope of this chapter to examine such relations in detail, it is, nonetheless, useful to sketch a few of the connections between the different strands of theorizing.

Primitive accumulation is the concept in Marxism that is used to designate various practices of expropriation that lead to the accumulation of wealth sufficient to serve as capital in the emerging mode of production, namely capitalism. Often this is theorized by Marx in terms of the transition from feudalism to capitalism, via processes such as the enclosure of common lands, or the formal subsumption of non-capitalist modes of production like artisanal or craft manufactures. Increasingly, factory-based industrial manufacture, with its gains in the productivity of labour, puts the self-employed craftsman out of work. As Marx writes in chapter 26 of the first volume of *Capital*:

> The process, therefore, that clears the way for the capitalist system, can be none other than the process which takes away from the labourer the possession of his means of production; a process that transforms, on the one hand, the social means of subsistence and of production into capital, on the other, the immediate producers into wage labourers.
>
> (1867/1976, p. 874)

However, force is also posited as a constant agent of primitive accumulation, not only in the enclosure of the commons, but also in repressive measures against vagrancy, the new rigid discipline of the working day and at its most extreme, in enslavement. In a well-known passage from chapter 36 of volume 1, Marx underlines the latter's centrality:

> The discovery of gold and silver in America, the extirpation, enslavement and entombment in mines of the aboriginal population, the beginning of the conquest and looting of the East Indies, the turning of Africa into a warren for

the commercial hunting of black-skins, signalised the rosy dawn of the era of capitalist production. These idyllic proceedings are the chief movements of primitive accumulation.

(Marx 1867/1976, p. 915)

It is the assertion of Cedric Robinson, the African American studies scholar who has devoted the longest study to Black Marxism, that despite an acknowledgement of the pivotal role of slavery in primitive accumulation, nonetheless Marx underplays the *continued* use of slavery after the establishment of the capitalist mode of production. He argues early on in the work:

> Certainly slave labour was one of [the] bases for what Marx termed 'primitive accumulation'. But it would be an error to arrest the relationship there, assigning slave labour to some 'pre-capitalist' stage of history. For more than 300 years slave labour persisted beyond the beginnings of modern capitalism, complementing wage labour, peonage, serfdom and other methods of labour coercion.
>
> (Robinson 1983, p. 4)

In Marx's defence, the aforementioned chapter 36 of the first volume of *Capital* makes very clear the importance, indeed indispensability, specifically of ongoing new world slavery for capital in Europe, as follows:

> Whilst the cotton industry introduced child-slavery in England, it gave in the United States a stimulus to the transformation of the earlier, more or less patriarchal slavery, into a system of commercial exploitation. In fact, the veiled slavery of the wage workers in Europe needed, for its pedestal, slavery pure and simple in the new world.
>
> (Marx 1867/1976, p. 925)

Robinson seems on more secure ground when alleging a possible *inconsistency* in emphasis in Marx's descriptions of primitive accumulation than in asserting an overall neglect of the ongoing role of slavery during capitalism 'proper'. Certain of Marx's definitions advanced imply that the removal of the means of production from producers, their transition from immediate producers to wage labourers is the crucial process, thus neglecting the dimension of producers who were themselves reduced to means of production, namely slaves. The qualifications that are added to include slavery into this process sometimes seem insufficiently integrated into the definition.

Robinson's key arguments in *Black Marxism* deny the compatibility of the subjectivity of slavery with capitalist oppression, on the one hand; and to underline the unacknowledged Eurocentrism of Marxist concepts, on the other. In this respect the work is foundational for some subsequent debates in Black studies. The work coined the term 'racial capitalism' (Robinson 1983, p. 2), for instance, which recurs in more recent studies such as Avery's *Ghostly Matters* aforementioned. This term seeks to provide a parallel genealogy for capitalism that derives as much from Western 'racialism' as it does from economic modes of production. Indeed, Robinson also uses a supernatural lexis to discuss this element in capitalism, when he refers to 'this "haunting" of radical European thought, and its Eurocentricism' (Robinson 1983, p. 53).

Perhaps more significantly still, Robinson argues that the subjectivity of the slaves is irreducible to resistance to capitalist oppression, and – crucially – draws on cultural traditions, however suppressed and oppressed, deriving from Africa. Some of these traditions, Robinson argues, reveal an internalization of violence in stark contrast to the external violence of Westerners practised on Africans conscripted into slavery. This was occasionally a death-haunted resistance, which Robinson (1983) characterized in the following terms:

> This violence was not inspired by an external object, it was not understood as a part of an attack on a system, or an engagement with an abstraction of oppressive structures and relations. Rather it was their 'Jonestown,' our Nongquase: *The renunciation of actual being for historical being; the preservation of the ontological totality* granted by a metaphysical system which had never allowed for property in either the physical, philosophical, temporal, legal, social or psychic senses.
>
> (p. 243, emphasis in original)

So, as well as Marxism being subject to a 'haunting' by the legacies of Western racialized conceptions, in Robinson's argument, the subjectivity of the slave was haunted by a sort of cultural death drive, a renunciation of the property-based actuality of chattel slavery in favour of an 'ontological totality' deriving from African cultural traditions. This radical expropriation continued, for Robinson, *during* the capitalist era, and not just in the primitive accumulation that paved the way for it. As we shall see, Gravediggaz themselves categorize the music industry in terms of a 'new plantation', signifying on the continuities between earlier and later experiences informed by the Black Atlantic.

Spectrality in the primal scene

In her 1997 work, *Scenes of Subjection*, Saidiya V. Hartman considers the various 'scenes' in which, in slavery, 'the exercise of power was inseparable from its display because domination depended upon demonstrations of the slaveholder's dominion and the captive's abasement' (p. 7). Among other things, the work considers how the ostensibly sympathetic direct representation of slavery can sometimes be counterproductive, either through desensitizing us to the horrors or through reinforcing the 'spectacular character of Black suffering' (p. 1). Another peril in consuming such representations is a spurious empathy that serves only to obscure the subjectivity of those rendered an object of the gaze rather than a subject. Here Hartman's position recalls some of the arguments from subaltern studies.

One episode in particular that is considered by various theorists in Black studies is the beating of Aunt Hester in Frederick Douglass's slave narrative. For Hartman, the overfamiliarity – or perhaps over-citation – of this episode risks precisely this desensitizing process or the reduction of suffering to spectacle (1997, p. 1). The episode also is crucial for Paul Gilroy in his (1993) theorizing of a Black Atlantic culture. Nonetheless, this episode, too, is acknowledged as something of a 'primal scene' for the aforementioned thinkers. Hartman describes it as 'an original generative act equivalent to the statement "I was born"' (p. 1).

The episode narrated by Douglass also serves as the basis of an elaboration by Fred Moten, who uses this primal scene to figure a complicated relation between performance, reproduction and disappearance. In relation to Aunt Hester's scream, the primal scene is, for Moten, inherently both sexual and phonic, something which lends the episode a general and generative import for interpreting African American expressive culture. Though the concepts advanced are involved, and bear the trace of certain post-structuralist styles of argumentation that would reward extensive unpacking, the articulation of these various elements, I would argue, offers a powerful framework in order to analyse Black popular culture.

Moten argues that both Douglass and Hartman wish to repress the primal scene of Aunt Hester's subjection, Douglass as the original subjectivity experiencing this scene as trauma, Hartman in order to ward off the 'specter of enjoyment' (Moten 2003, p. 4). Nonetheless, they both return to the episode in order to bear witness to its originary power. Now, Moten wishes to argue that this episode can also figure the disavowed or repressed performativity underlying mechanical reproduction, be it in print, photography or music recording: 'Douglass and Hartman confront us with the fact that the *conjunction* of reproduction and disappearance is performance's condition of possibility, its ontology and its mode of production' (Moten 2003, p. 5).

Moten's next rhetorical move is to invoke Karl Marx's analysis of the commodity in the first volume of *Capital*, in order to uncover 'the impossible material substance of the commodity's impossible speech' (2003, p. 9). In particular, Moten points to Marx's thought experiment where he imagines a scenario in which commodities could 'speak'. Marx ventriloquizes, enunciating the commodity's assertion of value (socially necessary labour time) over the *exchange* value under which it is classified in capitalism. However, for Moten, Aunt Hester, being property, herself bears witness to 'the irreducible materiality – the broken and irreducible maternity – of the commodity's scream' (p. 12). In other words, Aunt Hester as a slave *just was* the commodity for which Marx elsewhere supplies the speech.

Moten underlines the centrality of this episode once more, in relation to Black US culture: 'enslavement – and the resistance to enslavement that is the performative essence of Blackness (and perhaps less controversially, the essence of Black performance) is a *being maternal* that is indistinguishable from a *being material*' (16, original emphasis). The musical term that Moten uses in order to bring out both the musical and the sexual dimensions of this primal scene is simply the 'cut'.

An example here may help illustrate this complicated logic of the cut. One of the scenes of subjection that Moten invokes is the mediated representation of the dead body of Emmett Till. Till was a fourteen-year-old boy who was killed and dumped in the river allegedly for whistling at a White woman. In some accounts, Till was castrated too. Here we have another conjunction of racial trauma, aurality and sexuality, which was both a contemporary trauma and part of a legacy of such atrocities. The widely circulated photograph of Till's corpse is alleged then indeed to 'bear the trace of a particular moment of panic when there was massive reaction to the movement against separation' (Moten 2003, p. 195). Nonetheless, the episode and image also bear the trace of a 'phonic substance' that testifies to the presence of such violence since time immemorial, so much so that in relation to Till, 'that death was already haunted' (Moten 2003, p. 196).

This being the case, a particular reading strategy is required in interpreting the visual culture associated with African American experience. This involves attributing a phonic substance to the apparently purely visual, as well as deconstructing the opposition between live performance and the recorded or mechanically reproduced. For Moten, this type of interpretation is described in unavoidably hauntological terms: 'So that you need to be interested in the complex, dissonant, polyphonic affectivity of the ghost, the agency of the fixed but multiply apparent shade, an improvisation of spectrality, another development of the negative' (Moten 2003, p. 196). The words 'dissonant', 'polyphonic' and 'improvisation' also underline the specifically sonic aspect to this complex articulation.

Message rap and the Five Percent

I have considered in the past three sections some of the complex interrelations of gothic imagery and Marxist-inspired theorizing; the relations of this problematic to slavery; and Fred Moten's assertion of a relation of the latter problematic to the sonic register. In order to relate this broad context to the musical case study for this chapter, we need finally to highlight the dominant political creed influencing Gravediggaz' music, that of the Five Percent Nation and the hardcore rap it influenced.

Eric Allen Jr's (1996) essay on message rap summarizes the Five Percenters and their influence on hip hop culture. The movement is an offshoot of the Black Muslim organization, the Nation of Islam, founded by Clarence 13X after apparently being expelled from the Nation for teaching that 'all Black men are gods' (Allen, Jr. 1996, p. 165). As well as 'relativising divine authority', the Five Percenters hold that 85 per cent of society are 'slaves from mental death', 10 per cent are the rich ('the bloodsuckers of the poor') and 5 per cent are the poor (righteous teachers). We can see here an obvious source for the Gravediggaz' repeated references to their freeing the mentally dead. The Five Percenters also have an esoteric Supreme Mathematics and Supreme Alphabet. The Five Percenters were active in recruiting Harlem street youth in the 1960s – and they have often been criticized as little more than a street gang. Some trace the origins of the Five Percenters to a street gang called the Blood Brothers. LL Cool J, formerly loosely following the Five Percent when younger, acknowledged: 'We were just using the Five Percent label as a shield to do our dirty work – fighting and eventually robbing' (Knight 2007, p. 150). Whatever the case may be, their influence on hip hop has been considerable. The 'G' that is the seventh letter of the Supreme Alphabet, signifying God, became a standard greeting among the hip hop generation. The Five Percent reject the existence of a 'mystical god', insisting on the identification of God with Black men.

Michael Muhammad Knight has written about the close connections between the Five Percenters and hip hop music. He describes RZA (RZArector in Gravediggaz) as 'widely recognized as the Five Percent's ambassador to pop culture' (Knight 2007, p. 186) as well as quoting RZA as saying: '*In a lot of ways, hip hop is the Five Percent*' (cited in Knight 2007, p. 177; emphasis in original). The connections between this political/religious group and rap music could not be clearer. It is no surprise, then, that 'Blood Brothers' was the title of a track on the Gravediggaz debut LP.

In some ways we could compare the Five Percenters to Rastafari, in that it is a syncretism that combines various doctrinal elements, including ideas from world religion, Pan-Africanism and mysticism, and being associated with music of the African diaspora. Felicia M. Miyakawa characterizes the Five Percent's ideas as follows: 'Five Percenter theology is multiply grounded in Black Muslim Traditions, Black nationalism, Kemetic symbolism, Masonic mysticism, and Gnostic spirituality' (Miyakawa 2005, p. 5). Miyakawa cites various lyrics by Gravediggaz that reflect key ideas from the creed (see pp. 2, 49, 60), as well as revealing the design influence of the disc face of *The Pick, the Sickle and the Shovel* CD in the Islamic calligraphic art from a tenth-century Persian bowl (p. 129).

In fact, though the conflation of gothic imagery and political aspects is common to this strain of hip hop and Marxism, the solutions to the ills of capitalism are different in each case. It's worth pointing out that Gravediggaz were not nearly as successful in commercial terms as the RZA's other group, the Wu-Tang Clan. In his analysis of the hip hop business, *The Big Payback*, Dan Charnas highlights RZA's business acumen in obtaining non-exclusive deals for the Wu-Tang artists' solo albums with a separate deal for the group as a collective entity:

> Wu-Tang not only kept the right to determine the destinies of its members individually, but – fatefully – they also retained their *brand*: their name, their merchandising, and their publishing. Never before had hip hop artists negotiated the kind of autonomy that RZA did.
>
> (Charnas 2010, p. 449)

Indeed, their clothing brand, Wu Wear, became a multi-million-dollar spin-off industry, paving the way for Jay-Z's Rocawear and P Diddy's Sean John brands. Mark Anthony Neal (1999) has therefore described these rap entrepreneurs as 'petit bourgeois exploiters of hip hop's popularity' (p. 148).

Reflecting on hip hop's history in his 2008 book *Somebody Scream*, Marcus Reeves highlighted the importance for young African Americans of rap music after the decline of Black Power in the 1970s. In hip hop, the zenith of message rap was represented by the group Public Enemy. Public Enemy espoused a Black Muslim/Black nationalist creed; Chuck D also at times described himself as a communist. The group eventually foundered after the controversy of anti-Semitic comments from an errant member, Professor Griff. Reeves underlines the burden placed on the group at the time: 'the Griff storm [...] helped expose a vacuum of Black leadership within Black America, so much so that African Americans would mistake a rap group (cultural icons) for *real* political leadership' (2008, p. 82).

In fact, Public Enemy themselves were aligned with another strain of the Black Muslim culture associated with political rap, namely the Nation of Islam, from which the Five Percenters are an offshoot. Chuck D blames a specific interview with Professor Griff by David Mills of *The Washington Times* for undoing the PR work the group had achieved for Nation of Islam and its leader; Louis Farrakhan: 'by 1989 we had helped turn that around with our own form of media – Rap music. That one interview with Griff and Mills wiped all that shit away and threw us back to 1985' (Ridenhour and Jah 1997. p. 229).

Consumption and hypermasculinity

The most popular records following the Professor Griff controversy were gangsta rap records from N.W.A. and their followers, which represent another relation to capital. The commercial marginalization of message rap that followed is summarized by Miles White (2011) in the following terms:

> In the aftermath of the controversy, record companies apparently decided that highly politicized rap was bad for business. The political, nation-conscious rap that Public Enemy had defined was ultimately made commercially irrelevant, relegated to an alternative lifestyle on the margins of hip hop culture as it began to mainstream on the strength of N.W.A.'s bad nigger street swagger.
>
> (p. 75)

Eric K. Watts (2004) has described the 'symbiosis among street dictates and market strategy' (p. 606) that 'provides mythic justification for spectacular consumption' (p. 605). The gangsta MC feeds into the myth of Staggerlee (or Stackolee) such as analysed by Greil Marcus (1975/1977a) in relation to a musician from a previous generation, Sly Stone, as well as the pimp archetypes of blaxploitation movies from the 1970s. Fulmer (2002) discusses the supernatural connotations sometimes linked to this badman archetype: 'Stackolee, one of the most famous African American "badmen" heroes, supposedly sold his soul to enhance his supernatural powers' (p. 231). This latter sense appears more in line with horrorcore artists than the more secular gansta realism.

Reeves cites two examples of the 'realist' badman in rap: Notorious B.I.G. 'as supreme urban hustler, interpreted the crack game – just another form of capitalism – as a hood level way of fighting for Black empowerment' (2008, p. 191), and Jay-Z as 'the hardcore rapper as ghetto advocate', 'positioning himself as the conductor through which the joys, fears, and capitalistic pleasures of Black popular culture flowed' (p. 208). We might consider this the hegemonic rap MC identity, which has proved appealing ever since.

In addition and in keeping with traditions of race and representation analysed more widely by Stuart Hall (1997), masculinity is commonly constructed in hip hop music as spectacle. This might occur in music video, album covers or stage concerts, all of which might foreground the performing body to uphold and maintain norms of masculinity – if not hegemonic, nonetheless hypermasculinized, heteronormative and invulnerable. Nicole R. Fleetwood (2011) summarizes:

> In the context of Blackness and masculinity, authenticity imbues the subject with a mythic sense of virility, danger, and physicality; in representations of hip hop, authenticity most often manifests itself through the body of the young Black male who stands in for 'the urban real'.
>
> (p. 152)

There are obviously extreme limits placed on this form of hip hop as critique of the system since it often unproblematically extols capitalism as a model for the drugs game and rap entrepreneurship. It endorses stereotypes of Black male hypermasculinity offered as spectacle.

Conversely, it could be argued that – with its mysticism and emphasis on mental death authorized by the Five Percenters – the gothic version of rap exemplified by Gravediggaz uses supernatural imagery to figure themes of ghetto life that at least partially escapes from the mutual complicity between marketable 'street' personae and the complacency of an industry happy to rake in the dollars. Politically radical discourse, unfashionable and problematic in the wake of Public Enemy's clashes with the media, is submerged into a gothic lexis that figures the urban environment as demonic. Too Poetic on 'Constant Elevation' responds to a critic's injunction to 'go to hell' with the observation that he is already there. Gravediggaz' music is certainly a variant of hardcore rap. At times the lyrics feature the braggadocio, saltiness and masculine self-assertion that is built into the genre. However, this is not the dominant note in their music, which although featuring violence and darkness throughout, articulates these with the folkloric and supernatural elements that are so distinctive in their recordings.

The gothic provides a code from which to continue to explore the political economy of Black life commodified by the music industry; at a time when 'message rap' faced a sustained backlash from the media. In addition, the Five Percenters' esoteric alphabet and gnostic figures offer a type of spiritual guidance that promises enlightenment and escape from the gothic scenarios associated with urban life and ongoing exploitation by the music industry or wider society. We can see Gravediggaz' dark lyricism and gothic structure of feeling as an imaginative synthesis, which manages to overcome a contemporary impasse to political messages in rap, while drawing on existing narratives and frameworks from folklore and Black Muslim traditions.

RZA's sinister but funky soundscapes offer 'the complex, dissonant, polyphonic affectivity of the ghost' that Moten (2003, p. 196) associates with the cut, sublating the contradictions between the visual and the phonic, the live and the recorded (or dead). In the analogue samples that preserve the 'crackle' of worn vinyl, we might allude to Mark Fisher's assertion: 'It's no accident that sonic hauntology begins with the Afrofuturist sonic sciences of dub and hip hop, for time being out of joint is the defining feature of the Black Atlantic experience' (Fisher 2013, p. 50). For Moten (2003) and Fisher (2013), the sonic is tied explicitly to the ghostly temporality evoked by a specific articulation of cultural memories and folklore.

Nowhere to run

Saidiya Hartman (1997) argues that it is often in the more quotidian culture, indeed in entertainment, that we can meaningfully discern – or find sufficient distance to discuss – forms of domination associated with slavery and its legacy:

Rather than glance at the most striking spectacle with revulsion or through tear-filled eyes, we do better to cast our glance at the more mundane displays of power and the border where it is difficult to discern domination from recreation.

(p. 42)

Hartman's argument implies that rather than pursuing a direct ethnographic gaze, making an oblique glance at the legacy of slavery could better avoid any voyeurism or reduction of suffering to spectacle. One discrete cultural product which we might approach through these reading strategies is in the music and video for Gravediggaz' track 'Nowhere to Run' from their debut LP. The music video by David Shadi Perez intersperses footage of the group performing their rhymes in an urban backdrop; with shots of a man running down the middle of a city street, which we take to be Manhattan given the yellow cabs, and skyscrapers briefly in shot. The running man is clad initially in denims; throughout the video, there are dissolves that transform him to a barefoot figure stripped to the waist, with wrists manacled and chained.

The runaway slave imagery is unmistakable and underlines Gravediggaz' characteristic fusion of gothic tropes and social commentary. Later scenes see the running man set upon by Gravediggaz in a wooded environment. Among them is Too Poetic got up as a scarecrow tied to a stake; and RZA lunging towards him from the trees. Frukwan is present in the urban scenes, standing by security shutters covered with graffiti. Prince Paul makes an appearance in the wooded scenes at the end, to deliver the outtro. There is a goofy humour in the group's performance style that acts as a counterpoint to this otherwise gloomy scenario.

The outtro of 'Nowhere to Run' makes clear the complicity of industry with continued exploitation of African American artists. Prince Paul offers a sarcastic shout to the dishonest denizens of the recording industry, including A&R men damned by association. He also explicitly identifies the owners of the industry as the 'White man'. There could be no clearer indication that the music industry is figured here specifically in terms of racial capitalism. That this follows a gothic escaped slave narrative articulates once more both the cultural imagery and lexis of gothic, as well as the political context of the plantation and of capitalism.

The music supplements the visual track of the music video, manifesting the phonic substance that Moten argues is the necessary supplement to the purely visual in African American music. Moten's usual focus is jazz; 'Nowhere to Run' is one of several tracks of the era sampling Eugene McDaniels's 'Jagger the Dagger' (sections of which also grace A Tribe Called Quest's debut LP at several points).

This jazzy, soulful track is supplemented by sampled horn riffs and beats. The improvization that Moten discusses as crucial to the 'cut' is supplied by the MCs' rhymes, which provide the doom-laden scenario and sense of claustrophobia that form the starting point for the music video. Of course, the song title also brings into mind Martha and the Vandella's Motown hit, 'Nowhere to Run'. The Gravediggaz' nod to this song might seem ironic given the horrorcore tone of the later track. However, brief shots in the video of a couple arguing might allude to the lyrics of the earlier track and its focus on a toxic relationship; the presence of a young boy in these scenes might be interpreted as traumatic flashbacks to an unspecified domestic drama.

One aspect of the video's mise en scène that might support my wish to articulate the group's music to debates surrounding the Marxist import of gothic imagery is the costume design. The group wears loose-fitting garments of all Black, bearing a hammer and sickle logo with a shovel superimposed on top. It is indeed convenient for my argument in this chapter that the group are wearing signs signifying (on) both communism and gravedigging on their clothing! It also brings to mind Sollee's argument that gothic fashion in hip hop videos might be 'akin to the incorporation of an unexpected or unique sample in a track' (Sollee 2015, p. 254).

I hope to have established, then, that in this track and its music video we can see dramatized the various concerns associated with horrorcore and the African American gothic in popular music. The mise en scène riffs heavily on the runaway slave trope, bringing in visual conventions from psychological thriller and horror cinema, as well as affording Gravediggaz plenty of opportunity to throw gothic shapes, clad in Black with contrasting hammer, sickle and shovel logo. The lyrics afford RZA, Frukwan and Too Poetic opportunities for bars that combine menacing self-assertion humorously leavened with supernatural imagery; at the end Prince Paul explicitly frames the music industry as the true culprits, reflecting the group's personal grievances and an argument about ongoing exploitation of African American artists more generally.

As a coda to this section, as this chapter was nearing completion, a highly imaginative response to African American gothic was published by Leila Taylor, in her (2019) book *Darkly: Black History and America's Gothic Soul*. In a thought-provoking and sustained combination of reminiscence and cultural analysis, Taylor reflects on gothic identity as a Black American woman. She offers the following analysis of the musical genre featured in this chapter: 'nothing quite encapsulates the sound of the contemporary Black gothic as horrorcore, a subgenre of hip hop in which the classic themes of racism, gang violence, drugs, police brutality, and poverty use the language of horror movies to tell their story' (p. 224).

Conclusion

This chapter has considered some weighty political contexts in which to discuss the African American gothic – as well as some cultural traditions that inform it in popular culture. Debates around ghosts and haunting, capital and primitive accumulation, as well as the ongoing legacy of slavery, have all been seen as valid frameworks through which to interpret contemporary rap music. For critics such as Moten (2003), Hartman (1997) and Fisher (2013), popular culture such as music provides a key instance through which to read wider political contexts – and primal scenes associated with them – even if mediated obliquely in forms such as the gothic. At a time when presenting political ideas directly in music faced a cultural backlash, Gravediggaz present an interesting case study of a group that, as well as drawing on folkloric traditions, exemplified a particular cultural turn to gothic imagery in hip hop music and ancillary media.

Ultimately, gothic and horror tropes provided an imaginative resource for Gravediggaz that broke with the highly repetitive street narratives of 'keeping it real' and disingenuously uncritical 'reality' rap. The latter dominant strain of hip hop music faced the dilemma of cultural realisms – what is presented initially as a raw representation of unmediated reality can become very quickly an accepted narrative and formal schema, running the risk of repetitiveness despite continual attempts at variation within the musical template. Perhaps the more oblique mediation of political messages through gothic themes is, however, responsible for the untimely, still-fresh appeal of Gravediggaz' music.

7

Masculinity on trial: Noir Désir and perverse narcissism

This chapter will consider one of the most notorious episodes in the popular music history of France, involving Bertrand Cantat, the singer of the successful band Noir Désir. Some musicians are happy to play up their alleged monstrous status – or perhaps utilize such imagery with subversive or entertaining intent. The case study in this chapter explores the shock produced when an iconic figure is shown to be a 'monster' with no prior warning.

Though Noir Désir had previously been discussed in romantic terms that might be linked to monstrous vocabulary, after the events in question, mythic, literary and dramatic archetypes – contrasted with much more prosaic recent discourses derived from social sciences – became conflicting frameworks in which to discuss the events in question. We shall also see that associated with these two vocabularies were two rival conceptions of masculinity – one as solid, gregarious and republican; the other as violent, narcissistic and perverse.

Sombre heroes

In 2010, the French edition of music magazine *Rolling Stone* published a special issue with a list of their 100 essential French albums (Discogs 2016). The band Noir Désir had two entries in the top 10: their 1992 LP *Tostaky* at number 2 and their 1989 second album, *Veuillez rendre l'âme (à qui elle appartient)* (*Kindly Return the Soul (to Its Owner)*) at number 10. The only other artist with two in the top 10 was their late friend, Alain Bashung. Noir Désir also had albums placed at numbers 12, 21, 60. This would imply that for Francophone music critics, the band have a central, canonical position in such round-ups that we might compare to the Beatles, Stones or Bowie in comparable British lists. This is not necessarily to appeal to the authority of *Rolling Stone* as an arbiter of cultural value – but since Anglophone audiences have proved resistant to rock from outside the English-speaking world, some measures of critical and commercial success are helpful in underlining the centrality of the band to French popular music culture of the last few decades.

In commercial terms, by 1998 *Tostaky* had sold 400,000 copies while its follow-up, *666.667 Club* (1996) sold a million copies (Besse 2012, p. 92). The final studio album, *Des visages des figures* would equal the sales of the latter in three months in 2001 (Besse 2012, p. 122). By this time Noir Désir were certainly the most feted French rock band; they had also attracted critical acclaim and a certain cultural cachet both for their music and for their principled stance to the music industry and their engagement with left/liberal causes. Marc Besse, their biographer and others would often argue that at last there was a French rock band that bore comparison with their Anglophone influences (Besse 2012, p. 60).

Coming from Bordeaux, the band were already apart from the Parisian music industry and media, with whom they maintained a diffident relationship. Television appearances were very occasional; instead the band developed a loyal base of supporters through long and punishing tours as well as through increasingly prominent radio play. Their second album, *Veuillez rendre l'âme (à qui elle appartient)*, was their breakthrough. Produced by Ian Broudie, former producer for Echo and the Bunnymen and later in the Lightning Seeds, it included their first big hit, 'Aux sombres héros de l'amer'. The record has a recognizably rock/new wave sound that is melodic and less intense than the brace of albums to follow. Their fourth LP, *Tostaky*, considered a classic of French rock, was produced by Ted Nicely, the former Fugazi producer. The latter band's influence on Noir Désir is apparent on this album in the tight rhythms and brittle lead guitars mixed loud, as well as the hoarse, submerged vocals that signal the French group's distance from the ideals of clarity and prominence of the voice conventional in the French *chanson* (Isola 2004, p. 86). It also reflects what Matthew Bannister argues was the trajectory from indie to indie rock – 'a hardening of style towards a purist, "white noise" autonomy' and an 'often reified homosocial solidarity of rock' (Bannister 2006, p. xxvi). The later albums *666.667 Club* and *Des visages des figures*, however, widen the musical palette with instruments from electronic and various world musics, with more laid-back vocals and guitars to suit the looser, less frantic instrumentation.

Apart from their musical output, one thing that gained the band admiration from fans later on was its engagement with civil society (*citoyenneté*). This involved them supporting the *sans papiers* or undocumented migrants in the country as well as anti-globalization and gay rights. By 1997 they were supporters of Act Up as well as the Zapatistas in Mexico. They were alongside 148 other signatories (including film directors Jean-Luc Godard and Patrice Chéreau) for a petition protesting against the conviction of Act Up's president, Philippe Mangeot, for the latter's opposition to a clampdown on ecstasy consumption in gay clubs (Besse 2012, pp. 90–1). Above all, their opposition to the far right Front National (FN) was unstinting and won them enemies from its supporters. In 2002, after the FN came second in the first round of the presidential elections, the band put on a festival in Lyon, one of the far right's heartlands, with other French artists such as Yann Tierson, les Têtes Raides, Dominique A and Thomas Fersen in order to rally opposition to the fascists (Isola 2004, pp. 179–80).

The band were also able to strike some oppositional poses in relation to the music industry, despite being signed to the Barclay record label, part of Universal and home to big Francophone artists such as Charles Aznavour, Jacques Brel and Bashung. As stated, they avoided interviews with the press and on television, preferring to build a following via concerts and through the strength of their recordings. This places them within familiar conventions for 'alternative' if not independent rock bands of the era, about which, as David Hesmonhalgh (2013) noted: 'The critique of commerce was often self-contradictory and naïve' (p. 249). In this sense, one can make a comparison between Barclay and some British independent labels that were later subsumed under the majors, such as One Little Indian or Creation, both examined by Hesmondhalgh (1999), who casts doubt upon any direct association between loss of autonomy in a record label and 'negative aesthetic consequences' (p. 32).

Nonetheless, the singer of 'Noir Dez', Bertrand Cantat, made a widely publicized speech denouncing Jean-Marie Messier, the CEO of Universal, on the auspicious occasion of the 2002 Victoires de la Musique awards ceremony. In 1997, when the group had won the awards for best group and best single, 'none of four had deigned to make the trip to collect the statuette' (Besse 2012, p. 122). This time around in 2002, Cantat used it as a soapbox to harangue Messier as part of the band's sometimes rather vague denunciation of globalization. Cantat was evidently resentful of Messier's name-checking of the band in his claim that one in four records of the company were being exported to the United States, a claim which for Cantat smacked of an attempt to cash in on Noir Désir's cachet to boost the conglomerate's share price.

Despite the irony of Noir Désir being signed to Barclay (which the band were at pains to describe as one of the small labels alluded to in the speech above), the speech was taken by sympathetic listeners as emblematic of Noir Désir's left/alternative credibility.

The 'drama' of Vilnius

Unfortunately, of course, Noir Désir's fame, or notoriety, rests on more than just their music. For the band's singer, Bertrand Cantat, was in 2004 found guilty by Lithuanian justice for the 'murder committed with indirect, undetermined intent' (Bouchet and Vézard 2013, p. 300) of his then partner, the actress Marie Trintignant. A journalistic account of the affair is provided by Stéphane Bouchet and Frédéric Vézard, whose *Mort à Vilnius* (2004), like the book by the victim's mother Nadine Trintignant, *Ma fille; Marie* (2003) was published before the trial of Cantat. Bouchet was the first French journalist to arrive in Vilnius to cover the case. His summary of the Lithuanian and French investigations, though questioned by those close to Cantat (see Cantat 2004), offers a reconstruction of the events leading up to and during the fatal attack on Marie Trintignant. Ed Vulliamy (2003a) also published a comprehensive account of the case and its cultural context in *The Guardian* newspaper.

Bertrand Cantat was introduced to Marie Trintignant by his sister Anne, who accompanied Trintignant to a concert by Noir Désir, in Vaison-la-Romaine on 3 July 2002 (Bouchet and Vézard 2004, p. 31). They met again at another concert on 27 July, on which date they exchanged numbers (p. 46). Their relationship developed via text message. By October, Cantat had left his wife Kristina Rady, mother of his two children, while Trintignant had left her husband, the film director Samuel Benchétrit, father of one of her four sons (p. 48). The practicalities of child care frequently complicated a relationship which was frequently described by friends and family in terms of 'adolescence' (pp. 23, 48). On 25 May 2003, the couple arrived in Lithuania, where Trintignant was to shoot her final film, a made-for-television biopic of the French writer Colette directed by her mother Nadine (Bouchet and Vézard 2004, p. 55).

According to Bouchet and Vézard, on the day of the attack of 26 July, Cantat had been unnerved by a text message received to Marie Trintignant's phone by her ex-partner Samuel Benchétrit, who was in post-production with another film he had shot, *Janis et John* (2003), with Trintignant in the first eponymous role. Benchétrit addressed Trintignant in the text message as 'Ma petite Janis' ('My little Janis'), an affectionate diminutive that prompted a jealous rage on the part of Cantat up to, during and even after the attack on Trintignant, an obsession described by Bouchet and Vézard as an *idée fixe* (p. 67). While Trintignant lay in a coma in a neighbouring room, Cantat had two long phone conversations with Benchétrit lasting 59 minutes and 24 minutes, between 1:46 and 3:15 in the morning following the assault (pp. 70–3). This followed an initial call of 7 minutes a few hours before, after 10:15 pm. Cantat had badgered Trintignant on the final day of shooting about the significance of the text message. The couple had been present at drinks party following the end of shooting (p. 63), consuming alcohol and smoking spliffs according to those present. The couple declined to follow some of the party to a nightclub but spent a while in the apartment of a Lithuanian who had been on set, Andrius Leliuga (p. 66).

Cantat's behaviour in the apartment was unsettling: at one stage he leapt to the neighbour's balcony, at another he smashed a glass against the wall of the apartment. All present consumed copious amounts of vodka; other substances were alleged to have been ingested though this was subsequently denied by Leliuga and Cantat himself. The assault took place after the couple's return alone to their apartment in the Domina Plaza hotel in Vilnius. The discussion returned to the text message and to the complicated relationships between Cantat and Trintignant and their ex-partners. Shouting of an 'aggressive' nature was heard by the resident of the neighbouring room, a UK national named Gary Tuck (p. 214). This was followed by a fierce assault by Cantat that left Trintignant in an irreversible coma. The cause of death according to the post-mortem examination was cerebral oedema.

The details of the assault are horrifying. Cantat admitted on arrest slapping Trintignant hard around the face, with the front and back of his hand, on which rings added to the injuries sustained. However, the pathologists undertaking the autopsy judged that slaps would not be sufficient to account for the full injuries sustained, which included damage consistent with violent shaking as well as a punch or head-butt to the face. The doctors noted the smashed and crushed bones to the nose sustained by Trintignant, which they deemed too severe to have been inflicted by a slap of the hand, however violent (Bouchet and Vézard 2004, p. 146).

As mentioned above, Cantat did not seek medical assistance for his partner after the brutal assault. His telephone conversations to Benchétrit continued Cantat's obsession with the nature of the former's relationship to Trintignant. Subsequent to these phone calls, Cantat was visited by Vincent Trintignant, whom he reassured about his sister's state. As he had with Benchétrit previously, Cantat appeared to want to engage Vincent Trintignant in an interminable conversation about their relationship rather than admitting what had occurred earlier that night, between himself and his injured partner lying in the adjoining room. The pathologists confirmed that the latter would have required immediate medical assistance were she to have any chance of surviving the injuries. It was only around 9 am that Marie Trintignant was finally admitted to hospital.

I will not linger further on the details of the attack, though it is necessary to note and not to minimize the severity of the assault upon Marie Trintignant. For our purposes here, it is the reaction on the part of the media, the band's fans and certain writers and academics, which are my focus in the rest of this chapter. As we shall see, reactions sometimes reflected a psychic splitting on the part of commentators between Cantat the man and the monstrous act with which he was now charged. Those struggling to account for the 'drama of Vilnius' at times preferred secular, psychological or sociological explanations; at others, a monstrous vocabulary drawing on literary and romantic precedents was invoked.

After Marie Trintignant was flown back to France from Lithuania to finish her life, the presence of the press at the airport of Bourget was deemed by one journalist cited in Bouchet and Vézard to be the biggest media frenzy since the death of Princess Diana (Bouchet and Vézard 2004, pp. 135–6). The relationship between one of France's biggest rock stars and the late actress became a national preoccupation during this time.

Reading accounts by writers sympathetic to, or especially those who knew Cantat before the events of Vilnius, is to become familiar with a discourse that stresses the importance of 'saving the honour' of the singer, or some similar formulation, who nonetheless is deemed on that night to have gone beyond the point of no return (*commis l'irréparable,* Beauvallet in Besse 2012, p. 15). There is an attempt to highlight Cantat's involvement in various left-wing causes as well as the band's principled approach to the music industry not as mitigating circumstances for his actions, certainly, but as something that would, somehow, be unjust to forget in formulating an overall opinion on him as a person.

Perverse narcissism

In his first interview with the music press since his release, Cantat stated, 'It is awful, abject to have become the symbol of violence against women' (Beauvallet 2014). Cantat's various attempts at comebacks have been met with controversy. *The Guardian* in the UK published pieces by Jessica Reed (2013) and Suzanne Moore (2012), the latter criticizing a collaboration of Cantat with Malian musicians Amadou and Mariam. French weekly *Le Point* (2014) quoted the victim's mother in 2014 denouncing a stage appearance of Cantat as 'obscene' (*très indécent*).

In fact, the killing of Marie Trintignant came at a time in which various social scientific discourses on violence against women were finding their way into mass media in France. I shall mention two paradigms seeking to contextualize such acts that were explicitly linked in media discussions with this particular case. The first of these is provided by the psychiatrist and psychotherapist, Marie-France Hirigoyen, whose 1998 book, *Le harcèlement moral, la violence perverse au quotidien* was a best seller as well as being alluded to explicitly by Nadine Trintignant, the mother of Marie, as a framework in which to understand domestic violence, in terms of which she saw the events of Vilnius (Trintignant 2003, p. 41). Vulliamy (2003a, 2003b) also discusses Hirigoyen's arguments in relation to the case. Such a framework provides a type of 'secular' account of everyday (*quotidien*) monstrous behaviour, which sometimes lapses into deadly acting-out.

Of course, narcissism, as a diagnostic category, finds canonical exposition in psychoanalytic literature, particularly in Freud's metapsychological essay of 1914, 'On Narcissism: An Introduction' (Freud 1914/1991a). Hirigoyen's work popularized the term *pervers narcissique* ('narcissistic pervert') as a category describing what we might call 'abusive partners' perhaps in English. Where Freud would often stress that his use of terminology such as that of perversion was designed to be merely classificatory, Hirigoyen appears to be using perversion in a moral sense – she speaks repeatedly of 'moral harassment' (*harcèlement moral*). As a culture more at home with psychoanalytic discourse, drawing on Freudian terminology is perhaps less surprising than it would be in the Anglophone world. The most lucid definition is provided in a quotation Hirigoyen makes from Alberto Eiguer:

> Narcissistic perverse individuals are those who, under the influence of their grandiose self, try to create a connection with a second individual, more

particularly by attacking the narcissistic integrity of the other in order to disarm it. They also attack the self-love, self-confidence, self-esteem and the self-belief of the other.

(cited in Hirigoyen 1998, p. 151)

The phrase *pervers narcissique* was explicitly used on French television to describe Cantat by the actress and singer Lio, friend of Marie Trintignant's mother, Marie. Lio appeared on France 2, TF1 and Canal Plus in order to discuss the case, to the disgust of Xavier Cantat, the accused's brother, who in his autobiographical account of the case has the following to say of Lio:

> This *passionaria* of the media who lived for many months with an alcoholic cocaine fiend who spent his time insulting her children and beating her (and whom she would end up convicting through the courts) thinks that she possesses all the moral qualities in particular to bear the titles of psychiatric expert, legal doctor, prosecutor and even music critic.
>
> (Cantat 2004, pp. 92–3)

The unsavoury implication of Xavier Cantat's words here seems to be that being involved in an abusive relationship would call for more discretion in discussing the relationships of others.

It is interesting here to quote the diagnosis made by a psychologist examining Bertrand Cantat towards the end of 2005. Cantat is described as having: 'a dependent personality, a narcissistic fragility … All these signs favoured a passionate relationship that activated intense anxieties that facilitated the acting out (*passage à l'acte*), then a secondary depressive phase (*passage*) after the death of his partner' (cited in Besse 2012, p. 179).

Some of the features of the narcissistic perverse position appear to model the behaviour of Cantat leading up to the events. Hirigoyen notes that perverse behaviour can be put in place when there is 'too great a proximity with the loved object' (Hirigoyen 1998, p. 22). One recalls the repeated description by their friends of the two forty-something lovers being in an 'amorous bubble' (*bulle amoureuse*, Bouchet and Vézard 2004, pp. 51–5). According to Denis Barthe, the band's drummer, this bubble was in part sustained through marijuana consumption (cited in Vulliamy, 2003a). This proximity becomes a 'relation of domination' (*emprise*) of the narcissistic pervert over his or her partner.

Another of Hirigoyen's assertions is that moments in which the victim threatens a separation or to flee the abusive relationship are in fact fraught with the danger of physical (not just psychological) violence: 'Perverse violence appears in moments of crisis when an individual who has perverse defences cannot assume the responsibility for a difficult choice' (Hirigoyen 1998, p. 28). In relation to the event of Vilnius, Cantat himself cited Marie Trintignant's repeated 'Go to your wife' ('*Va chez ta femme*') just before the tussle he alleges preceded his fatal assault on her. According to the French sociologist Maryse Jaspard, in fatal cases, 'Break-up is the principal motive of the murderers: they cannot stand a separation wished for by the other party' (Jaspard 2011, p. 48); furthermore, one-third of these murders is committed under the influence of alcohol (p. 53).

Continuing in this vein, some of the characteristics of this alleged personality type identified by Hirigoyen chime with subsequent revelations about Cantat's behaviour upon release from prison. I will mention two particular episodes that hint at an ongoing pattern of behaviour that fits this scheme.

The first of these emerged in reporting of the suicide of Cantat's wife, Kristina Rady, who had stood by Cantat during the trial and afterwards. Cantat's child found her body around midday on 10 January 2010; she had hanged herself (Bouchet and Vézard 2013, p. 329). It was not until 27 February 2013 that *Voici* magazine published excerpts from a message left by Rady on her parents' voice mail while they were on holiday. Among the transcription are the following two, troubling extracts:

> Yesterday, I almost lost a tooth, this thing that I don't know how to name is going so much worse [words inaudible] … He seized my telephone, my glasses, he threw something at me. My elbow is completely swollen, I even broke a cartilage, but that is not important provided I can still speak about it.
>
> What I am feeling is difficult to imagine: Bertrand is mad, he thinks that I am the great love of his life and that, apart from some small slips, everything is going well. In the street, of course, everyone considers him as an icon, as an example; as a star. Everyone hopes that he is happy. But when he returns to the house, he makes me suffer horrible things in front of our children (cited in Bouchet and Vézard 2013, p. 323).

Rady's parents were interviewed in *Paris Match* on 22 November 2012; the title of the article was: 'He Terrorised Her' (p. 326). It should be noted that the couple sued *Paris Match* for libel on 6 December 2012 though they did not sue *Voici* from whom the extracts above are quoted.

The second instance, less chilling perhaps but still consistent with this diagnosis, is reported by the band's biographer, Marc Besse, in relation to the group's split at the end of 2010. According to Besse, rehearsals were strained with the band due to Cantat's writer's block – in contrast to the time before his incarceration, Cantat was unable to write lyrics. The decisive rupture took place in the Brasserie des Arts in the band's native Bordeaux. Later, the band's guitarist Serge Teyssot-Gay revealed the reasons for his departure and the group's subsequent break-up:

> We were all sat here. All at once, in the discussion, Bertrand changed completely and behaved like a shit. He told us about everything. He positioned himself as a victim. All at once, he was the victim of everything. Vilnius was not his fault … As if Marie had slipped on a bar of soap. Kristina, that wasn't his fault … It was she who was unhappy, etc. He accused all of us of needing his fame.
> (Besse 2012, p. 213)

Teyssot-Gay noted his familiarity with this strategy of Cantat's to cause a rupture in a relationship by provoking his ex-partners to split with him – and then blaming them for the split. This self-centred refusal to accept responsibility and to pose as the victim is characteristic of the narcissism that Hirigoyen outlines. This also places Cantat firmly in a line of indie or alternative rock narcissists discussed by Matthew Bannister. Drawing on Michael Azerrad's account of Dinosaur Jr's J. Mascis, Bannister summarizes this personality as follows: 'an almost textbook male narcissist – a sadistic voyeur who although apparently passive and blank, causes others to act out and injure themselves mentally and physically' (Bannister 2006. p. 149).

Of course there are dangers in pursuing pop-psychoanalysis-at-a-distance in this manner; it is nonetheless a pertinent framework in which to discuss the case since it was itself heavily mediated, as stated, in Nadine Trintignant's best-selling book about her daughter as well as in her friend Lio's numerous television interviews. One should conversely point out Cantat's repeated admissions of his guilt and of 'having done what cannot be undone' (*commis l'irréparable*) in press and in court, which is incompatible with the narcissistic position as described by Hirigoyen.

The second theoretical framework to make some inroads to the public sphere was feminist-informed sociological analysis of domestic violence, or 'violence against women' – the researchers were keen to extend their analysis to public spaces and the workplace, as well as to psychological as well as physical abuse. This is the second 'secular' perspective that was presented in the public sphere to account for the monstrous behaviour evident in this particular case.

According to Maryse Jaspard, in the 1980s, despite some opposition by feminists opposed to reformism, the Left government institutionalized 'State feminism' and actively supported feminist research (Jaspard 2011, p. 13). In a country that had conducted little systematic research into the question, the time was now ripe for an extensive questionnaire survey into women's experience of violence. This is what occurred in 2000 with the publication of the Enveff report (Jaspard, Demur and Enveff 2002) following the survey of violence against women in France. The preliminary results were published in the beginning of 2001, with the first findings disseminated at the end of 2000 (Jaspard 2011, p. 24). Florence Maillochon highlights the partial reporting of the results of the survey in the media, who were keener to reproduce a single headline figure of 1 in 10 women being victims of domestic violence, construed in physical terms. Despite the subsequent usefulness of this round statistic in political and policy debates, the Enveff survey sought to emphasize continuities between physical and psychological violence, the latter of which this figure included; the press discussion however focused solely on 'battered women' (Maillochon 2007, p. 50).

In addition, subsequent fuller reporting and analysis was largely passed over or even opposed in anti-feminist diatribes. The sociologist Éric Fassin discusses the interesting implications of these polemics against Enveff, as part of a republican refusal of all attempts to politicize sexuality. In France, these polemics would argue, sexuality is a part of the private sphere, not part of public life (Fassin 2007, p. 288). Partly informing this, according to Fassin, was a conception of France contrasted with Anglo-Saxon tabloid culture: 'to denounce the politicisation of sexuality, is also to oppose the Americanization of French culture' (p. 290).

Fassin (2007) also links the reluctance to take the Enveff findings on board partially to an us-and-them attitude in the wider culture that would seek to attribute violence (including sexual violence) to particular ethnicities (p. 291). In part, he argues, this is at the basis of the widespread praise at this time for the grassroots feminist movement Ni Putes Ni Soumises (literally 'Neither Whores Nor Submissive'); the media were according to him more welcoming of a feminist movement against violence based in the multiracial *banlieux* than with a feminist sociological study of such violence observing its effects among the entire nation. It was easier for the media and public commentators to see the need for feminism in the multiracial suburbs – than among the population of France at large.

It was in fact the Cantat-Trintignant case itself that ended the mediated backlash against the Enveff survey (Jaspard 2011, p. 26). As Maillochon (2007) observes:

> It was thus necessary to wait for another 'event' for the Enveff survey paradoxically to win its spurs and finally to be the object of a genuine scientific review: the hospitalisation and tragic death of an actress under the blows of her lover.
>
> (p. 48)

Maillochon observes that it was only after Trintigant's fate that the quality newspaper *Le Monde* finally published an in-depth article on the question of domestic violence. So far from the killing of Marie Trintignant serving merely as a repellent illustration of the phenomena registered in the survey, it in fact helped disseminate the survey's findings at a time when it had faced either indifference or reactionary polemics against it. Vulliamy (2003b) notes the boost that the publicity for the case provided for Ni Putes Ni Soumises and another feminist group, La Fédération Nationale Solidarité Femmes. The singer of Noir Désir may have thought it 'awful, abject to have become the symbol of violence against women' – yet by late 2003 this is exactly what he had become in public and media discussion.

Critical stupefaction and fan mourning

Critics and fans sympathetic to the band faced a dilemma in the immediate aftermath of the killing. Bertrand Cantat was not only the charismatic frontman of the band, but he was also admired for his civic virtues and political engagement. Though it may seem lazy to make the comparison, and though the personnel and national context are very different, the story seems to restage Sid Vicious's killing of Nancy Spungen while recasting the murderer not as the nihilist Vicious but rather as Joe Strummer. Such was the impact of this event for French rock fans, which seemed to issue in the downfall not only of a talented singer but also of someone who had been admired as a human being. How to deal with the revelation that one's idol is not only a killer, but apparently a misogynist one to boot? Bouchet and Vézard (2013) point to the lack of home-grown precedents for this and, after mentioning Vicious and Phil Spector, claim that these Anglophone artists are at odds with Cantat's image 'of the contented father (*père tranquille*) who walks with his family in the markets of Bordeaux' (Bouchet and Vézard 2013, p. 169).

One of the publications most sympathetic to Noir Désir and to Cantat, to this day, is the French music paper *Les Inrockuptibles* (the name is a pun on *incorruptibles*). We can follow the reactions of some of the band's staunchest advocates in the press – and some of their devoted fans – in the articles and letters pages that followed the murder in the issues that followed.

The first editorial after the news broke, from the issue dated 6–12 August 2003, is entitled 'Black night' ('*Nuit noire*'). Describing their reaction as 'stupefaction and pain', the piece first of all underlines the state of uncertainty as to what precisely has happened at the time of going to press. Nonetheless, the editorial advances the following preliminary verdict: 'The simple thing that one has the right to affirm is that it is a matter of love, passion and death. An intimate, private affair. Whence the obligation to approach it with sobriety, discretion and respect' (*Nuit noire* 2003, p. 3).

Cantat and Trintignant are further described in the following terms: 'two exceptional (*hors du commun*) personalities and artists: unbending, upright, generous, totally sincere, uncompromising'. One can see here perhaps the Republican attitude to relationships described by Éric Fassin above – a reluctance to 'politicise' intimacy, while nonetheless paying tribute to the characters of Cantat and Trintignant. Less generously perhaps, we might describe it as a near denial of the brutality of Cantat's actions. A repeated trope in the coverage that follows was that domestic violence is a banal albeit repellent news item (*fait divers*), but that here we have a crime of passion (*crime passionnel*) whose actors transcend the quotidian.

The journalist Arnaud Vivant, writing in the same issue, states that upon hearing the news 'there are very many of us who were immediately traumatised. Profoundly shattered' (Vivant 2003, p. 11). What follows is worth quoting at length:

> Bertrand Cantat is not just the singer of Noir Désir: he has become for many the spokesperson of our generation of idealists. He fights for the good, he is engaged, generous, upright, uncompromising, one of the big voices, always ready, always prepared as they say in the scouts, for anti-globalisation, in other words the often idealistic and sometimes clumsy fight for a better world. And now he has committed an absolute evil, now he has perhaps killed someone.
>
> (p. 11)

It would be hard to find a better characterization of the reaction by many in the pages of *Les Inrocks*, the contraction by which the paper is often known.

One way of broadly characterizing such responses is in terms of mourning, especially if, following Freud's 1915 essay on 'Mourning and Melancholia', we observe that 'Mourning is regularly the reaction to the loss of a loved person, or to the loss of some abstraction which has taken the place of one, such as one's country, liberty, an ideal, and so on' (Freud 1991b, pp. 251–5). Cantat's position as public figure engaged with progressive causes is added in many responses to the personal significance of the singer's music. The mourning of the ideal of an engaged political artist is added to the loss of a band soundtracking the fans' everyday lives.

The next issue of 13–19 August 2003 publishes letters received to the paper from fans of Noir Désir. One of the most personal reactions comes from a fan signing as Overmarsapril:

> Everyone's dying this summer. My aunt, my grandmother, Marie Trintignant. Strangely, it is the passing of the person who is least close to me which has most devastated me (*démoli*). Because it's an enormous waste, and because her death is the act of a person who was for me like an example on the musical and civic level.
>
> (*Ping-Pong* 2003a, p. 16)

Once again we have the combination of shock, mourning and disillusionment that pervades the immediate reaction by advocates of the band, professional or fan.

One fan refers to a letter received to the letters pages of the paper *Libération*, in which a fan has pledged to get rid of his Noir Désir records following the death. The fan writing to *Les Inrocks*, a certain Clément Masse, writes:

> We thought we were going to grow old with Noir Désir, with their values, their music and the words of Cantat [...] I will not send back my records like the reader of *Libération*. Impossible. Their music is too much part of me and of what I love. I just want to understand.
>
> (*Ping-Pong*, 2003a, p. 16)

This is echoed by Christophe (p. 18), who feels for Cantat and fears no longer hearing the band on the radio or seeing their videos. A correspondent signing as Barbara states her lack of surprise at the downfall of the tormented singer but asserts that she listened to the band night and day while recovering from a suicide attempt. For Debby C, the band helped her pass her happiest years as a youth and young adult: 'And I am not the only one' (p. 17). Demo, who respects Cantat as much as Serge Gainsbourg or Neil Young, writes 'We love you despite what you have done' (p. 16).

In fact, as well as *Les Inrocks*, the left-wing paper *Libération* was largely sympathetic to the band and their politics. The newspaper's editorial on Friday 1 August was by the journalist and film critic Antoine de Baecque, who describes the events as 'A tear-jerking (*triste à en pleurer*) drama of passion', as well as speaking of the mixed feelings of 'betrayal' and 'compassion' felt by the newspaper staff (cited in Bouchet and Vézard 2004, p. 138). We can see once more the lexis of drama and tragedy to describe the events.

Some admirers of the band used the letters page as a forum to defend the reputation of their idol. Gaetano writes the following: 'To be a fan, or simply to like Noir Désir, is to vibrate with the essence of Rock itself. Rock in its noble sense: revolt, violence, anger against injustice, the system. Everything that produces inequalities' (*Ping-Pong*, 2003a, p. 16). And Sébastien Tricart wishes to defend Cantat against the non-music press: 'Never has the word "rock" sounded as negative (*péjoratif*) as in the mouth of these fucking mainstream (*généralistes*) journalists who are going to massacre Bertrand's image once more, like wild animals' (p. 17). We note in passing here the bestialization not of Cantat but of journalists, likened to wild animals in their reporting of the case.

There is at least one person who takes a less sympathetic view of the affair. More in line with feminist commentators, and sympathizers with the Trintignant family, someone writing as Patrick points out: 'Let's not talk about love in this story. You don't destroy the brains of someone whom you love with your fists' (p. 17).

Published correspondence to *Les Inrockuptibles* dated 20–26 August 2003 opens with a letter signed by Claude Faber, journalist and writer; Armand Gatti, author and playwright; and Hélène Châtelain, film director and writer. The correspondents defend Cantat as 'worthy of being considered as a brother' and state that they refuse the role of 'spectators, voyeurs and judges' that they feel imposed upon them. In addition, they take the characterization of the murder as a drama of passion to new heights:

> Bertrand is today on a stage which is not his own. In the skin of a character who is not written for him. The actor in a tragedy that does not correspond to him and from which nonetheless he cannot struggle free. A tragedy where everything seems unreal.

> As in Greek tragedies, two families must henceforth carry burdens of pain within them. And henceforth history will recall (*retient*) that Marie and Bertrand are tied more than ever. United and inseparable. Other than that she is dead and he, living. The drama is complete.
>
> (Faber, Gatti and Châtelain 2003, p. 15)

The letter signed jointly by these three did not go without challenge. Two issues later a reader from Lyon signing herself Emanuelle reads back the writers' own words with a telling rejoinder:

> *Our companion needs to recover his honour. In the name of what he really is. A man worthy of being considered as a brother.* For me, nothing other than a man who has killed, with his own hands, a woman whose speech, behaviour – it matters little – upset him.
>
> (*Ping-Pong*, 2003b, p. 14; emphasis in original)

We see a similar letter of defence to that of Gatti et al. in the letters pages of the next issue, 27 August to 2 September 2003, by the writer Bernard Comment. Like others, Comment considers Cantat 'a friend' and resists calls to stop listening to Noir Désir 'out of decency'. In addition, he rejects the subsumption of what he sees as an individual case under the wider feminist concern with violence against women. Once more he prefers to see this as private tragedy:

> As for the Swiss daily *Le Temps* or the weekly *Elle* and even *Le Monde*, there was an editorial do-gooder (*très bonne âme*) there each time, under the guise of analysis, debating the drama of beaten women ... Are they so sure that Marie Trintignant would have appreciated being claimed as this type of icon and that she would subscribe to this condemnation which reveals a tendency to repress the singular tragedy under sociological statistics?
>
> (Comment 2003. p. 15)

It is with some relief that the reader comes to the final letter that I will cite in this correspondence, towards the end of the discussion that had been going on in August and September in the music paper. Nelly Kaprèlian, a journalist for the paper, heads her letter, 'Cantat, a romantic hero?' Her opening is scathing: 'This act is not that of Bertrand Cantat, but the consequence of his absolute love for Marie Trintignant. What a ridiculous romanticisation of the situation: in France, romanticism excuses everything' (Kaprèlian 2003, p. 26). Continuing in this vein, she describes as inexcusable the 'retrospective aestheticisation' of the death of Trintignant. She concludes: 'It's up to the courts to judge the act of a man in all his complexity. Not a left-wing singer who reads Rimbaud' (Kaprèlian 2003, p. 26). We will see in the next section how monstrous imagery from romanticism and symbolism was drawn on by some as a sort of 'poetic' framework for the case more widely.

Nadine Trintignant, the mother of Marie, also highlighted this tendency to appeal to Cantat's left-wing sympathies as an attempt to appeal to his better instincts, in her book published shortly before the trial of Cantat in Vilnius. She notes the assertion of a friend who in his letter describes Cantat as 'This false apostle of the big causes' and, apostrophizing her deceased daughter throughout the text, here she has the following observation:

> Of course, I do not know the circumstances well, but it is impossible for me not to make the link between the horrible act that has afflicted you and the forms of machismo that, to my mind, persist in milieus that are artistic and assimilated to the left. Each time I have made this remark in the past, my interlocutors have been flabbergasted, outraged, as if belonging to a certain cultural family definitively dissociated them from any form of barbarism, of racial or sexual discrimination.
>
> (Trintignant 2003, p. 17)

As an afterword to the discussion that took place in the immediate weeks after the event in *Les Inrocks*, it is interesting to compare the line taken by Jean-Daniel Beauvallet in his interview with Cantat a decade later, Cantat's first for the music paper since the events of 2003. In his introduction, Beauvallet describes the editorial line of the paper in wishing to conduct an interview with Cantat after his release:

> If we wanted to speak to him, it was that beyond the consternation caused by the death of Marie Trintignant, beyond the terror in the face this absurd murder of passion (*meurtre passionnel*), we did not recognise the Bertrand Cantat described by a certain press that had largely beaten in lousiness (*dégueulasserie*), lynchings and summary trials, the English tabloids that France knows so well how to point the finger at.
>
> (Beauvallet 2014)

In many ways the terms of reference are unchanged – the 'passionate' nature of the crime, the fundamental decency of Cantat despite his act, and the republican opposition to the public discussion of relationships (Fassin's 'politicisation of sexuality' discussed above), here identified with the Anglophone press.

Romantic monsters and cursed poets

Candice Isola's study of the band from a musicological perspective written before the events of Vilnius begins from the premise that 'the most common term to qualify the group remains that of "romantic"' (Isola 2004, p. 9). She considers the roots of this adjective in the Romantic movement of the eighteenth and nineteenth centuries, particularly in relation to French poetry, of which Cantat was a noted admirer. Isola traces a line from the nineteenth-century 'cult of the ego' in Romantic poetry to the importance of the first person singular in rock, in this case particularly singer of Noir Désir: 'Without wishing to deny the importance and the value of the other members, if there is someone who can incarnate the Romantic "I," it is Bertrand Cantat' (pp. 29–30).

Other French commentators allude to the 'cursed poets' (*poètes maudits*) of Symbolist poetry that also find an echo in the band's lyrics and statements. Besse (2012, p. 21) quotes the group's first interview in French music paper *Les Inrockuptibles* in which although Cantat likens his band to Faulkner, Selby or Tenessee Williams, the terms he cites seem applicable to the generations of Baudelaire or Rimbaud: 'In their books, in our pieces too, people are damned from the beginning [*dès l'origine*].' Besse also reminds us of the lyrics from 'Bouquet de nerfs', which similarly allude to themes of culpability and damnation present in Symbolism and Decadence.

Unsurprisingly, tropes from literature and myth, as well as from loosely romantic archetypes found their way into discussion of the events of Vilnius and the relationship of Cantat and Trintignant beforehand. We have already seen Nelly Kaprèlian's criticism of this framework evident in the letters in *Les Inrocks* and other publications sympathetic to Noir Désir.

Romanticism in the more quotidian sense of idealizing love relationships informs some of the discussion of the relationship between Cantat and Trintignant. In their journalistic reconstruction of the events leading up to and taking place in Vilnius, Bouchet and Vézard (2004) refer to the fatal events as a 'night of madness' (*nuit de folie*) (p. 11) for an 'extraordinary couple' (*couple hors normes*) (p. 15). As is almost a formula for many reports of the event at the time, there it is noted that such events are familiar from 'sadly banal news items' (p. 13), but that here the extraordinary protagonists elevate this 'tragedy' above the everyday. Later on the relationship of these forty-somethings is described as 'a form of eternal adolescence with a stormy destiny' (p. 23).

We can see such frameworks in a lineage of representations of *amour fou* (mad love) that pervade French (and European) culture. From the world of literature one might mention the Surrealist poet André Breton, who as well as writing a book entitled *L'Amour fou* (1937), gave one of the enduring representations of such doomed love in his 1928 book *Nadja*, based on the poet's own relationship with a woman with mental illness. Closer to the time of Cantat and Trintignant, one of the most successful films of the 1980s glossy *cinema du look* featured another such doomed heroine in *Betty Blue* (*37°2 le matin*) (Jean-Jacques Beineix 1986), in which the eponymous character, played by Béatrice Dalle, after a descent into mental illness, is finally smothered by her boyfriend. Around the same time as this case, Bruno Dumont's *Twentynine Palms* (2003) provides another example of the trope. For Vulliamy (Vulliamy 2003a), the Trintignant case put cultural notions of the 'crime of passion' (*crime passionel*) itself on trial.

Elsewhere, tropes of monstrosity or bestiality, or of the past coming back to haunt its protagonists, are used to characterize the relationships and occasionally the characters of those concerned. One of the most troubling instances of this imagery was allegedly given in a conversation with Cantat's late wife, Kristina Rady, whom Cantat had left to pursue his relationship with Marie Trintignant. After the arrest of Cantat, the other band members of Noir Désir as well as Rady took a private flight to Vilnius to arrive on Sunday, 27 July 2003, beating most of the French press to the destination.

One of Marie Trintignant's circle, the makeup artist for the shoot in Vilnius, Agnès Tassel, sat next to Rady in the hotel in order to ask her about her ex-partner. Tassel made a subsequent statement to the crime squad in Paris, in which she reported asking Rady, 'Was Bertrand violent with you?' to which she received the response 'Yes'. When asking Rady why she had stayed with Cantat for eleven years, Tassel got the response, 'Because he was also capable of great tenderness, but when I felt the violence coming, I left.' Tassel then asked, 'But then he's Doctor Jekyll and Mister Hyde?' to which Rady again replied 'Yes' (Bouchet and Vézard 2004, p. 95).

Bouchet and Vézard (2004) describe the French police as 'haunted' (p. 167) by this characterization of Cantat as Jekyll and Hyde, while never being able to find evidence of violence to any of Cantat's previous partners. Rady herself later qualified her statements by saying that she referred to 'a violence of speech' (p. 96). When Tassel later went to the press reiterating the conversation, Rady appeared on television channel M6 in an interview with Laurent Delahousse in order to counter the accusations of physical violence made against Cantat in relation to previous partners (p. 252). It is noteworthy that one of the aims of the Enveff researchers, in any case, was to establish a continuity between physical and verbal abuse against women, and Robert Louis Stevenson's (1886/2003) monstrous protagonist bears something in common with the psychological bully character type described by Hirigoyen in *Le harcèlement moral*.

Evidence of a looser sort was hinted at by an official witness in the Vilnius case, as reported by the band's biographer Marc Besse. As the member assigned to the case from the French embassy, the witness going by the pseudonym of Sandro Ferretti met the other band members soon after their arrival at Vilnius. Here Ferretti appeared anxious that in relation to the case, the lyrics from the most recent album might be incriminating. He reports his discussion with the band's bassist, Jean-Paul Roy: 'I told him about the premonitory and worrying character of the texts of the album *Des visages des figures*. He replied to me: "If you'd only seen all those that weren't recorded"' (Besse 2012, p. 167). Here the implication seems to be that Cantat's lyrics themselves might have been coming back to haunt him.

Xavier Cantat, as we have seen, was one of those keen to defend his brother from at least some of the charges made by the press and public. His book is particularly marked with monstrous vocabulary, much of it to characterize the media discourse surrounding the case. The account takes the form of a diary of Cantat's activities related to the case from his first hearing of the assault on Trintignant on the television. Recalling his emotions of the morning before Marie's funeral, he goes on to characterize the subsequent media discussion in the following florid terms:

> 'White angel' and 'black eagle,' desperate confrontation between the incarnation of fragility and the guru of bestiality, freedom and oppression, etc. The reality becomes myth constructed with great slugs of rumour distilled by journalists adept at fabulation.
>
> (Cantat 2004, p. 48)

The following January, Xavier Cantat offered an interview in the weekly news magazine, *L'Express*, where he reiterated this idea: 'There is not a cold-blooded monster on one side and a white angel on the other' (p. 144). It is not just the press, for Cantat, who are trying to bestialize his brother; this is also the aim of the prosecution for the defence, and notably of Marie's mother Nadine, often the target of Cantat's ire in his journal: 'The other party does not seek to know the truth, it wants to wipe Bertrand out, transforming him into a monster since it can't pump him full of lead' (p. 165).

At times, Xavier Cantat's journal sees him on the defensive to the extent that he appears petulant towards the deceased and her family. He refers to Nadine Trintignant throughout as Nadine Marquand, her maiden name, despite the fact that she is known by all other sources, and in her book and films, as Trintignant. Her marriage to Jean-Louis Trintignant, the famous actor, ended in 1976 but she still uses the surname. One wonders whether this might be linked to Cantat's repeated observation in his book that each of Marie Trintignant's children is by a different partner; this might contrast to Bertrand, who despite his affair with Marie, is supported by Kristina Rady, who, 'Like us all, [...] fights to the end for the dignity of Bertrand' (p. 53). Cantat observes that the press are finding their own stereotypes for Rady:

> A lot of the media are literally going to beatify Kristina who is becoming a new icon in the affair. A symbol of 'Mothers Courage' and of 'scorned women who forgive,' the ex-wife of Bertrand is thus finding herself despite herself reduced to these journalistic stereotypes.
>
> (p. 151)

Nonetheless, by implication the contrast is made between the Trintignant clan with their serial relationships and children by numerous partners; and the Cantat family, who – dalliances aside – are largely settled family units.

Related to this is Xavier Cantat's verdict on the deceased herself, whom he thinks has also been selectively remembered:

> Marie had chosen the life of a bohemian, cultivated emotional disorder, sometimes made light of moral constraints, was capable of serious excesses. In short, she was a woman filled with humanity with its faults and good qualities. Her orchestrated beatification under the auspices of the cinematic microcosm, a world whose depravities are known, is unworthy.
>
> (p. 51)

There is an interesting implication here that it is the world of cinema that is (and is known to be) the degenerate one, not that of rock'n'roll.

In order to boost this thesis, Cantat is keen to bring in testimony given to the French crime brigade from a former partner of Marie's, a certain Sébastien, whose verdict is that Bertrand Cantat 'has let himself be trapped in the spider's web that Marie spun'. Furthermore, Xavier Cantat recalls an interview by the deceased's father Jean-Louis Trintignant in *Libération* a few years previously, in which the latter, speaking of his daughter, said: 'I am fascinated by her praying mantis side' (p. 80). The words cited by Sébastien parallel those written by Nadine Trintignant herself about Bertrand Cantat in her own book. Once again apostrophizing Marie, she writes: 'He wove around you his spider's web in order to isolate you from us' (Trintignant 2003, p. 28). We find the relations of each partner characterizing the other in the pair as predatory insects and spiders.

Of course, the difference is that one of the sides was in mourning a woman beaten to death while the other was supporting the man who admitted the killing. Though by his own admission not an impartial observer, to the impartial reader Xavier Cantat does himself no favours by appearing to attempt to gain sympathy for his brother through denigrating the family of the deceased, and indeed the deceased herself.

Probably the most disturbing voice in reactions to the case – and in the 'literary' discourse on the affair – is provided by the French novelist Muriel Cerf, who died in 2012. Cerf initiated correspondence with Cantat after the killing, when he was in custody in Vilnius. Her book, *Bertrand Cantat, ou le chant des automates* (2006) reproduces her letters to him in prison as well as framing narratives both recreating in literary terms the events in question and adding reflections of her own, often about her own relationship with a controlling and occasionally violent partner.

At one point in the book she characterizes her own relationship with this partner as follows: 'it is not *The Night Porter* that I would have to mention here, but Stockholm Syndrome: I am trying to make a pact with the jailer' (Cerf 2006, p. 105). Reading the book, with its romanticized portrayal of the relationship between Cantat and Trintignant, one has the queasy sense of reading correspondence from someone who has an infatuation with a killer, such as those discussed in the media in relation to Ted Bundy or Ian Huntley (for instance, see Mina 2003). The admission of Stockholm Syndrome underlines here the sense of a possibly pathological fascination with Cantat on the part of the writer. When she later appears to argue for the claims the rights of romantic love over all other considerations, her description of the lovers during the film shoot in Vilnius sees them in the following terms: 'they are no longer anything but a monster with two heads, they are no longer *normal*' (Cerf 2006, p. 28).

Cerf spends much time alluding to what she sees as the mythical, literary and dramatic dimensions of the relationship between Cantat and Trintignant, as indicated in the opening words of her prologue: 'One could make a portrait of Bertrant Cantat as Prince of Denmark (Hamlet); as a lover (Romeo); as a jealous man (Othello); as a murderer (Macbeth); as a condemned man (the same, the same ones); as a shaman (Orpheus)' (Cerf 2006, p. 16). Elsewhere the latter comparison is taken up again: 'he is Orpheus again, dismembered in the snow of the mountains of Thrace, torn to pieces, devoured by the fingers and teeth of the bacchantes that have chased him, at night' (pp. 65–6). One of the few available figures of myth that Cerf rejects in her florid prose is Narcissus: making explicit reference to Hirigoyen's book, Cerf argues 'Cantat is anything but Narcissus, still less the narcissistic pervert described by Marie-France Hirigoyen' (p. 58).

Cerf's (2006) rather dismaying book seems to want to appeal to allegedly universal archetypes of romance, creation and passion in order to absolve Cantat, who 'will outstrip terrestrial justice' (p. 48). 'As for Marie', Cerf states, 'you had premeditated nothing but to make her happy' (p. 119). Such arguments met evident contempt from Nadine Trintignant's friend Lio, whose scorn is unhidden when both were invited as guests on Thierry Ardisson's chat show on France 2 (*France 2*, 2006). Georges Kiejman, lawyer for Trintignant's parents, also criticized such romantic construals of the case: 'People who refer to Romeo and Juliet should remember that Romeo did not kill Juliet' (Gentleman 2003).

Media relations

It will be evident from the discussion so far that reactions from the families of both Trintignant and Cantat were heavily mediated after the arrest of Cantat. The Trintignants and their friends had an obvious advantage in terms of the sympathy that the killing of Marie would evoke in the general public. There are other notable factors that gave them an advantage in the media and public discourses, and which put the Cantat clan at a disadvantage. Xavier Cantat in his memoir nonetheless argues, in relation to those close to Bertrand: 'To belong to the "wrong side," that of guilt, of culpability, of destruction, doesn't reduce the unspeakable suffering at all' (Cantat 2004, pp. 11–12).

Accounts of the aftermath of the arrest and of the media debate before the trial in Vilnius often point to the differences in class, region and professions of the two clans. We have seen that Xavier Cantat wanted to paint the world of stage and screen as the truly decadent one; and that Nadine Trintignant attacked the problematically macho world of some strains of the cultural Left, here identified with French rock. The Trintignants, as prosperous bourgeois Parisians well established in the performing arts, were seen to be at an obvious advantage over the more provincial, petit-bourgeois family in Bordeaux, in their proximity to the media and the facility with which they were able to present their sides of the story. In addition, a voluntary radio ban of Noir Désir came in after the events (Bouchet and Vézard 2004, p. 173) effective for a month or so before a slow resumption of airplay by some stations. One of the preoccupations of the media following the events was the record sales for the band, which observed a spike in the aftermath of Cantat's arrest, despite the broadcast silence (pp. 174–7).

Emblematic in this regard is the publication on 1 October 2003 of Nadine Trintignant's book, *Ma fille, Marie*, before the trial in Vilnius. The book addresses the deceased directly throughout and mixes biography and autobiography, memoir and polemic about the case. Cantat is not named by Trintignant but is referred, according to the count of Bouchet and Vézard, as 'your murderer' eighty-five times and as 'your assassin' twice (2006, pp. 253–4). The journalists describe Trintignant's media coup in these terms: 'The enterprise of demolition is complete, unsubtle (*sans nuance*). The priestess of feminism in a crusade against the "butcher (*bourreau*) of Vilnius." In a few lines, the cursed artist in quest for redemption has become the macho brute again' (p. 254).

Coming before the trial, this book not only was a best-seller for a curious French public but also underlined the Trintignant clan's ready access to the media. Fayard had published two books by Nadine Trintignant already. Fayard was a subsidiary of the publisher Hachette-Lagardère; the two interviews that Nadine Trintignant accorded to the weeklies, *Elle* and *Paris Match*, were for publications owned by the same conglomerate. Finally, the company producing the telefilms *Colette* on which Nadine and her daughter had been working in Vilnius, Studio International, was also owned by Hachette-Lagardère (p. 255). This is in contrast to the battles Xavier Cantat (2004) complains of in securing coverage for the *partie adverse*.

Bouchet and Vézard's description of Nadine Trintignant as the 'priestess of feminism' alludes in part to her being one of the signatories of the so-called Manifesto of the 343 Sluts (*salopes*) written by Simone de Beauvoir in the *Nouvel Observateur* in 1971 in favour of abortion (p. 25); the nickname for this document was coined by *Charlie Hebdo*. The fact that Trintignant had just filmed a biopic of the socially unconventional writer Colette with her daughter in the title role added to the media narrative, with some justification, of the 'feminist' versus the 'macho bruiser' (*cogneur*) that was current leading up to and during the trial.

Conclusions

It should be evident from the foregoing that the Cantat–Trintignant affair exposed numerous fault lines in French public life at the time. For our purposes here, we can point above all to two versions of masculinity that were proposed and appealed to variously by the defenders of and those condemning Cantat for his actions. Critics (and some fans) sympathetic to Cantat and writing in *Les Inrockuptibles* or perhaps *Libération* appealed to a version of masculinity construed as gregarious, engaged and republican as true of the singer despite his killing of Marie Trintignant. On the other hand, the violence of the case as well as emerging discourses from feminist-inspired psychiatry and sociology made the case an emblem for alternative and troubling ways of viewing masculinity in terms of 'macho bruisers' or 'narcissistic perverts'.

Furthermore, in discussing the case, time-honoured frameworks inspired by romanticism were mixed with a vocabulary informed by monstrosity, in seeking to make sense of the relationship as well as the crime. Sometimes these archetypes were challenged by a newer social science lexis that wanted to construct violence as something social rather than individual; at other times they were unproblematically reproduced by the media or writers supportive of Cantat. Reactions from some advocates and fans of the band appeared to be tinged with a certain fan mourning; conversely, suspicion was sometimes placed on the world of rock and its alleged pretensions to progressive causes from those more sympathetic to other cultural spheres. Cantat's 2013 interview in *Les Inrockuptibles* – and his erstwhile band's high placing in the 2010 *Rolling Stone* album survey – indicates that, to various extents, his or his band's work has been rehabilitated by sections of the French music press.

8

Jingle Jangle Man: Jimmy Savile, paedophilia and the music industry

In October 2012 the London Metropolitan Police began an investigation into the sexual offences of one of Britain's most famous pop DJs, the late Jimmy Savile. It is hard, if not impossible, for anyone outside of the UK to imagine the scale of Savile's celebrity from the 1960s to 1990s, and the shock of his crimes. According to feminist media scholar Karen Boyle, who investigated his changing posthumous news coverage, there was 'a need to cast Savile in black and white terms': before the scandal broke he was a 'national treasure', after a 'monster' (p. 1574). The famous character from Leeds was born in the mid-1920s and conscripted to work in coal mines during the Second World War. By the end of the 1950s, Savile had forged a career as a dance hall manager in the north of England and started moving from music events into broadcast entertainment. After entering the BBC, he hosted the first episode of the perennial chart show *Top of the Pops* in 1964, and many later weekly episodes. Following a spell at Radio Luxembourg he became a BBC Radio 1 DJ in 1968, presenting shows on various national radio and television channels until at least 1989. He also had his own BBC1 primetime Saturday children's series, *Jim'll Fix It* (Bishop 1975–1994). In the 1980s, he furthered his charity fundraising and celebrity connections, becoming a fixture at Stoke Mandeville Hospital, the psychiatric hospital Broadmoor and Leeds General Infirmary. Savile received a knighthood in 1990. His various TV and radio catchphrases, and advertising slogans – including 'Now then, now then', 'Clunk click every trip' and 'This is the age of the train' – became household sayings. In October 2011, at the age of eighty-four, he died of natural causes after being hospitalized for pneumonia. Drawing on Dan Davies's (2014) extensive biography, what follows will discuss Savile's crimes, image, and how they have been interpreted.

In plain sight

Child sex abuse (CSA) is the crime of sexually assaulting children. It leaves a psychological trauma which can haunt its victims for life. A few months after Savile died, *The Oldie* magazine ran a story examining why the BBC had dropped a segment from its *Newsnight* programme investigating allegations made against the celebrity from ex-pupils of Duncroft Approved School. Its author said, 'The BBC has serious questions to answer ... Surely the BBC had a duty to inform police about these disclosures? Yet there is no indication that it has done so, and the BBC have refused to answer questions about this' (Goslett 2012, p. 48). Then, almost a year after the DJ's passing, ITV aired a documentary, *Exposure: The Other Side of Jimmy Savile* (Gardiner 2012), in which former detective Mark Williams-Thomas accused the DJ of a series of sex assaults. A police investigation into the offences, Operation Yewtree, followed immediately. Yewtree had three strands: around the sexual offences committed by Savile himself, around alleged crimes committed by those associated with him, and around those committed by celebrities and others unconnected to him. A joint Metropolitan Police Service and child abuse charity NSPCC report, *Giving Victims a Voice* (January 2013), was issued in the police operation's wake. Yewtree revealed a total of 450 allegations against Jimmy Savile himself, which related to 214 criminal offences (see Davies 2014, p. 534). A series of organizations connected with the Leeds DJ rapidly mounted investigations and began to write reports detailing what he had done in each context, and what they had or had not done in response. The most famous of these were the Director of Public Prosecution Alison Levitt's report, *In the Matter of the Late Jimmy Savile* (January 2013), Her Majesty's Inspectorate of Police's inspection report, *Mistakes Were Made* (March 2013), the NSPCC's own report, *Would They Actually Have Believed Me?* (September 2013), *The Report of the Investigation into Matters Relating to Savile at Leeds Teaching Hospitals* (April 2014), the *Jimmy Savile Investigation: Broadmoor Hospital* (June 2014), *A Further Investigation into Allegations of Abuse by Jimmy Savile at Leeds General Infirmary* (December 2014), two Stoke Mandeville Hospital reports (February 2015) and *The Dame Janet Smith Review Report* for the BBC (February 2016). There were actually many others.[1]

Beyond any insights they contained, some of the reports read like their aim had been to exonerate the institutions concerned. Many came to similar conclusions: that there was a lack of hard evidence at the time, that victims never came forward as they feared they would not be believed, that institutional issues – from incompetence and bureaucracy to hierarchical deference and sexism – prevented the circulation of vital information and that bosses or senior staff simply did not know what was happening. Every wrongdoing seemed to have happened without much of a trace. Despite the Metropolitan Police Service's Paedophile Unit being aware of Savile since the mid-1960s, Mark Erooga (2013c) of NOTA observed there was a failure to join the dots. Beyond the police services there was also *a lack of dots to join*. Erooga (2013c, p. 3) explained that over half of all female assault victims tell someone around them of the crime, yet neither Barnardo's, the National Association for People Abused in Childhood (NAPAC), nor NSPCC/ChildLine had any clear records of allegations made against Savile. Though many people came forward to Yewtree, between all the UK's police forces, just five allegations went on record during Savile's lifetime.

Giving Victims a Voice (Gray and Watt 2013) was a joint report written by representatives of the children's care charity, the NSPCC and the Metropolitan Police. It described Jimmy Savile, who had by then cast a dark shadow over one cohort's generational memory in Britain, as hiding 'in plain sight': a kind of paedophilic version of the famous evidence from Edgar Allan Poe's 1844 story *The Purloined Letter*:

> It is now clear that Savile was hiding in plain sight and using his celebrity status and fundraising activity to gain uncontrolled access to vulnerable people across six decades. For a variety of reasons the vast majority of his victims did not feel they could speak out and it's apparent that some of the small number who did had their accounts dismissed by those in authority including parents and carers.
> (Gray and Watt 2013, p. 6)

The term 'in plain sight' became the title of Savile's biography (Davies 2014). His crimes were an open secret. Certainly, the Leeds DJ seemed both untouchable and uncanny. He may have become 'hidden', in part, because his suspected crimes – paedophilia, and perhaps even necrophilia – were so monstrous, so far beyond the pale (Davies 2014, p. 373). Savile's predilection for underage girls was an open secret on Fleet Street by 1990 (p. 428).[2] He was 'the man who could do anything' (p. 13).

In a 1978 BBC radio interview, John Lydon, who found fame as Johnny Rotten of the Sex Pistols, was asked the idea of making a movie where he would kill those he hated. Asked who would be on his dream hit list, Lydon said, 'On film, I'd like to kill Jimmy Savile. I think he's a hypocrite. I think he's into all kinds of seediness we all know about, we're not allowed to talk about. I know some rumours. I bet none of this will be allowed out' (*I Am Incorrigible*, 2015).

How could an individual DJ have committed so many offences? Why was Savile able to get away with committing them for so long? From the various institutional reports, a number of readings of Jimmy Savile emerged, pointing to reasons why such a recognizable figure might have gained control of his victims. Almost universally, these official reports painted Savile simply as a predator, opportunist and conman. When she announced the findings of the BBC report, for example, Dame Janet Smith revealed a litany of horrors. Discussing both Savile and another offender, the presenter Stuart Hall, Dame Smith explained:

> Both of these men used their fame and positions as BBC celebrities to abuse the vulnerable. They must be condemned for their monstrous behavior, but the culture of the BBC certainly enabled both Savile and Stuart Hall to go undetected for decades. I have identified five occasions when the BBC missed an opportunity to uncover their misconduct.
>
> (*Sky News*, 2016)

Smith described Savile as a serial sexual predator who was opportunistic, shameless and dangerous. At the BBC alone he had seventy-two victims. Thirty-four were under the age of consent, the lowest aged just eight years old. Of the eight incidents of rape that he perpetrated at the channel, the youngest victim was ten years old. Dame Smith's report carefully exonerated senior staff at the broadcasting institution: news of Savile's misdeeds never, it was claimed, reached Heads of Department or anyone further up the management hierarchy. Police reports about Savile similarly claimed opportunities were missed because of a lack of co-ordination between constabularies. However, claims of ineptitude were somewhat suspicious, because they could not exclude the alternative reading, that in the face of mounting evidence things were never taken further because the reporting situation had been rigged in Savile's favour. Indeed, Jimmy Savile regularly held court with local police and others on a Friday morning at his Leeds flat. When West Yorkshire police investigated its own culpability for instance, it concluded, among other things, that 'Friday Morning Club' meetings were innocent affairs. The force encouraged officers to interact more with those on their beats, and Savile had invited his local community officer, DCS Knopwood, for a coffee. The sergeant claimed that nothing had occurred at the regular Friday morning meetings he had with Savile. Attending them never compromised his role as a serving officer. Nevertheless, when victims made accusations elsewhere, Savile used West Yorkshire police to send internal messages to other constabularies. Dame Smith blamed BBC culture:

> There was a culture of not complaining or of raising concerns. BBC staff felt, and were sometimes told, that it was not in their best interests to pursue a complaint. Loyalty to, and pride in, a programme could hinder the sharing of concerns. There was a reluctance to rock the boat. The management structure of the BBC was not only hierarchical, but deeply deferential. Staff were reluctant to speak out to their managers, because they felt it was not their place to do so. Also there was a culture of separation, competition and even hostility between different parts of the BBC, so that concerns arising in one part would not be discussed in another. There was also a macho culture, in particular in Radio 1 and light entertainment. There were very few women in management positions; women found it difficult to report. All the problems of report were compounded in the case of the talent. Celebrities were treated with kid gloves and were virtually untouchable. One witness told me that the talent were more valuable to the BBC than their own values ... These are all factors which the BBC must now address.
>
> (*Sky News*, 2016)

The claims of Dame Smith's report point to industrial and cultural factors – general shortfalls, as it were, of the workplace. Savile's 'freedom' to abuse was blamed on class deference, sexism, internal competition and the urge for profit, to the detriment of locating any kind of deliberate corruption or cover-up.

Another evident but somewhat partial explanation was that Jimmy Savile was someone who systematically capitalized on a range of opportunities. The 'conman' reading was exemplified in DCS Knopwood's (2013) report for West Yorkshire Police, quoted in Erooga (2013d, p. 19):

> Savile's celebrity status spanned many decades and he was seen by the public as a man who 'did good'. He was able to manage his public persona in such a way that he deceived most people he met. He was a manipulative man who exploited to the worst possible degree the trust people placed in him.

The abuse of trust took a variety of forms. First, there was the matter of his own fame. By the late 1960s, he was a TV and radio star who received hundreds of fan letters per week (Davies 2014, p. 229). Savile had his own fan club, and teenagers were star-struck when they met him (p. 215).[3] He used his appeal as a famous DJ to enter into the orbit of young girls (p. 154). In the *Daily Mirror*, he rebranded the sort of stories that circulated around Elvis to serve his own image, claiming that girls went to 'great lengths' to find out where he lived and camped on his doorstep (p. 271). His studio at BBC Broadcasting House was called 'The Surgery' 'because of the waifs, strays and unfortunates who flocked to bask in his aura' (p. 373). Savile sometimes played upon the familiarity of his celebrity persona to hoodwink teens into sexual assaults (p. 279).

Girls also got close to Jimmy because he had a lot of famous contacts. In the 1960s, his appeal occurred in part because he was on friendly terms with a lot of pop idols, including the Beatles (p. 217). On his TV show *Jim'll Fix It*, he arranged for three female fans to meet the Osmonds (p. 311). He occasionally exploited his connections with music icons to sexually entrap their fans (p. 152). For instance, Savile capitalized on meeting Elvis Presley: he had the picture of their encounter framed and placed in his specially commissioned DJ box (p. 215). After visiting Presley in the United States, the disc jockey lured one female Elvis fan club member by saying that the Memphis singer had given her a present (p. 222).

Savile also capitalized on young peoples' dreams and career aspirations. He entrapped at least one girl who was driven to get on TV (p. 268). At Duncroft Approved School, he lured one victim by promising her he could get her a job as a nurse at Stoke Mandeville (p. 470). Savile's modus operandi was revealed in a NOTA summary of Operation Ornament, which questioned Jimmy about his meetings with girls from Duncroft:

> He said that he believed these allegations were simply people trying to get money from him and were unfounded. He explained that he had contacts within the police at Leeds and whenever he received letters alleging that he had done something he gave them to his contacts who 'get rid' of them.
>
> (Erooga 2013a, p. 3)

Some sets of victims, such as the girls at the Duncroft school, therefore seemed to be chosen because they would be perceived as celebrity opportunists or unreliable witnesses who only had themselves to blame. To borrow from Fred Vermorel's recent London noir *Dead Fashion Girl*, Savile may have played upon the widespread perception that 'Such women were up to no good and therefore came to no good' (2019, p. 51). While employee deference, sexism and celebrity may have been enabling factors in Savile's predatory career at the BBC, they do not fully explain his continual evasion of the law.

Doorway to the cesspool?

Rossi: I was 17 or 18 so it didn't seem that ridiculous. Lots of people told me.
Sackur: When you first came across Savile, you were 17 or 18?
Rossi: Yeah, and that thing went on that I told you about. Because we just – [raises eyebrows and shrugs]
Sackur: You can tell me about it on air. Why not?
Rossi: I can't. I don't think I can. I think that's gross. Anyway, something went on, as I said, during the show, and he said, 'Come and see these. They're only 12 years old.' And you kind of ignore it. You're new to the [music business] thing, and you've just got into the system yourself.
Sackur: You're a teenager yourself.
Rossi: Yes. To be honest, back then, they were 15 or 12 year olds, and it didn't seem as gross as it does now, obviously. But you didn't realize what they were doing. You didn't realize the gravity of it, if you wish. All of those acts of my generation, you ask them; they all had an inkling, but we were, like, ssssh – told to watch out for the Leeds mafia. And even when Louis Theroux had him cornered on camera, Jimmy Savile was that confident. He looked straight at him and the camera. He [Savile] knew, somehow – and he still must have something in the system that's covering him, or covering what's gone on. We all know it, we just can't find it. (*QuoTelevision* 2018)

When Status Quo first appeared on *Top of the Pops* in 1968, Jimmy Savile invited Francis Rossi to his dressing room by saying, 'Come and see me tarts. Some fucking tarts we've got in' (Davies 2014, p. 249, also see Hall 2012). Years later, in 2014, Stephen Sackur, presenter of the BBC's show *Hardtalk*, asked Rossi about Status Quo's first *Top of the Pops* performance and whether he knew anything of the presenter's sexual activities. Rossi noted that 'the Leeds mafia' and other agencies unknown were making sure his crimes were covered up. Beyond the restricted reporting of the mainstream media, theories began to circulate about why Savile was so untouchable.

Marshall McLuhan (1970/2015) once noted, 'World War III is a guerilla war with no division between military and civilian participation.' In recent years, Russian media outlets such as *Sputnik* and *Russia Today* have been targeting Western countries and offering facts and viewpoints which question their establishment narratives. The same or associated agencies likely pursue covert operations online. In Britain, while alternative media outlets are not necessarily overtly pro-Russian, they constantly critique the Anglo-American political Establishment and rarely complain about Moscow. Savile's posthumous scandal erupted at a point in time when social media emerged to become a platform for conspiracy theories that connected a popular distrust of authority, with a postmodern focus on mediated evidence, an enchanting resurgence of religious superstition and the reformulation of popular discussion as online entertainment. As television began to lose ground to social media platforms, figures such as David Icke and Alex Jones found larger audiences, in part by reactivating and combining ideas of older provenance. While in some ways they were dissident figures, critical of the use of the reach of surveillance technology in everyday life, Icke's work sometimes diverted public opposition into a post-political realm: dark entertainment based on tropes made of 'what-if' and 'could-be'.[4] Their reading of stories like Savile's case is that corruption is endemic in the highest levels of British politics, and the system is in a state of constantly covering up its misdeeds. The emphasis of this reading has been that entertainers such as Savile have been the objects of investigation in order to deflect public attention away from paedophilic politicians. It exacerbates a 'post-political' environment in which ordinary people have, perhaps rightly, lost faith in the ability of politicians to serve them ahead of unelected agents of business or global governance (see Wilson and Syngedouw 2015). The result is that those who rightly campaign for justice and clarity have sometimes become interested in, or associated with, agents of destabilization. A good example of this is the British investigative journalist Sonia Poulton, who has simultaneously written for the *Daily Mail*, appeared on *Russia Today*, and releases her own self-made YouTube documentaries such as *Paedophiles in Parliament* (2018), which starts with a shot of Savile. It is notable that Poulton was a music journalist in the 1990s and has adapted her career to cover this new middle ground of conspiracy which unites political commentary with news entertainment and celebrity scandal. In some cases, alternative media outlets have given a platform to mavericks, rebels or individuals simply looking to end corruption. However, any general aim to destabilize the interests of Western national identity is not necessarily shared by the same ordinary citizens whose distrust has been carefully levered.

It is important to briefly contextualize the place of the Savile story in the globalized mediascape which is consumed by both British and other citizens. Here, like in the United States, as Uscinski and Parent (2014, p. 156) suggest, the popular media is 'awash in conspiracy imagery … News outlets, talk radio, music, and books all traffic in conspiracy theories.' The two authors also note, 'Yet simply because conspiracy theories are discussed prominently does not mean they are discussed favourably' (p. 156). Not everyone believes them without firm evidence. In a multimedia environment where the line between different media forms and sources has been breached, the Savile case was valuable for showing to innocent viewers that everything about Western democracy was not as it seemed. His case acted as scandalous entertainment with serious implications.

One of the key things that conspiracy theory seemed to get right about Savile was that his crimes appeared to be attempts to see what he could get away with. He could not easily be profiled as a man with a clear psychosexual predilection. Jimmy Savile's celebrity and charity work gave him a reputation that made the stories of his victims seem less credible. If his 'charm' could so easily be used to lever money for his preparatory publicity and charity efforts, then the question becomes one of precisely why he was so tolerated and supported. He hardly looked the part. The DJ had a struggle of bleached white hair, and would usually appear with his eyes glowing behind 'granny glasses', his hands clutching a large cigar. His body, meanwhile, was often festooned with a loud shell suit, accessorized by clunky necklaces and bracelets. The look was deliberately striking – bordering on psychedelic, gaudy, and to some, perhaps, vulgar – it was an eccentric and bizarre look, assembled from precisely the kind of clothing that middle class British people would never wear. His modus operandi, meanwhile, was not constant. Like a sociopath, he never held his victims in high regard. In fact, victims seemed to be unimportant to Savile: pawns in a game designed to emphasize and lever his obvious untouchability. Opportunism and institutional shortfall did not quite seem enough to account for Jimmy Savile's continual, utter untouchability and the way he brandished his free status during his lifetime. An alternative explanation offered in the public sphere was to suggest that the DJ was protected by the British Establishment. Playing upon associations between the live music industry and organized crime, Savile sometimes jokingly asserted he was part of the mafia (Theroux 2019, p. 362). Marcus Erooga's (2014, p. 2) additional NOTA summary of the NSPCC report also noted, 'he manipulated some of those around him to access potential victims and by real or implied threats used his status and position to prevent his activities being made public'. This, however, is not quite as nefarious as it seems: some of his threats were of using his legal team to meet victims head on at the Old Bailey. The Levitt Report concluded, however, that when victims came forward to the Crown Prosecution service – while the choice not to prosecute was not consciously influenced by any improper motive on the part of either police or prosecutors – they could have done much more to build a case. In fact, 'the police treated the alleged victims and the accounts they gave with a degree of caution that was neither justified nor required' (Erooga 2013b, p. 3).

One notion that has gained ground in recent years is the idea of the organized crime of the 'deep state'. Originally associated with twentieth-century governance in Turkey, the term was lifted by former Republican Congressional aide Mike Loftgren to describe American politics and has been adopted by President Trump. Lofgren borrowed his definition from John Le Carré's 2013 espionage novel *A Delicate Truth* which used the term to highlight pacts that allowed finance capital to control politicians and bypass democracy. It was 'the ever-expanding circle of non-governmental insiders from banking, industry and commerce who were cleared for highly classified information denied to large swathes of Whitehall and Westminster' (Le Carré 2013, p. 252).

It is important to realize that both Left- and Right-wing thinking has attempted to specify powerful business interests that dominate society.[5] The idea of the 'deep state' has prospered in neoliberal society, in political climate cynical about the positive possibilities of democratic governance. It points to corruption that is, by definition and necessity, never fully named. While rightly highlighting that politicians now mediate between powerful capitalists and the electorate rather than democratically serving the people, by entrenching popular disillusionment and refusing to suggest peaceful, practical ways forward, the idea either encourages citizens to withdraw from the democratic process or leaves them open to Trump-style populist appeals. It has therefore been associated with a kind of alt-right appropriation of electoral politics: 'Instead of anti-elitism, we are ending up with anti-politics' (Glaser 2017, p. 30).

According to biographer Dan Davies, writing about Savile:

> He had spent a lifetime drawing attention to himself without ever really revealing who, or what he really was. At our first meeting he told me, 'I am the man who knows everything but says nothing. I get things done but I work deep cover.'
> (2014, p. 365)

For Savile's eightieth birthday, Prince Charles sent Cuban cigars and a note saying, 'Nobody will ever really know what you have done for this country Jimmy' (Davies 2014, p. 462). CSA seemed tailor-made for conspiracy theorists in its capacity to evoke panic without necessarily proving specificity or evidence. Theories abounded which connected politicians and celebrities to paedophile rings operating at locations such as Elm Guest House and Dolphin Square in

London. Depending on their different versions, these rumours implied not only that child sex trafficking rings operated internationally and that abusers in positions of social power could freely indulge their horrifying predilections, but also that such moments were engineered by the secret services to enable the blackmailing of perpetrators into service of the deep state. More recently, Carl Beech, a man who accused a range of Establishment figures of CSA, including Edward Heath, triggering Operation Midland, was found to be creating false stories and perverting the course of justice (*Carl Beech* 2019). Beech's claims were widely discredited in the media.

One variant of such stories suggested that victims were directly being trafficked through the very social services designed to protect them. Another suggested that any whistleblowers were being hounded, made into unreliable witnesses through intimidation or mental destabilization tactics. Yet other variants combined this trope with satanic panic, suggesting that high level diplomats were coerced after they found themselves attending ceremonies that included ritualized child abuse and sacrifice. Read specifically in relation to the idea of the 'deep state', Savile did *appear* to ultimately be protected, especially as other celebrities with money, power and good reputations had been prosecuted. Wealth can buy off some victims, can buy strong legal defence and – if used unethically – can also cause corruption, buying institutional ignorance, deliberate ineptitude, threat and intimidation. Yet as the cases of public figures accused of sexual offences – such as the Lostprophets singer Ian Watkins in 2013, and the African American comedian Bill Cosby in 2018 – demonstrated, celebrity, connections and money do not alone grant immunity from prosecution.

'Deep state' theories explained why the many reports about what happened in various institutional settings could be read, effectively, almost as exonerations, never quite seeming to unearth the full roots of any cover up. While some of these scenarios stretch the bounds of credibility, others are at least possible and worth investigating. Recent controversy over the death of Jeffrey Epstein suggests the possibility, at least, that certain individuals involved in serial sexual assaults can be sponsored and allowed to continue their misdeeds because they are assets to the intelligence services: people who can incriminate and blackmail high profile figures. Could that ever have happened in the UK and Ireland? The Channel 4 series *After Dark* aired an episode in 1988 that began to explore the extent of the murky connections between abuse at the Kincora boys home, loyalist paramilitary organizations and the proprietary interests of the British intelligence, MI5. The journalist Robin Ramsay (in Tookey 1988) suggested:

> At the far edge of this network, somebody was bringing, procuring boys for this homosexual network. Now, it's not Kincora because the boys were too old – sixteen plus I think – but some of the other homes had younger people. So I assume that people with paedophilic inclinations made use of the other homes.

After suggesting that there was a 'procurer' for illicit abuse rings, the writer Robert Harbinson, who had been a friend of Anthony Blunt – a spy who had a fondness for visiting Northern Ireland – explained when pressed by Gary Murray (in Tookey 1988):

> Harbinson: There are people who literally kicked [former British Prime Minister] Wilson out of office.
> Murray: What did they do to kick him out of office?
> Harbinson: They kicked Wilson out of office and they got themselves into high places. This is why Mrs Thatcher consults them today.
> Murray: How did they go about that?
> Harbinson: Because they were blackmailed.
> Murray: Over what?
> Harbinson: Sex!

Reviewing a biography of Blunt's Cambridge spy-ring friend Guy Burgess, another commentator noted, 'Burgess was addicted to "rent boys" … On one occasion he wrote … "Small boys are cheap today, cheaper than yesterday"' (de Búrca 2018).

It is not impossible there was ambiguously sanctioned abuse at Kincora and other places. Reporting on why Dr Morris Fraser, who had examined Kincora victims like Richard Kerr, was allowed to keep practising after a sex conviction with a thirteen-year-old boy in London, *The Guardian* noted a report claimed Fraser remained on the medical register 'due to a series of cover-ups by the authorities … It also emerged that freedom of information requests for documents on Fraser were turned down on national security grounds. His victims included boys sent to Kincora boys' home in Belfast, where a paedophile ring operated, some of whose members were being blackmailed by MI5 and the RUC.' As the report's writer, Dr Niall Meehan noted, 'Children were abused while the authorities knew they were being abused' (McDonald 2016). Ireland's

Historical Institutional Abuse Enquiry into Kincora and other locations found, however, that the intelligence services were interested in the Kincora housemaster William McGrath, because he founded the Ulster loyalist organization TARA. They knew, and ignored, a rumour that he had assaulted small boys. However, McGrath was not an agent of the state. It concluded:

> There have been frequent allegations that various individuals, including Sir Maurice Oldfield, a former head of the Secret Intelligence Service who was later the Security Coordinator in Northern Ireland, and a number of named and unnamed Northern Ireland Office Civil Servants, and unnamed business men and other prominent figures, resorted to Kincora for sexual purposes. We are satisfied there is no credible evidence to support any of these allegations (11) … We are satisfied that Kincora was not a homosexual brothel, nor used by any of the intelligence agencies as a "honey pot" to entrap, blackmail or otherwise exploit homosexuals.
> (*Report of the Historical Institutional Abuse Enquiry*, 2017, p. 12)

One of the surviving Kincora victims, Richard Kerr, who claimed that he had been trafficked to Westminster, pulled out of the enquiry after his law firm said they were given very little time to prepare. They explained, 'The State bodies/agencies that are Core Participants to the inquiry appear to have been provided with bundles of documents of up to 16,000 pages. In contrast, Mr Kerr was provided with around 740 pages' (Preston 2018).

Variously speculating that Savile was a 'procurer of children', 'blackmailer', 'fixer' or 'ambassador', conspiracy theories found their own answers to the question of why the upper echelons of the British society, from Mrs Thatcher to the Royal family, embraced such a bizarre entertainer. They appealed to the question of why Savile both seemed immune from prosecution and arrogant about it. Yet they also did ideological work, suggesting pervasive corruption, and thus connecting child abuse to electoral politics in something other than an incidental way. They were based on unproven suppositions which could lever popular cynicism, pushing audiences into further acceptance of disturbing fantasies. It turned Jimmy's industrial scale efforts at abuse into entertainment, extending the tropes of true crime shows in ways that pessimistically viewed contemporary society as experiencing its own prolonged fall from grace.

Embroidering the notion that Jimmy Savile served the deep state has been the equally entertaining idea that he used occult powers. Conspiracy theorist David Icke (2013, p. 284) reported:

I have been saying for decades that paedophilia and Satanism are fundamentally connected and the cement that holds the [global political] system together, and so it was no surprise when stories emerged of Savile's Satanism. The UK *Daily Express* reported how Savile had raped a 12-year-old girl in a satanic ritual at Stoke Mandeville Hospital in 1975.

The story in question contained a quote from Dr Valerie Sinason (reproduced in Icke 2013, p. 284), who said the victim recalled, 'Several adults were there, including Jimmy Savile who, like the others, was wearing a robe and a mask. She recognized him because of his distinctive voice and the fact that his blond hair was protruding from the sides of the mask.' Icke was not the only one exploring the idea that Savile worshipped the devil. A 47-minute documentary by poster 5ocietyX on YouTube explored the possibility in more detail. There was, of course, a slim thread of circumstantial evidence for Savile's alleged Lucifarian interests. After all, he had been born on Halloween and was supposedly a seventh son. He had familiarity with religious rites and hospital cadavers. He had joked that his co-workers down the mine had thought he was a witch. 5ocietyX spun this in further directions: among Savile's possessions were wizard's robes and a crystal ball; his catchphrases acted like hypnotic chants; and Stoke Mandeville could even have been built on ley lines. This rather slim chain of points, furthermore, made at least some hypothetical sense for those who wanted to believe it. Savile's appeal as an entertainer could attract a supply of young virgins and perhaps make him a procurer. His supposed lack of emotional empathy, paedophilia and necrophilia would, furthermore, also have been useful assets in such rituals. Finally, satanic rituals could then be used to implicate and blackmail public leaders, rendering them open to manipulation by the 'dark forces' who were supposed to actually run society. Savile's supposed Satanism had emerged from more politicized issues too: his uncanny level of success, close links to the Establishment, and now-revealed identity as Britain's most notorious sexual predator – a monster who had 'groomed the nation', committed paedophilia on an industrial scale and arrogantly managed to hide in plain sight for his entire career.

Claims of Satanic Ritual Abuse (SRA) could be used to make questionable points about the issues that Savile's case raised. The prominent human rights barrister Barbara Hewson (2013), for example, published an online piece in the contrarian journal *Spiked* arguing 'Yewtree Is Destroying the Rule of Law.' Its tagline clarified her interpretation, 'With its emphasis on outcomes over process, the post-Savile witch-hunting of aging celebs echoes the Soviet Union.' Hewson compared the post-Savile era to the 1880s Social Purity movement, a campaign which got the age of consent raised from thirteen to sixteen and criminalized gay relationships as a matter of gross indecency. In Hewson's view 'moral crusaders' such as the NSPCC had 'a vested interest in universalizing the notion of abuse … But the most remarkable facet of the Savile scandal is how adult complainants are being asked to act like children. Hence we have witnessed the strange spectacle of mature adults calling a children's charity to complain about the distant past.' Hewson further argued that behavioural norms around sex from past decades were quite different, that victims' allegations were now taken as solid despite a lack of evidence, and that there was still a legal difference between minor sexual assaults and 'serious' charges like rape. Lamenting what she saw as an emerging therapeutic model of jurisprudence, Hewson argued that the objective impartiality of judges was being over-ridden by emotional demands from victims for results. Finally, Hewson advocated a US-style statute of limitations to discount past offences, removing claimant anonymity and returning of the age of consent to thirteen, partly on the basis that puberty was now averagely happening for girls at the age of ten.

Needless to say, Hewson's views were highly controversial and provoked a firestorm in the British press and on social media. While some people *were* concerned with the way that the urge to 'give victims a voice' was compromising due process, damaging reputations and potentially prioritizing affect over careful, rational jurisprudence, few agreed with Hewson's solutions. Instead, she was seen as defending the wrongdoings of the British Establishment. Two months after the piece was published, presenter Krishnan Guru-Murthy interviewed Hewson on *Channel 4 News*. The conversation began:

Guru-Murthy: You began this article saying that 'I wouldn't support the persecution of old men.' So you wouldn't have gone after Jimmy Savile if he was still alive?
Hewson: Well, it depends what he's alleged to have done.
Guru-Murthy: We know what he's alleged to have done – a variety of sexual crimes.
Hewson: Including Satanic ritual abuse – huh! (laughs)
Guru-Murthy: You find it funny?
Hewson: I do.
Guru-Murthy: Which bit?
Hewson: Satanic ritual abuse doesn't exist. It's like alien abduction.

> Guru-Murthy: So are you saying that the people who have made these allegations are just making it up?
> Hewson: I would think so.
> Guru-Murthy: Everything?
> Hewson: The Satanic ritual abuse allegations?
> Guru-Murthy: We're talking about hundreds of people here who have made allegations.
> Hewson: They've made allegations, but that's not evidence.
> Guru-Murthy: Are you saying you just don't believe them?
> Hewson: What I'm saying is that it's pointless to conduct an investigation of this kind into someone who's dead because they can't answer.
> (*TopTellyFan*, 2013)

The notion of SRA was being used here as a way to discredit victims, diminish more founded allegations and calls for justice. It was an obvious example which could be wheeled out and pointed at in order to say that individuals could claim victim status by telling all manner of tall stories, and nobody should believe all that they heard without firm evidence. This self-evident position could then be used to support other views that were, to say the least, unpopular.

SRA was taken as the 'fake smoke' used to say that there was little or no fire. This raises the issue of why claims about Savile and SRA emerged at all, especially as they could so easily be used to discredit his victims. Savile's supposed Satanic majesty offers insights into conspiracy theory itself as a mode of vernacular theorizing – the question that should be asked here is *not* whether SRA was fantasized or covered up, but rather what functions the story had beyond its capacity to register the deep sense of injustice felt on behalf of victims that went unnoticed by the law while Savile had been allowed to hide 'in plain sight'.

What conclusions might we draw from all the speculation? In the end, the evidence for Savile being a high magus or even the possibility of him procuring for one or more high level paedophile rings was rather limited. On one hand, while certain lodgings and children's homes became synonymous with the idea of Established paedophile rings, only in a few cases (notably Haute de la Garenne in Jersey) was Savile connected to the properties. On the other hand, the idea of SRA has itself become a kind of collective fantasy fuelled by representations from popular culture and propagated by Christian fundamentalists among others. The cases relating ritual abuse to care homes have concerned youngsters being taken into care after their families were accused of abusing them, not organized rituals inside the care homes themselves. Claims of organized ritual abuse have collapsed through lack of evidence. There has never been significant evidence of any unbroken tradition of organized Satanism (secret or not) in politics recorded in recent Anglo-American history; Satanic rituals have been practised either in isolated cases or by self-publicists. Nevertheless, the British public had been relatively unaware that Savile was a prolific sex offender while he was alive, and there was a sense in which the revelatory nature of his case made the impossible seem possible.

Ultimately, however, a deep state explanation for Savile's untouchability is not entirely needed. As Dan Davies explained:

> But still [in 1981] there was no apparent appetite for examining the murkier aspects of Jimmy Savile's life, not least while he was all-powerful within the BBC, working unofficially for the royals and leading the charge to build a hospital unit for the nation, a project undertaken on the behalf of a reluctant but grateful government.
>
> (2014, p. 374)

Given the logic of such explanations, they raise the proliferation of conspiracy theory as a puzzle. Back in 1992, as part of his history of media controversies over CSA and SRA in Britain, *Intimate Enemies*, media sociologist Philip Jenkins described what he called a 'symbolic politics' or 'politics of substitution' in which traditionalists who wished to stigmatize 'moral offences' associated with public permissiveness – notably public homosexuality and the sale of pornography – drummed up moral panics about crimes against children 'as by definition, children could not legally give informed consent to sexual activities'. He continued:

> In the 1980s, therefore, we find morality campaigns directed not against homosexuality, but pedophilia; not so much against pornography in general, but child pornography; not against Satanism, but against ritual child abuse. In each case, the claims-makers raised the stakes by arguing, first, that real physical harm results from these offences, and second, that the crimes were the work of organized groups. Children were not only ritually abused, they were sacrificed; they were not only photographed nude, or molested by pedophiles, they were murdered. And in each case, the perpetrators were tightly-knit conspiratorial gangs, child sex rings, or devil-worshipping covens.
>
> (1992, p. 10)

The mechanisms of displacement and exaggeration that Jenkins outlines are persuasive and could account for elements of the reactivation of panic that occurred after Savile died. Legislation supporting same-sex marriage, for instance, was passed in the UK in the summer of 2013 after much debate about the merit of civil partnerships. However, claims about SRA were also used to rubbish the worth of existing evidence.

As a mode of thinking, conspiracy theory is not simply a form of superstition with the 'tendency to impute false meaning and significance into an essentially contingent situation' (Taylor 2013, p. 11). It is guided by goals which emerge from a compromise between different forms of public discourse. Its persistence stems from a conjunction of entertainment, politics, religion and paranoia *already* emerging in spaces of contemporary media dominated by political scandal (from Watergate to Leveson) and uncanny geopolitics (from the 'war on terror' to 'weapons of mass destruction'). In this environment, audiences have almost inevitably lost faith in the democratic process; conspiracy theory both reflects and promotes their cynicism. Savile's case was useful in that process. As a celebrity, he came to symbolize betrayal on multiple levels. Not only had he betrayed the trust of his victims, but he had also betrayed the British public as his celebrity image was not as it seemed. Finally, he had also hoodwinked, withdrawn, controlled and – though legal means – coerced media institutions into again betraying the public by relenting on their role as guardians of the public interest. Satanist or not, Jimmy Savile was already synonymous with the idea of cover up.

Conspiracy theorists have been dismissed by progressive thinkers and rational scholars both for creating arguments that lack rigour and for forwarding repugnant ideologies (such as anti-Semitism). Despite these problems, conspiracy theory remains a popular, appealing mode of vernacular theorizing that cannot be so easily dismissed. As a strategy, it does not adhere to traditional standards of logic and rigour, but instead pushes lines of speculation and semi-educated guesses to their furthest limits in order to see what may or may not come into view if more substantive evidence appears. The coordinates of this territory are not only – as in some academic work – already proven assertions (such as the fact that 9/11 happened), but also things that are potentially scandalous and, however absurd they appear, *hard if not impossible to disprove* (such as hypothesizing 9/11 was secretly conceived as a giant occult ritual). For those who entertain such suppositions, rigorous theorizing can appear inhibited, or, worse still, inadvertently supporting mechanisms dedicated to hiding the truth. Savile's case not only showed that some truths were being hidden, but also that there were forces such as libel law and celebrity reputation that could be used to maintain a cover-up. The problem for conspiracy theorists is not that the media covers up certain things; conspiracy theory thrives on the notion of cover-ups. Instead the problem is that, as Paul Taylor writing about the media has said, public cynicism and complicity can go hand in hand. The horror for conspiracy theorists is not to be met by opposition, but by a great, collective 'So what?' After all, it is already common knowledge that political systems can be corrupt, that they can be swayed by external agents, that the democratic process can be compromised. The idea that politicians are involved in social transgressions and faux occultic or hazing rituals – such as the annual 'Cremation of Care' at Bohemian Grove – are already in the public sphere. The 2012 Leveson enquiry showed that British politics, the media and the police could be corrupted. Neither these, nor growing degrees of material inequality, have precipitated a revolution. Paedophilia, however, is a personalized crime which breaks deep social taboos. It centres on the innocence of children. The Savile case was used to suggest the possibility that CSA could have been the very glue that bonded the Establishment.

Orientalism and the music industry: Misadventures in the seedy world of pop

One of the interesting things about Jimmy Savile's story is the way it drew on his involvement in the world of popular music. In this milieu, Jimmy Savile played on the idea that he was an outrageous spectacle, a freak and a clown. In the 1960s, as his media career took off, he would dress like the Joker from *Batman*:

> One side of his clothing would be all black and the other side would be all white; he'd have one black shoe on and one white shoe. His hair would be dyed black on one side and white on the other. Or everything he wore would be tartan and he'd have his hair sprayed tartan as well.
>
> (Davies 2014, p. 143)

Like the Joker, Savile was a loner, a riddle, a mystery. *The New York Times* said Jimmy spouted 'patter that in its manic intensity verged on Dada' (Davies 2014, p. 502). He could also use his bizarre visual image to great advantage. When he operated on behalf of a Broadmoor Psychiatric Unit task force, Savile said, 'It would be beneath anybody's dignity to be frightened of someone dressed like this' (p. 406). In later years, about what he meant to the Royals, Savile maintained, 'I was [perceived as] a freak with long hair' (p. 282). The royal biographer Andrew Morton said, 'As the unofficial court jester, he articulates opinions that courtiers can only think' (in Davies 2014, p. 436). One vulgar joke Jimmy told was, 'How can you tell a Scotsman's clan? Pull up his kilt and if he's got two quarter pounders then he's a McDonald' (Brown 2012a). Savile was, above all, a 'jingle jangle' man. He used the term 'jingle jangle' to describe the flashy jewellery that he wore, but its associations went further. In street slang, the term 'Jingle jangle' is used to signify the physical noise of alpha masculinity: the sound that 'big balls' make when their male owner struts. 'Jingle jangle' also refers, in street parlance, to female genitalia. Following the Byrds 1965 success with Bob Dylan's 'Mr Tambourine Man', 'Jangle' became used to label the droning, arpeggiated sound of an electric guitar and the music styles associated with it, from 1960s psychedelic rock to indie rock and 1990s Britpop. It signified a surface of pleasurable, enchanting sound, behind which there was the 'jingle jangle' of a music industry profiteering. This section will discuss how the ever-familiar concept of music industry permissiveness arguably functioned as a 'front' or more correctly a 'fig leaf' for various parties to explain away the open secret of Savile's misdeeds. It connects with the state of mind explored by Stanley Cohen in his book *States of Denial* (2001): 'The psychology of "turning a blind eye" or "looking the other way" is a tricky matter … We are vaguely aware of choosing not to look at the facts, but not quite conscious of what it is we are evading. We know, but at the same time, we don't' (p. 5). He might have added, 'Or we don't want to.'

The posthumous scandal that defined Savile as Britain's biggest sex offender prompted a climate in the media and social institutions in which past crimes were investigated, and a large string of late middle-aged figures from the world of British popular music were brought in for questioning and sometimes put on trial. Popular music had been associated with paedophilia in the past: in Britain the DJ, promoter and novelty artist Jonathan King and glam rocker Gary Glitter were among the most prominent cases, while in the United States, Michael Jackson's two trials challenged his reputation. What was new in the 2010s was that a whole generation of entertainers from the baby boomer cohort faced charges for crimes largely perpetrated during the era of the permissive society. Two women who claimed they were Savile's girlfriends said on Louis Theroux's documentary episode, *Savile* (Cary 2016), which reframed the 2000 show *When Louis Met ... Jimmy*: 'All Jim's girlfriends knew each other. There was never jealousies.' They were in their forties and had met at the BBC. One of them had been fifteen years old when her liaison started. She explained, 'At the time,

I took the relationships to be symptomatic of a different era: the show business world of the '60s and '70s.'

It is easy to forget the foregrounding of permissiveness which characterized rock music during its 1960s and 1970s heyday. Consider, for example, Led Zepplin's infamous fish incident, immortalized on 'The Mud Shark' from Frank Zappa's summer 1971 live album, *Fillmore East*. The incident has been used as a bench mark for the height of rock'n'roll debauchery. In the Mud Shark incident, which allegedly took place while Led Zeppelin were on tour in Seattle, the band's tour manager Richard Cole was supposed to have penetrated a groupie with a small fish caught from out the window of their room at the Edgewater Hotel in Seattle. The act seems to have been consensual and featured a woman who was above the age of consent, but it involved allusions to intoxication, nudity, bestiality, voyeurism and, in some versions, other animals (alive or dead) in the room, bondage, S&M and perhaps gang-banging. The Edgewater Hotel incident is the stuff of legend. Some versions of the story say it was filmed. The female participant has never come forward, nor has the film surfaced. Indeed, the Edgwater now features a 'Beatles Suite' on its website and mentions a photograph of *that group* fishing out the window (*Luxury Suites* 2011).

The Mud Shark story is not exceptional. In 1972, for example, the same year that *Deep Throat* played in mainstream cinemas across America, the Rolling Stones contested the showing of Robert Frank's backstage tour documentary, *Cocksucker Blues*, on account that the free sex and drug-taking might incriminate them. In other words, though *getting prosecuted* for criminal acts was not especially hip, louche and lascivious behaviour that pushed the bounds of permissiveness was not just accepted, it was politicized: celebrated as an emancipatory act of self-expression and audacious display of progressive social attitudes. While, at least in public perceptions, British rock bands like Led Zepplin and the Stones epitomized this libertine attitude, it extended across a range of entertainment industries and other cultural milieux, including radio and television. Glam rock, meanwhile, followed the lead set by the Beatles, and courted female fans of very young ages: early teen and tweenaged years. As the Status Quo singer Francis Rossi explained to Stephen Sackur during an interview on the BBC show, *Hardtalk*, 'I find it interesting that if we go to rock'n'roll, or DJs, or whatever, if you want to find out where there's paedophiles, they're going to be where children are' (*QuoTelevision* 2018). Seen in this way, the music industry was framed as a place where the glittering world of popular music hid an underside of seedy attitudes and practices.

On one hand, the story of Savile's paedophilia played into conspiracy notions that the glossy world of pop was not as it seemed. It was not just that media events became used as recruiting grounds, rather like schools or hospitals, as Savile abused the public trust placed in him as a celebrity. For conspiracy theorists, it was also that the world of entertainment itself was finally unmasked as something that was not as it had first seemed. This was associated with notions of the permissive society era of the 1970s, symbolized by the frivolity of *Top of the Pops*, being 'on trial' as a smokescreen for all manner of predators. According to Joan Bakewell, who worked as a BBC studio manager in the 1960s:

> These men, people like Jimmy Savile, were treated like rock stars … and sexually many of those men lived in a self-contained culture … People were at the top of their form and many were jubilantly having affairs … [And Jimmy Savile?] Later, yes. Repellent, you know. He once tried to get me to go to his hotel room. But many of the young girls who did go I'm afraid went willingly … You can't re-create the mood of an era … You just can't get into the culture of what it was like, transfer our sensibilities backwards from today. It would be like asking Victorian factory owners to explain why they sent children up chimneys. It's the same with the BBC that I first entered. It had habits and values that we just can't understand from the point of view of where we are now. What we now find unacceptable was just accepted back then by many people.
>
> (O'Hagan 2012, p. 5)

This statement suggests that the era's culture of celebrity and permissiveness were to blame. Savile's era was one of youth pop acts and young people's television and radio programming. On Theroux's documentary episode, *Savile* (Cary 2016), the DJ's female BBC producer explained why she saw no evidence:

> The music industry was like that – sex, drugs and rock'n'roll – people could get away with that … My relationship with Savile was in the workplace … I was a bit 'walnutish' [too old, in her mid-twenties] … part of his persona was that he would tread very close to the line … I once had a conversation with him about the perfect crime … I sometimes wonder whether he was teasing the world in an effort to be discovered.

In Savile's case, however, something beyond 1970s permissive pop and TV celebrity culture seemed to be at play. He painted a picture of himself emerging from a 'Godfather' role in the seedy world of club land and achieving the status of a legitimate public hero who raised millions for charity, seduced prime ministers and entertained a nation. According to his critical biographer Dan Davies (2014, p. 41):

> As he memorably put it in his autobiography, [as a child growing up at the Mecca Locarno ballroom in Leeds] he became 'the confidant of murderers, whores, black marketeers, crooks of every trade – and often the innocent victims they preyed upon'. He recounted how the body of a regular female patron was found in several plastic bags in a ditch, reflecting, 'It was all part of the strange adult world that I never tried to understand.' It was here, under the lights and amid the spit and sawdust that Savile claimed to receive his formal education.

In light of the Savile scandal, a common view of the music industry was evoked to help justify or explain what happened. Its culture centred on the social process of male stage performers inciting collectively expressed female desire, something which was potentially a cause for anxiety: initially for its superficiality and permissiveness, then for its sexism and potential to include predation. However, in this case, it appears that there were occasions when art, which almost certainly had been inspired by the worst possibilities and aspects of life, was again paralleled by reality. For instance, one girl who was a member of Savile's fan club wrote to him in 1968. Two years later a Rolls Royce arrived to pick her up, and she met Jimmy outside a local Town Hall. When they went inside a caravan, he told her he could get her a job on *Top of The Pops* and, without any prior invitation, he pushed her on to a bed and tried to have sex with her. As she left, he asked if she had her bus fare home, and said she could take something from the caravan as a memento (Erooga 2013b, p. 2).

Mulling over the *London Review of Books*' consideration of the BBC's research reports on Savile's first *Top of the Pops* appearances, Mark Fisher (2014) noted that Savile's emergence was greeted by negative comments such as 'this revolting spectacle', 'this nutcase' and 'this obnoxious "thing"'. For Fisher, such indications of aversion were evidence that Savile's 'ticket to fame was grotesquerie itself … [and] after the '60s, if you belonged on television, there was nowhere that wasn't open to you' (p. 91). This approach is an attempt to critique the emerging commercial vacuity of light entertainment as it positions Savile as a kind of garish spectacle in Daniel Boorstin's (1962/1997) classic sense: performing 'larger than life' celebrity as the act of garnering attention for attention's sake.[6] However, BBC viewers expressed the opposite. They were not just interested in anything flashy; they were being over-ridden by the broadcaster.

Savile's profile was arguably developed not because of his awkward, 'larger than life' persona, but *in spite of it*. As the NSPCC's report into Savile's abuse explained:

> In a 1990 interview for *The Independent on Sunday*, journalist Lynn Barber asked him about rumours that he liked young girls. Savile's reply was that, as he worked in the pop music business, 'the young girls in question don't gather round me because of me – it's because I know the people they love, the stars, I am of no interest to them.'
>
> (Gray and Watt 2013, p. 8)

In other words, Savile exploited his celebrity capital. He transmuted the currency of pure celebrity into sex appeal: as one women who pondered whether her son was his love child explained, 'Let's be honest, I only went out with someone looking like he did because of the people I could meet' (Hall 2012). This reading, however, makes the DJ a strange, pop art type of celebrity – certainly famous for being famous, but also a star and yet a kind of nobody, attractive for his connections. He was aligned more closely to music industry moguls (hence the cigar) and management than with pop musicians: exploiting others' fame for his own gain, though not necessarily financial reward.

Questions of industry raise the issue of whether Jimmy operated as part of a wider community. The 2013 NSPCC report on his crimes attempted a degree of closure over the issue:

> There is no clear evidence of Savile operating within a paedophile ring although whether he was part of an informal network is part of the continuing investigation and it's not therefore appropriate to comment further on this at this time.

The next year, Channel 5's *Crimes that Shook Britain* documentary series offered an episode on Savile (Nolan 2014) which suggested otherwise. In 1968, Savile's nephew Guy Marsden travelled from Leeds to London with three friends. They were approached by two men at Euston station. Marsden explained:

> I would have said about 30 years old, rock'n'roll: with leather jackets and long hair. They were just saying, 'Do you want to come to our place?' You've got to try and remember that there was no such thing as perverts. There was, but you didn't hear of them … We just thought they liked us, so we ended up going with these back to their flat.

Marsden found out that children enticed in this way could then be trafficked to other interested parties from 'higher up the chain … to take them elsewhere, to do what they were going to do with them'. When Savile arrived at the flat, Marsden thought he was being taken home, but then he realized the encounter was accidental:

> When my Uncle Jimmy came in, he was with this vicar and some kids ... I think he didn't catch me. I caught him ... He didn't seem to speak to us or acknowledge us. Every now and then you might have got a nod. He just seemed to come in, flitter about, do whatever he was doing – bringing little ones in, and stuff like that – and then he'd go. I recently found out I was getting what the police were calling 'groomed' to do what the people down London were doing, ie. getting the kids ... to go to these parties.

The documentary voice-over explained that Savile, 'far from being a lone predator, seemingly played an active role in supplying children to a network of child abusers in London'.

The version of the pop business associated with Savile was a seedy one where young runaways were apprehended by perverts at London train stations, plied with music, drugs and brushes with stardom, then treated as worthless human sex toys. While 'Uncle Jimmy' may well have been involved in such parties, it is important to also understand that the popular idea of them plays upon notions of the metropolitan music business as louche, shallow and exploitative. Two years after Marsden's trip to London, director Derek Ford released the exploitation feature, *Groupie Girl* (aka *I Am a Groupie*) (1970), which focused on the plight of Sally, a young fan who romantically fantasizes about getting close to the lead singer of her favourite band, but ends up passed between roadies and feeling jaded. With its loss of innocence narrative, *Groupie Girl* restructures this mass cultural notion of pop as swindle for the emergent era of the permissive society, locating it as a matter of sexual rather than financial exploitation. *Groupie Girl* reformulated a classic critique of popular music targeted, for example, at fans of the Beatles in 1964 by Paul Johnson:

> While the music is performed, the cameras linger savagely over the faces of the audience. What a bottomless chasm of vacuity they reveal! The huge faces, bloated with cheap confectionery and smeared with chain-store makeup, the open, sagging mouths and glazed eyes, the broken stiletto heels: here is a generation enslaved by a commercial machine.

This interpretation – which found its echo in Fred Vermorel's (1985/2011, p. 249) more concise claim that 'Pop is a frustration machine' – hints at an industry based on a con trick that constantly evokes (female) desire, but never authentically satisfies it.

Savile was a 'jingle jangle man' *par excellence* insofar as his garish and mesmeric exterior – the loud shell suits, the long white hair, acid-tinged 'granny' glasses and acid-tongued quips – superficially reflected youthful hedonism and working-class rebellion, but actually signified an almost psychic process of misdirection, in which he arrogantly crossed boundaries and underhandedly pillaged rewards, both financial and sexual, that he had not 'earned'. In light of this approach, Savile's charity work might be explicable less as penance and more as camouflage, an extension of his 'jingle jangle' smoke screen. Not only did Jimmy use his charity work to get closer to vulnerable people; anyone who raised millions would be harder to brand in public as a monster. As a clergyman explained, orating his funeral, 'His life story was an epic of giving – giving of time, giving of talent and giving of treasure' (*ITV News*, 2011).

The music industry is not, however, simply a monstrous circle of male predators and associated set of victims. Ironically, it was actually figures within the music scene – such as Francis Rossi – who, getting closer to the presenter himself, and without vested interests, were free to say more than many others about Savile and his misdeeds.

Savile as Spiv: 'All I ever wanted was to stop in bed'

Class difference is heavily signified in Britain by clothing and visual markers. They play a role in extending middle class prejudice and anxiety, which became focused in the early 2000s on the figure of the 'chav' (Jones 2011, p. 16). Commenting on the combination of economic progress and what he saw as a moral descent from a class-divided, workplace orientated, Britain – once characterized by deference, community and the stiff upper lip, Jeffrey Richards (1997, p. 20) claimed:

> Chivalry and sportsmanship were rejected in the 1960s on the grounds that they inhibited free expression and were class-based ... Instead of modelling themselves on such graceful and stylish gentlemen as Ronald Coleman and Leslie Howard, today's young Britons choose as their cinematic role models the muscle-bound thugs Arnold Schwarzenegger and Sylvester Stallone. Indeed, the very notion of heroism has been devalued and anti-heroes have become the order of the day.

While we might read Richards's interpretation as rather curmudgeonly, it is worthy of attention. His take on the age of affluence and associated consumer boom pinpoints some important shifts:

> In a delirious upsurge of Romanticism similar to that which overtook the early nineteenth-century, the rebel and deviant became heroes, the self was exalted, spontaneity was encouraged and rules, restrictions, conventions and traditions in both life and art ditched. The old structure, old values and old certainties (notably the doctrine of respectability) were increasingly derided and rejected … Violence, profanity and sexuality, hitherto rigorously suppressed, became prominent in both high culture and low culture. Personal style, cool, chic, cynical and consumerist, became the ideal: self-rather than service, immediate gratification rather than long-term spiritual or intellectual development. In the 1960s it became fashionable for the first time in British history to be young and working class.
>
> (1997, p. 18)

Savile epitomized this slide in Britain from the world of *Brief Encounter* (Lean 1945) and received pronounciation, through Elvis and the Beatles, and on to the neoliberal world of the 1980s where 'the young British now go round in baseball caps, eating McDonalds, using American slang, watching American films' (Richards 1997, p. 22). When the infamous Leeds DJ was considered for presenting *Juke Box Jury* (Potter 1959), Tom Sloan, who later became head of Light Entertainment said, 'I don't want that man on the television.' The show's producer, Johnny Stewart said, 'Sorry baby, but that man is box office. In his own sweet way – boy is he box office' (O'Hagan 2012, p. 8). Such portrayals are important because Savile emerged as a figure who symbolized commercial entertainment at precisely the time when it was becoming courted by the BBC. He was initially dismissed as 'a mere fairground huckster' by some at the corporation (p. 258). His case therefore cuts to the heart of the issue of public service broadcasting. After all, while the middle class metropolitan bastions of the public corporation nicknamed 'Auntie' had not only acquiesced to the evident financial value of an entertainer who was flash, brash, common and yet 'box office' – more naturally a candidate for the commercial populism of ITV – they had, in doing so, actually harboured a 'monster'.

Compassion was not Savile's forte and he had a characteristically ambiguous and exploitative relationship to the working class. For his *Clunk Click* series, which was named after his road safety campaign slogan, he mused, 'It seems to me that there are so many people doing such valuable jobs who have never been heard of. Why not give them the chance to speak?' (Davies 2014, p. 295) This apparent class solidarity, however, was over-ridden by Jimmy's *urge to exploit*.

A typical place to go for understanding the acts of an individual is to explore their approach to life. Jimmy Savile sometimes contrasted his self-conception with his image of his father. Vincent Savile was a figure that Jimmy described as scrupulously honest and scrupulously broke (Parkinson 1968). Instead, his son saw himself as 'tricky'. As the radio DJ explained in his last major interview:

> I never ever thought, for instance, that I was clever. Tricky? Yes – I'm a very tricky fella – but tricky is much better than being clever … If you are clever, you can slip up because you are clever, but if you're tricky you don't slip up. You never slip up if you're tricky. If something comes in front of you, whoa, you can get out of it, because you're tricky. You can skirt round it.
>
> (*Celebrity Radio by Alex Belfield* 2013)

In combination, Savile's contrast to his father and notion of trickiness implies that one of the archetypes Jimmy inhabited was that of the spiv. After all, he was a 'fixer of things' (Davies 2014, p. 19). Embodied by the characters played by British film and TV actors like George Cole and James Beck – who was Private Joe Walker on the BBC series *Dad's Army* – a wheeler dealer whose ability to hustle goods on the black market made him popular with everyone during the post-war era, a time of rationing and austerity. When asked in his last major interview whether it was good being Jimmy Savile, the DJ replied:

> I have been other people. When I worked down the pit, for instance, and I got 74 pence a week – 13 and nine pence in old money – I was somebody else then, because I didn't know that this world existed. It didn't exist because there was something on called a war … When I came out of the pit, and joined a scheme called *Lend A Hand On The Land*, which meant you could volunteer because you needed food, you needed this, that and the other … I thought, no, the clock of life is ticking away and I think I need a few quid, somehow, and so I started to run dances and discos … I got a name as a promoter, an entrepreneur.

Of his career as a dancehall DJ, Savile explained to biographer Dan Davies, 'It wasn't about the music or the power, it was about opportunity' (2014, p. 391). As Davies (2014) had it, 'To Jimmy Savile, pop music was nothing but business' (p. 220). Even with his charity work, Savile was arguably more interested in the process of making money than helping those who would benefit (p. 440). His efforts involved not only asking the public for donations, but also combining them with large sums requested from private companies and the government. He called the Duke of Edinburgh 'Boss' (p. 376) and saw his charity exploits as a case, in a sense, of blagging the co-operation of respectable businesses and representatives of the aristocracy, conning them into working for a good cause (p. 282). A spiv reading therefore explains something about Savile's career and approach to life.

The spiv is a loveable rogue, both 'dodgy' and appealing, because he offers a service that cannot function without the unethical participation of ordinary folk. As well as playing the role of a broker, he is, secondarily, an entertainer, egocentrically toying with the idea that his appeal primarily rests on personal charm. Above all, the spiv is a kind of cheat who gives the lie to the basis of the British class system because he refuses to become exploited labour. As a trader, his dictum is that 'only mugs work' (Ritchie 2014). Savile was especially interested in serving his own interests. In his final interview, he explained on Radio 2:

> Shall I tell you a quick Beatles story? I was going to America on an aeroplane to meet Elvis ... On the same plane that I got on, by some amazing fluke, were the Beatles ... John [Lennon] comes and sits down and says, "Alright, King Solomon – what are we doing wrong?' ... I said, 'Well, John, you're flying 3000 miles to work'. ... [They did it] to earn money for promoters, to earn money for agents, but what were they doing for themselves, except travelling 3000 miles?
>
> (*Celebrity Radio by Alex Belfield*, 2013)

Savile's intuitive instinct for self-service was not simply framed as a personal trait, however, but something he dreamed up as an antidote to the injustices of the class system. In the same interview, he contrasted the hardship of his formative years with the entertainment industry life that he engineered:

> I started off life down the pit and I used to get up at half past four in the morning, walk a mile and a half to catch a bus, get to the pit, and I'd walk another mile and a half, bent double, banging me head on the girders. So all I ever wanted was to stop in bed. How can you stop in bed? You can't stop in bed if you're a plumber. You can't stop in bed if you're a builder, or anything like that. So the only thing I found where you could stop in bed was to run a disco or a dance hall ... because at least you could stop in bed until 12 o'clock. That suited me down to the ground. I turned it into a bit of fun. I thought, stopping in bed is terrific. What else is there? I thought, I know, a bit of fun. So I had a bit of fun, at nobody's expense.

Jimmy Savile's own visual and verbal inhabitation of the spiv role located it in the commercial opportunities of the pop era. Crucial here is that he was grounded in the world of musical entertainment, yet had no direct discernable musical talent, except perhaps as a DJ. Savile's perspective on show business referenced both innocent pleasure and commercial exploitation:

> It's a business that promotes and sells pleasure, so there's no reason why all that pleasure cannot enter your own life ... If you have a good time, that is addictive and that is communicative, and other people have a good time, so you all have a good time .... If you've got a pound in your pocket, someone, somewhere wants it, and they will come up with all sorts of reasons why you should give them that pound ... It wasn't like that sixty years ago, but it is today.
> (*Celebrity Radio by Alex Belfield*, 2013)

In 1959, the actor Lawrence Harvey played his career-defining role as the aspirational, Northern social climber Joe Lampton in Jack Clayton's realist melodrama, *Room at the Top*. Lampton, who hails from a lowly fellside village in Cumbria, pursues an industrialist's daughter in his efforts to marry up. During one scene he explains to one factory boss, 'Dufton's not much of a place, but we're not exactly savages there, you know, Mr Hoylake.' Just under a year later, Lawrence Harvey was back on British cinema screens, this time as the fast-talking wheeler-dealing talent spotter Johnny Jackson in Val Guest's 1959 Cliff Richard vehicle, *Expresso Bongo*. Notions of the shady, opportunistic music manager were well established by this point. Consider the figure of Hunk Haughton in Richard Thorpe's 1957 Elvis film *Jailhouse Rock*. Savile merely capitalized on a long-held myth that the music business was a place where older men preyed upon talented and innocent youth. Like social climber Joe Lampton, he was a poor Northerner who aspired to better. Like talent spotter Johnny Jackson, he was a spiv character. However, Savile was, by his own words, also a 'freak' and he exploited that persona to draw on perceptions of the entertainment industry in which he worked. He seemed hard to locate: playful, obfuscating, uncanny and capricious. By the 1970s, perceptions had changed, too, of the industry to which he belonged. Cultural sociologist Nick Couldry (2000, p. 112) has described a widespread public perception of the media and film industries as a kind of glamorous other world that stands in stark contrast to most people's everyday life. Here the music industry does not just appear glamorous, however. It appears seedy. In other words, it may be more appropriate to consider Edward Said's (1978/2003) notion of Orientalism.

Said (1978/2003) argued that Western nations projected desire and fear on to the territories that they colonized, framing 'the Orient' as both sexually permissive and threatening, a place where captured, vulnerable, young, White women could be enslaved and exploited; a place where even full grown, White, male adventurers could be harmed. It could be argued that in the postcolonial period, rock'n'roll, with its cross-racial connotations, became associated with the social 'dangers' of sexual liberation, and such perceptions remained – even once rock became 'White-washed' as an introspective form of musical expression. Sometime soon after Beatlemania, a perception had emerged that stars were not the only young people exploited by the pop machine. Following the tenor of mass cultural criticism, young female pop fans were perceived of as vulnerable and exploited too. Sometimes that exploitation was portrayed as having a sexual dimension. While a range of magazine articles and documentaries appeared at the end of the 1960s and very early 1970s showing groupies as liberated and acquisitive, other portrayals suggested there was a price to pay. Returning to Derek Ford's notion of the music business as an exciting and exotic, but potentially dangerous and damaging place, Francis Rossi told *Hardtalk*:

> I still find the fascination – if you look at the *X Factor* generation: they wanna get round here [points behind hand]. They see this front of showbiz. It looks fabulous. Well, of course it looks fabulous; it's show business! You don't want to see the real bit at the back here. I find I get on people's –, I cheese them off, because I say, 'You don't want to see what's back here. It's grim. It's just ordinary and mundane'.

As Savile extended his audience and celebrity image, he became a family entertainer who could then play knowingly upon his roots in the seedy netherworld of the pop business. At this point, Joseph Conrad's classic novella, *The Heart of Darkness* (1899/1995), makes a useful comparison. In Conrad's famous fictional story, Marlow is appointed as a steamboat captain in Africa and sent down the Congo river to trade ivory. Along the way he hears rumours about a powerful, mystical figure called Mr Kurtz. As Marlow finds out when they meet, Kurtz is a White man who has had a lot of success trading ivory, but has also 'gone native'. He is worshipped by the locals. Marlow finds Kurtz psychologically overwhelming, even though the infamous trader's physical and mental health is in decline. In the narrative, Mr Kurtz comes to embody the dark side of Western projections about colonialism. Kurtz appears to have become infected by African madness, but he is really the product of Western projections. By suggesting that European powers were not 'immune to the gothic potentialities of their colonized territories', *The Heart of Darkness* therefore questions whether they were 'civilized' at all. Powerful and seductive, in his madness, Kurtz acts out an Orientalist conception of colonial Africa.

In 1971, Philip Norman wrote, 'Such an ectoplasm exists around [Savile] that it has become difficult to perceive the actual man at all.'[7] According to biographer Dan Davies (2014, p. 505): 'like Conrad's Kurtz, he [Savile] was supremely controlling'. He added, 'there was never any doubt in my mind that arriving at the real Jimmy Savile would entail a journey into the heart of darkness. Hence the title I'd planned for my book, and now its opening chapter: "Apocalypse Now Then"' (p. 506).

Like Mr Kurtz, Savile had a reputation for being powerful, underhand and monstrous: potentially violent stemming from his days as a dancehall manager. In reality, he was also absolutely Mr Kurtz: willing to display a vicious and violent streak, or opportunistically perform sexual assaults on innocent youngsters, assaults which appeared to demonstrate no aim other than to affirm his own untouchability. In 1972, he boasted to the newspapers 'of his days as a black market operator in Leeds' (Davies 2014, p. 277). Savile celebrated his promotion by ordering a brand new Rolls Royce from Jack Barclay's in London. He went in to collect it in person wearing a pair of fur slippers. According to a newspaper report, the vehicle was fitted with a 'record player, radio, fridge and a shillelagh, the reason for the latter being in the dance hall business, possession of a blunt instrument is nine tenths of the law' (p. 184). Biographer Dan Davies observed:

> As he memorably put it in his autobiography, he became 'the confidant of murderers, whores, black marketers, crooks of every trade – and often the innocent victims they preyed upon'. He recounted how the body of a regular female patron was found in several plastic bags in a ditch.
>
> (2014, p. 41)

By the early 1960s, Savile reportedly had six bodyguards (Davies' 2014, p. 185). His assortment of aids included at least one giant wrestler (p. 132), an even bigger one in Leeds (p. 139) and three Hungarians who had worked for the Nazis (Davies' 2014, p. 139). Savile was not afraid of issuing threats to troublemakers at the Plaza (Davies' 2014, p. 133). In *God'll Fix It*, Savile recalled 'how he took troublemakers in his dancehall downstairs to the boiler room whereupon they'd be tied up and gagged. After everyone else had gone home, his minders would beat them' (p. 343). 'I was the meanest man in Manchester,' he once claimed (p. 191). At one 1960s gig where the Rolling Stones did not have their instruments and were reluctant to play, Savile told them, 'If you're not going to play you're going to be unconscious because my minders are going to chin all of you ... And I'll throw you to the fucking audience' (p. 218). In the mid-1980s, one double page spread was headlined, 'My Violent World by Jim the Godfather', with the tag-line, 'How I fixed it the night I wanted someone beaten up' (p. 381). The story explained how Savile had ordered his minders to kick a man's head in, and that he also humiliated another man he caught trying to seduce his girl. He added, 'He thought he was going to have his legs broken – it wouldn't be anything unusual' (p. 382). Dan Davies even wondered whether Savile might have been a murderer (p. 544).

Savile's reputation for violence was only matched by his bantering claims to being a ladies man. For his payment in 1967 to help the Otley Civic Ball, the DJ wanted 'a guard of honour of six young ladies – in another tent of course – to keep me safe'; Dan Davies called this a 'barefaced' demand for payment in girls (Davies 2014, p. 237). Savile plied them with vodka and made advances on them (p. 241). Just after he was awarded an OBE in 1972, the *People* ran with, 'Me and My 3,000 birds – At last! Jimmy Savile's Own Story' (p. 242). In 1972, Savile wrote in one newspaper of a scene with six girls in his caravan appearing like 'a cross between a double-X film set and multi-legged octopus', and that he had to bluff the next say when the parents of one girl arrived (p. 278). The DJ explained in a 1974 *People* story called 'Why I Never Married – I can have my pick of 25 dollies any night,' 'In my game the girls abound like summer flowers' (p. 306). He told the *News of the World* that same year, 'I'm no saint. I want it to be known that I'm a great crumpet man' (p. 306). Ironically, in the mid-1980s, 'the claims about his promiscuous sex life, allied with the thuggish aspects of his dancehall career, meant it was again decided that it would be wise to consider him for a future [not present Knighthood] list' (p. 387).

According to biographer Dan Davies:

> So, far from being a dirty secret that Jimmy Savile strove to conceal, his desire to have sex with teenage girls, and the frequency with which he was able to satisfy his desire, had mutated into an expression of power.
>
> (2014, p. 229)

This excessive, Kurtzian reputation for violence and permissiveness was reflected in posthumous rumours about Savile's private life, some of which suggested that he participated in, or perhaps even orchestrated, organized child abuse. He was known to visit houses associated with vice rings, like the one on Battersea Bridge Road in London thought to be used by absconders from the Duncroft Approved School (p. 223). In Scarborough, Savile was thought to be 'a member of a group of older men known locally as "The Club" ... Some alleged the Club's members attended sex parties for which local youngsters were procured' (p. 286).

While Davies' claim of Savile being a Kurtz-like figure frames the biographer himself as a kind of Marlow, there, however, is another way to see it. In the 1970s Savile successfully managed to diversify his media career beyond the teenage market and become a family and children's entertainer. By 1973, 'Jimmy Savile was now seen as a man who could communicate with the population at large' (Davies 2014, p. 294). In 1974, Savile appeared in party political broadcasts by both the Conservatives and Liberals; he was marked as a potential vote winner (p. 304). He was liked at the BBC for his ability to bridge generations and social classes (p. 257). In the preface to *God'll Fix It*, Reverend Colin Semper pondered, 'Who is this blond-haired eccentric who can help a prostitute with a problem on the same day as he introduces [the Christian show] *Songs of Praise*?' (p. 342). At its peak, his signature show *Jim'll Fix It* had 15 million viewers per week and 'made its host an icon for daydreaming children everywhere' (p. 319).

If the music industry had become an Orientalized place, then 'Uncle Jimmy' the family entertainer could also play a kind of tour guide, Marlow role, charming the tabloids with stories of shock and violence from his days in the Northern live music industry. One part a monstrous criminal and the other a benign children's entertainer, Savile revealed in this 'jingle-jangle' a switching of hats. His Radio 1 colleague Paul Gambaccini claimed that the Leeds disc jockey played the tabloids 'like a Stradivarius' (Davies 2014, p. 385). As Savile explained it to the *Daily Express*, 'Well, 19 or 20 year olds with some experience of the world might look upon me as a sexual object. But the younger ones, the 14 to 16 year olds, don't even think about sex. In fact they would be most offended if you suggested anything sexual to them' (p. 271). Of *Top of the Pops*, he explained it was 'remarkably free of seductions and drug taking, but there are lots of dates made by everybody' (p. 269). In his role as music industry tour guide, Savile explained in another story in 1973, 'Say what you want about the pop scene, but I have never done anything which I believe would corrupt anyone' (p. 295). For a mid-1980s press story he also explained, 'I never take advantage of a fan. If a girl asks me for an autograph I don't say, "You're nice, come home with me for three days" ... Parents can trust their 17-year-old daughters with me ... I'll never take advantage' (p. 383). In another story from around the same time:

> He freely admitted that in his early days there were girls and groupies camped outside his home. He didn't deny that he had enjoyed them. 'But that's all changed now,' he insisted. 'Ever since I started my hospital and charity work, it all stopped. People began to look at me differently.'
>
> (p. 385)

In a further *Sun* tabloid story he explained in the mid-1980s, 'They [female fans] may idolize me but they're not coming into my gaff' (p. 418).

The Thatcher connection

> Child abuse is now a national obsession, but in 1963 it scarcely came up as a subject of public concern. That doesn't mean it was fine back then and we were all better off, but it allows one to see how much the public understanding of what isn't all right, or more or less all right, has changed. There have always been genuine causes for concern, but overall, nowadays there is an unmistakable lack of proportion in the way we talk about the threat posed to children by adults. (It's hard not to imagine that the situation has to do with a general estrangement from the notion of a reliable community.) The 1960s, on the other hand, seem like a sexual kaleidoscope made of unusual colours, out of focus, out of order, but not 'out'. There is always a dark lining to permission – asking for it, granting it – and 1963 was a moment of blurring more than a moment of clarity. Women might have worn shorter skirts and gone on the pill but society still didn't – and still doesn't – sexually know itself as well as it might. (O'Hagan 2012, p. 7)

In the *London Review of Books*, Andrew O'Hagan (2012) condemned the actuality of predatory incidents at any point in time, but also argued that the reporting of child abuse had a moral panic dimension. He suggests that contemporary public anxiety about it can be read as a symptom of neoliberal culture: 'a general estrangement from the notion of a reliable community'. It is worth considering this argument in more detail. O'Hagan's reading is associated with what Mark Fisher has described as a moment of cancellation, associated with the attempted erasure of footage of Savile from television reruns. Fisher explains, 'the period since 1979 in Britain has seen the gradual but remorseless destruction of the very concept of the public ... Public space has been consumed and replaced by something like the third place exemplified by franchise coffee bars' (2014, p. 137). He also elaborates:

> Someone, I don't remember who, says it's like the '70s have gone on trial. Yes, that very particular strand of the '70s that is under investigation – not the officially debauched rock'n'roll '70s, not Zeppelin or Sabbath, but the family entertainment '70s … Murdoch and the *Daily Mail* wasted no time in pushing the idea that the abuse was an institutional pathology – it was the BBC, and, more broadly, the paternalistic media culture of the '60s and '70s, which had incubated Savile's corruption. The BBC, now in a permanent state of confusion about its role in a neoliberal world, duly went into a neurotic, narcissistic collapse.
>
> (2014, p. 92)

The line of reasoning Fisher attributes to media mogul Rupert Murdoch and the *Daily Mail* is not true. It was not a case of public service bodies incubating Savile's corruption due to their own institutional pathologies. His monstrosity was a case of his own elaborate making or acquiescence, and it was a selfish signifier of the neoliberal regime to come.

Ultimately, whether Savile was an agent of the 'deep state' or had simply inveigled his way into the British Establishment was immaterial. He was protected by them. In that context, his alibis and excuses were also *theirs*. Blaming the inadequacies of 1970s institutional culture – as a place that bred deference to wealth, celebrity or men – does not account for Savile, any more than the idea he was a conman who groomed the nation. The culture that simply accepted what he did because he was untouchable was abetted by perceptions of the music scene which labelled it as a space of wildness that was simultaneously a joke about an open secret. Modes of explanation of the sort that Savile span out to front his operation have not entirely disappeared. A good example of this was given by the television documentary maker, Louis Theroux, who met Savile as part of his BBC series *When Louis Met* … Theroux capitalized on Savile's creepiness – making him a documentary subject and asking him on screen about rumours of paedophilia – and then had the awkward task of deflecting criticism that he really knew about it, but never worked on behalf of victims to bring the Leeds DJ to justice. Once the scandal came to light, Theroux made another documentary called *Louis Theroux: Savile* (Cary 2016), in which he interviewed some of the victims. What this new documentary did, in part, was perform the cultural work of exonerating the BBC, providing alternative frames that would avoid the question of cover-up and corruption. During the second documentary he explained of Savile, 'In his time, he charmed Royalty and Prime Ministers, and millions of us who listened to him, and saw him on the TV. So, to understand his crimes, we should all remember how we were beguiled.' To frame Jimmy Savile as a conman who *beguiled the nation* seems somewhat misguided, as it suggests he pulled the wool over everyone's eyes using nothing more than his own charm and appeal, when in fact the Leeds DJ had fluctuating levels of both. In a more recent memoir, Louis used the idea of music industry permissiveness to maintain that all *he* knew for sure were rumours:

> His private life was famously obscure. For almost as long as I can recall – certainly since my early teens – I'd heard there was something sexually untoward about Jimmy Savile. But one didn't attach any more significance to these rumours than to the idea that a certain film star had a furry animal removed from his rectum or that a rock star collapsed on his way to a gig and had his stomach pumped of six pints of semen.
>
> (Theroux 2019, p. 137)

While the discussion came within an extended section on Savile and seeing his friends and victims, with Louis sensitively assessing their changing moods over a period of time, what is striking is the *insensitivity* of this in comparison. Theroux is asking us to understand why he was in denial, but the function of this word-picture of mythologized vulgarity seems to be to stop us, as readers, from considering real CSA. It is as if the music industry has become a kind of alter-ego or 'alternative universe' for the Establishment: a place of hidden permissiveness, where corruption could operate with public knowledge, while ordinary observers, like punters waiting in the line-up for their local nightclub, accepted it as part of the game.

The sociologist Stanley Cohen has claimed that, due to wars and other wrong doings, 'Denial ... is built into the ideological façade of the state' (2001, p. 10). Jimmy Savile's success predated, but continued with Margaret Thatcher's period in office as Britain's political leader. Cultural studies theorist Stuart Hall (1980, p. 26) said her ascent to power was part of a radical, global move to the Right that forwarded 'a wide range of social and political issues under the social market philosophy'. He added, 'It is the only parliamentary political force resolutely committed to the view that "things cannot go on in the old way." It knows that it must de-struct in order fundamentally to reconstrust' (p. 26). Well known for her union-crushing stance, the 'Iron Lady' entered into a pact of mutual support with Savile. He 'wooed' her by enabling her to present a £10,000 cheque to the

NSPCC in 1980 (p. 355). Stoke Mandeville Hospital nearly closed because the NHS could not afford its refurbishment before Jimmy Savile stepped in and raised the funds for its new National Spinal Injuries Centre (p. 356).

Ultimately, Savile's spiv-like, disingenuous and borderline psychopathic qualities were invaluable in the alliance he created with Thatcher. While attempting to return to family values, economically, Mrs Thatcher increased inequality when she rejected Britain's Keynesian consensus, privatized industry and started to dismantle the welfare state. She made her individualist creed very clear:

> I think we have been through a period when too many people have been given to understand that when they have a problem it is government's job to cope with it. 'I have a problem, I'll get a grant. I'm homeless, the government must house me'. They are casting their problems on society. And, you know, there is no such thing as society. There are individual men and women and there are families. And no governments can do anything except through people, and people must look to themselves first. It is our duty to look after ourselves and then, also, to look after our neighbours. People have got their entitlements too much in mind, without the obligations.
>
> (Brittan 2013)

In relation to such positions, Savile was, in a sense, Thatcher's awkward remainder. Unlike her in so many ways, he was notionally, at least, an embarrassment. Yet enchanted by whatever he used as his spell, she battled to get him his knighthood. Ultimately, Savile epitomized Thatcher's entrepreneurial stance, but also taking it further and unmasking it as a step towards a slide into indecent behaviour: 'there is no such thing as society ... people must look to themselves first'. At one point, the *Sun* ran a Stanley Franklin cartoon featuring Jimmy Savile in a pin-striped gangster's suit and fedora, sitting comfortable in front of a sign which says, 'Godfather Jim'll Fix It.' Mrs Thatcher gives him the profiles of various labour leaders – Michael Foot, Dennis Healey, Arthur Scargill, David Steel and Tony Benn – and says, 'Bump off this lot and I'll see you get a knighthood' (p. 347). As Mrs Thatcher had it, 'Jimmy is a truly great Briton. He is a stunning example of opportunity Britain, a dynamic example of enterprise Britain and an inspiring example of responsible Britain' (2014, p. 49). In turn, she was loyal to Jimmy, accepting his invitation, for instance, to appear on *Jim'll Fix It* (p. 374). Dan Davies said Mrs Thatcher and Jimmy made a natural pair because both were outsiders who took on the Establishment: 'Both were prepared to do what it took, and neither seemed to care what anyone thought of them' (p. 375). However, psychiatrist Dr Anthony Clare noted that Jimmy was uninterested in altruistic concepts like sharing or sacrifice (p. 439). According to Dan Davies, 'he was and remained a money grabber to his core' (p. 221). In the world of the spiv, everything is potentially an opportunity, and every opportunity is potentially a con. There is thus an ethical parallel between financial and sexual.

Jimmy Savile combined a trickster's sense of fun and frivolity with arrogance and entitlement. This transferred to matters of romance. On his sex life, he once explained:

> Savile: My game was not to have one wife, but to have a thousand. A thousand wives makes your hair go white. Did you know that? It keeps you slim, and you get people looking for you, who want to chin you, and all that sort of stuff, but all there was, was an oil drip, and that's where you were yesterday, and you've gone.
> Belfield: Are you saying you were a stud muffin?
> Savile: No, no, no, no – I don't even know what that is. All I know is, most people want one wife, I quite liked having a thousand, like King Solomon. It was terrific. I think of them sheiks of old, when they had the harems and all that.
> Belfield: Why could you never find one special person. Did you dream of that, or did it never matter?
> Savile: Yeah, I tried every day. Then by five o'clock, I found that wasn't the special person, but I might find her tomorrow. In fact, my case comes up on Thursday.

In a characteristically mischievous performance on the Radio 4 show *In the Psychiatrist's Chair*, Savile talked to Dr Clare about his approach to life. The DJ made statements such as:

> I'm not constrained, pretty well, by anything. The tough thing in life is ultimate freedom. That's when the battle starts. Ultimate freedom is what it's all about for people, but you've got to be very strong to stand for ultimate freedom … With doing the things that I do, wearing the caps that I wear, I've got some considerable clout as well, all over, so that's where the battle is … I've got everything.
>
> (*tartantroozers* 2011)

This rather Nietzschean statement seems cryptic and nonsensical, but placed in the context of Savile's sexual misdeeds, it suggests psychopathic and sociopathic traits. Clare concluded the Leeds DJ was 'a man without feelings' ('Professor Anthony Clare' 2007). He was certainly a figure who lived by his own creed, regardless of any moral or social opposition. In that sense, Western popular music, with its promotion of the rebel, the sexually and psychologically free subject, was a useful tool or cover for Jimmy Savile. However, it is also clear from his statement that 'free' acts would inevitably bring about resistance, which could only be countered by being 'very strong' and using social 'clout'. Savile's knighthood was not granted until 1990, after Margaret Thatcher made repeated attempts to make it a reality. She had become Britain's prime minister in May 1979. Within a year, after one of their personal meetings, Jimmy Savile had written to her, signing his letter, 'Jimmy Savile, OBE'; such was the calibre of his 'brazen charm' (Bowcott 2012). Some of the interactions between the DJ and prime minister provoked enquiries from civil servants asking if she had promised to give money to Stoke Mandeville or to appear on *Jim'll Fix It*. Material released from the archives in 2012 contained a letter and telephone call between Savile and Thatcher that have been withheld from the public and would not be released for another decade (Bowcott 2012).

Central to Savile's thinking was an exploitative, 'something for nothing' mentality, which extended into both the worlds of business and sex, and often put both together in a consistent kind of calculus. In other words, Savile brought the same approach to his sexual offences as he did to his music business dealings. Both were pursued with a ruthless, calculating, systematic opportunism. As a dancehall manager, he cut costs by replacing bands and spinning records instead. According to Dan Davies (2014), 'he said he often let girls in free because he knew they would be good for business' (p. 145). His live music shows at the Plaza became successful in part because he included 'Smooch time' for jiving teenagers (p. 129). At one point he advertised them with posters that said, 'Saturday night is crumpet night'. Savile also saw his DJ work as a way to qualify his live audience, in effect to select out a steady stream of willing female company (p. 145). When he started exploiting the media, having a halo of teens around him made Savile seem young (p. 186). He used promises of sex with women to attract the company of men (p. 152). Typical of this calculus was a moment at one point in 1973 when Savile's love life was shielded by fabricated news of an affair with Polly James of the group Pickettywitch, but 'it was "a set up for publicity" designed to promote the band's new single' (p. 294).

As religious studies scholar Linda Ceriello (2018) has noted, 'In many monster narratives, the monster is deployed to symbolize that which threatens or has gone wrong in society or within an individual – that which, once "fixed," will result in the restoration of the social order' (p. 207). Dr Ceriello also suggests much academic research on the cultural work of monsters also makes this assumption (p. 207). High on the Leeds DJ's exploitative logic was the idea of 'the ledger': a concept that suggested his excess of good deeds (as a charity fund raiser) might counterbalance any bad deeds (such as the exploitative sexual demands he placed on young people).[8] This idea was prominent in his thinking, and may, to some degree, be a reworking of Catholic or perhaps esoteric doctrines. More importantly, what it suggests is that a large amount of good deeds – and Jimmy certainly did plenty of those – could be used to exonerate any sinner and, in effect, 'buy off' his wrong doings. This idea gave him license to molest girls without seeking any form of help to address his monstrous predilections. Ultimately, though, the ledger never fully added up. Even if it neutralized the work involved in denial by making Savile an 'admitter' instead (see Cohen 2001, p. 62), it could never quite be used to offer comfort, let alone anything like justice. Despite financial gains and legal immunity, Savile never escaped from a world of total emotional poverty. In one mid-1980s press story, he explained, 'I don't allow myself the luxury of personal feelings. It's the same with my ladies' (Davies 2014, p. 382).

As a final note, it should be mentioned that Savile's heyday paralleled the discovery and popularization of CSA as a crime against the individual. According to the sociologist Frank Furedi (2013, p. 56), 'In the 1960s the word "victim" became associated with the subjective experience of an identity.' In Britain, the early 1970s are associated with the first use of the term 'child abuse' and it has spread exponentially since then, limited only by the backlash against fabricated memories in the 1980s. CSA is a murky crime insofar that the act itself can mentally destabilize its victims, and evidence for it can easily be hidden. Children are not always taken as reliable witnesses. It has also been positioned as a hidden epidemic and social scourge. These things are true, but what is also worth considering is that increasing media coverage of them has emerged in parallel with the neoliberal era. From this perspective, a media focus on hidden corruption and abused – often anonymized – victims generates endless speculation and hides less magnetic state crimes, including spending on war (currently formulated, in part, as a fight against terrorism), the doctrine of austerity (against public spending) and the effort that goes into freeing the way for capital to further increase class inequality. Growing recognition of the extent of child abuse as a social problem has been informed by a confessional media culture, where figures such as Oprah Winfrey built their business empires by helping victims to speak out and find their healing. Here, in relation to CSA, it is relevant to note that the figure of the innocent child, specifically, is a symbol of 'futurity' (Edelman 2004): an indication of the state of society through suppositions about the future. As exponential technological development encourages us to look to the future, as the figure of the abused child has become prominent, citizens in neoliberal society face greater competition, stress and inequality than previous generations. In that sense, beyond a shared need to address the repressed horrors of actual child abuse, popular anxiety over the subject may perhaps also reflect the anxious sense of 'no future' experienced by millennials. As it tainted generational memory, Savile's case pointed to personal horrors, and systemic corruption, but *its portrayal* suggests there may be further things it has helped us avoid.

Despite all the institutional reports, the tragic truism of the #MeToo era is that serial abuse could still be happening, and might well happen again in the future, because cunning combined with privilege can still buy increased freedom from criminal justice. What this helps to generate is, in a sense, free floating affect. It could therefore be argued that the sensationalism around Jimmy Savile has plunged audiences a small step further into an abstract realm where emotion is socially orchestrated in part for *capital's* end. The problem of the inherent lack of justice for Savile's victims has made a quiet contribution to cancel culture (see Fisher 2014). Drawing attention to this might sound like a ploy to downplay the meaning and significance of Jimmy's crimes. That is not the present intention. Tragically and undeniably, *he had real victims*. As a recent article by Karen Boyle (2018) made clear, decades of acceptance of 'everyday sexism' was part of what shielded the DJ even as his posthumous scandal broke in the early 2010s: any 'recasting of Savile as monster' was 'not as immediate or as wholesale as previous commentators have claimed … understandings of Savile as a prolific child sexual abuser jostle[d] with debates about sexual morality which had previously fit, relatively comfortably, with Savile's media image' (p. 1571). My argument concurs with Boyle, adding that Savile's entitled stance benefited not only from a slippage between permissiveness and domestication associated with a safely Orientalized 1970s music industry, but also from the self-interest propagated by Thatcherism. *As well as* paying attention to Savile's monstrous crimes, we should, *also* consider the *recent* mediascape as an ideological context in which he was posthumously evoked to symbolize a sense that *the past has betrayed the present*, cultivating intense, shared, outrage: a shout of collective protest at injustice for the heartbreaking horrors he caused.

Notes

Chapter 1

1. Gothic novels were associated with just such a reader at the time. Contemporary discourses stressed the excessive 'sensibility' of its (female) readers (liable to emotional excess and associated nervous ailments); and the sensationalist content of the novels. Jane Austen's *Northanger Abbey* includes references to gothic fiction (*The Monk, Udolpho*), parodying the genre and its (female) readers. The 'highly strung imagination' of Christine seems very much in line with Austen characters such as Margaret Dashwood in *Sense and Sensibility*.
2. In relation to Erik's extortion … Dead labour primarily matters as an experience that displaces living workers. In Leroux's version of the Phantom story, the issue is highlighted when Erik, in his guise as the Opera ghost, attempts to extort a fortune from its managers, giving them the ultimatum that he will otherwise blow up the whole edifice. Evidently, he is both a blackmailer and terrorist – the music market's impulse to creative destruction played out through a phantom. Erik's go-between in this process of extortion is the working-class usher Madam Giry. The Opera's management team begin to question the very idea of a ghost and start to place the blame on Giry herself, in the end firing her from her role. In that sense, we might argue that as technology moves forwards and changes the grounds for competition, businesses which struggle to survive often slash their costs, starting with labour, perhaps blaming wage demands as the source of their difficulty.
3. ASCAP is an acronym for the American Society of Composers, Authors and Publishers, while BMI stands for Broadcast Music, Inc.
4. It could even be hypothesized that Erik's disfigurement is itself a form of castration; see Freud's discussion of 'The Sandman' (Freud 1919/1997b).
5. Diminutive in stature, Paul Williams was chosen to play Swan as a grasping, egocentric figure. De Palma was undoubtedly aware of the ironic casting: the actor was himself a talented songwriter whose material had already been used on David Bowie's *Hunky Dory* LP.
6. One reading here might be that Devereaux, in his shamed and despised predicament, at least – though not his personality – resembled 'Tricky Dicky', the 'bad father' of the nation: a post-Watergate President Nixon.
7. While it might be tempting to see a band replaced by clones as a kind of early indication of the tribute artist phenomenon, my point in this chapter is that there

has, in one form or another, been perpetual anxiety about the replacement of 'authentic' live musicians throughout the era of recorded music.

8. When Seymour reclines on a bed, her styling in the film bears a strong resemblance to the cover photo from Madonna's *Like a Virgin* album, which was released the following year.

Chapter 2

1. Some readings of *King Kong* include the idea that Kong *is* the media (as there are a lot of screen-within-screen shots) or that he represents new media corporations (he has to scale the RKO tower).
2. Aside from a slew of sequels and other movie releases, which included a Japanese version called *King Kong Returns* in 1968, the myth of the big gorilla had also made its mark on popular music. One hit wonder Big T Tyler had retold the story in a rockabilly style in 1957. The Kinks recorded a song with the same title around the time of their 1968 LP *The Kinks are the Village Green Preservation Society*.
3. Lead Belly wanted to play Gene Autry's 1935 hit 'That Silver-Haired Daddy of Mine', for example, but John Lomax wrote, 'We held him to the singing of the music that first attracted us to him' (Filene 1991, p. 613).
4. See Long (2019).

Chapter 3

1. This was the copy in a PDF synopsis for the film from around 2017, but it has since been replaced by the more moderate 'to most people Colonel Parker was the shady hustler who took half of Elvis' fortune and worked his protégé into an early grave. But was this an image that the Colonel deliberately cultivated?' It is worth noting, too, that Stone was Presley's tour producer. See: http://www.seanchaifilms.net/media/Seanchai_catalogue.pdf
2. Parker was, famously, High Potentate of the 'Snowmen's League of America', a club skitting the Showmen's League of America that he created, based on the idea that people should be 'snowed' – conned, fogged, bamboozled, confused with false information – in order to get things done (see Nash 2003, p. 155).
3. See Duffett (1998, p. 86).
4. Chapters on Elvis's generosity include 'Its Only Money' (Yancey 1977, p. 79–98) and 'A Natural Resource' (Lacker et al. 1979, pp. 144–61).
5. Charlie Hodge put this point speaking to fans at the Official Elvis Presley Fan Club of Great Britain's Mabelthorpe event in 1996.

6   For a different perspective, see Duffett (2018).
7   For a discussion of recent neoliberal era self-branding see Marwick (2015).

Chapter 5

1   In focusing on these topics, I am deliberately ignoring, for example, the conspiracy theories that suggested John was killed by the CIA, or the popular notion that his death marked the end of the 1960s dream. These topics may deserve research.
2   The cynical narrator of *The Catcher in the Rye* used the word 'killed' mostly in a cynical way, to suggest he was amused about things. This usage itself dissociates the term from the act of killing, transporting it into the expression of flippancy: saying that the situation 'killed me' suggests that the narrator viewed it as an ironic joke.
3   In Chapter 4 of Freud's (1913/2001) book *Totem and Taboo*, young, upcoming males attempt to wrest the control of women from the clutches of the tribal patriarch: a dominant older male figure. For Freud, this scenario reflects the plight of brothers marginalized by their alpha-male father.
4   For a more detailed discussion of the idea of imagined memories, see Duffett (2010a, 2010b).
5   The first side of *Unfinished Music #2: Life with the Lions* from 1969, for example, contained just one 26 minute art composition called 'Cambridge 1969'. It consisted of Yoko shrieking over a continuous bed of feedback. Compared to the Beatles music, 'Cambridge 1969' was an endurance test for listeners. However, what should also be noted is that George Harrison entered similar, experimental territory, notably on his 1969 solo album, *Electronic Sound*.
6   John's words can be heard in *The U.S. vs John Lennon* (Leaf and Scheinfeld 2006).
7   What the 'hell was other people' reading ignores is that negativity may occasionally have come from John towards Yoko, as he struggled to square the distrust for women he carried from his upbringing with the intensity of his love for her.
8   A good example of this is 'John & Yoko' from *The Wedding Album* in 1969, where the couple say each other's names, moving through various mutually responsive intonations, over a sound bed that resembles a beating heart. The result seems undeniably intimate, playfully performing the emotional dynamics that couples experience at close range.

Chapter 6

1   In between the first two albums was an interesting 1995 EP released with the Bristol trip hop artist Tricky, significantly entitled *The Hell E.P.*, which entered the UK singles charts at number 12.

Chapter 8

1. Other reports included over forty local NHS enquiry reports based on specific hospitals, two reports into the BBC and its *Newsnight* show – which pulled a Savile story – Ken McQuarrie's *Findings of the Editorial Standards Committee of the BBC Trust: Newsnight, BBC2, 2 November 2012* (December 2012) and *Pollard Report* (December 2012) – Surrey Police's *Report into Operation Ornament* (January 2013), Kate Lampard's *Independent Oversight of NHS Department of Health Investigations into Matters Relating to Jimmy Savile* (June 2014), Peter Wanless and Richard Whittam's *An Independent Review of Two Home Office Commissioned Reviews looking at Information Held in Connection with Child Abuse from 1979–1999* (November 2014), the Department of Education's *Independent Oversight of Investigations into Matters Relating to Jimmy Savile at Schools and Children's Homes* (February 2015), the Department of Health's *NHS Savile Legacy Unit: Oversight Report* (February 2015) and a report into Savile's activities at Duncroft Approved School (April 2015). Many of these were collected and summarized by the National Organization for the Treatment of Abusers (NOTA) who offer a timeline of Yewtree related occurrences: http://www.nota.co.uk/wp-content/uploads/2019/01/June-2017.pdf

2. Savile was constantly under suspicion during his career. For instance, the DJ's relationship with P&O ferries ended later when he was thrown off the company's flagship *SS Canberra* after complaints from the parents of a fourteen-year-old girl (Davies 2014, p. 340). As was typically, the story was not reported because the press feared Savile would use libel laws (p. 341).

3. It is notable that reference to Savile's Fan Club and its members has been erased from Google under European legislation that protects individuals' rights to be forgotten.

4. The mainstreaming of conspiracy theory was reflected in parodies such as 'Weird Al' Yankovic's 2014 pop video 'Foil', a cover of Lorde's 'Royals' which saw the comedian position himself as a TV chef before aping a paranoid conspiracy believer, mentioning the Illuminati and donning a tin hat. At the end of the video, after he has left, his TV director reveals himself to be a lizard.

5. There is a long-standing variant of Marxist state theory that is pertinent here. Lenin's (1966) *Imperialism: The Highest Stage of Capitalism* argues that joint stock companies (finance capital) now subsume industrial capital (and are now the most powerful elements in bourgeois society). Ralph Miliband's (1973) *The State in Capitalist Society* makes points about the state as heavily affected by concentration of capital in 'giant enterprise', with the state effectively colluding with finance capital. There is also the sociology of elites of C. Wright Mills (2000) that is

pertinent to conceptions of the state. The 'deep state' phrase itself seems to come from the online Right, or 'alt-right' it is often called.
6   This makes Savile akin to a kind of pre-Trumpian troll, as the same kind of criticism has been levelled against the US president and his undignified spearheading of an era of politics garishly remade as mass entertainment.
7   Reproduced from Davies (2014, p. 259).
8   See, for instance, Davies (2014, pp. 221, 247, 275, 343, 500, 544).

Reference List

All translations from sources in French in the bibliography are by the authors unless otherwise stated.

'1,400 "Lifers" Released from California Prisons in Last 3 Years' (25 February 2014). *CBS News*. Retrieved from https://www.cbsnews.com/news/1400-lifers-released-from-california-prisons-in-last-3-years/

5ocietyX [Screen name]. (13 January 2014). 'Was Jimmy Savile a Wizard?' [Video file]. Retrieved from https://www.youtube.com/watch?v=-QUuCWNyvv8

Adams, A. M. (2009). What's in a Frame?: The Authorizing Presence in James Whale's Bride of Frankenstein. *The Journal of Popular Culture*, 42(3), 403–18. doi:10.1111/j.1540-5931.2009.00687.x

Adler, L. (Producer), White, M. (Producer) and Sharman, J. (Director). (1975). *The Rocky Horror Picture Show* [Motion Picture]. United States: Michael White Productions.

Agamben, G. (1998). *Homo Sacer: Sovereign Power and Bare Life*. Stanford, CA: Stanford University Press.

Albrecht, M. M. (2016). *Masculinity in Contemporary Quality Television*. Abingdon, England: Routledge.

'Album Signed by John Lennon for Mark Chapman on Sale for £500,000'. (23 November 2010). *The Telegraph*. Retrieved from http://www.telegraph.co.uk/culture/music/the-beatles/8152937/Album-signed-by-John-Lennon-for-Mark-Chapman-on-sale-for-500000.html

Alexander, H. (16 September 2016). 'John Lennon's Killer Revealed Details of Shooting as He Was Denied Parole for the Ninth Time'. *The Telegraph*. http://www.telegraph.co.uk/news/2016/09/16/john-lennons-killer-revealed-details-of-shooting-as-he-was-denie/

Alexander, J. (2004). Toward a Theory of Cultural Trauma. In J. Alexander, *et al* (eds), *Cultural Trauma and Collective Identity* (pp. 1–30). Berkeley: University of California Press.

Allen, Jr., E. (1996). Making the Strong Survive: The Contours and Contradictions of Message Rap. In W. E. Perkins (ed.), *Droppin' Science: Critical Essays on Rap Music and Hip Hop Culture* (pp. 159–91). Philadelphia, PA: Temple University Press.

Aparin, J. (1988). *He Never Got above His Raising: An Ethnographic Study of a Working Class Response to Elvis Presley*. (Doctoral dissertation). University of Pennsylvania, Philadelphia.

Argento, C. (Producer), Colombo, G. (Producer), Sipos, A. (Producer) and Argento, D. (Director). (1998). *The Phantom of the Opera* [Motion Picture]. Italy: Focus Films.

Argento, C. (Producer), Rubinstein, R. (Producer), Cuomo, A. (Producer) and Romero, G. (Director). (1978). *Dawn of the Dead* [Motion Picture]. United States: Laurel Group Inc.

Argento, D. (2019). *Fear: The Autobiography*. Godalming, England: FAB Press.

Asma, S. T. (2009). *On Monsters: An Unnatural History of Our Worst Fears*. Oxford, England: Oxford University Press.

Auslander, P. (2006). *Performing Glam Rock: Gender and Theatricality in Popular Music*. Ann Arbor, MI: University of Michigan Press.

Aviram, A. F. (1992). 'Postmodern Gay Dionysus: Dr. Frank N. Furter'. *Journal of Popular Culture*, 26(3), 183–92.

Babilas, D. (2018). 'Monstrosity and Suffering in the Roles of Lon Chaney'. In A. Łowczanin and K. Małecka (eds.), *Gothic Peregrinations: The Unexplored and Re-explored Territories*. New York: Routledge.

Badiou, A. (2009). *Pocket Pantheon: Figures of Postwar Philosophy*. London, England: Verso.

Baker, H. and Taylor, Y. (2007). *Faking It: The Quest for Authenticity in Popular Music*. London, England: Faber and Faber.

Baker, J. (1997). 'Perfectly Normal'. *Memphis Flyer*, 442, 30–4.

Baldick, C. (1987). *In Frankenstein's Shadow: Myth, Monstrosity, and Nineteenth-century Writing*. Oxford, England: Clarendon.

Bannister, M. (2006). *White Boys, White Noise: Masculinities and 1980s Indie Guitar Rock*. Aldershot, England: Ashgate.

Barfe, L. (2005). *Where Have All the Good Times Gone? The Rise and Fall of the Record Industry*. London, England: Atlantic Books.

Bari, M. (2007). *Mass Media Is the Message: Yoko Ono and John Lennon's 1969 Year of Peace* (PhD thesis). Maryland, DC: University of Maryland.

Barthes, R. (1977). 'The Grain of the Voice'. In R. Barthes (ed.), *Image Music Text* (pp. 179–89). London, England: Fontana Press.

Barthes, R. (2013). *Mythologies*. New York: Hill and Wang. (Original work published in 1957)

Batey, A. (2011). 'DJ Kool Herc DJs His First Block Party (His Sister's Birthday) at 1520 Sedgwick Avenue, Bronx, New York'. *The Guardian*. https://www.theguardian.com/music/2011/jun/13/dj-kool-herc-block-party

Bayton, M. (1998). *Frock Rock: Women Performing Popular Music*. Oxford, England: Oxford University Press.

Beauvallet, J. (14 April 2014). 'Bertrant Cantat: "Rêver m'est impossible."' *Les Inrockuptibles*. https://www.lesinrocks.com/2014/04/11/musique/actualite/bertrand-cantat-rever-mest-impossible/

Beineix, J. J. (Producer and Director). (1986). *Betty Blue (37°2 le matin)* [Motion Picture]. France: Gaumont.

Bennett, A. (2007). 'The Forgotten Decade: Rethinking the Popular Music of the 1970s'. *Popular Music History*, 2(1), 5–24. doi:10.1558/pomh.v2i1.5

Berman, M. (1981). *All That Is Solid Melts into Air: The Experience of Modernity*. New York: Simon & Schuster.

Berman, P. (Producer) and Thorpe, R. (Director). (1957). *Jailhouse Rock*. United States: Metro-Golwyn-Mayer.

Bertrand, M. (2011) 'How Much Does It Cost if It's Free? The Selling (out) of Elvis Presley'. In E. Barfoot-Christian (ed.), *Rock Brands: Selling Sound in a Media Saturated Culture*. Lanham, MD: Lexington Books.

Besse, M. (2012). *Noir Désir: à l'envers, à l'endroit*. Paris, France: Ring.

Besser, S. (Producer), Maddalena, M. (Producer) and Craven, W. (Director). (1991). *The People under the Stairs* [Motion Picture]. United States: Alive Films.

Beverburg Reale, S. (2012). 'A Sheep in Wolf's Corset: Timbral and Vocal Signifiers of Masculinity in *The Rocky Horror Picture/Glee Show*'. *Music, Sound & the Moving Image*, 6(2), 137–62. doi:0.3828/msmi.2012.17

Bishop, P. (Director). (1975–1994). *Jim'll Fix It* [TV series]. England: BBC.

Blom, P. (2015). *Fracture: Life and Culture in the West, 1918–1938*. London, England: Atlantic Books.

Bloom, H. (2000). *J.D. Salinger's Catcher in the Rye*. New York: Chelsea House.

Blum, J. (Producer), Cooper, I. (Producer), McKittrick, S. (Producer) and Peele, J. (Producer and Director). (2019). *Us* [Motion Picture]. United States: Monkeypaw Productions and Perfect World Pictures.

'Book Review: *Who shot John Lennon?* by Fenton Bresler'. (11 September 2016). *Beatle-Freak's Reviews Blog*. Retrieved from https://beatles-freak.com/2016/09/11/book-review-who-killed-john-lennon-by-fenton-bresler/

Boorstin, D. (1997). *The Image: A Guide to Psuedo-events in America*. New York: Vintage Books. (Original work published 1962)

Botting, F. (2003). 'Metaphors and Monsters'. *Journal for Cultural Research*, 7(4), 339–65. doi:10.1080/1479758032000165020

Bouchareb, R. (Producer), Bréhat, J. (Producer) and Dumont, B. (Director). (2003). *Twentynine Palms* [Motion Picture]. France, United States and Germany: 3B Productions, The 7th Floor & Thoke Moebius Film Company.

Bouchet, S., and Vézard, F. (2004). *Mort à Vilnius*. Paris, France: l'Archipel.

Bouchet, S., and Vézard, F. (2013). *Bertrand Cantat, Marie Trintignant: L'amour à mort*. Paris, France: l'Archipel.

Bowcott, O. (28 December 2012). 'Jimmy Savile's Extraordinary Access to Margaret Thatcher Detailed in Secret Files'. *The Guardian*. https://www.theguardian.com/uk/2012/dec/28/jimmy-savile-access-margaret-thatcher

Boyle, D. (20 July 2017). 'Album Signed by John Lennon for His Murderer Mark Chapman Hours before the Killer Struck Has Gone on Sale for $1.8 Million'. *Daily Mail*. Retrieved from http://www.dailymail.co.uk/news/article-4714250/Album-signed-John-Lennon-killer-sale-2m.html#ixzz4w4QlyAIr

Boyle, K. (2018). 'Hiding in Plain Sight: Gender, Sexism and Press Coverage of the Jimmy Savile Case'. *Journalism Studies*, 19 (11), 1562–78. doi:1080/146167 0X.2017.1282832

Brackett, D. (2016). *Categorizing Sound: Genre and Twentieth-century Popular Music*. Oakland, CA: University of California Press.

Breit, H. (23 July 1950). 'Talk with Alan Lomax'. *New York Times*, p. BR7.

Breton, A. (1928). *Nadja*. Paris: NRF.

Breton, A. (1937). *L'amour fou*. Paris: Gallimard.

Brewer-Giorgio, G. (1990). *The Elvis Files: Was His Death Faked?* New York: Shapolsky.

Brittan, S. (18 April 2013). 'Thatcher Was Right – There Is No Society'. *Financial Times*. https://www.ft.com/content/d1387b70-a5d5-11e2-9b77-00144feabdc0

Broeske, P., and Brown, D. (9 July 1997a). 'He Binged on Junk Food'. *Daily Mail*, pp. 32–4.

Broeske, P., and Brown, D. (11 July 1997b). 'Once Priscilla Gave Birth, Elvis Rejected Her'. *Daily Mail*, pp. 52–3.

Brown, J. (2012a). 'Ows about that then, Guys and Gals: Snap up Jimmy's "Jingle Jangle"'. *The Independent*, 31 July. https://www.independent.co.uk/news/uk/this-britain/ows-about-that-then-guys-and-gals-snap-up-jimmys-jingle-jangle-7988041.html

Brown, S. (2012b). 'Scream from the Heart: Yoko Ono's Rock'n'Roll Revolution'. *Volume!*, 9(2), 107–23. https://doi.org/10.4000/volume.3415

Bryant, C. G. (2005). '"The Soul Has Bandaged Moments": Reading the African American Gothic in Wright's "Big Boy Leaves Home", Morrison's *Beloved*, and Gomez's "Gilda"'. *African American Review*, 39(4), 541–53.

Burk, B. (1997). *Early Elvis: The Sun Years*. Memphis, TN: Propwash.

Buskin, R. (1995). *Elvis: Memories and Memorabilia*. London, England: Salamander.

Bustard, A. (2013). 'I'm Sick of This Gothic, Hip-Hop, Nasty Look'. *The Boombox*, http://theboombox.com/pusha-t-play-cloths-fall-2013-kanye-west-drake/

Butler, J. (2006). *Gender Trouble*. New York: Routledge. (Original work published 1990)

Byrne, D. (26 May 2015). 'A Good, Bad, Hard, Easy Life'. *Boston Review*. http://bostonreview.net/books-ideas-literature-culture-arts-society/dave-byrne-good-bad-hard-easy-life

Cagle, V. (2000). 'Trudging through the Glitter Trenches: The Case of the New York Dolls'. In S. Waldrep (ed.), *The Seventies: The Age of Glitter in Popular Culture*. New York: Routledge.

Calafell, B. (2015). *Monstrosity, Performance, and Race in Contemporary Culture*. New York: Peter Lang.

Canguilhem, G. (1991). *The Normal and the Pathological*. New York: Zone Books.

Canguilhem, G. (2008). *Knowledge of Life*. New York: Fordham University Press.
Cantat, X. (2004). *Méfaits divers: Journal d'un frère*. Paris, France: Editions Michalon.
'Carl Beech: Liar, Fraudster and Paedophile'. (2019). *BBC News*, 26 July. https://www.bbc.co.uk/news/uk-49048972
Carrigan, T., Connell, R. and Lee, J. (1985). 'Toward a New Sociology of Masculinity'. *Theory and Society*, 14(5), 551–604.
Cary, A. (Director). (2016). *Louis Theroux: Savile* [TV show]. England: BBC.
Caughey, J. (1984). *Imaginary Social Worlds: A Cultural Approach*. Lincoln: University of Nebraska Press.
Celebrity Radio by Alex Belfield [Screen name]. (15 July 2013). 'Jimmy Savile Last/Final Exclusive 40 min BBC Interview "I Got away with It" – BBC Radio 2'. [Video file]. Retrieved from https://www.youtube.com/watch?v=_kOGqQbE3xE
Cerf, M. (2006). *Bertrand Cantat, ou le chant des automates*. Paris, France: Ecriture.
Ceriello, L. (2018). 'The Big Bad and Big 'aha!': Metamodern Monsters as Transformational Figures of Instability'. In M. Heyes (ed.), *Holy Monsters, Sacred Grotesques* (pp. 207–33). Lanham, MD: Lexington Books.
Chapman, I. (2016). 'Alice Cooper: Glam Rock's Problem Child'. In I. Chapman and H. Johnson (eds.), *Global Glam and Popular Music: Style and Spectacle from the 1970s to the 2000s* (pp. 113–28). New York: Routledge.
Chapman, I., and Johnson, H. (Eields.) (2016). *Global Glam and Popular Music: Style and Spectacle from the 1970s to the 2000s*. New York: Routledge.
Charnas, D. (2010). *The Big Payback: The History of the Business of Hip-Hop*. New York: New American Library.
Chess, M. (Producer), Seymour, D. (Director) and Frank, R. (Director). (1972). *Cocksucker Blues* [Motion Picture]. United States: Videobeat.
Chion, M. (1994). *Audio Vision: Sound on Screen*. New York: Columbia University Press.
Clawson, M. A. (1999). 'Masculinity and Skill Acquisition in the Adolescent Rock Band'. *Popular Music*, 18(1), 99–114.
Clawson, M. A. (1999a). 'When Women Play the Bass: Instrument Specialization and Gender Interpretation in Alternative Rock Music'. *Gender and Society*, 13(2), 193–210.
Clayson, A. (1994). 'Snowmen: The Manager and His Client'. In A. Clayson and S. Leigh (eds.), *Aspects of Elvis* (pp. 50–5). London, England: Sidgwick and Jackson.
Click, M., Lee, H., and Willson Holladay, H. (2013). 'Making Monsters: Lady Gaga, Fan Identification, and Social Media'. *Popular Music and Society*, 36(3), 360–79. doi:10.1080/03007766.2013.798546
Cocks, J. (29 August 1977). 'Last Stop on the Mystery Train'. *Time*, pp. 24–7.
Cohen, J. J. (1996). 'Monster Culture (Seven Theses)'. In J. J. Cohen (ed.), *Monster Theory: Reading Culture*. Minneapolis: University of Minnesota Press.
Cohen, R. (Producer) and Lumet, S. (Director). (1978). *The Wiz* [Motion Picture]. USA: Motown Productions.

Cohen, S. (1991). *Rock Culture in Liverpool: Popular Music in the Making*. Oxford, England: Clarendon Press.

Cohen, S. (2001). *States of Denial: Knowing about Atrocities and Suffering*. Cambridge, England: Polity.

colujomes [Screen name]. (31 January 2009). 'Leadbelly Newsreel' [Video file]. Retrieved from https://www.youtube.com/watch?v=QxykqBmUCwk

Comment, B. (27 August 2003). 'Je n'oublie pas qui est Bertrand Cantet'. *Les Inrockuptibles*. 15.

Conn, P. (1983). *The Divided Mind: Ideology and Imagination in America, 1898-1917*. New York: Cambridge University Press.

Connell, R. W. (2000). *The Men and the Boys*. Cambridge, England: Polity.

Conrad, J. (1995). *Heart of Darkness & Other Stories*. London: Wordsworth Editions. (Original work published in 1899)

Conrad, P. (1998). *Modern Times, Modern Places: Life & Art in the 20th Century*. London, England: Thames and Hudson.

Cook, N. (2000). *Music: A Very Short Introduction*. Oxford, England: Oxford University Press.

Cooper, B. L. (2006). 'These Ghoulish Things: Horror Hits for Halloween, Various Artists, 2005 [review]'. *Popular Music and Society*, 29(5), 621-31. doi:10.1080/03007760600884650

Cooper, M. (Producer and Director) and Schoedsack, E. (Producer and Director). (1933). *King Kong* [Motion Picture]. United States: Radio Pictures.

Cooper, M. (Producer) and Schoedsack, E. (Director). (1949). *Mighty Joe Young* [Motion Picture]. United States: RKO Radio Pictures.

Cornwall, A., Karioris, F., and Lindisfarne, N. (eds) (2016). *Masculinities under Neoliberalism*. London, England: Zed Books.

Cornwall, A. and Lindisfarne, N. (eds) (2017). *Dislocating Masculinity: Comparative Ethnographies*. Abingdon, UK: Routledge.

Corona, V. (2011). 'Memory, Monsters and Lady Gaga'. *Journal of Popular Culture*, 44(2), 1-20. doi:10.1111/j.1540-5931.2011.00809.x

Cortez, D. (1978). *Private Elvis*. Stuttgart, Germany: Fey.

Cosimini, S. (2017). '"I'm a Motherfuckin' Monster!": Play, Perversity, and Performance of Nicki Minaj.' *Feminist Formations*, 29(2), 47-68. doi:10.1353/ff.2017.0016

Cott, J. and Dounda, C. (1982). *The Ballad of John and Yoko*. Rantoul, IL: Doubleday.

Cotten, L. (1995). *Did Elvis Sing in Your Hometown?* Sacramento, CA: High Sierra Books.

Cottom, D. (1980). *Frankenstein* and the Monster of Representation. *Sub-Stance*, 28, 60-71.

Couldry, N. (2000). *The Place of Media Power*. London, England: Routledge.

Coward, N. (Producer), Havelock-Allan, A., Neame, R. (Producer) and Lean, D. (Director). (1945). *Brief Encounter* [Motion Picture]. UK: Eagle-Lion Distributors.

Crane, L. (30 April 1956). 'Rock Age Idol: He's Riding the Crest of a Teenage Tidal Wave'. *Daily Mirror*, 9.

Creed, B. (1993). *The Monstrous-feminine: Film, Feminism, Psychoanalysis*. New York: Routledge.

Crumbaker, M. and Tucker, G. (1981). *Up and down with Elvis Presley*. Sevenoaks, England: New English Library.

Crysell, A. (20 September 1997). 'Gloom! Shake the Room!' *New Musical Express*, 16.

Curtin, J. (1998). *Elvis: Unknown Stories behind the Legend, Volume 1*. Nashville, TN: Celebrity Books.

Darling, J. (2009). 'Becoming Bare Life: Asylum, Hospitality, and the Politics of Encampment'. *Society and Space*, 27(4), 649–65. https://doi.org/10.1068/d10307

Dash, M. (24 February 2012). 'Colonel Parker Managed Elvis' Career, But Was He a Killer on the Lam?' *Smithsonian Magazine*. Retrieved from https://www.smithsonianmag.com/history/colonel-parker-managed-elvis-career-but-was-he-a-killer-on-the-lam-108042206/

'David Bowie Departs This Plane'. (11 January 2016). *Famous Monsters of Filmland*. https://famousmonsters.com/david-bowie-departs-this-plane/

Davies, D. (2014). *In Plain Sight: The Life and Lies of Jimmy Savile*. London, England: Quercus.

Davies, H. (2001). 'All Rock and Roll Is Homosocial: The Representation of Women in the British Rock Music Press'. *Popular Music*, 20(3), 301–19.

Davies, H. (ed.) (2016). *The John Lennon Letters*. London, England: Weidenfeld & Nicholson.

Davis, C. (2009). 'Holy Saturday or Resurrection Sunday? Staging an Unlikely Debate'. In S. Žižek and J. Milbank, edited by C. Davis, *The Monstrosity of Christ: Paradox or Dialectic* (pp. 2–23). Cambridge, MA: MIT Press.

de Búrca, J. (14 June 2018). 'Stalin's Englishman on Trial in Ireland'. *Village Magazine*. https://villagemagazine.ie/index.php/2018/06/stalins-englishman-on-trial-in-ireland/

Deeley, M. (Producer), Spikings, B. (Producer) and Roeg, N. (Director). (1976). *The Man Who Fell to Earth* [Motion Picture]. UK: British Lion Films.

Delbosc, O. (Producer), Missonnier, M. (Producer) and Benchetrit, S. (Director). (2003). *Janis et John* [Motion Picture]. France: Fidélité Productions & France 3 Cinéma.

Deleuze, G. and Guattari, F. (1987). '1914: One or Several Wolves?'. In *A Thousand Plateaus* (pp. 26–38). Minneapolis: University of Minnesota Press. (Original work published in 1980)

Deleuze, G. and Guattari, F. (1992). *A Thousand Plateaus*. London, England: The Athlone Press.

Derrida, J. (2006). *Specters of Marx: The State of the Debt, the Work of Mourning and the New International*. New York: Routledge. (Original work published in 1993)

Discogs. (2016). '100 Greatest French Rock Albums'. *Rolling Stone*. http://www.discogs.com/lists/Rolling-Stone-100-Greatest-French-Rock-Albums/247807

Dolgin, A. (2009). *The Economics of Symbolic Exchange*. Moscow, Russia: Springer.

Doss, E. (2011). 'Remembering 9/11: Memorials and Cultural Memory'. *OAH Magazine of History*, *25*(3), 27–30. https://doi.org/10.1093/oahmag/oar018

'"Double Fantasy" signed by John Lennon for Mark Chapman'. (2012). *Moments in Time*. Retrieved from http://momentsintime.com/double-fantasy-album-signed-by-john-lennon-for-mark-chapman/#.WgX99LDQr1K

Du Bois, W. E. B. (1973). *The Souls of Black Folk*. Millwood, NY: Kraus-Tomson Organization. (Original work published in 1903)

Du Chiallu, P. (1985). *Explorations and Adventures in Equatorial Africa*. New York: Time Life. (Original work published in 1862)

Duffett, M. (1998). *Understanding Elvis: Presley, Power and Performance* (Doctoral Dissertation). University of Wales, Aberystwyth.

Duffett, M. (2 February 1999). 'Prof. Kindamuzik: The Ballad of Mark Chapman'. *Kindamuzik*. Retrieved from www.kindamuzik.net/features/article.shtml?id=8099

Duffett, M. (2001). 'Caught in a Trap? Beyond Pop Theory's "Butch" Construction of Male Elvis Fans'. *Popular Music*, *2*(3), 395–408.

Duffett, M. (2010a). 'Imagined Memories: Webcasting as a 'Live' Technology and the Case of Little Big Gig'. *Information, Communication and Society*, *6*(3), 307–25. https://doi.org/10.1080/1369118032000155267

Duffett, M. (2010b). 'What Are Imagined Memories? [blog post]'. *Pop Research Links*. http://pop-music-research.blogspot.com/2010/07/what-are-imagined-memories-and-how-are.html

Duffett, M. (2013). *Understanding Fandom*. New York: Bloomsbury.

Duffett, M. (2018). *Counting Down Elvis: His 100 Finest Songs*. Lanham, MD: Rowman and Littlefield.

Dundy, E. (1995). *Elvis and Gladys*. London, England: Pimlico.

Dyer, R. (1979). *Stars*. London, England: BFI Publishing.

Dyer, R. (1998). 'Resistance through Charisma: Rita Hayworth and *Gilda*'. In E. A. Kaplan (ed.), *Women in Film Noir* (pp. 115–22). London, England: BFI.

Easthope, A. (1990). *What a Man's Gotta Do: The Masculine Myth in Popular Culture*. New York: Routledge.

Eberle-Sinatra, M. (2005). 'Readings of Homosexuality in Mary Shelley's Frankenstein and Four Film Adaptations'. *Gothic Studies*, *7*(2), 185–202.

Edelman, L. (2004). *No Future: Queer Theory and the Death Drive*. Durham, NC: Duke University Press.

Elliot, A. (1999a). *The Mourning of John Lennon*. Berkeley: University of California Press.

Elliot, A. (1999b). 'Celebrity and Political Psychology: Remembering Lennon'. *Political Psychology*, *19*(4), 833–52.

Ellis, M. (2000). *The History of Gothic Fiction*. Edinburgh, Scotland: Edinburgh University Press.

Erooga, M. (11 January 2013a). 'Summary of Report into Operation Ornament, by Detective Superintendent Jon Savell, head of public protection Surrey police'. *NOTA News*, July, 1–4. https://www.nota.co.uk/wp-content/uploads/2019/01/January-2013-3.pdf

Erooga, M. (11 January 2013b). 'Summary of "in the Matter of the Late Jimmy Savile" Report to the Director of Public Prosecutions by Alison Levitt QC'. *NOTA News*, 70, 1–4 July. https://www.nota.co.uk/wp-content/uploads/2019/01/January-2013.pdf

Erooga, M. (12 March 2013c). 'Summary of Mistakes Were Made: Her Majesty's Inspectorate of Constabulary's Review into Allegations and Intelligence Material Concerning Jimmy Savile'. *NOTA News*, 1–5 November. https://www.nota.co.uk/wp-content/uploads/2019/01/March-2013.pdf

Erooga, M. (May 2013d). 'Summary of the "Knopwood Report" for West Yorkshire Police about "Operation Newgreen"'. *NOTA News*, November, 71. https://www.nota.co.uk/wp-content/uploads/2019/01/May-13.pdf

Erooga, M. (2014). 'Summary of "Giving Victims a Voice": A Joint Metropolitan Police Service (MPS) and NSPCC Report into Allegations of Sexual Abuse Made against Jimmy Savile under Operation Yewtree, published 11 January 2013'. *NOTA News*, July, 1–2.

Esposito, J. (1994). *Good Rockin' Tonight*. New York: Simon & Schuster.

Faber, C., Gatti, A. and Châtelain, H. (20 August 2003). Bertrand Cantat, l'homme digne d'être un frère. *Les Inrockuptibles*, 15.

Fairchild, C. (2007). 'Building the Authentic Celebrity: The "Idol" Phenomenon in the Attention Economy'. *Popular Music and Society*, 30(3), 355–75. doi:10.1080/03007760600835306

Farren, M. (1981). *Elvis in His Own Words*. London, England: WH Allen.

Fassin, É. (2007). 'Une enquête qui dérange'. In N. Chetchuti and M. Jaspard (eds), *Violences envers les femmes, trois pas en avant deux pas en arrière* (pp. 287–97). Paris, France: L'Harmattan.

Filene, B. (1991). '"Our Singing Country": John and Alan Lomax, Lead Belly, and the Construction of an American Past'. *American Quarterly*, 43(4), 602–24.

Filene, B. (2000). *Romancing the Folk: Public Memory and American Roots Music*. Chapel Hill, NC: University of North Carolina Press.

Finlay, J. (Director). (2001). *Sound It Out* [Motion Picture]. England: Glimmer Films.

Firth, V. (1965). 'Presley and Playmates in the World Playgrounds'. *ABC Film Review*, 15(8).

Fisher, M. (2013). 'The Metaphysics of Crackle: Afrofuturism and Hauntology'. *Dancecult: Journal of Electronic Dance Music Culture*, 5(2), 42–55. doi:10.12801/1947-5403.2013.05.02.03

Fisher, M. (2014). *Ghosts of My Life: Writings on Depression, Hauntology and Lost Futures*. Alresford, England: Zero Books.

Fleetwood, N. (2011). *Troubling Vision: Performance, Visuality, and Blackness*. Chicago, IL: University of Chicago Press.

Flippo, C. (1994). *Graceland: The Living Legacy of Elvis Presley*. London, England: Hamlyn.

Fogo, F. (1994). *I Read the News Today: The Social Drama of John Lennon's Death*. Maryland, DC: Rowman and Littlefield.

Fortas, A. (1992). *Elvis from Memphis to Hollywood: Memories from My Twelve Years with Elvis Presley*. Ann Arbor, MI: Popular Culture, Ink.

Fortas, A. and Nash, A. (2008). *Elvis from Memphis to Hollywood*. London, England: Aurum.

Foucault, M. (2003). *Abnormal: Lectures at the College de France 1974–1975*. London, England: Verso.

France 2. [Screen name]. (19 June 2006). 'Tout le monde en parle' [Video file]. Retrieved from https://www.youtube.com/watch?v=2fWVQVsI-F4

Franklin, L. (2012). *Gender*. New York: Palgrave.

Frankovich, M. J. (Producer), Self, W. (Producer) and Siegel, D. (Director) (1976). *The Shootist* [Motion Picture]. United States: Paramount.

Freud, S. (1991a). 'On Narcissism: An Introduction'. In S. Freud (ed.), *Penguin Freud Library, vol. 11: On Metapsychology: The Theory of Psychoanalysis* (pp. 55–97). Harmondsworth, England: Penguin. (Original work published in 1914)

Freud, S. (1991b). 'Mourning and Melancholia'. In S. Freud (ed.), *Penguin Freud Library, vol. 11: On Metapsychology: The Theory of Psychoanalysis* (pp. 245–68). Harmondsworth: Penguin. (Original work published in 1917)

Freud, S. (1997a). *The Interpretation of Dreams*. London, England: Wordsworth Editions. (Original work published in 1900)

Freud, S. (1997b). 'The Uncanny'. In *Writings on Art and Literature* (pp. 193–233). Stanford, CA: Stanford University Press. (Original work published in 1919)

Freud, S. (2001). *Totem and Taboo: Some Points of Agreement between the Mental Lives of Savages and Neurotics*. London, England: Routledge. (Original work published in 1913)

Frith, S. and McRobbie, A. (1990). 'Rock and Sexuality'. In S. Frith and A. Goodwin (eds), *On Record: Rock, Pop and the Written Word* (pp. 371–89). New York: Routledge. (Original work published 1978)

Fulmer, J. (2002). '"Men Ain't All": A Reworking of Masculinity in *Tales from the Hood*, or, Grandma Meets the Zombie'. *The Journal of American Folklore*, 115(457/458), 422–42.

Furedi, F. (2013). *Moral Crusades in an Age of Mistrust: The Jimmy Savile Scandal*. London, England: Palgrave.

Gaines, J. (1992). *Contested Culture: The Image, the Voice, and the Law*. London, England: BFI Publishing.

Gains, J. (9 March 1987). 'Mark Chapman Part III: The Killer Takes His Fall'. *People*, 27(10). https://people.com/archive/mark-chapman-part-iii-the-killer-takes-his-fall-vol-27-no-10/

Gardiner, L. (Director). (2012). *Exposure: The Other Side of Jimmy Savile* [TV show episode]. England: ITV.

Gates, H. L. (2019). *Stony Is the Road: Reconstruction, White Supremacy and the Rise of Jim Crow*. New York: Penguin.

Geller, L. (1989). *If I Can Dream: Elvis's Own Story*. London, England: Century.

Gentleman, A. (14 September 2003). 'France Gripped as a Showbusiness Story of Doomed Love Unravels'. *The Guardian*. https://www.theguardian.com/world/2003/sep/14/film.france

Gilbert, J. (2016). 'What Kind of Thing Is Neoliberalism?' In J. Gilbert (ed.), *Neoliberal Culture* (pp. 10–32). London, England: Lawrence & Wishart.

Gilbert, R. and Gilbert, P. (2017). *Masculinity Goes to School*. Abingdon, England: Routledge.

Gilroy, P. (1993). *The Black Atlantic: Modernity and Double Consciousness*. London, England: Verso.

Glaser, E. (2017). *Anti-politics: The Demonization of Ideology, Authority and the State*. London: Repeater Books.

Glover, T. (1973). 'New York Dolls: *New York Dolls* [review]'. *Rolling Stone*. www.rollingstone.com/music/albumreviews/new-york-dolls-19730913

Golan, M. (Producer) and Towers, H. (Producer) and Little, D. (Director). (1989). *The Phantom of the Opera* [Motion Picture]. United States: Columbia.

Gold, A. (2013). 'Dave Grohl's SXSW Keynote Speech: "The Musician Comes First"'. *Rolling Stone*. http://www.rollingstone.co/music/news/dave-grohls-sxsw-keynote-speech-the-musician-comes-first-20130314

Goldbaum, J. (10 September 2003). 'Hamburg Man at Center of Dispute over Lennon Album'. *New Jersey Herald*. Retrieved from http://www.beatlesnews.com/news/the-beatles/200309100101/hamburg-man-at-center-of-dispute-over-lennon-album.html

Goldman, A. (1982). *Elvis*. London, England: Penguin.

Goldman, A. (1988). *The Lives of John Lennon*. New York: Bantam Books.

Golin, S. (Producer), Sighvatsson, S. (Producer), Poul, A. (Producer) and Rose, B. (Director). (1992). *Candyman* [Motion Picture]. United States: Propaganda Films and PolyGram Filmed Entertainment.

Goodman, F. (24 August 2003). 'Without You I'm Nothing'. *New York Times*, Section 7, 11.

Gordon, A. (2008). *Ghostly Matters: Haunting and the Sociological Imagination*. Minneapolis, MN: University of Minnesota Press. (Original work published in 1997)

Gordon, R. (1996). *The King on the Road: Live on Tour 1954 to 1977*. London, England: Hamlyn.

Goslett, M. (March 2012). 'Savile Row'. *The Oldie*, 12.
Gracyk, T. (2007). *Listening to Popular Music: Or, How I Learned to Stop Worrying and Love Led Zeppelin*. Ann Arbor, MI: University of Michigan Press.
Gray, D. and Watt, P. (2013). 'Giving Victims a Voice: Joint Report into Sexual Allegations Made against Jimmy Savile'. *Metropolitan Police and NSPCC*. https://www.nspcc.org.uk/globalassets/documents/research-reports/yewtree-report-giving-victims-voice-jimmy-savile.pdf
Gray, J. (2005). 'Antifandom and the Moral Text: Television without Pity and Textual Dislike'. *American Behavioral Scientist*, 48(7), 840–58. https://doi.org/10.1177/0002764204273171
Green, L. (1997). *Music, Gender, Education*. Cambridge, England: Cambridge University Press.
Gregory, G. (2002). 'Masculinity, Sexuality and the Visual Culture of Glam Rock'. *Culture and Communication*, 5(2), 35–60.
Gunter, B. (2014). *Celebrity Capital: Assessing the Value of Fame*. New York: Bloomsbury.
Guralnick, P. (1995). *Last Train to Memphis: The Rise of Elvis Presley*. London, England: Abacus.
Hackett, J. (2015). 'Art, Artifice and Androgyny: Roxy Music's Dandy Modernism'. *Clothing Cultures*, 2(2), 167–78. doi:10.1386/cc.2.2.167_1
Hackett, J. and Harrington, S. (2018). *Beasts of the Deep: Sea Creatures and Popular Culture*. East Barnet, England: John Libbey.
Hackett, J. and Harrington, S. (2019). *Beasts of the Forest: Denizens of the Dark Woods*. East Barnet, England: John Libbey.
Haining, P. (ed.). (1987). *Elvis in Private*. New York: St. Martin's Press.
Halberstam, J. (1995). *Skin Shows: Gothic Horror and the Technology of Monsters*. Durham, NC: Duke University Press.
Halberstam, J. (2012). *Gaga Feminism: Sex, Gender and the End of the Normal*. Boston, MA: Beacon Press.
Hall, A. (2009). *Phantom Variations: The Adaption of Gaston Leroux's* Phantom of the Opera, *1925 to the Present*. Jefferson, IA: McFarland.
Hall, J. (5 November 2012). 'Status Quo Frontman Francis Rossi: Savile Invited Me to "Sex Party" in His Dressing Room'. *The Independent*. https://www.independent.co.uk/news/people/news/status-quo-frontman-francis-rossi-jimmy-savile-invited-me-to-sex-party-in-his-dressing-room-8282508.html
Hall, S. (February 1980). 'Thatcherism – A New Stage?' *Marxism Today*, p. 26.
Hall, S. (1997). 'The Spectacle of the "Other"'. In S. Hall (ed.), *Representation: Cultural Representations and Signifying Practices* (pp. 223–9). London, England: Sage.
Halttunen, K. (2001). *Murder Most Foul: The Killer and the Gothic Imagination*, Cambridge, MA: Harvard University Press.
Haraway, D. (1991). 'A Cyborg Manifesto: Science, Technology, and Socialist-feminism in the Late Twentieth Century'. In D. Harraway (ed.), *Simians, Cyborgs, and Women: The Reinvention of Nature* (pp. 149–81). New York: Routledge.

Haraway, D. (1992). 'The Promises of Monsters: A Regenerative Politics for Inappropriate/d Others'. In L. Grossberg, C. Nelson and P. Treichler (eds.), *Cultural Studies* (pp. 295–336). New York: Routledge.

Hartman, S. V. (1997). *Scenes of Subjection: Terror, Slavery, and Self-making in Nineteenth-century America*. New York: Oxford University Press.

Harvey, R. (Producer), Heller, P. (Producer), Segan, L. (Producer) and Dickerson, E. (Director). (2001). *Bones* [Motion Picture]. United States: New Line Cinema.

Hawkins, S.(2009). *The British Pop Dandy: Masculinity, Popular Music and Culture*. Abingdon, England: Ashgate.

Hawkins, S. and Nielsen, N. (2020). 'Gaahl: Monster or Postmodern Prometheus? Masculinity, Class and Norwegian Black Metal'. In I. Peddie (ed.), *The Bloomsbury Handbook of Popular Music and Class* (pp. 185–204). New York: Bloomsbury.

Hawks, H. (Producer and Director). (1948). *Red River* [Motion Picture]. United States: United Artists.

Haynes, C. (1997). 'Elvis: In the Twilight of Memory'. *Official Elvis Presley Fan Club of Great Britain Magazine 7*, 18–19.

Hazen, C. and Freeman, M. (1997). *Memphis Elvis-style*. Durham, NC: John F. Blair.

Hebdige, D. (1987). *Subculture: The Meaning of Style*. London, England: Routledge.

Herzog, W. (Producer and Director) (1977). *Stroszek*. Germany: Werner Herzog Filmproduktion.

Hesmondhalgh, D. (1999). 'Indie: The Institutional Politics and Aesthetics of a Popular Music Genre'. *Cultural Studies*, 13(1), 34–61. doi:10.1080/095023899335365

Hesmondhalgh, D. (2013). *The Cultural Industries*. London, England: SAGE.

Hessler, G. (Director). (1978). *Kiss Meets the Phantom of the Park* [Motion Picture]. United States: Hanna-Barbera Productions.

Hewson, B. (8 May 2013). 'Yewtree Is Destroying the Rule of Law'. *Spiked*. https://www.spiked-online.com/2013/05/08/yewtree-is-destroying-the-rule-of-law/

Hiller, S. (ed.) (1991). *The Myth of Primitivism: Perspectives on Art*. Abingdon, England: Routledge.

Hinds, A. (Producer), Keys, B. (Producer) and Fisher, T. (Director). (1962). *The Phantom of the Opera* [Motion Picture]. England: Hammer Films.

Hirigoyen, M. F. (1998). *Le harcèlement moral, la violence perverse au quotidien*, Paris, France: Syros.

Hitchcock, A. (Producer and Director). (1958). *Vertigo* [Motion Picture]. United States: Paramount.

Hodge, C. (1988). *Me 'n' Elvis*. Memphis, TN: Castle Books.

Hofman, P. S. and Newman, A. (2014). 'The Impact of Perceived Corporate Social Responsibility on Organizational Commitment and the Moderating Role of Collectivism and Masculinity: Evidence from China'. *International Journal of Human Resource Management*, 25(5), 631–52.

Holden, S. (9 July 1981). 'Yoko Ono: "Season of Glass"'. *Rolling Stone*. Retrieved from http://www.rollingstone.com/music/albumreviews/season-of-glass-19810709

Holley, J. A. (26 August 1997). Gravediggaz beyond the Grave. *Blues & Soul*, 24.

Hopkins, J. (1974). *Elvis*. London, England: Abacus.

Hopkins, J. (1980). *Elvis: The Final Years*. London, England: WH Allen.

Horton, D. and Wohl, R. (1956). 'Mass Communication and Parasocial Interaction: Observations on Intimacy at a Distance'. *Psychiatry*, 19, 215–29.

Hoskyns, B. (1998). *Glam! Bowie, Bolan and the Glitter Rock Revolution*. New York: Pocket Books.

Howe, C. (Director). (2014). *The Jonathan Ross Show* [TV show]. England: ITV, 6 December.

Huet, M. H. (1983). 'Living Images: Monstrosity and Representation'. *Representations*, 4, 73–87.

Huet, M. H. (1991). 'Monstrous Imagination: Progeny as Art in French Classicism'. *Critical Inquiry*, 17(4), 718–37.

Hughey, M. (2014). *The White Savior Film: Consent, Critics and Consumption*. Philadelphia, PA: Temple University Press.

Hurwitz, M. (2011). 'Classic Tracks: The Edgar Winter Group, "Frankenstein"'. *Mix*, 35(7), 18–19. https://www.mixonline.com/recording/classic-tracks-edgar-winter-groups-frankenstein-366279

Hutchins, C. (26 January 1997). 'No, I Don't Take Half of What Elvis Earns …'. *The People*, pp. 6–8.

I Am Incorrigible [Screen name]. (26 September 2015). 'BBC Banned Johnny Rotten in 1978 for Telling the Truth about Jimmy Savile' [Video file]. Retrieved from https://www.youtube.com/watch?v=esKnWAIgpLY

Icke, D. (2013). *The Perception Deception*. Ryde, England: David Icke Books.

Ishita, S. (2016). 'Construction of the Public Memory of Celebrities: Celebrity Museums in Japan'. In P. Marshall and S. Redmond (eds), *A Companion to Celebrity* (pp. 135–53). Oxford, England: Blackwell.

Isola, C. (2004). *Noir Désir: Le creuset des nues*. Paris, France: Les Belles Lettres/Presses universitaires de Valenciennes.

ITV News [Screen name]. (9 November 2011). 'Sir Jimmy Savile's Funeral' [Video file]. Retrieved from https://www.youtube.com/watch?v=O6eUV2Uz2PU

James, R. (2015). *Resilience & Melancholy: Pop Music, Feminism, Neoliberalism*. Alresford, England: Zero Books.

Jarman-Ivens, F. (ed.) (2007). *Oh Boy! Masculinities and Popular Music*. New York: Routledge.

Jaspard, M. (2011). *Les violences contre les femmes*. Paris, France: La Découverte.

Jaspard, M., Demur, A. F. and l'équipe Enveff. (2002). *Enquête nationale sur les violences envers les femmes en Ile-de-France*. Paris: IDUP.

Jelassi, T. and Enders, A. (2008). *Strategies for E-business: Creating Value through Electronic and Mobile Commerce – Concepts and Cases*. Harlow, England: Prentice-Hall.

Jenkins, H. (1992). *Textual Poachers: Television Fans and Participatory Culture*. New York: Routledge.

Jenkins, P. (1992). *Intimate Enemies: Moral Panics in Contemporary Great Britain*. Hawthorne, NY: Aldine Dr Grutyer.

'John Lennon's Final Autograph to His Killer Part of PNE Exhibition'. (24 August 2015). *CBC News*. Retrieved from http://www.cbc.ca/news/canada/british-columbia/john-lennon-s-final-autograph-to-his-killer-part-of-pne-exhibit-1.3202553

Johnson, B. (Producer), Kosove, A. (Producer), Netter, G. (Producer) and Hancock, J. (2009). *The Blind Side* [Motion Picture]. United States: Warner Brothers.

Johnson, P. (28 August 2014). 'The Menace of Beatlism'. *New Statesman*. https://www.newstatesman.com/culture/2014/08/archive-menace-beatlism (Original work published 1964)

Jones, O. (2011). *Chavs: The Demonization of the Working Class*. London, England: Verso.

Jordan, W. (1974). *The White Man's Burden: Historical Origins of Racism in the United States*. New York: Oxford University Press.

Judy. (2 March 2014). 'Archive for the 3 – Modern Art and Still Life Category'. *Fibres of Being*. Retrieved from: https://fibresofbeing.wordpress.com/category/oca/western-art/3-modern-art-still-life/

Kael, P. (1982). *5001 Nights at the Movies*. London, England: Arena.

Kaprèlian, N. (3 September 2003). 'Cantat, un héros romantique?' *Les Inrockuptibles*, 26.

Kass-Gergi, Y. (2012). *Killer Personalities: Serial Killers as Celebrities in Contemporary American Culture (BA thesis)*. Middletown, CT: Wesleyan University.

Kearney, R. (2003). *Strangers, Gods and Monsters: Interpreting Otherness*. New York: Routledge.

Keightley, K. (2015). 'Hogan's Tin Pan Alley: R.F. Outcault and Popular Sheet Music'. *The Music Quarterly*, 98(1), 29–56.

Kelley, M. (2000). 'Cross Gender/Cross Genre'. *PAJ: A Journal of Performance and Art*, 22(1), 1–9. https://eastofborneo.org/archives/cross-gender-cross-genre-by-mike-kelley/

Kennedy, M. E. (27 December 1936). 'The "King of the Twelve-string Guitar Players": Negro Folksongs as Sung by Lead Belly [review]'. *New York Times*, BR7.

Kimmel, M. (2017). *Angry White Men: American Masculinity at the End of an Era*. New York: Bold Type Books.

Knight, M. M. (2007). *The Five Percenters: Islam, Hip Hop and the Gods of New York*. London, England: Oneworld.

Knopwood, D. (2013). 'Operation Newgreen [report]'. *West Yorkshire Police*, 1–59.

Koncienzcy, R. (27 June 2016). 'Shirt Stained with John Lennon's Blood Sold at Auction'. *Liverpool Echo*. Retrieved from http://www.liverpoolecho.co.uk/news/liverpool-news/shirt-stained-john-lennons-blood-11531893

Kristeva, J. (1982). *Powers of Horror: An Essay on the Abject*. New York: Colombia University Press.

Kuhn, D. (Producer), St John, C. (Producer) and Jarecki, E. (Director). (2017). *The King*. United States: Oscilloscope Laboratories.

Kulkarni, N. (2004). *Hip Hop: Bring the Noise: The Stories behind the Biggest Songs*. London, England: Carlton.

Lacker, M. et al. (1979). *Elvis: Portrait of a Friend*. Memphis, TN: Wimmer Brothers Books.

Laemmle, C. (Producer) and Julian, R. (Director). (1925). *The Phantom of the Opera* [Motion Picture]. United States: Universal.

Laemmle Jr., C. (Producer) and Whale, J. (Director). (1931). *Frankenstein* [Motion Picture]. United States: Universal Pictures.

Laemmle Jr., C. (Producer) and Whale, J. (Director). (1935). *Bride of Frankenstein* [Motion Picture]. United States: Universal Pictures.

Landau, J. (Producer) and Cameron, J. (Director and Producer). (2009). *Avatar* [Motion Picture]. United States: 20th Century Fox.

Lane, A. (3 January 2004). 'Unmasked'. *New Yorker*. https://www.newyorker.com/magazine/2005/01/03/unmasked-3

Lang, J. (Producer) and Goldstone, J. (Director). (1977). *Rollercoaster* [Motion Picture]. United States: Universal.

Laplanche, J. and Leclaire, S. (1972). 'The Unconscious: A Psychoanalytic Study'. *Yale French Studies*, 48, 118–75.

'Larry King Live Weekend: Mark David Chapman' [TV programme]. (30 September 1992). *CNN*.

Latour, B. (1993). *We Have Never Been Modern*, trans. by C. Porter. Cambridge, MA: Harvard University Press.

Lawrence, K. (2005). *John Lennon: In His Own Words*. Kansas City, MI: McMeel Publishing.

Le Carré, J. (2013). *A Delicate Truth*. London, England: Penguin.

Leaf, D. and Scheinfeld, J. (Directors). (2006). *The U.S. vs John Lennon* [Motion Picture]. United States: Lionsgate.

Lee, G. (ed.) (2018). *Rethinking Difference in Gender, Sexuality, and Popular Music*. New York: Routledge.

Leland, J. (2004). *Hip: The History*. New York: HarperCollins.

Lenin, V. (1966). 'Imperialism, the Highest Stage of Capitalism'. In *Essential Works of Lenin* (pp. 177–270). New York: Bantam. (Original work published 1917)

Lentini, P. (2003). 'Punk's Origins: Anglo-American Syncretism'. *Journal of Intercultural Studies*, 24(2), 153–74. doi:10.1080/0725686032000165388

Leonard, M. (2007). *Gender in the Music Industry: Rock, Discourse and Girl Power*. Farnham, England: Ashgate.

Leroux, G. (2011). *The Phantom of the Opera*. London, England: Harper Press. (Original work published in 1909)

LeRoy, M. (Producer), Fleming, V. (Director) and Vidor, K. (Director). (1939). *The Wizard of Oz* [Motion Picture]. United States: Metro-Goldwyn-Mayer.

'Letters Written by John Lennon's Killer Up for Sale'. (19 February 2013). *The Telegraph*. Retrieved from http://www.telegraph.co.uk/news/worldnews/northamerica/9879177/Letters-written-by-John-Lennons-killer-up-for-sale.html

Levy, A. (1962). *Operation Elvis*. London, England: Consul Books.

Lifton, D. (9 December 2012). 'Album Signed by John Lennon for Killer up for Sale'. *Ultimate Classic Rock*. Retrieved from http://ultimateclassicrock.com/john-lennon-mark-chapman-album-auction/

Linson, A. (Producer), Chaffin, C. (Producer), Bell, R. (Producer) and Fincher, D. (Director). (1999). *Fight Club* [Motion Picture]. United States: 20th Century Fox.

Lloyd Webber, A. (Producer) and Schumaker, J. (Director). (2004). *The Phantom of the Opera* [Motion Picture]. United States: Warner Bros.

Locke, A. (1997). *The New Negro*. New York: Touchstone. (Original work published in 1925)

Lofgren, M. (21 February 2014). 'Essay: Anatomy of the Deep State'. *Moyers & Company*. http://www.gatherthepeople.org/Downloads/Deep_State.pdf

Long, S. (3 May 2019). 'Pete Seeger at 100: Revisiting a Classic Hot Press Interview with the Folk Music Legend'. *Hot Press*. Retrieved from https://www.hotpress.com/music/pete-seeger-100-revisiting-classic-hot-press-interview-folk-music-legend-22772389 (Original work published in 2001)

Long, S. (Producer) and Ford, D. (Director). (1970). *Groupie Girl* [Motion Picture]. England: Salon Productions.

Loza, S. (2017). *Speculative Imperialisms: Monstrosity and Masquerade in Postracial Times*. Lanham, MD: Lexington Books.

Luxury Suites. (2011). *Edgwater Hotel* [website]. http://www.edgewaterhotel.com/luxury-seattle-suites.aspx

Mackie, V. (2016). 'Yoko Ono's Magical Thinking'. *Portal*, *13*(1). Retrieved from: http://epress.lib.uts.edu.au/journals/index.php/portal/article/view/4779/5203

Maillochon, F. (2007). '"Chiffres noirs" contre "chiffres ronds": L'enquête enveff dans la press quotidienne française (2000–2004)'. In N. Chetchuti and M. Jaspard (eds.), *Violences envers les femmes, trois pas en avant deux pas en arrière* (pp. 41–57). Paris, France: L'Harmattan.

Mäkelä, J. (2004). *John Lennon Imagined: Cultural History of a Rock Star*. New York: Peter Lang.

Mäkelä, J. (2005). 'Who Owns Him? The Debate on John Lennon'. In S. Jones and J. Jensen (eds.), *Afterlife as Afterimage: Posthumous Fame* (pp. 179–90). New York: Peter Lang.

Malchow, H. L. (1993). 'Frankenstein's Monster and Images of Race in Nineteenth-century Britain'. *Past & Present, 139*, 90–130.
Marcus, G. (1977a). 'Sly Stone: The Myth of Staggerlee'. In G. Marcus (ed.), *Mystery Train: Images of America in Rock'n'Roll Music* (pp. 75–111). New York: Omnibus Press. (Original work published in 1975)
Marcus, G. (1977b). 'Presliad'. In G. Marcus (ed.), *Mystery Train: Images of America in Rock'n'Roll Music* (pp. 137–206). New York: Omnibus Press. (Original work published in 1975)
Markowitz, R. (Director). (2002). *The Phantom of the Opera* [TV movie]. United States: Robert Halmi.
Marsh, D. (1992). *Elvis*. London, England: Omnibus Press.
Marshall, P. David. [Screen name]. (9 November 2016). 'Marshall and Redmond on Celebrity' [Video file]. Retrieved from https://www.youtube.com/watch?v=WEbFTChNv5s.
Marwick, A. (2015). *Status Update: Celebrity, Publicity, and Branding in the Social Media Age*. New Haven, CT: Yale University Press.
Marx, K. (1976). *Capital: A Critique of Political Economy, volume one*. London, England: Penguin Books. (Original work published in 1867)
Marx, K. (1993). *Grundrisse: Foundations of the Critique of Political Economy*. London, England: Penguin. Written in 1857. (Original work published in 1939)
Marx, K. (2010). 'A Contribution to the Critique of Political Economy, Third Chapter: The Process of Production of Capital'. In K. Marx and F. Engels (Eds.), *Marx & Engels Collected Works, Volume 30: Marx 1861–63* (pp. 9–171). Chadwell Health, England: Lawrence & Wishart.
Marx, K. and Engels, F. (1968). *Selected Works in One Volume*. London, England: Lawrence & Wishart.
Maxile Jr., H. J. (2011). 'Extensions on a Black Musical Tropology: From Trains to the Mothership (and beyond)'. *Journal of Black Studies, 42*(4), 593–608. doi:10.1177/0021934710386225
McCann, I. (17 September 1994). 'Doom! Shake the Tomb!' *New Musical Express*, 22.
McCutcheon, M. A. (2007). 'Techno, *Frankenstein* and Copyright'. *Popular Music, 26*(2), 259–80. doi:10.1017/S0261143007001225
McDonald, H. (31 March 2016). 'Doctor Convicted of Sex Assault Allowed to Keep Working, Report Reveals'. *The Guardian*. https://www.theguardian.com/uk-news/2016/mar/31/northern-ireland-dr-morris-fraser-report-alleges-cover-up
McGoohan, P. and Markstein, G. (Creators). (1967–1968). *The Prisoner* [TV series]. England: ITC Entertainment.
McIntosh, D. (2018). 'Monstrosity, Performance and Race in Contemporary Culture [review]'. *Quarterly Journal of Speech, 104*(1), 115–18.

McKittrick, S. (Producer), Blum, J. (Producer), Hamm Jr., E. (Producer) and Peele, J. (Producer and Director). (2017). *Get Out* [Motion Picture]. United States: Blumhouse Productions, QC Entertainment and Monkeypaw Productions.

McLuhan, M. (2015). *Culture Is Our Business*. Eugene, OR: Wipf and Stock. (Original work published 1970)

McNally, D. (2012). *Monsters of the Market: Zombies, Vampires and Global Capitalism*, Chicago, IL: Haymarket Books.

Mead, M. (5 February 1961). 'Letters to the Editor: Father and Son'. *New York Times*, p. BR44.

Means Coleman, R. (2011). *Horror Noire: Blacks in American Horror Films from the 1890s to Present*. New York: Routledge.

Mellor, A. K. (2003). 'Making a "Monster": An Introduction to *Frankenstein*'. In E. Schor (ed.), *The Cambridge Companion to Mary Shelley* (pp. 9–25). Cambridge, England: Cambridge University Press.

Mercer, K. (1986). 'Monster Metaphors: Notes on Michael Jackson's "Thriller"'. *Screen*, 27(1), 26–43.

Messerschmidt, J. W. (2018). 'The Salience of "Hegemonic Masculinity"'. *Men and Masculinities*, 22(1), 85–91. doi:10.1177/1097184X18805555

Michaels, L. (Producer) and Spheeris, P. (Director). (1992). *Wayne's World* [Motion Picture]. United States: NBC Films.

Middleton, R. (2007). 'Mum's the Word: Men's Singing and Maternal Law'. In F. Jarman-Ivens (ed.), *Oh boy! Masculinities and Popular Music* (pp. 103–24). New York: Routledge.

Miliband, R. (1973). *The State in Capitalist Society: The Analysis of the Western System of Power*. London: Quartet. (Original work published 1969)

Millett, K. (1970). *Sexual Politics*. New York: Doubleday.

Mills, R. (2015). '"Transformer": David Bowie's Rejection of 1960s Counterculture Fashion through His Glam Reinvention and Stylings in the Years 1969–1972'. *Clothing Cultures*, 2(2), 179–92. doi:10.1386/cc.2.2.179_1

Mina, D. (2003). 'Why Are Women Drawn to Men behind Bars?' *The Guardian*, 13 January. https://www.theguardian.com/world/2003/jan/13/gender.uk?CMP=aff_1432&utm_content=The+Independent&awc=5795_1589219580_f367ad4ebc254c87f112476f6eb29ac0

Mittman, A. (2012). 'Introduction: The Impact of Monsters and Monster Studies'. In A. Mittman (ed.), *The Ashgate Research Companion to Monsters and the Monstrous* (pp. 1–16). Farnham, England: Ashgate.

Miyakawa, F. M. (2005). *Five Percenter Rap: God Hop's Music, Message, and Black Muslim Mission*. Indianapolis, IN: Indiana University Press.

Moore, S. (1997). *That's All Right Elvis: The Untold Story of Elvis' First Guitarist and Manager*. New York: Schirmer Books.

Moore, S. (6 April 2012). 'No Beautiful Malian Music Will Make Marie Trintignant's Death Go Away'. *The Guardian*. https://www.theguardian.com/commentisfree/2012/apr/06/malian-blues-marie-trintignant

Morant, K. (2011). 'Language in Action: Funk Music as the Critical Voice of a Post–civil Rights Movement Counterculture'. *Journal of Black Studies*, *42*(1), 71–82.

Morrison, T. (1987). *Beloved*. New York: Alfred A. Knopf.

Morton, R. (2005). *King Kong: The History of a Movie Icon from Fay Wray to Peter Jackson*. New York: Applause Theatre & Cinema Books.

Moten, F. (2003). *In the Break: The Aesthetics of the Black Radical Tradition*. Minneapolis, MN: University of Minnesota Press.

Mulvey, L. (1975). 'Visual Pleasure and Narrative Cinema'. *Screen*, *16*(3), 6–18.

'Nadine Trintignant juge "indécent" que Cantat remonte sur scène'. (30 April 2014). *Le Point*. www.lepoint.fr/people/nadine-trintignant-juge-indecent-que-cantat-remonte-sur-scene-30-04-2014-1817834_2116.php

Nash, A. (2003). *The Colonel: The Extraordinary Story of Colonel Tom Parker and Elvis Presley*. London, England: Aurum.

Neal, M. A. (1999). *What the Music Said: Black Popular Music and Black Public Culture*. New York: Routledge.

Nehring, N. (1997). *Popular Music, Gender and Postmodernism: Anger Is an Energy*. Thousand Oaks, CA: Sage.

Newitz, A. (2006). *Pretend We're Dead: Capitalist Monsters in American Pop Culture*. Durham, NC: Duke University Press.

Niva, S. (2019). 'Tough and Tender: New World Order Masculinity and the Gulf War'. In M. Zalewski and J. Parpart (eds.), *The 'Man' Question in International Relations* (pp. 109–28). London, England: Routledge.

Nolan, D. (Director). (2014). *Crimes That Shook Britain: Jimmy Savile* [TV show episode]. England: Channel 5.

Northcutt, W. (2006). 'The Spectacle of Alienation: Death, Loss, and the Crowd in "*Sgt. Pepper's Lonely Hearts Club Band*"'. In K. Womack and T. Davis (eds.), *Reading the Beatles: Cultural Studies, Literary Criticism, and the Fab Four* (pp. 129–46). Albany: State University of New York.

'Nuit noire'. (6 August 2003). *Les Inrockuptibles*, 3.

O'Hagan, A. (2012). 'Light Entertainment'. *London Review of Books*, *34*(21), 5–8.

O'Neal, S. (1996). *Elvis Inc: The Fall and Rise of the Presley Empire*. Rocklington, CA: Prima.

O'Rawe, D. (2006). 'Ten Minutes of Silence for John Lennon'. *Film Studies*, *9*(1), 64–7.

Parkenham, C. (4 June 1939). 'Recent recordings'. *New York Times*, A6.

Parker, E. (1978). *Inside Elvis*. Orange, CA: Rampart House.

Parkinson, M. (14 January 1968). 'Honest Jim'. *The Sunday Times Magazine*.

Parry, B. (1994). 'Problems in Current Theories of Colonial Discourse'. In B. Ashcroft, G. Griffiths and H. Tiffin (eds.), *The Post-colonial Studies Reader* (pp. 36–44). London, England: Routledge.

Pennington, J. (Producer) and Guest, V. (Director). (1959). *Expresso bongo* [Motion Picture]. England: British Lion.

Perry, I. (2004). *Prophets of the Hood: Politics and Poetics in Hip Hop*. Durham, NC: Duke University Press.

Pih, D. (ed.) (2013). *Glam: The Performance of Style*. Liverpool, England: Tate Publishing.

Ping-Pong [Letters]. (13 August 2003a). *Les Inrockuptibles*, 16–18.

Ping-Pong [Letters]. (3 September 2003b). *Les Inrockuptibles*, 14.

Pinsdorf, M. (2002). 'Greater Dead Heroes than Live Husbands: Widows as Image-makers'. *Public Relations Review*, 28(3), 283–99. https://doi.org/10.1016/S0363-8111(02)00132-7

Poe, E. (2016). *Edgar Allan Poe: The Purloined Letter*. Scotts Valley, CA: CreateSpace. (Original work published in 1844)

Poignant, R. (2004). *Professional Savages: Captive Lives and Western Spectacle*. Newhaven, CT: Yale University Press.

Porterfield, N. (2001). *Last Cavalier: The Life and Times of John A. Lomax, 1867–1948*. Urbana, IL: University of Illinois Press.

Potter, P. (Creator). (1959). *Juke Box Jury* [TV show]. England: BBC.

Presley, D. et al. (1980). *Elvis, We Love You Tender*. London, England: New English Library.

Presley, P. (1985). *Elvis and Me*. London: Century.

Pressman, E. (Producer) and De Palma, B. (Director). (1974). *Phantom of the Paradise* [Motion Picture]. United States: 20th Century Fox.

Preston, A. (15 June 2018). 'Kincora Survivor Richard Kerr Brands Inquiry "Unfair" and Stops Giving Evidence'. *Belfast Telegraph*. https://www.belfasttelegraph.co.uk/news/northern-ireland/kincora-survivor-richard-kerr-brands-inquiry-unfair-and-stops-giving-evidence-34802146.html

'Professor Anthony Clare' (obituary). (30 October 2007). *The Daily Telegraph*. Retrieved from https://www.telegraph.co.uk/news/obituaries/1567778/Professor-Anthony-Clare.html

Quinn, M. (1990). 'Celebrity and the Semiotics of Acting'. *New Theatre Quarterly*, 6(22), 154–61.

QuoTelevision [Screen name]. (6 October 2018). 'HARDtalk with Francis Rossi' [Video file]. Retrieved from https://www.youtube.com/watch?v=47xGz97vaxk

Ravalli, R. (2007). 'Snoop's Devil Dogg: African American Ghostlore and "*Bones*"'. *The Journal of American Culture*, 30(3), 285–92.

Reed, J. (25 July 2013). 'Bertrand Cantat Is Back. But Should Music Fans Boycott Him?' *The Guardian*. https://www.theguardian.com/commentisfree/2013/jul/25/bertrand-cantat-back-music-fans-boycott

Reeves, M. (2008). *Somebody Scream! Rap Music's Rise to Prominence in the Aftershock of Black Power*. New York: Faber and Faber.

Rennell, T. (4 December 2010). 'Was John Lennon's Murderer Mark Chapman a CIA Hitman? Thirty Years on, There's an Extraordinary New Theory', *Daily Mail*. Retrieved from http://www.dailymail.co.uk/news/article-1335479/Was-John-Lennons-murderer-Mark-Chapman-CIA-hitman-Thirty-years-theres-extraordinary-new-theory.html

'Report of the Historical Institutional Abuse Enquiry'. (2017). 9(2). Retrieved from https://www.hiainquiry.org/historical-institutional-abuse-inquiry-report-chapters

Reynolds, H. (2 March 1947). 'Collecting Our Living Folksong'. *New York Times*, p. BR7.

Reynolds, S. (2006). 'Haunted Audio'. *The Wire* 273, November. http://reynoldsretro.blogspot.com/2012/05/

Reynolds, S. (14 May 2012). 'HAUNTED AUDIO, a/k/a SOCIETY OF THE SPECTRAL: Ghost Box, Mordant Music and Hauntology'. *ReynoldsRetro* [blog]. http://www.reynoldsretro.blogspot.com/2012/05/(Original work published 2006)

Reynolds, S. (2016). *Shock and Awe: Glam Rock and Its Legacy from the Seventies to the Twenty-first Century*. London, England: Faber and Faber.

Richards, E. (1999). 'A Political Anatomy of Monsters, Hopeful and Otherwise: Teratogeny, Transcendentalism, and Evolutionary Theorizing'. *Isis*, 85(3), 377–411.

Richards, J. (1997). *Films and British National Identity: From Dickens to Dad's Army*. Manchester, England: Manchester University Press.

Richards, M. (Producer) and Marshall, R. (Director). (2002). *Chicago* [Motion Picture]. United States: Miramax.

Ridenhour, C. and Jah, Y. (1997). *Fight the Power: Rap, Race, and Reality*. Edinburgh, Scotland: Payback.

Ritchie, C. (2014). '"Only Mugs Work": The Spiv in British Comedy'. *Comedy Studies*, 2(1), 13–20. doi:10.1386/cost.2.1.13_1

Robbins, B. and Myrick, R. (2000). 'The Function of the Fetish in The Rocky Horror Picture Show and Priscilla, Queen of the Desert'. *Journal of Gender Studies*, 9(3), 269–80. doi:10.1080/713677997

Robinson, C. J. (1983). *Black Marxism: The Making of the Black Radical Tradition*. London, England: Zed Press.

Rollefson, J. G. (2008). 'The "Robot Voodoo Power" Thesis: Afrofuturism and Anti-anti-essentialism from Sun Ra to Kool Keith'. *Black Music Research Journal*, 28(1), 83–109.

RZA, The. (2009). *The Tao of Wu*. New York: Riverhead Books.

Said. (2003). *Orientalism*. London, England: Penguin. (Original work published in 1978)

Salinger, J. (2010). *The Catcher in the Rye*. London, England: Penguin. (Original work published in 1945)

Salter, A. and Blodgett, B. (2017). *Toxic Geek Masculinity in Media: Sexism, Trolling, and Identity Policing*. Cham, Switzerland: Springer.

Sandbrook, D. (3 October 2015). 'A Cruel, Greedy, Selfish Monster: A Peace-loving Visionary? No, Argues a Blistering Book. John Lennon Was a Nasty Piece of Work Who Epitomized Our Age of Self-obsession'. *Daily Mail*. Retrieved http://www.dailymail.co.uk/news/article-3258235/A-cruel-greedy-selfish-monster-peace-loving-visionary-No-argues-blistering-book-John-Lennon-nasty-piece-work-epitomised-age-self-obsession.html

Sandvoss, C. (2005). *Fans: The Mirror of Consumption*. Cambridge, England: Polity Press.

Sante, L. (1981). 'Relic'. *New York Review of Books*, 28(20), 22–4.

Sargent, C. (2009). 'Playing, Shopping, and Working as Rock Musicians: Masculinities in "De-skilled" and "Re-skilled" Organizations'. *Gender & Society*. 23(5), 665–87.

Savilonis, M. F. (2013). 'Got to Get over the Hump: The Politics of Glam in the Work of Labelle and Parliament'. In N. Cook and R. Pettengill (eds), *Taking It to the Bridge: Music as Performance*. Ann Arbor: University of Michigan Press.

Scarborough, D. (1968). 'American Ballads and Folksongs'. In *New York Times Book Review* (p. 2). New York: Arno Press. (Original work published in 1934)

Schneider, S. (1999). 'Monsters as (Uncanny) Metaphors: Freud, Lakoff, and the Representation of Monstrosity in Cinematic Horror'. *Other Voices*, 1(3), 167–91.

Schoedsack, E. (Producer and Director). (1933). *Son of Kong* [Motion Picture]. United States: RKO Radio Pictures.

Schur, R. L. (2009). *Parodies of Ownership: Hip-hop Aesthetics and Intellectual Property Law*. Ann Arbor, MI: University of Michigan Press.

Scott, D. (Producer) and Cundieff, R. (Director). (1995). *Tales from the Hood* [Motion Picture]. USA: 40 Acres and a Mule and Filmworks.

Scott, N. (2007). 'God Hates Us All: Kant, Radical Evil and the Diabolical Monstrous Human in Heavy Metal'. In N. Scott (ed.), *Monsters and the Monstrous: Myths and Metaphors of Enduring Evil* (pp. 201–12). Amsterdam, Netherlands: Rodopi.

Shank, B. (1994). *Dissonant Identities: The Rock'n'roll Scene in Austin, Texas*. Hanover, NH: University Press of New England.

Shapiro, R. and Shapiro, S. (Creators) and Moore, I. et al. (Directors). (1981–1989). *Dynasty* [TV series]. USA: ABC.

Shaviro, S. (2002). 'Capitalist Monsters'. *Historical Materialism*, 10(4), 281–90.

Shelley, M. (1986). 'Frankenstein: Or, the Modern Prometheus'. In P. Fairclough (ed.), *Three Gothic Novels* (pp. 257–498). Harmondsworth, England: Penguin. (Original work published 1818)

Shenson, W. (Producer) and Lester, R. (Director) (1964). *A Hard Day's Night* [Motion Picture]. England: United Artists.

Shenson, W. (Producer) and Lester, R. (Director) (1965). *Help!* [Motion Picture]. England: United Artists.

Shumway, D. (2011). 'LennonNYC'. *Journal of American History*, 98(1), 301–3.

Sky News [Screen name]. (25 February 2016). 'Dame Janet Smith Delivers Savile Report Findings' [Video file]. Retrieved from https://www.youtube.com/watch?v=Y8FHb08pc44

Slaughter, T. (1995a). 'Why I Chose Not to Ride with Elvis'. *Elvis Monthly*, 423, 1–5.

Slaughter, T. (1995b). 'Buddy, Can You Spare Some Bread?' *Elvis Monthly*, 425, 1–4.

Smethurst, J. (2001). 'Invented by Horror: The Gothic and African American Literary Ideology in "Native Son"'. *African American Review*, 35(1), 29–40.

Snead, J. (1994). *Black Screens/White Images: Hollywood from the Dark Side*. Abingdon, England: Routledge.

Sollee, K. (2015). 'All Black Everything: Gothic Cloak and Swagger in Contemporary Hip Hop'. *Fashion, Style & Popular Culture*, 2(2), 241–56.

Sonia Poulton [Screen name]. (2 August 2018). 'Paedophiles in Parliament' [Video file]. Retrieved from https://www.youtube.com/watch?v=PnZiDxkwgrU

Spivak, G. (1985). 'Three Women's Texts and a Critique of Imperialism'. *Critical Inquiry*, 12(1), 243–61.

Stevenson, R. L. (2003). *The Strange Case of Dr Jekyll and Mr Hyde and Other Tales of Terror*. London, England: Penguin Classics. (Original work published 1886)

Stewart, J. (Producer). (1964–2018). *Top of the Pops* [TV series]. England: BBC.

Stowe, A. (1987). 'Elvis the Man'. *Elvis Monthly*, 325, 15.

Stratton, J. (1986). 'Why Doesn't Anybody Write Anything about Glam Rock?' *Australian Journal of Cultural Studies*, 4(1). http://espace.library.curtin.edu.au/R/?func=dbin-jump-full&object_id=145813&local_base=GEN01-ERA02

Strausbaugh, J. (2006). *Black Like You: Blackface, Whiteface, Insult & Imitation in American Popular Culture*. New York: Tarcher.

Straw, W. (1997). 'Sizing Up Record Collections: Gender and Connoisseurship in Rock Music Culture'. In S. Whiteley (ed.), *Sexing the Groove: Popular Music and Gender* (pp. 3–16). New York: Routledge.

Streiner, R. (Producer), Hardman, K. (Producer) and Romero, G. (Director). (1968). *Night of the Living Dead* [Motion Picture]. USA: Image Ten.

Sullivan, M. (1987). '"More Popular than Jesus": The Beatles and the Religious Far-right'. *Popular Music*, 6(3), 313–26.

Surkis, J. (2018). *Sexing the Citizen: Morality and Masculinity in France, 1870–1920*. Ithaca, NY: Cornell University Press.

tartantroozers [Screen name]. (31 October 2011). 'Jimmy Savile & Dr. Anthony Clare – Radio 4' [Audio file]. Retrieved from https://audioboom.com/posts/526151-jimmy-savile-dr-anthony-clare-radio-4

Taylor, I. and Wall, D. (1976). 'Beyond the Skinheads: Comments on the Emergence and Significance of the Glamrock Cult'. In G. Mungham and G. Pearson (eds.), *Working Class Youth Culture*. London, England: Routledge & Kegan Paul.

Taylor, L. (10 December 2012). 'Album Signed by John Lennon for His Killer Could Be Yours for $650,000'. *The Star*. Retrieved from https://www.thestar.com/entertainment/2012/12/10/album_signed_by_john_lennon_for_his_killer_could_be_yours_for_650000.html (accessed 9 November 2017).

Taylor, L. (2019). *Darkly: Black History and America's Gothic Soul*. London, England: Repeater Books.

Taylor, P. (2013). *Žižek and the Media*. Cambridge, England: Polity.

Theroux, L. (2019). *Gotta Get Theroux This: My Life and Strange Times in Television*. London, England: MacMillan.

TheUnauthorizedStory [Screen name]. (9 November 2015). 'Mark David Chapman' [Video file]. Retrieved from https://www.youtube.com/watch?v=KR9xx2vDC5c

Tickle, V. (2014). 'Gender Performativity and "*The Rocky Horror Picture Show*"'. *Film International*, 69, 147–50. doi:10.1386/fiin.12.3.147_7

Titon, J. (2014) *Early Downhome Blues: A Musical and Cultural Analysis*. Chapel Hill: University of North Carolina Press.

Tobler, J. and Wootton, R. (1983). *Elvis: The Legend and the Music*. London, England: Optimum Books.

Tookey, C. (Director). (1988). *After Dark: British Intelligence* [TV series episode]. England: Channel 4.

TopTellyFan [Screen name]. (8 July 2013). 'Barbara Hewson Interviewed over Her Controversial Child Sex Abuse Comments (Channel 4 News, 8.7.13)' [Video file]. Retrieved from https://www.youtube.com/watch?v=3DR6EEl0H64

Trintignant, N. (2003). *Ma fille, Marie*. Paris: Fayard.

Tschmuck, P. (2012). *Creativity and Innovation in the Music Industry*. Vienna, Austria: Springer.

Turner, A. W. (2004). *Biba: The Biba Experience*. Woodbridge, England: Antique Collectors' Club.

Turner, A. W. (2013). *Glam Rock: Dandies in the Underworld*. London: V&A Publishing.

Uscinski, J. and Parent, J. (2014). *American Conspiracy Theories*. New York: Oxford University Press.

Valenzuela, L. (1977). *Como en la guerra*. Buenos Aires: Sudamericana.

Van Upp, V. (Producer) and Vidor, C. (Director). (1946). *Gilda* [Motion Picture]. USA: Columbia Pictures.

Varriale, S. (2012). 'Is That Girl a Monster? Some Notes on Authenticity and Artistic Value in Lady Gaga'. *Celebrity Studies*, 3(2), doi:10.1080/19392397.2012.679481

Vermorel, F. (2011). *Starlust: The Secret Fantasies of Fans*. London, England: Faber and Faber. (Original work published 1985)

Vermorel, F. (2019). *Dead Fashion Girl: A Situationist Detective Story*. Cambridge, MA: Strange Attractor Press.

Vivant, A. (6 August 2003). 'Les histoires d'A'. *Les Inrockuptibles*, 11.

Vulliamy, E. (16 November 2003a). 'When Love Dies'. *The Guardian*. https://www.theguardian.com/film/2003/nov/16/features.magazine

Vulliamy, E. (16 November 2003b). 'When Love Dies (Part 2)'. *The Guardian*. https:www.theguardian.com/film/2003/nov/16/features.magazine1

Waggner, G. (Producer) and Lubin, A. (Director). (1943). *The Phantom of the Opera* [Motion Picture]. USA: Universal.

Walker, W. [Letter to the editor]. (14 July 2016). 'Terrorist Novels'. *London Review of Books*. Retrieved from https://www.lrb.co.uk/the-paper/v38/n14/letters

Wapole, H. (2002). *The Castle of Otranto*. London, England: Penguin. (Original work published in 1764).

Watts, E. K. (2004). 'An Exploration of Spectacular Consumption: Gangsta Rap as Cultural Commodity'. In F. Forman and M. A. Neal (eds.), *That's the Joint: The Hip-hop Studies Reader* (pp. 593–607). New York: Routledge.

Weiss, A. S. (2004). 'Ten Theses on Monsters and Monstrosity'. *TDR/The Drama Review*, *48*(1), 124–5.

Wertheimer, A. (1994). *Elvis '56: In the Beginning*. London, England: Pimlico.

West, R. et al. (1977). *Elvis: What Happened?* New York: Ballantine.

Westmoreland, K. (1987). *Elvis and Kathy*. Glendale, CA: Glendale House.

White, M. (2011). *From Jim Crow to Jay-Z: Race, Rap, and the Performance of Masculinity*. Urbana: University of Illinois Press.

Whitehead, S. M. (2002). *Men and Masculinities*. Cambridge, England: Polity.

Whiteley, S. (ed.) (1997). *Sexing the Groove: Popular Music and Gender*. New York: Routledge.

Wiene, R. (Director). (1920). *The Cabinet of Doctor Caligari* [Motion Picture]. Germany: Decla-Bioscop.

Wilderson III, F.B. (2009). 'Grammar & Ghosts: The Performative Limits of African Freedom'. *Theatre Survey*, *50*(1), 119–25. doi:10.1017/S004055740900009X

Willhardt, M. and Stein, J. (1999). 'Dr; Funkenstein's Supergroovalisticprosifunkstication: George Clinton Signifies'. In K. J. H. Dettmar and W. Richey (eds.), *Reading Rock and Roll: Authenticity, Appropriation, Aesthetics*. New York: Columbia University Press.

Williams, G. (ed.) (2007). *'The Gothic: Documents of Contemporary Art'*. London, United Kingdom: Whitechapel Gallery.

Williams, K. (1993). *The Kenneth Williams Diaries*. New York: Harper Collins.

Williams, R. (1977). *Marxism and Literature*. Oxford, England: Oxford University Press.

Wilson, J. (4 April 1959). 'Program Given by Alan Lomax'. *New York Times*, p. 13.

Wilson, J. and Swyngedouw, E. (2015). *The Post-political and Its Discontents: Spectres of Depoliticization, Spectres of Radical Politics*. Edinburgh, Scotland: Edinburgh University Press.

Wilson, S. (2013). 'Give Peace a Chance'. In G. Matthews and S. Goodman (eds.), *Violence and the Limits of Representation* (pp. 28–48). Basingstoke, England: Palgrave.

Wise, S. (1987). 'Sexing Elvis'. *Women's Studies Forum*, *7*(1), 13–17.

Wolff, E. (1948). *La science des monstres*. Paris, France: Gallimard.

Wood, R. (2003). 'The American Nightmare: Horror in the '70s'. In R. Wood (ed.), *Hollywood from Vietnam to Reagan ... and Beyond* (pp. 63–84). New York: Columbia University Press.

Woolf, J. (Producer), Woolf, J. and Clayton, J. (Director). (1959). *Room at the Top* [Motion Picture]. England: British Lion.

Worrell, M. (2014). 'The Commodity as the Ultimate Monstrosity: Capitalism and the Four Horsemen of the Apocalypse, or, Reading Marx's *"Capital"* through Durkheim's *"Suicide"'. Fast Capitalism*, 11(1), 61–5. https://doi.org/10.32855/fcapital.201401.008

Wright, A. (2013). *Monstrosity: The Human Monster in Visual Culture*. London, England: I.B. Tauris.

Wright, J. (1989). 'The New Negro Poet and the Nachal Man: Sterling Brown's Folk Odyssey'. *Black American Literature Forum*, 23(1), 95–105.

Wright Mills, C. (2000). *The Power Elite*. Oxford, England: Oxford University Press. (Original work published in 1956)

Wright, R. (1972). *Native Son*. Harmondsworth, England: Penguin. (Original work published 1940)

Yancey, B. (1977). *My Life with Elvis*. London: WH Allen.

Yapp, W. (Director). (2000). *When Louis Met ... Jimmy* [TV series episode]. England: BBC.

Žižek, S. (2001). *Enjoy Your Symptom! Jacques Lacan in Hollywood and Out*. New York: Routledge.

Index

50 Cent 20
6 Feet Deep 140
666.667 Club 162

A Hard Day's Night 122
acousmatic listening 31
Act Up 163
Adams, Nick 75
adolescence 1, 10, 17, 28, 58, 112, 164, 178
Adventures of a Ballad Hunter 67
Africa 51, 53–4, 58–9, 61, 145–7, 149, 153, 217–18
    pan-Africanism 153
African Americans
    Black gothic, *see* gothic
    Black Marxism 147–8
    Black music 41, 52, 61, 104, 157,
        also see blues, disco, funk, hip hop,
        jazz, p-funk
    Black Power movement 58, 154
    Black studies 139, 146, 149–50
    civil rights 41, 57, 58, 104
    expressive culture 150
    folklore 142–3
    Harlem Renaissance 52–3
    Jim Crow era 50–4
    music industry exploitation 157
    musical creativity 59, 67
    race movies 56
    racist stereotyping 53, 59, 63–4, 67
    Reconstruction era 50–1, 54
    segregation in music 66
    self-definition 105
    social experience 138, 142
    taboo on interracial sex 57
    urbanization of 51
    visual culture 152
    womanhood 158
Afrofuturism 103–5, 156
After Dark 197
Agamben, Giorgio 132–3
Albrittan, Dub 72
Alden, Ginger 70
alt-right 196
American Society of Composers, Authors and Publishers (ASCAP) 39, 230
Americanisation 171
amour fou 179
'Angola, La!' 61–3, 65
Anohni 108
anti-fandom 114, 134
Archive of American Folksong. *See* Library of Congress
Ardisson, Thierry 183
Argento, Dario 44–5
Arnold, Eddy 71, 75
art
    interpretation 117
    as metaphor 109
    music as 126, 232
    pop art 210
    relation to life 209
    tradition 60
    visual 125, 127, 131, 153
ASCAP. *See* American Society of Composers, Authors and Publishers
Astronaut 46
'Au clair de la lune' 32
Audiard, Jacques 6
Austen, Jane 230
    Northanger Abbey 230
    Sense and Sensibility 230
authenticity
    and adaption 90
    and class 60, 92
    celebrity 60, 122, 123
    commodities 60, 80
    gender 20, 122
    musical 18, 43, 60, 106, 212, 231
    personal 82, 112, 117, 123
    and race 60, 103
    and region 82 64

Autry, Gene 231
'Aux sombres héros de l'amer' 162
Avatar 66
Aznavour, Charles 163

baby boomers 206
Badiou, Alain 10
badman archetype 155
Baker, Jackson 74, 76
Baker, Josephine 52
Bakewell, Joan 208
'Ballad of Dwight Fry' 99
Bangs, Lester 101
banlieux 171
Barclay label 163–4
bare life 132, 134
Barthes, Roland 12, 18
Bashung, Alain 161, 163
BBC 187–93, 203, 206–9, 213–14, 220, 222, 233
Beatles, the 41, 75, 109, 113–14, 118, 121–3, 128–9, 131, 134, 161, 192, 207, 213, 215, 232
    fans 125–6, 128, 132, 134, 211, 217
    'More popular than Jesus' comment 122
Beauvoir, Simone de 184
Beck, James 214
Beckford, William Thomas 138
Beech, Carl 197
Beethoven, Ludwig van 29
Beineix, Jean-Jacques 179
Benchétrit, Samuel 164–6
Berliner, Emile 32
Bertelsmann Music Group 46
Bertrand Cantat, ou le chant des automates 182
bestiality
    savage behaviour 53, 179–80
    sexual 207
bestialization 175
Betty Blue (37°2 le matin) 179
Biba 102
'Big Beast' 137
Big T Tyler 231
Bigelow, Kathryn 6
Bildungsroman 96–7
Black Atlantic 149, 150, 156
Black gothic. *See* gothic
Black Marxism. *See* African Americans

'Black night' 173
Black Power. *See* African Americans
Black studies. *See* African Americans
Blackface minstrelsy 52, 65
Blood Brothers (gang) 152
'Blood Brothers' 153
Bloom, Harold 112–13
blues 41, 61, 65, 104
BMI. *See* Broadcast Music, Inc.
Bohemian Grove 205
Bolan, Marc 94, 106, 108
Bone, Thugs and Harmony 138
Bones 143
Bowie, David 1, 2, 20, 87–8, 92–5, 102, 104, 108, 121, 161, 230
    Aladdin Sane 104
    Ziggy Stardust 104
Boy George 98
Boyle, Robert 107
'Boys Keep Swinging' 1
Brasserie des Arts 170
breakbeats 139
Brel, Jacques 163
Breton, André 179
    L'Amour fou 179
    Nadja 179
Bride of Frankenstein 91
Brief Encounter 213
Britpop 206
Broadcast Music, Inc. (BMI) 39, 84, 230
Brontë, Charlotte 138
    Jane Eyre 138
Broudie, Ian 162
Bundy, Ted 182
Burgess, Guy 198
Burke, Edmund 89
Butler, Judith 4, 96

'Cambridge 1969' 232
Cameron, James 66
Canal Plus 168
cancel culture 221, 228
Candyman 143
Canguilhem, Georges 9–10
Cantat, Bertrand 161, 163–4, 168–70, 172–83, 185. *Also see* Noir Désir
Cantat, Xavier 168, 180–4

capital 5–6, 13, 34, 46–7, 81, 85, 146–8, 154, 159, 196, 228, 233
capitalism 5–7, 13, 15, 19–20, 43, 114, 138, 142–4, 146–9, 151, 153, 155, 157, 196
   casino capitalism 82
   consumer 42
carnival 22, 76, 85, 99
Cavalcade of American Song 61
celebrity 71–3, 77, 81, 110, 120–1, 127, 192, 194–5, 197, 209–10
   attention economy 113–15
   bare celebrity 121
   celebrity capital 210
   commodification 81–2, 84–6, 138, 156
   experience of audience 120–1
   genealogy 70–1
   image 12, *see* individual celebrities
   infamy 115, 204, *also see* objectification
Centre for Contemporary Cultural Studies 91
Cerf, Muriel 182–3
Chaney, Lon 38
Channel 4 197, 201
Channel 4 News 201
chansons 162
Chapman, Mark David 109–20, 127–8, 131–5
   agency 131
   infamy 129
   mental health 110, 112, 119, 133
   parole hearings 127, 133
Charlie Hebdo 184
Châtelain, Hélène 175
Chéreau, Patrice 163
Chicago 46
Child, Francis 60
Child Sex Abuse (CSA). *See* paedophilia
children 28, 73, 76, 78, 82, 85, 117, 142, 164, 169, 181, 187–9, 197–9, 201–3, 205, 207–11, 220–1, 227–8, 233
   as symbols of futurity 228
Chuck D. *See* Public Enemy
cinéma du look 179
civil society 62, 163
Clare, Anthony 225–6

Clarence 13X 152
class 60–1, 73, 78, 85
   middle 6, 41, 73, 92, 122, 195, 212–13
   working 7, 92, 189, 213
      White trash stereotype 73, 77–8
Clayton, Jack 216
Clinton, Bill 19
Clinton, George 103–5
Clipse 137
Clunk Click 213
Cocksucker Blues 207
Cohen, J. J. 11–12
Cohen, Lyor 140
Cohen, Stanley 206, 223, 227
Cole, George 214
commodification 80, 84, 116–17, 138, 156
   self-commodification 43
Connell, R.W. 5–7, 15–16
Conrad, Joseph 217–18
conspiracy theory 69, 194–6, 199, 202–5, 208, 232–3
'Constant Elevation' 156
Constrictor 99
consumption 15–16, 39, 42, 81, 142, 213
   drugs 163, 165, 168
   media 111, 194 and race 150, 155
   and race 150, 155
   music 17–18, 35, 39, 47, 92
Cooper, Alice 88, 98–100, 102
Cooper, Merian Caldwell 49–50, 54–7, 96
Cosby, Bill 197
country music 39, 71, 75, 79
Craven, Wes 143
Creation label 163
Creem 101
Cremation of Care ceremony 205
Crimes That Shook Britain 210
criticism 49, 109, 172, 217, 222
cultural capital 18
cultural hierarchies 37, 47, 52, 117
Cundieff, Rusty 142
Curry, Tim 95, 97

Dad's Army 214
Daily Express 220
Daily Mail 113, 194, 222
Dalle, Béatrice 179
Darwin, Charles 14

Das Cabinet des Dr. Caligari 38, 72
Datebook 122
David Bowie Is exhibition 88
Davis, Oscar 75
Dawn of the Dead 142
De La Soul 140
De Palma, Brian 41, 230
Decadent movement, arts 178
deep state 196–7, 199, 203, 222, 234
Deep Throat 207
Def Jam 140
Derrida, Jacques 11, 13, 32, 37, 143–5
   Specters of Marx 143, *also see*
     différance, hauntology
Des visages des figures 162, 180
Diana. *See* Spencer, Diana
Dickerson, Ernest 143
différance 11, 143
Dinosaur Jr 170
disco 103
DJ Kool Herc 100
Dolphin Square 196
Dominique A 163
Doo Dew Man Records 140
Double Fantasy 113, 117, 126
Douglass, Frederick 150–1
Dr. Dre 20
Dracula 146
Du Bois, W.E.B. 51, 147
du Chiallu, Paul 54
   Explorations and Adventures in
     Equatorial Africa 54
Dumont, Bruno 179
Duran Duran 46
Dyer, Richard 97, 124
   Stars 124
Dylan, Bob 41, 206
Dynasty 43

Eastwood, Clint 6
Echo and the Bunnymen 162
ecstasy (drug) 163
Edgar Winter Group 100
Edison, Thomas 32
eerieness 32
Electric Sound 232
Elle 184
Elm Guest House 196

Elvis. *See* Presley, Elvis
Engels, Friedrich 144
Enter the Wu-Tang (36 Chambers) 140
Enveff (National Survey on Violence
   Against Women in France)
   171–2, 180
Epstein, Jeffrey 197
Esposito, Joe 70, 79
Exposure: The Other Side of Jimmy
   Savile 188
Expresso Bongo 216

Faber, Claude 175
fans 20, 29, 33, 41–3, 58, 70, 74–5, 79–83,
   85–6, 93, 98, 101–2, 107, 114, 119,
   125–6, 128, 130–1, 134, 163, 172–4,
   185, 192, 197, 211, 217, 221, 231
   Beatlemania 122
   extreme 23, 113–14
   fictionalized 30–1
   mass culture stereotypes 29, 31,
     113–14, 123
Farrakhan, Louis 154
Federal Theatre Project 61
Fédération Nationale Solidarité Femmes,
   La 172
'Feed My Frankenstein' 99
femininism 4–5, 11, 13, 175–6, 184–5, 187
   French feminism 170–2
   Ni Putes Ni Soumises 171–2
Ferry, Bryan 106
Fersen, Thomas 163
Fight Club 6
Fillmore East: June 1971 207
Fincher, David 6
Finlay, Jeanie 33
Fisher, Mark 13, 156, 159, 209, 221–2,
   228
Five Percent Nation 103, 141–2, 152–6
Flatlinerz 140
Fleming, Victor 104
'Foil' 233
Folk music 19, 32, 49, 58–67
Folklore 50, 142, 143
Foo Fighters 100
Ford, Derek 211
Foucault, Michel 5, 9–10, 89
France 2 channel 168, 183

Frankenstein 87–108, 146
  as metaphor and myth 88–91
  and science 89–91
'Frankenstein' 99, 100–2
Frankenstein (film) 91
Frankenstein (novel) 88–90, 94, 98–99, 103
Freud, Sigmund 3, 11, 14–16, 19, 27–8, 77, 115, 167, 174, 230, 232
  death drive 35, 149
  id 85
  'Mourning and Melancholia' 174
  narcissism theory 167
  Oedipus complex 3, 11, 15–16, 27, 40
    bad father 40, 43, 70, 77, 230
    spousification 73
  'On Narcissism' 167
  'Rat Man' 11
  repression 11, 34, 82
  The Interpretation of Dreams 27
  'The Sandman' 230
  Totem and Taboo 14–15, 77, 115, 232
  'Wolf Man' 11, *also see* Oedipus complex
Frith, Simon 16–20
Front National 163
Frukwan. *See* Gravediggaz
Fugazi 162
Fuller, Rob 70
funk 41, 103–5
Funkadelic 103–4
'Funkentelechy' 105
Funkentelechy vs. the Placebo Syndrome 103, 105
funkentelechy, idea 106–8

Gambaccini, Paul 220
gangsta rap. *See* hip hop
Gates, Henry Louis 50–2
Gatti, Armand 175
gay culture 95, 101, 201
  gay rights 163
  New Queer Cinema 98
  same-sex marriage 204
gender
  and musical performance 17–21
  and musical spaces 17–18
  as performance 1–2, 4, 96, *also see* masculinity
Get Out 143
Geto Boys 140
G.I. Blues 70
Gilda 97
Gilroy, Paul 150
Ginsberg, Allen 109, 135
'Girls, Girls, Girls' 20
'Give Peace a Chance' 124
glam rock. *See* rock
Glitter, Gary 92, 104, 206
globalization 5, 19, 58, 84, 121, 163, 173, 194
'God' 126
God'll Fix It 22, 218
Godard, Jean-Luc 163
Godzilla 43
Goldman, Albert 72, 123, 130
Goldstone, James 42
'Goodnight Irene' 61–2
Gordon, Avery F. 143, 145, 146, 149
  Ghostly Matters 143, 145–6, 149
goth (music genre) 100, 102, 108
gothic, the 13, 28, 30, 41, 45, 88–91, 99, 105, 110, 137–46, 153, 155–9, 230
  Black gothic 137–8, 158–9
  fiction 88–90, 105, 138, 141, 230
  imagery 13, 137, 144, 152–3, 158–9
Graceland. *See* Presley, Elvis
Gramsci, Antonio 5
Gravediggaz 137–44, 149, 152–3, 155–9
  Frukwan/Gatekeeper 139–40, 157–8
  Prince Paul/Undertaker 139–40, 157–8
  RZA/RZArector 140, 142, 153, 156–8
  Too Poetic/Grym Reaper 139–40, 156–8
Great Depression 58
Grohl, Dave 100
Groupie Girl 211
Guardian, the 164, 167, 198
Guest, Val 216

Hackworth, Ernest 75
Halberstam, Jack 20, 88, 105, 108
Hall, Stuart 155, 190, 223
Hancock, John Lee 66
Hanna-Barbera 42–3

Haraway, Donna 13
Hardtalk 193, 207, 217
Harmony, Dotty 77
Harper, Jessica 41
Harrison, George 121, 232
Hartman, Saidiya V. 150, 156–57, 159
hauntology 13, 32, 37, 143–5, 152
Hawks, Howard 14
Haynes, Todd 98
Heath, Edward 197
Hebdige 92, 95–6
Hell EP, The 232
Help! 122
Herzog, Werner 72
Hey Stoopid 99
hip hop 19–20, 100, 137–59
    gangsta rap 154–6
Hirigoyen, Marie-France 167–70, 180, 183
Hitchcock, Alfred 44
Hobbes, Thomas 107
Hodge, Charlie 70, 231
Hopkins, Jerry 72, 74
horrorcore 137, 140, 155, 158
Hunky Dory 230
Huntley, Ian 182
'Hurt' 74
Hutchins, Chris 72–3

Icke, David 194, 199–200
Illuminati, the 233
'Imagine' 123
In the Psychiatrist's Chair 225
Intimate Enemies 203

J Mascis 170
Jackson, Michael 12, 20, 206
'Jagger the Dagger' 157
Jagger, Mick 19, 101. *Also see* Rolling Stones, the
Jailhouse Rock 76–7, 216
James, C.L.R. 147
Janis et John 165
Jarecki, Eugene 82
Jay-Z 20, 154–5
jazz 52, 60, 139, 157–8
Jekyll and Hyde 179–80

Jenkins, Henry 111
Jenkins, Philip 203
Jim'll Fix It 187, 192, 220, 224, 226
'John & Yoko' 232
Johnson, Lyndon 58
Johnson, Nobel 56
Johnson, Paul 211
Jones, Alex 194
Jones, Tom 75
Jordan, Winthrop 53
Juanico, June 71, 74, 77
Juke Box Jury 213
Jungle Rhythms 56
juvenile delinquency 112, 122

Kanter, Hal 71
Karloff, Boris 90–1, 95
Killer Mike 137
King Kong 49, 50, 53–8, 63, 96, 231
'King Kong' 57–8
King Kong Returns 231
King, Jonathan 206
King, Martin Luther 58
King, Stephen 117
Kinks, the 231
Kiss 42–3
Kiss Meets the Phantom of the Park 43
Klein, Melanie 58
Kool Herc 100
Kristeva, Julia 11

L'Express 180
Labelle 104–5
Labor Party, American 60
Labour Party, British 60, 224
labour 5
    dead labour 32–3, 144, 230
Lacan, Jacques 15–16
Lacker, Patsy 81
Lady Gaga 20, 108
Laemmle, Carl 38
Larry King Live 110–13, 115–16, 119–20
Latour, Bruno 12–13, 106–7
Le Carré, John 196
    A Delicate Truth 196
Le Monde 172, 176
Le Point 167

Lead Belly 49–50, 53, 58–67, 78, 231
Leaf, David 127
Lean, David 213
Led Zepplin
  Mud Shark incident 207, *also see* Plant, Robert
Lenin, Vladimir 233
Lennon, John 109–15, 117–35, 215, 232
  activism 123–4
  celebrity image 111, 120, 122–3, 125, 127, 130, 133
  murder 109–10, 113–15, 117–21, 127, 129, 131–3
    nihilist readings 120, 133
    and social trauma 128
Leroux, Gaston 27–8, 31–6, 38, 40, 42, 45, 230
Les Inrockuptibles 173–8, 185
Lester, Richard 122
Levitt Report 188, 195
Lewis, Matthew 138
Libération 174–5, 181, 185
Library of Congress, Archive of American Folksong 49, 62, 65
Like a Virgin 230
Lincoln Motion Picture Company 56
LL Cool J 152
Locke, Alain 51
Lofgren, Mike 196
Lomax, Alan 58–60, 63–4, 66–7
Lomax, John 49–50, 53, 58–67, 231
  American Ballads and Folksongs 59
London Review of Books 209, 221
Lorde 233
Lostprophets, the 197
Louisiana Hayride 78
Love It to Death 99
Lubin, Arthur 39
Lumet, Sidney 104
Lydon, John. *See* Sex Pistols

M6 television channel 179
Ma fille, Marie 184
Madonna 231
'Mama Weer All Crazy Now'
Mangeot, Philippe 163
Manifesto of the 343 Sluts 184

March of Time newsreel. *See* 'Angola, La!' newsreel
Marcuse, Herbert 11
Markowitz, Robert 44
Marsh, Dave 83
Marshall, Rob 46
Martha and the Vandellas 158
Marx, Karl 5, 13, 47, 139, 143–9, 151–3
  A Contribution to the Critique of Political Economy 32
  Capital 144, 147–8, 151
  and the gothic 24, 143–6, 158
  and monstrosity 13
  primitive accumulation 146–9, 159
  state theory 233, *also see* capital, labour, and African Americans, Black Marxism
  The Communist Manifesto 144
  The Eighteenth Brumaire of Louis Bonaparte 144
  The Grundrisse 33, 144
Mascis, J. *See* J Mascis
masculinity 2–8, 17–18, 206, 212
  in crisis 5–6
  as gender project 5
  hegemonic masculinity 5
  hypermasculinity 154–5
  and monstrosity 14–16
  and patriarchy 4–6
  toxic masculinity 7–8, 21
  transnational business masculinity 6, 16
mass culture critique 30, 34, 37, 43, 86, 111
McCartney, Paul 120, 132, 135
McDaniels, Eugene 157
McLaren, Malcolm 102
McLuhan, Marshall 193
McNally, David 13, 146
McRobbie, Angela 16–20
media concentration 46
#MeToo 21
memorabilia, ethics 117–18
memory
  flash bulb 109
  imagined 119
Memphis Mafia. *See* Presley, Elvis and names of individual members
Mended Cups 131

mental illness 110–11, 114, 116, 120, 133, 179, 217, 227
Mercer Arts Centre 101
Mercer, Kobena 12
Messier, Jean-Marie 163
MGM 76, 83
Midnight Globe, The 78
Mighty Joe Young 56
Miliband, Ralph 233
    The State in Capitalist Society 233
millennials 228
Millett, Kate 4
Milligan, Spike 122
Mills, C. Wright 233
Minaj, Nicki
modernity 3, 9–10, 14–15, 28, 42, 47, 49, 51, 62, 65, 82, 89, 91, 94, 106–7, 131, 145–6
'Monster' 137
monstrosity 1–3, 8–14, 20–1, 28–9, 35, 40, 43, 47, 50, 56, 65, 69, 72–3, 78, 88–91, 107–9, 114–16, 133, 135, 146, 161, 179, 185, 187, 200, 212–13, 222, 227–8
    and interdisciplinary 2
    and masculinity 14–16
    and race 50, 65, 142
    secularisation 9
Moore, Scotty 75, 80
Morrison, Toni 141, 143, 145
    Beloved 143, 145
Moss, Albert 61
Moten, Fred 150–2, 156–9
'Mother' 126
Mothers of Invention 57
Mothership Connection 104
MTV 43–4
Mulvey, Laura 17
murder 35, 40, 49, 53, 64, 69, 110–11, 113–21, 127, 129, 131–4, 164, 169, 172–3, 175, 183–4, 219
    crime of passion 173, 177, 197
music
    day the music died 33
    digital 34, 44, 46–7, 88
    live 33, 43–4, 60–1, 63, 71, 76, 79, 98, 101–2, 155, 163–4, 195, 219–20, 226

    popularity 125, 232
    recorded 32, 33, 60, 65
    sound in relation to vision 45

N.W.A 154
NAPAC. *See* National Association for People Abused in Childhood
narcissism 167–170, 183, 185
Nation of Islam 103, 152, 154
National Association for People Abused in Childhood 189
National Society for the Prevention of Cruelty to Children 188–9, 195, 201, 210, 224
Neal, Bob 75
Neal, Mark Anthony 154
necrophilia 189
Negro Folksongs as Sung by Lead Belly 63
Negro Music: Past and Present stage show 61
Negro People's Theatre 61
neoliberal society 84–5, 196, 221–2, 227–8, 232
New Romantics 108
new wave music 162
New York Dolls 88, 100–2
New York Post 118
New York Times 59–60, 63, 67, 69, 125, 205
New Yorker 45
News of the World 219
Newsnight 188, 233
Nicely, Ted 162
Niggamortis 140
Night of the Living Dead 142
Nirvana 100
Nixon, Richard 230
Noir Désir 161–4, 172–6, 178–9, 184. *Also see* Cantat, Bertrand
Nollywood 146
Notorious B.I.G. 155
Nouvel Observateur 184
'Nowhere to Run' 157–8
NSPCC. *See* National Society for the Prevention of Cruelty to Children
'Nuit noire'. *See* 'Black night'

objectification
    celebrity 71–3, 76, 79–81, 85
    labour 32–3, 85

occult 94, 199–200, 204–5
Oedipus complex. *See* Freud, Sigmund
Oldie, The 188
One Little Indian label 163
One Nation under a Groove 103
Ono, Yoko 117, 123–9, 131, 133
   art 129, 131
   celebrity image 126–8
   widowhood 128
Operation Midland 197
Operation Ornament 192, 233
Operation Yewtree 188–9, 200, 233
Orientalism 35, 39, 54–5, 216–18, 220, 228
Osbourne, Ozzy 19
Othering 12–13, 50, 54, 58, 66, 105, 110
Our Man in Nirvana 57

P Diddy 154
p-funk 103–5
P-Funk Earth Tour 105
'P.I.M.P.' 20
P&O ferries 233
paedophilia 187–9, 194, 196–208, 210, 221–3, 227–8
   Haute de la Garenne children's home 202
   Kincora boys' home 197–9, *also see* Satanic Ritual Abuse (SRA)
pan-Africanism 153
Paris Match 169, 184
Parker, Colonel Thomas Andrew 69–86, 231
   celebrity image 71
   Snowman's League 74, 231
Parker, Ed 70, 75
Parliament. *See* Clinton, George
patriarchy 4–6, 12, 16
   patriarchal dividend 6, 16
Pearl, Minnie 71
Peele, Jordan 143
People magazine 72–3, 133, 143, 219
Perryman, Bill 75
perverse narcissism. *See* narcissism
Phantom of the Opera. See The Phantom of the Opera
Phantom of the Paradise 41–2
Phillips, Dewey 75

Picasso, Pablo 109, 135
Plant, Robert 19. *Also see* Led Zepplin
Poe, Edgar Allan 99, 189
   The Purloined Letter 189
Pokémon Go 112
Pop, Iggy 55, 102
postcolonial period 66, 138, 217
postindustrial society 5
postmodernity 5, 12, 95, 194
post-structuralism 5, 8, 10–12, 150
Presley, Elvis 33, 69–86, 192, 213, 216, 231
   army service 70, 76–7, 82
   career 82–3
   celebrity image 82
   Comeback Special 78
   Country Fan Club 79
   Elvis Week 79
   Elvis: A Biography 72
   finances 84
   funeral 79
   generosity 79
   Graceland 70, 76, 78
   Memphis Mafia 72–3, 81, *also see* names of specific members
   merchandising 84
   self-commodification 81–2, 84, 86
Presley, Gladys 70, 72–4, 78, 85
Presley, Lisa Marie 70, 77
Presley, Minnie Mae Hood 70
Presley, Priscilla 70, 78
Presley, Vernon 70, 73–4, 77–8, 81, 85
Presley, Vester 70
Primitivism 50, 53, 59, 60
Prince Paul. *See* Gravediggaz
Prince Rakeem 140
Prisonaires, the 78
Professor Griff. *See* Public Enemy
Psycho 43
Public Enemy 154, 156
   Chuck D 154
   Professor Griff 154
Pusha T 137
Putin, Vladimir 16

Queen (group) 104, 108
queer theory 22, 98

Radcliffe, Ann 89, 138
Radio 38–9, 47, 60, 75, 162, 174, 184, 187, 189, 191, 194, 207–8, 214, 215, 220, 225
    Radio City Music Hall 56
Rady, Kristina 164, 169, 179, 181
Rains, Claude 39
Randle, Bill 75
Raw Power 93
Rawls, Alex 109
RCA 75–7, 81, 84
Red River 14
Reynolds, Simon 13, 34, 37, 87–8, 93–94, 106
Rhys, Jean 138
    Wide Sargasso Sea 138
Richard, Cliff 122, 216
RKO 49, 56, 231
Robeson, Paul 52
Robinson, Cedric 147–9
Rocawear 20, 154
rock music 16–21, 41–3, 87–8, 91–104, 106, 108, 116, 120–1, 162–3, 172, 175, 178, 183, 185, 206–7, 217
    art rock 121, 232
    cock rock 19–20, 97
    glam rock 19, 87–108, 206–7
    and magic 93–95
    as subculture 91–3
    indie rock 18, 162–63, 170
    punk 99, 101–2, 108, 172
    stardom 41–2, 71, 97, 113–14, 123, 126, 131, 166, 170, 217
rock'n'roll 1, 41–2, 63, 82, 100, 102, 106, 118, 121–2, 181, 207–8, 210, 217, 222
rockabilly 231
Roeg, Nicolas 1, 102
Rollercoaster 42
Rolling Stone magazine 101, 129, 161–2, 185
Rolling Stones, the 101, 161, 207, 219. *Also see* Jagger, Mick
Romanticism 29, 176–8, 182, 185, 213
Romero, George A. 142
Room at the Top 216
Rose, Bernard 143
Rossi, Francis 193, 207, 212, 217
Rotten, Johnny. *See* Sex Pistols
Royal Family, British 123, 166, 196, 199, 205, 215

'Royals' 233
Roxy Music 92, 106, 108
Ruff, Chuck 100
Rundgren, Todd 114
Russia Today 193–4
RZA. *See* Gravediggaz

Said, Edward 35, 216
Salinger, J. D. 112–13, 117
sampling 139–40, 156, 158
Sandbrook, Dominic 123
Sands, Julian 44–5
Sands, Tommy 75
Saperstein, Hank 84
Satanic Ritual Abuse (SRA) 200, 202–4
Savile, Jimmy 187–229
    and Broadmoor Hospital 187–8, 205
    celebrity image 192, 204, 217
    class 191, 195, 200, 212–15
    clothing 195, 205
    and Duncroft Approved School 188, 192, 220, 233
    fan club 191, 209, 233
    Friday Morning Club 190
    institutional reports about crimes 188–92, 199, 210, 233
    Marsden, Guy (nephew) 210
    and Stoke Mandeville Hospital 187–8, 192, 200, 224, 226
Savile, Louis Theroux episode 206, 208, 222
Scarborough, Dorothy 59
Scary Monsters (and Super Creeps) 1
Scheinfeld, John 127
Schoedsack, Ernest 49–50, 56–7, 96
'School's Out' 102
Schumacher, Joel 45–7
Scooby-Doo 43
Season of Glass 129–30
Seeger, Pete 67
Sex Pistols, The 102, 189
    Rotten, Johnny 189, *also see* Vicious, Sid
Seymour, Jane 44, 231
Sharman, Jim 95
Shaviro, Steven 146
Shelley, Mary 88–91, 94, 96, 98–9, 103, 107
Shootist, The 115
Simmons, Gene 42–3

Siouxsie Sioux 98
Slade 92–3
slavery 53–4, 58, 104, 138–9, 145–52, 156–9
Smith, Billy 70
Smith, Dame Janet 188, 190–1
Smithsonian magazine 69
Snoop Dogg 143
Snow, Hank 75
Social Democrats 60
Son of Kong 56
Songs of Praise 220
Sony Music Entertainment 46
Sound It Out 33
Sparks 108
Spector, Phil 172
spectrality 34, 37–8, 44, 46–7, 120, 145, 150
Spencer, Diana, Princess of Wales 166
Spheeris, Penelope 99
Spiked 200
spiv archetype 212, 214–16, 224–6
Spungen, Nancy 172
Sputnik News 193
SS Canberra 233
Stanley, Dee 81–2
Stanley, Paul 42
States of Denial 206
Steele, Tommy 122
Stetsasonic 139
Stevenson, Robert Louis 180
Stewart, Johnny 213
Stockholm Syndrome 182
Stone, Charles 69, 231
Stone, Sly 104, 155
Stroszek 72
Studio International 184
Sun Ra 104
Sun Records 75, 78
Sun, The 221, 224
Surrealism 179
Symbolism, art movement 178
SXSW festival 100

Tales from the Hood 142–3
teenage 40, 53, 99, 191, 193, 219, 220
'Teenage Frankenstein' 99
Tennant, Neil 98
Têtes Raides, les 163

TF1 channel 168
'That Silver-Haired Daddy of Mine' 231
Thatcher, Margaret 199, 223–4, 226, 228
The Big Payback 153
The Blind Side 66
The Catcher in the Rye 112, 115, 232
The Clones of Dr. Funkenstein 103–4
The Colonel 69, 72
The Heart of Darkness 217–18
The Jonathan Ross Show 120
The King 82
The Kinks are the Village Green Preservation Society 231
The Man Who Fell to Earth 1, 102
The Monk 230
'The Mud Shark' 207
The New Negro essay 51–2
The People under the Stairs 142
The Phantom of the Opera (1925 film) 38–40
The Phantom of the Opera (1943 film) 39–40
The Phantom of the Opera (1983 film) 44
The Phantom of the Opera (1998 film) 44
The Phantom of the Opera (2004 film) 45–6
The Phantom of the Opera (novel) 27–8, 33–4, 37, 41, 230
The Pick, The Sickle and the Shovel 140, 153
The Prisoner 42
The Rocky Horror Picture Show (film) 41–2, 95–6, 98, 102
The Rocky Horror Picture Show (play) 88
The Tao of Wu 142
The U.S. vs John Lennon 127, 232
The Wedding Album 232
The Wiz 104
The Wizard of Oz 104
They Only Come Out at Night 100
Thorpe, Richard 76, 216
Three 6 Mafia 140
Three Feet High and Rising 140
Tierson, Yann 163
Till, Emmett 151
Time magazine 71–2
Tin Pan Alley 40–1
Tommy Boy Records 140
Too Poetic. *See* Gravediggaz
Top of the Pops 102, 187, 193, 208–9, 220

Tostaky 161–2
trauma
    personal 56, 131, 150, 158, 188, 228
    social 128–9, 131, 150–1, 227–8
Tribute artists 230
Tricky 232
Trintignant, Jean-Louis 181–2
Trintignant, Marie 164–8, 170, 172–85
Trintignant, Nadine 164–70, 177, 180–4
trip hop 232
Trolling 7, 234
Trump, Donald 16, 19, 196, 234
Tual, Blanchard 77
Tucker, Gabe 72
'Turkey in the Straw' 71
'Twelve Jewelz' 142
Twentynine Palms 179
Two Virgins 126
Tyler the Creator 137

Uncle Meat 57
Unfinished Music #2: Life with the Lions 232
Universal (movie studio) 38–9, 43
Universal Music Group 163
Us 143

Valenzuela, Luisa 145
    Como en la Guerra 145
Velasco, John 61
Vermorel, Fred 192, 211
    Dead Fashion Girl 192
Vertigo 44
Veuillez rendre l'âme (à qui elle appartient) 161–2
Vicious, Sid 172
victim culture 227–8
Victor Records 39, 46
Vidor, Charles 97
violence
    domestic 165, 171, *also see* murder
Voici 169
voyeur role 55, 157, 170, 175, 207

Wapole, Horace 28, 138
    The Castle of Otranto: A Gothic Story 28
Washington Post 85
Washington Times 154
Washington, Booker T. 63

Watkins, Ian 197
Wayne's World 99
We Have Never Been Modern 12, 106–7
Webber, Andrew Lloyd 45–7
Weine, Robert 38
'Weird Al' Yankovic 233
Welch, Raquel 77
Wertheimer, Alfred 76
West Yorkshire Police 190–1
West, Kanye 137
Westmoreland, Kathy 70–1
Whale, James 90–1
When Louis Met … Jimmy 206, 222
Whitehead, Stephen 4–6, 19
Whitehouse, Mary 102
Whiteness 21, 41, 49–60, 62, 65–7, 73, 77–8, 103, 138–9, 151, 157, 217
    White saviour trope 66
Wide Sargasso Sea 138
Wilderson III, Frank B. 145
Williams, Kenneth 123, 125
Williams, Paul 41, 230
Williams, Raymond 145
Wills, Bob 71
Winfrey, Oprah 228
Winter, Edgar 100
Wire, the 34
Wizzard 88
'Woman Is the Nigger of the World' 126
Wood, Robin 11
Wood, Roy 88, 106
World's Fair 61
Wray, Fay 55–7
Wright, Richard 141, 147
    Native Son 141
Wu-Tang Clan 140, 153–4
    RZA, *see* Gravediggaz

Yankovic, 'Weird Al'. *See* 'Weird Al' Yankovicv
'Yonkers' 137
youth. *See* adolescence, teenage, juvenile delinquency

Zapatistas 163
Zappa, Frank 57–8, 207
Žižek, Slavoj 15
zombies 146

www.ingramcontent.com/pod-product-compliance
Lightning Source LLC
Chambersburg PA
CBHW072129290426
44111CB00012B/1838